Slave-Wives, Single Women and "Bastards" in the Ancient Greek World

Law and Economics Perspectives

Morris Silver

OXBOW | books
Oxford & Philadelphia

Published in the United Kingdom in 2018 by
OXBOW BOOKS
The Old Music Hall, 106–108 Cowley Road, Oxford OX4 1JE

and in the United States by
OXBOW BOOKS
1950 Lawrence Road, Havertown, PA 19083, USA

Paperback Edition: ISBN 978-1-78570-863-3
Digital Edition: ISBN 978-1-78570-864-0 (epub)

A CIP record for this book is available from the British Library

Library of Congress Control Number: 2017958327

Typeset in India by Lapiz Digital Services, Chennai

For a complete list of Oxbow titles, please contact:

UNITED KINGDOM
Oxbow Books
Telephone (01865) 241249, Fax (01865) 794449
Email: oxbow@oxbowbooks.com
www.oxbowbooks.com

UNITED STATES OF AMERICA
Oxbow Books
Telephone (800) 791-9354, Fax (610) 853-9146
Email: queries@casemateacademic.com
www.casemateacademic.com/oxbow

Oxbow Books is part of the Casemate Group

Front cover: Photograph of Athenian red-figure cup interior of fifth century BCE featuring man leading woman (Odysseus and Penelope?), British Museum London, 1843.1103.11 (reproduced with permission of the British Museum).

To my wife Sondra, my best friend for 60 years

Contents

List of Plates

Acknowledgments

My research benefited greatly from the conscientious assistance of Evelyn Bodden and her staff of the Interlibrary Loan Department in the Cohen Library in the City College of New York. I am most grateful to Julie Gardiner, Hannah McAdams and Katie Allen of Oxbow Books for their editorial assistance.

Abbreviations

AthPol	Aristotle, *Athenaion politeia (Athenian Constitution)*
CEG	Peter Allan Hansen (1983) *Carmina epigraphica Graeca*
CIL	*Corpus Inscriptionum Latinarum*
Digest	*The Digest of Justinian*
FGrH	Fragments of Greek History
fr.	Fragment
Hesychius.	Hesychius of Alexandria. *Lexicon.* Available for download at: https://archive.org/details/hesychiialexand00schmgoog
IG	*Inscriptiones Graecae*, 1873–2003
LCL	Loeb Classical Library
PCL	*Pericles's Citizenship Law*
P.Colon	*Papyrus Cologne* (inv. 7511)
P.Eleph	*The Elephantine Papyri*
P.Giss	*The Papyri Giessen*
P.Hibeh	*The Papyri Hibeh*
P.Oxy	*The Oxyrhynchus Papyri*
LSJ	H.G. Liddell, R. Scott, and H.S. Jones (1996). *Greek-English Lexicon* (9th ed.). London Oxford University Press
Pollux	*Onomasticon.* Julius Pollux of Naucratis, *Onomastical.* Available for download at: https://archive.org/details/onomasticon01polluoft
SEG	*Supplementum epigrahicum Graecum*, 1923
Suda	Byzantine Lexicography. Available at: http://www.stoa.org/sol
tr.	translator
Watson	Alan Watson (1985) *The Digest of Justinian*

In the Interests of Disclosure

The conclusions in this study about Greek nuptial institutions are based on a preponderance of evidence drawn from different genres (epic, tragedy, comedy, novel, myth, forensic, epigraphic, onomastic and iconographic) from different historical periods (mainly Classical but also Archaic, Hellenistic and even Mycenaean) and cultures (especially Rome but also the ancient Near East).

It would take additional volumes to expound on the advantages and disadvantages of each type of evidence. It should be obvious, however, that in the ancient Mediterranean world there emerged a shared culture in which visual literacy compensated for gaps in verbal literacy. Specialized symbols also substituted for words in lowering transaction costs (Silver 2009: 252–53). Thus, in Aeschylus's *Agamemnon* 1061, Clytemnestra expects Cassandra to communicate with her "barbarian hand". Today, everyone comprehends the meaning of the emblem used by barbers, the pole with red and white stripes. The ancient Greeks (and Romans) very much relied upon a rich vocabulary of non-verbal signs—posture, gesture, clothing, tools employed and many more to lower transaction costs (Pipili 2000: 157–62; Sage 1916: 206; Trimble 2017).

It should also be obvious that answers to complex questions cannot always be found by confining the search to the path followed by a single academic discipline. Beyond these brief observations, I will rely for justification of diverse kinds of evidence mainly on the authority of several outstanding scholars of antiquity.

First, François de Polignac's (2008) has observed that "[t]he problem ... is not to decide whether one is authorized or not to use material of various times and places, but to see how it can help understanding both continuity and evolutions, coherence and differences." This advice I have sought to heed. Second, with respect to learning social history from Greek drama, Cynthia Patterson (2012: 392) believes "we can read Sophocles as social history if we understand that his plays neither imitate reality nor propagate an ideology, but rather portray essential social values and human conflicts through characters who act in ways that would be most unlikely in the 'real world', but are nonetheless 'necessary' given who these characters are...." Third, we can be sure that "Heroic Greece"/"Homeric Greece" antedates Classical Greece and that while much of this material is concerned with the fictionalized lives of gods of various ranks, it is unlikely (because unnecessary and prohibitively expensive) that the author(s) bothered to invent completely ahistorical sets on which to stage the epics. That is, it should be possible to learn something about pre-Classical nuptial systems and other artifacts of everyday social life by studying the scenery, if not the main actors.

Finally, the late great Assyriologist I.J. Gelb (1965: 62) famously declared: "As all man's ideas about the divine are human, it is my firm belief that we shall never know what was the nectar of the gods until we learn what was the daily bread of the people" (somewhat anticipated by Xenophanes fragments 14–15). The other side of this profound insight is that when myth or cultic text provides some details about the god's nectar we are positioned to offer an informed estimate of the people's daily bread. This vantage point applies of course not only in respect to the food of the gods but to their socioeconomic relationships generally.

Greek and Latin scholars have produced a vast body of evidence bearing on nuptial practices that has yet to be analyzed by a professional economist. By standing on their shoulders the present author proposes and tests new interpretations of three important status groups in Greek history: the *pallakē*, the *hetaira*, and the *nothos*. The shoulders I refer to are the translations and commentaries on the original sources produced by classics scholars to deepen their own understanding as well as to support the research of scholars in other disciplines.

The approach throughout this book is analytical not judgmental or prosecutorial. There is no blame, no shame, no heroes, no villains, no applause and, hopefully, there are no "-isms" and no political correctness. There is, I trust, only the sense of wonder at the diverse ways in which it is possible for human beings to shape a fundamental institution to cope successfully with the challenges of the transaction costs that impede social cohesion.

The findings summarized hereafter may evoke a state of disbelief in some readers. However, the first chapter is not intended to be an invitation to readers to close this book. Rather, it is an invitation to scholars who enjoy the challenge of new ideas to read the entire work including the recommendations for future research.

I. Overview and Summary of Main Conclusions

A primary subject of the present study is the *pallakē* or slave-wife institution, which was prevalent in the ancient Greek world generally, and more specifically in classical Athens. The evidence indicates that the rules governing this nuptial institution were remarkably stable from Heroic Greek times to Greek Egypt making it to synthesize a near-complete picture of *pallakia*.[1]

The Greek word *pallakē* whose etymology is unknown is often misleadingly translated as "concubine" (see, however, Rabin 1983). In 1937, Radin (1937: 601) asserted that "[t]he Greek concubine, the *pallakē*, was not a wife in any sense." More recently, E. Cohen (2015: 100–01) dismissed *pallakia* as a "live-in relationship." It is tempting to elide several other important differences and reply that for the ancient Greeks the *pallakē* was a wife in every sense with the exception that her children lacked the right of inheritance from her husband.

It is fair to say, however, that Radin's perspective remains, with some notable exceptions (e.g. Sealey 1984; Patterson 1990), the *communis opinio* among contemporary scholars who recognize as legal marriage only the form the Greeks designated as "legitimate marriage"—that is, the form that may be understood as marriage by *loan* of the bride to the groom (Wolff 1944). This is especially the position taken in an important study by Ogden (1996). However, the present shows that *pallakia*—that is, the form that may be understood marriage by *sale* of the bride to the groom, was a legally recognized form of marriage in classical Athens and elsewhere in the Greek world.[2] This conclusion is supported by a preponderance of evidence drawn from the orators, comedy (especially Menander), drama (especially Euripides) and poetry (especially Pindar) as well as by characteristic features such as the use of metronymics for offspring and by overly detailed expressions of legal qualification, such as *gametēs gunaikos gnēsious*—"legitimate married women"—, that would have been pointless if they did not refer to a only a *subset* of legally recognized "married

1. Due to the paucity of direct sources and, more importantly, the dangers of "invented history," I largely exclude Classical and Hellenistic Sparta from generalizations about ancient Greek marriage practices. For a recent discussion and references to the literature, see Scott 2011.

2. In Roman legal terminology, the *pallakē* is best compared not with the *concubina* but rather with the wife in the *manus* of her husband (and/or possibly with *contubernium*). Children born to the wife *cum manus* were not legally entitled to receive either their father's name or his property by inheritance. The two-branch Roman marriage system is explained concisely by Cicero (*Topics* 3.14): "For the wife is the genus: there are two kinds of wife; one being those mothers of a family [*materfamilias*] which become wives by *coemptio*; the other kind are those which are only considered wives [*uxores*]" (tr. Yonge *LCL*).

women." I realize that some readers will agree with me only to the point of regarding *pallakia* as a legally recognized "domestic partnership." The problem with this kind of intellectual compromise is that the Greeks often used the same nuptial words for the *pallakē* as for the *gnēsia*. Thus, both might be termed *gunē*—"wife"—and both might be *gamein*—"married".

As has become well known, legitimate marriage or marriage by loan of the bride is made recognizable by a distinctive betrothal terminology cognate to the verb *eggmalizein* (Wolff 1944; Ferrari 2002). Pindar *Pythian* 9.13, however, indicates that *pallakia* or marriage by sale/self-sale of the bride also relied on a distinctive terminology involving use of the verb *harmozein*—"to fit together"—in *gamos*—"marriage". It is not entirely clear whether *harmozō* refers only to betrothal or to completed marriage but it is clear that the term has no linguistic connection to the loan market. Note the example of the mythical Harmonia, whose name (cognate to *harmozein*) reveals that she was "fitted-together with/joined to" Cadmus who became her husband by purchase.

The Greek *pallakē* is a woman sold into marriage to a man by her *kurios*—"master," or, more accurately, "owner" (Wohl 1998: xvii), typically her father or brother—or who, as *kuria*, sold herself (auto-*ekdosis*). Women were passively traded into wifeship, but also actively traded themselves. The Athenian evidence shows that such traded women were legally designated by the purchaser as wife for the production of children who are freeborn (*eleutheros*) and also "illegitimate"/"bastards" (*nothoi*). The *pallakē* herself was assigned by her husband and *kurios* to manage a household, including the husband's children by her. It is discussed in passing whether some women called *pallakai actually* remained undesignated by their owners/husbands.

The legally recognized status of the *pallakē*'s marriage is demonstrated not only by the routine acquisition of citizenship by her children, but also by her sexually protected status. A non-husband who had sexual relations with her, just as with a legitimate wife, was guilty of the grievous crime of adultery. In addition, in Athenian social practice, taken as revealed in Menander's plays, the *pallakē* may be represented as a wife. The men sharing households with Menander's heroines clearly intended to be married to them. *Pallakia* is a lasting relationship or, better, a commercially-formed familial relationship, wherein the man's wife is also his slave (compare Sommerstein 2014: 13). Thus, Themistocles's father "took to wife"/"married" (*gamein*) Habrotonon *ex agoras*—"from the marketplace."[3] More famously, there are grounds for concluding that Xanthippe was a sexually active single woman who contracted to become Socrates's *pallakē*.

Sometimes the sale of a woman into slave-wifeship is made explicit but often sale must be inferred from the (otherwise unexplained) property the *pallakē* carries with

3. Revealingly, in Roman law it was as much a delict (*furtum*) to steal a man's wife in *manus* as to steal his slave (*servus*) or "judgment debtor" or gladiators "who, though nominally free, take a solemn oath [*auctoramentum*] that placed them entirely at the disposal of their employer" (Gaius *Institutes* 3.199; Frier and McGinn 2004: 229).

her either into or out of the marriage or by still other considerations. In contractual form, the Athenian *pallakē*-wifeship transaction is a sale into slavery with a restrictive covenant calling for the sold woman to be employed as a wife. Restrictive covenants, as will be explained, were recognized by Roman law and Athenian law, and were common in business practice.[4] Of course, a husband might demote his *pallakē* from wife status if she deviated from standard or expected wifely behavior. In addition, there is evidence from Greek Egypt (but perhaps hinted in classical Athens) that a slave-wife might divorce her husband if he deviated from proper husbandly behavior.

Although the *pallakē* was acquired as the *ktētai*—"property"—of her husband she was not often referred to by the usual terms for "[female] slave" (e.g. *doulē*). In emotional terms, the *pallakē* was one's wife, not one's slave (Schaps 1998: 165). In the same way, a son or daughter over whom the father was *kurios* was regarded as his child, not his slave. However, despite the inevitable penetration of law by emotional considerations, it is demonstrable that the *pallakē* might legally be treated *as if* she were a slave. Specifically, like a slave, her husband might sell his *pallakē* to another man and, as in the *Homeric Hymn to Aphrodite* (5.136–40) and, arguably also, as in Euripides *Electra* (1284 ff.), he might receive a "ransom" or "reward" for releasing her. A *pallakē*, unlike a free person, could be subjected to judicial torture (*basanos*). In addition, an analysis of the relationship between Zeus and Hera in the *Illiad* supports the view that, unlike a legitimate wife, a *pallakē* was subject to physical discipline, like the husband's child[5] or his ordinary slave. Hence, rather than referring to the *pallakē* as a "quasi-slave," or as an "owned-wife," this study understands her to be as a specific kind of slave—that is, she is a "slave-woman with wife (*gametē*)-status," for which the shortened form is "slave-wife".

Thus, the *pallakē* is both wife and slave. Needless to say, her position as "treasurer" (*tamias*) or "steward" (*oikonomos*) of the *oikos*—"household"—is one of immense responsibility that, in the wider economy (e.g. in private banks), was held by slaves. A major economic advantage of *pallakia* is that since her husband owned the pallakē she, unlike the legitimate wife, could legally act as her husband's business agent.[6] Agency behavior is illustrated by the sizeable loan made by a wife on behalf of her husband in Demosthenes 41.9.

4. Note is taken below of Roman slave sale contracts incorporating restrictive covenants such as a legally recognized manumission clause (*ut manumittatur*), or a clause calling for the slave to be exported (*ut exportetur*) (or not to be exported) or, especially relevant for the present study, a clause which forbade the buyer to prostitute the slave (*ne serva prostituatur*).

5. Note Zeus' threats of physical force against his daughter/creation in the *Illiad* (Synodinou 1986).

6. For this and other reasons discussed below, I disagree with Lape (2002–03: 126) when she says: "When legitimacy became the *sine qua non* of socio-political and familial status there were no longer any positive benefits to be gained from supporting concubines and fathering children by them."

It should be clear that, as a wife, the *pallakē* is not an ordinary slave. As the manager of a household, her husband's agent and the mother of free, citizenship-qualified children, she is a privileged slave. Her status resembles Demosthenes's (4.36–37) *chōris oikountes*—"[those] living apart"—who were arguably "autonomous slaves" (*apeleutheroi*; Silver 2014, 2015). Because she had so much control over her lifestyle, the *pallakē*, like other autonomous slaves, might be referred to as "free." Such reference is appropriate because she enjoyed "lifestyle freedom." Significantly, the *pallakē* might have slaves of her own like Euripides's Andromache and (it is argued the *pallakē*) Clytemnestra. Nevertheless, like other autonomous slaves, the *pallakē* lacked important rights/protections possessed by a juridically free person.

A very similar pattern of lifestyle freedom for the *pallakē* is found in Homer and in the Hesiodic *Catalogue of Women* (Heroic Greece) wherein, as will be shown, marriage rules seem to have much in common with those in classical Athens. Most importantly, the distinction in inheritance rights between offspring of the legitimate wife and of the *pallakē*-wife is recognized in the *Odyssey* (14.199–210) wherein Odysseus fabricates details of his personal history.

As noted earlier, in becoming a *pallakē*, a free foreign or citizen woman either gave herself up for sale into wifeship or was given up for sale by her male *kurios*. In the latter case, the father of the bride received a bride-price (termed *hedna*) from the groom; in the former case, the bride, a single woman, received a bride price (termed *dōra*) from the groom. That is, seller of the bride received the groom's payment. The father needed/wished to be compensated for the loss of control over his daughter and the single woman needed/wished to be compensated for surrendering her juridical freedom. That some single women sold themselves into wifeship finds interesting support in Meander's Glycera and in the myth of the bride Stratonice as told in the Hesiodic *Catalogue of Women*. The study casts light on a number of related problems including the nuptial role of the "old woman" (sometimes resembling the Roman *materfamilias*) by considering the marriage of Glycera to Polemon and of Persephone to Hades.

The payment for the bride terminology (*hedna*/*dōra*) is well attested in Heroic Greece. If references to sale of ordinary goods and services are infrequent in the Homeric poems, this is certainly not the case for the slave market and the marriage market. Sealey (1990: 115) proposes: "It is not likely that a well-established custom of marriage would be modeled on a merely embryonic practice of sale." It is not clear why Sealey thinks that marriage markets needed to be evolved from other kinds of markets rather than leading the way in the spread of markets. It is possible to defend the proposition that the sale of wives is everywhere the fundamental market.

It appears that the technical terminology of sale into wifeship changed in classical Greece but the practice remained. The *pallakē* carried part or all of her sale price into wifeship as a kind of *peculium*—"purse." *Peculium* is of course a Latin word but a variety of evidence shows that Greek slaves certainly had "purses." The slave-wife also carried the purse with her out of wifeship, perhaps augmented by her *kurios*, in the event of divorce or emancipation. In this way, the purse of the *pallakē* resembles the dowry (*proix*) given by her *kurios* to a legitimate bride. However, unlike the dowry, which belonged to the legitimate wife, the *peculium* of the *pallakē* belonged legally to the husband and might be confiscated by him if her nuptial performance was deemed unsatisfactory.

Why was wealth typically transferred *to* the husband in the case of legitimate marriage by means of a kind of groom-price called *proix*—"dowry"—and transferred *from* the husband in the case of *pallakia*? One major consideration is that, *other things remaining equal*, the greater the bride's geographic distance from him, the higher the cost to the father of exercising his ownership option and, hence, the lower its net value. At the same time, the groom typically has a definite preference, economic and emotional, to form his new household in his ancestral community. Hence, predictably, the likelihood of bride purchase rises with increases in the geographic distance between the groom's ancestral *oikos* and the father's *oikos* and it declines—that is, the likelihood of groom purchase rises—with proximity between the groom's household and the father's. A second consideration in wealth transfers is that the father of the bride might place value, even great value, on having his son-in-law nearby. In such cases, the likelihood of groom purchase (legitimate marriage) increases.

These propositions are confirmed by testing them against a variety of evidence including Hephaestus's bride-price for Aphrodite and *P.Eleph.* 1. The myths of the shape-shifting bride Mestra in the Hesiodic *Catalogue of Women* and the sources for the marriage of Penelope with Odysseus offer clear guidance attesting to the role of distance in determining the form of marriage (with groom-price/dowry or with bride-price). Thus, it is not required to postulate a difference in socioeconomic structure between societies mostly practicing groom-price and those mostly practicing bride-price. Whether a society exhibited mostly one or mostly the other might depend mainly on whether native women were mostly marrying native men or mostly marrying foreigners.

Relying on the forceful nature of the gesture itself, on its use in the acquisition of slaves wives such as Briseis in the *Iliad* (in Musée du Louvre G 146), on a scene depicted on the Shield of Achilles, on the etymology of the name Hera and on explicit Roman evidence that the coemption required the husband to grasp in his hand (*manus*) his new wife, it is proposed that a distinguishing ritual of a *pallakē*'s marriage is that the groom led the bride in a procession while grasping her left wrist in his right hand. Most importantly, in the marital relationship between Odysseus and Penelope, the wrist-grasping gesture serves to authorize behavior that is inconsistent with legitimate marriage. That is, the *cheir' epi karpoi* gesture indicates that the bride had been removed from her own authority or from her father's *oikos* to become the groom's property (i.e. that he become her *kurios*). It has not been possibe to rigorously exclude that *cheir' epi karpoi* is a universal nuptial symbol. However, up to now, I have not found an example of a legitimate marriage in which the gesture is attested.

Turning to another nuptial ritual, it has been claimed that a distinguishing symbol of legitimate marriage is a handshake (*dexiosis*) between the groom and the bride's father who remained the bride's *kurios*. Even so, and there is no literary evidence for this practice, a handshake between father and groom is also expected in the sale of the daughter into *pallakia*. A handshake between father and groom is attested only iconographically. However, when the woman was a single woman—that is, when she was outside a male-headed household—meaning that she was her own *kuria*, the *pallakia* marriage ritual featured a handshake between the bride and the groom indicating that, as in the Roman *dextrarum iunctio*, she had consented to become the groom's property—that is, his slave-wife. This handshake between bride and groom is attested in literature and in iconography.

The offspring of a designated citizen *pallakē* qualified for Athenian citizenship as did the offspring of a foreign *pallakē* prior to the passage of Pericles's Citizenship Law (PCL). Nevertheless, the legal status of the *pallakē*-wife, whether Athenian or foreign, was distinctly inferior to that of a legitimate (*egguētē, gnēsia*) wife (*gunē, damar*). Most importantly, her children (*nothoi*) did not have the legal right to inherit the estate of their father (*kurios*)—that is, they lacked the quality of *anchisteia*—"being next." Thus, *nothoi*, representing the second thrust of this study, were necessarily "bastards" in the important sense of inheritance rights.

Nothoi were not, or were not necessarily, illegitimate in the sense of having unmarried parents or parents of unequal status. Neither were they necessarily illegitimate in the sense of having "dark" (*skotioi*) fathers, meaning that their fathers were unknown and/or did not recognize them. The *pallakē* is a wedded woman whose children are *nothoi*. The child of an *unwedded* citizen mother is called *a parthenios*.[7] There is, however, some reason to believe that in classical Athens, probably in post PCL times, *parthenioi* began to be called *nothoi* (see Patterson 1990: 51). This blurring of nomenclature is evident in Euripides's *Ion*, especially in line 1472 with its reference to *nothon me partheneuma* "bastard of an unmarried woman." Evidence suggests that, in all times, *nothoi* belonged to their mothers and, consequently bore metronymics, rather than the patronymics borne by legitimate children.[8]

The *pallakē* institution primarily represents a legal accommodation to the sexual and emotional needs of Athenian men (and Homer's heroes) who often spent large blocks of time away from their primary or legitimate households. Indeed, these needs may well explain the origin of the Greek word *pallakē* as well as Latin *paelex* and Hebrew *pi(y)legeš* (note *Judges* 19.1 ff.), all of which mean something like "additional wife".[9] The division in residence explains, for example, why Hephaestus has two wives, Cabeiro on Lemnos and, certainly as a *pallakē*, Aphrodite on Mount Olympus.

7. Compare Patterson (1990: 50–51). For *parthenios*, note Eudorus in Homer *Iliad* 16.179–84 and, more generally, the Spartan *partheniai* "virgin boys" (Quiller 1996).

8. For *nothoi*, the only apparent exception of which I am aware is *Iliad* 11.490, in which a *nothos* has a patronymic adjective (see Ogden 1996: 94–96; Chapter XVII). For the children of unknown fathers to unmarried citizen mothers, see Homer *Iliad* 16.179–84, Sophocles *Oedipus Tyrannos* 1062–63 (discussed by Dugdale 2015: 429) and Euripides *Ion* 1472.

9. See Levin (1983) who notes the perfect Indo-European structure of *pi(y)legeš*.

To some extent, the institution also represents an accommodation to citizen women who wished to marry but rejected the more constrained (but not entirely restricted) lifestyle expected by husbands of wives whose children had inheritance rights. Ancient Greek men were probably not aware of genetic science, but they did possess the "selfish gene" (Dawkins 1976)—that is, they were motivated to ensure that they had biologically fathered their legal heirs. The woman's *aidos*, as demonstrated in the cover image of this book, helped to lower the groom's ex-ante paternity uncertainty. In addition, some citizen women became *pallakai* simply because they were not legally eligible to be given in legitimate marriage.

The *hetaira* institution represents the third major thrust of this study. The term *hetaira* is usually rendered as "prostitute," "not a simple prostitute," "mistress," or "courtesan," so it is a term that appears to mean something like "gold-digger"—that is, a woman who makes herself sexually attractive/available to rich men for the sole purpose of sharing in their wealth.[10] Some discussions leave *hetaira* undefined. Sometimes the meaning is unstable, as the word shifts meanings within a single discussion. Concededly, there were prostitutes and gold-diggers among Athens's *hetairai* and, indeed, it appears they were sufficiently numerous and/or newsworthy that among elite Athenians they virtually monopolized the *hetaira* designation. *Hetaira* as a sociologic status (about which below) was dominated in elite conversation by *hetaira* as a set of (disreputable) behaviors (Kennedy 2015: 61–62).

Some of the *hetairai* women were demonstrably independently living citizens. Others, perhaps many, were *nothai*, the daughters of *pallakai* who were under the *kuria* of their mothers (the "old women") and hence necessarily excluded from male-headed households. There is, indeed, evidence, including a speech by Electra in Euripides's *Electra* (930–35) that the children of *pallakē*-wives were identified by metronymics. More generally, probing beneath the surface we detect evidence, applicable to the fourth century and later, that the ranks of *hetairai* included some who had sexual relations not for economic gain but for enjoyment and even some celibate women. These "respectable" *hetairai*—that is, those who did not support themselves by selling their sexual favors—constituted an occupational cross-section including *talasiourgoi*—"wool workers,"—musicians and a variety of other paid workers (*mistharnousai*) who performed manual labor ("made a living from their bodies"). The evidence does not suggest that the meaning of the term *hetaira* changed over the centuries (compare Kennedy 2015: 63).

Most generally and fundamentally, the term *hetaira refers* to a *single woman*. Note that "single woman" is not a *translation* of the Greek word. Rather, "single woman" is intended to describe her social and legal status. The single woman was probably a citizen, *who was legally recognized* as being under the *kuria* of her mother or was her

10. "If anyone's ever grown attached to a *hetaira*—could you name a more criminal bunch?... And isn't Phyrne [presumably of Thespiae] behaving just like Charybdis by grabbing the ship-owner and gulping him down boat and all?" (Athenaeus 13.6 p.558a, citing Anaxilas' *Neottis*; tr. Olson *LCL*).

own *kuria*. The only necessarily excluded status being that of wife.[11] Thus, in this study, a *hetaira*/single woman is of course an "unmarried woman" (*parthenos*) but an "unmarried woman" who resides in a male-headed household or has a male *kurios* is not a *hetaira*/single woman.[12] Not all unmarried women are *hetairai*. The presence of geographically mobile, sexually active, husband-seeking single women is attested in literary sources ranging in time and space and genre from Homer's *Odyssey* (6.270–87) to Chariton's *Callirhoe* (3.2.8–9). It is simply not true that premarital sexual relations were forbidden in ancient Greek society. Probably, many *pallakē*-wives had originally been *hetairai*. The transformation is hinted by the expression "married as a *hetaira*" in Isaeus 3.

The received model of classical Athenian society in particular takes the "courtesan" to be an aberration or a special case lacking roots in respectable society while the normal woman lives in seclusion in the house of her *kurios*. This model is defective. We may be sure that the "courtesan" and the prostitute did not emerge fully-formed from the head of Solon.

Myth is an especially rich source, providing the names of single women such as Stratonice, Atalanta and the Protids. The latter women are explicitly placed outside the household of their fathers *and* situated in meadows (*leimōnes*), in which they often are depicted picking flowers.[13] In various seminal studies, Kirk Ormand has studied these women and provided a solid foundation for developing my research. Placement in the "wild" signifies not only readiness to marry but also that the bride to be is outside a male-headed household. To this list of single women, we may add the sixth–early fifth century poet Anacreon's work, *Herotime*. Indeed, picking flowers in a meadow is taken in this study as a proxy for single woman status in the examples of Hera, Europa, Persephone and other mythical brides.

Keeping in mind the legal status of the Danaids, whom Aeschylus portrays as being implacably opposed to being under the authority of a husband, it is suggested that in classical Athens, suppliant status (*hiketeia*) was understood as providing a legal foundation for *hetaira* status. A similar understanding may be developed from

11. Assuming that the *korai* "young girls" constitute a limited group dedicated to the cult—that is, they are *korai-numphai*—then it is significant that the goddess Helen could no longer participate in their activities at the Eurotas River because she was married to Menelaus (Theocritus *Eighteenth Idyll* 38–48).

12. In an as yet unpublished study, Huebner utilized Roman Egypt census returns to measure the number of "unmarried women" generally—that is, without considering household status. She roughly estimated that some 26.4% of females over the age of 15 were unmarried. This estimate constitutes an upper limit on the proportion of unmarried women living outside male-headed households. It is difficult to say more at this point. However, if I understand correctly, Huebner does not recognize the existence of unmarried women in their own power.

13. Several mythical women who are obviously outside male-headed households reside in flowery meadows. The list includes the sexually liberated nymph or goddess Calypso (*Odyssey* 5. 70 ff., 194–225) and the Sirens (*Odyssey* 12.159).

the mythical invasion of Attica by the Amazons and their subsequent defeat and surrender = integration into Athenian society.

In much of the scholarly literature, however, the status of "single woman" is ignored, or only vaguely sensed, or is attributed only to foreign women (*xenei*), or else denied altogether in accordance with the counterintuitive (and contrafactual) proposition that citizen women spent their lives sequestered in a few chambers in their spacious houses. Even the grandest Greek women would not, like Euripides's Andromache (*The Trojan Women* 645–55), volunteer to be cooped up with nothing to do but weave and bear children. The inborn human desire for socialization and for self-realization had to motivate wealthy Athenian women and had to matter to their husbands (for a very different perspective, see Gould 1980: esp. 48–49). Thus, "In [Euripides]fragment 1063 (= Stob. 4.23.26a), the wise (*sophos*) husband is told not to keep his wife indoors (line 3), since giving her access to the world beyond the *oikos* will in fact satisfy her and make sure she stays out of trouble (lines 6–7). In contrast, the husband who controls his wife too much, as fragment 463 suggests, is called foolish (*mataios*, line 11) and helpless (*achreos*, line 16). This stands out for its contradiction of the usual Greek ideal of the sequestered upper-class woman and in fact suggests a positive, rather than disastrous, outcome when a wife is granted some freedom" (Funke 2013: 60; transliterations mine). In addition, most citizen women could not afford to live in spacious houses and never go shopping or have to perform other household chores or sell goods and labor power in the market.[14] Of course, we do not know the percentage of wealthy Greek husbands who were in fact *sophos*.

Single women (*hetairai*) lacked the protection of a male *kurios* and orators smeared them as "prostitutes" and/or as "budget-breaking luxuries" (McClure 2003: 16). Moreover, the legal penalty for sexual assault against single women was much less severe than for married and unmarried women living within a male-headed household. The defensive adaptation of single women to an outsider and hence relatively dangerous status finds a reflection in Greek myth in their grouping into packs. The latter are often called *numphē* "bride, unmarried young woman" and they

14. In the seventh century BCE, Semonides of Amorgos (Poem 7 64–69) spoke of the wife "who always wears her hair combed-out, and dressed with overhanging flowers. Such a wife is beautiful to look at *for others*, for her keeper she's a pain—unless he is a king or head of state who can afford extravagant delights" (tr. Svarlien *Diotima* available for download at http://www.stoa.org/diotima/anthology/sem_7.shtml; emphasis added).

Aristotle (*Politics* 1300a 4–7) comments: "But a Superintendent of Children and a Superintendent of Women, and any other magistrates that exercise a similar sort of supervision, are an aristocratic feature, and not democratic (for how is it possible to prevent the wives of the poor [*aporōn*] from going out [*exienai*] of doors? [to go to work?]) nor yet oligarchic for the wives of oligarchic rulers are luxurious" (tr. Rackham *LCL modified*). Note that Aristotle's "poor" women who are being contrasted with aristocrats probably comprise the majority. Averted glance and downcast eyes together with the veil (Llewellyn-Jones 2007: 256) made it possible for unescorted women to negotiate streets crowded with male strangers. Indeed, I suspect that the conception of *Aidos* was born on the streets.

are frequently depicted in Attic vase paintings in non-urban settings where they are both sexually active with and sexually harassed by crude figures called "satyrs" or "silens". In addition, there are *parthenoi* "virgins" who in myth are abducted as they roam free outside normal society in distant mountains and meadows. "Amazons" refers to the most extreme and most famous mythical pack of the outsider *parthenoi* (see Hardwick 1990). The "untamed" *numphai* and *parthenoi* are reflections of women outside male-headed households, not of unmarried women generally. A variety of evidence—textual, symbolic representations (iconography), and archaeological—is utilized to trace the role of real world single women (*hetairai*) who, like the mythical *numphai* and *parthenoi*, courted in the "wild". There is evidence that cults of Aphrodite and Artemis participated in the courtship/marriage of mortal single women.

As suggested by the name "*hetaira*" (male form *hetairos*) these women were "companions," but this does not mean that they were "sexual companions/ companions to men." Rather, it implied that they were *companions to one another*. One important manifestation of their companionship was to serve together as live-in workers producing woolen textiles for the market. Comparable "houses of women" are found in the ancient Near East and probably at Bronze Age Pylos. Some scholars classify Building Z in Athens as a brothel but others see the structure as "factory" for cloth production. On the former view, customers went from the central courtyard to one of the ten smaller rooms after viewing the "merchandise" and paying the manager. On the latter view, textile production took place in the central courts and the smaller rooms housed the workers. The problem with the brothel understanding is that the street entrances in the rooms would have made it most difficult for the manager of a brothel to monitor the entry and exit of customers. Another candidate for the role of single women's "house of textile work" is the sanctuary of Artemis at Brauron where textiles played a central role. Unfortunately, the available evidence for commercial textile production remains entirely circumstantial.

With respect to the iconographical problem of the "spinning *hetaira*" depicted on Attic vase paintings, it is concluded that she represents neither housewife nor prostitute. Instead, she is a respectable single woman being "propositioned" with a money pouch for the status of *pallakē*-wife. Other spinning women depicted on Attic vases that are usually said to be prostitutes of one kind or another are actually single women (*hetairai*) who are full-time textile workers (*talasiourgoi*). The women may have had sexual relations with their dates, but they were motivated by pleasure rather by material gain.[15]

15. In much contemporary scholarship, the existence of such women is implicitly denied. Note, for example, the sinuous discussion of New York, Metropolitan Museum of Art 07.286.50 in which a fashionably dressed young woman embraces an essentially nude young male: "The youth's wreath indicates that we are at a symposium and thus that the woman is a hetaira (prostitute). Indeed, no woman other than a prostitute would be depicted in an embrace and in direct contact with a man. This woman is, in fact, minimally attentive to modesty; although her body is concealed by her garments, she eagerly encloses the man's neck in her arms and

The study also casts light upon the marital status of Homer's Penelope, of Hesiod's Mestra, Europa and Stratonice, of Apollodorus's Atalanta, of Menander's Glycera, Pamphile and Crateia, of the banker Pasiōn's wife Archippe (who, it is suspected, acted as her husband's business agent), of Plangon the wife of Mantias, and of the two wives of Socrates. In addition, it is argued that PCL was intended to limit competition among citizens for transfer payments distributed by the Athenian state.

presses his head down to her as she reaches up to kiss him" (Reeder 1995: 192). In London, British Museum 1865, 1118.401865, 1118.40, a fully dressed man stands a discreet distance apart from a fully dressed woman who wraps both hands around his neck and appears to be speaking to him; the man lifts up both arms around her shoulders sides of her without making contact (his hands are open with fingers pointed upward). The woman is classified as a "hetaera," meaning courtesan.

II. Socioeconomic Foundation of the *Pallakē* Institution

The *pallakē* institution is foremost a social and legal accommodation to the needs of men who often spent large blocks of time away from their primary or legitimate households. Displaced Athenians (and others) sought by marrying a secondary wife, or several secondary wives, to enjoy a stable sexual/familial life and/or to support their businesses without, as we shall see, diluting the inheritance of children by their primary wives. Given this perspective, it becomes understandable why Terence (*Andria* 146, 273) renders *pallakē* as *pro uxore*—"for a wife."[1]

Griffith (2011: 187) notes

> a type of "quasi-marriage" must have occurred quite frequently in the case of elites who spent lengthy periods abroad, perhaps visiting their own family's estates in various parts of the Mediterranean or Black Sea region, negotiating trade and business deals ... While abroad, these men ... would sometimes be accompanied by—or would themselves capture or woo—other women to be their sexual partners ... Foley [2001: 87–103] sees the prominence of concubines in Athenian tragedy as a kind of aristocratic male "nostalgia" for an imagined Homeric past: but I am suggesting that present realities were more open-ended.

The practice of taking secondary wives was a practice of real marriage, it was not a matter of nostalgia and not only elites participated.

In Terence's *Phormio*, a play based on a Greek original by Apollodorus, a wealthy Athenian named Chremes has, under the name Stilpo, a secondary family in Lemnos that he visits regularly. The other side of the coin is that foreign visitors sometimes took Athenian women as secondary wives (Demosthenes 24.202–03). Athenian men who regularly spent blocks of time in the city or countryside away from their primary households also formed secondary households (Cox 2002).

Of course, some men, such as widowers and divorcés, who were relatively immobile or lacked primary households but wished to protect their inheritances, also took advantage of the *pallakē* institution. In addition, some Athenian men preferred a *pallakē* to a legitimate wife (see below) including some who lacked sufficient wealth to be

1. The double household is vaguely recalled in *Digest* 50.16.144, Paul: "Massurius writes in his book of memoirs that among earlier generations a '*pellex*' was regarded as someone who lived with someone even if she was not his wife; whom now one calls by the true name of friend [*amicam*] or the slightly more honorable concubine" (citing Granius Flaccus; tr. Watson). For Roman "illegitimacy" see Rawson (1989) and Evans-Grubbs (2015).

very much concerned about inheritances and some who saw business advantages in taking a local woman as a *pallakē* (see Chapter X.1 on wives as agents).

Practices among humans are reflected in the supernatural world. Gods who divided their time between distant residences (temples) took *pallakē* wives. Thus, Hephaestus had wives in both Lemnos and Mount Olympus. Note also that Poseidon, a god with numerous wives, regularly spent blocks of time away from his primary home. For example, Pindar (*Nemean* 5.36–7) tells that the god "often comes from Aegae to the famous Dorian Isthmus" (tr. Svarlien *Perseus Project*).

> But Hercules is the man who appears to have had more wives [*gunaikas*] than anyone else, for he was very much addicted to women; and he had them in turn, like a soldier, and a man employed at different times in different countries. And by them he had also a great multitude of children (Athenaeus 13.4 p. 557a; tr. Yonge *Perseus Project*).

The Athenian Theseus had reasons to sojourn in Crete. We may extract from the sources that Theseus was visualized as having abandoned his Cretan *pallakē* Ariadne on Naxos/Dia (near Crete) and having taken the Athenian Meliboea/ Eriboea to be his legitimate wife (Athenaeus 13.4 p. 557a; Jackson 1999, Skempis 2011: 261–64, both with references). In no version of the myth does Ariadne ever arrive in Athens.

Webster (1966: 26) provides insight into how Athenians viewed the abandonment of Ariadne.

> The solution is shown on a number of red figure vases: Theseus deserted Ariadne because it was his duty to return to Athens and her destiny to become the bride of Dionysus. The earliest is a cup probably by the Foundary painter Hermes leads Theseus away from the sleeping Ariadne over whom a winged boy hovers. If the winged boy is Eros rather than Hypnos, Eros is preparing the bride for Dionysos. On a *lekythos* near the Pan painter it is Athena who comes quietly to rouse a reluctant Theseus, while a tiny Sleep squats on Ariadne's head. Two vases, a *skyphos* by the Lewis painter [Vienna, Kunsthistorische Museum 1773] and a *hydria* by the Syleus painter [Berlin, Antikensammlung 2179], show Athena sternly driving Theseus off against his will.

In Boston Museum of Fine Arts 00.349a, Theseus, at Athena's direction, leaves behind a sleeping Ariadne to return to his ship (for discussion, see http://www.mfa.org/collections/object/jar-stamnos-154074). There are other versions in which Theseus resists or in which he "retires hastily when he sees the god (Dionysus) or even draws his sword to prevent the god attacking him" (Webster 1966: 28; cf. Isler-Kerényi 2015: 113–21).

The point of the images is that the time had come for Theseus to return to his legitimate household in Athens. The abandoned *pallakē* Ariadne, daughter of King Minos and goddess, recollects the many ordinary local wives who were destined to be divorced when foreign husbands departed for good. Some, like Ariadne, found new husbands.

Plate 1. Athenian red-figure lekythos from Taranto, Italy of the fifth Century BCE featuring Ariadne, Athena and Theseus. Taranto, Museo Archeologico Nazionale 4545 (De Agostini Picture Library/G. Dagli Orti/Bridgeman Images).

Amphimetric disputes are prominent in Euripidean tragedy and in the orators (Ogden 1995: 221–24). Thus, for example, the Chorus in Euripides's *Andromache* (465–70, tr. Kovacs *LCL*) laments:

> Never shall I praise doubleness of marriage among mortals nor sons with two mothers [*amphimatoras korous*]. It is strife and pain for a house. May my husband [*posis*] be content in marriage [*gamos*] with a single mate and a bed undivided.

In Homer's *Iliad* 9.449–51 (tr. Murray *LCL*), Phoenix explains:

> I left Hellas, the home of fair women, fleeing from strife with my father Amyntor, son of Ormenus; for he waxed grievously wroth against me by reason of his fair-haired concubine [*pallakidos*], whom himself he ever cherished, and scorned his wife, my mother. So she besought me by my knees continually, to have dalliance with that other first myself, that the old man might be hateful in her eyes.

Ogden (1995: 222) explains:

> In practice different wives and their children must always be kept separately in different houses, the idea of bringing two women together under one roof is in poor taste or worse, the principle that one set of siblings may help and support another is a contradiction of the principle of amphimetric strife so prevalent in Greek culture (cf. Patterson 1991a: 284).

However, the separation of such households might be functional and not mainly or solely a matter of good taste. Usually the different houses were located in different places and their separation may have facilitated economic co-operation between the households.[2]

The above discussion has focused entirely on the desires of men who spent large blocks of time away from their primary or legitimate households and desired to form secondary households. However, there are always two sides in a market. Why did local

2. The best example of this kind of familial specialization comes from the Near East. The prominent position of women in Assur's (in Assyria) business life in the early second millennium BCE is predictable once account is taken of that city's flourishing trade and the dispersal of many of its businessmen to commercial stations in Anatolia and Syria and along the connecting caravan routes (Veenhof 1972: 102–23). The Assyrian merchants often took secondary wives in places where they did business and wrote to their primary wives remaining in Assur to send them the kinds of textiles (and other goods) in demand where they were. For a translated example of a merchant's letter to his wife, see Michel (2001: no. 307). It has been suggested (Silver 1991: 249–52) that in the Argonaut myth the Lemnian women are portrayed as being involved in the finishing of textiles for which their absent husbands sought international markets and raw materials. Interestingly, Lemnian men visiting Brauron, arguably a center for the production and distribution of textiles (Chapter XIV.4), "seized" (*harpazō*) Athenian women gathered there to be their *pallakas* in Lemnos (Herodotus 4.145.2, 6.138.1). It is in Chapter VI.2 that *harpazō* signifies not abduction but marriage by purchase. I very much doubt that Lemnos was the destination of the "abducted" wives.

women agree to become the slave-wives of resident aliens? In strictly materialistic terms, the answer is that such marriages had the potential to improve a local woman's lifestyle. In addition, by building on the purchase price a local wife would be able to accumulate a "peculium," which would be her legal property when the *kurios*, upon his retirement, divorced her to return to his primary home. Finally, the purse would be the inheritance of the *pallakē*'s children. Thus, for example, the Athenian woman Archippe enjoyed significant material advantages from being sold into marriage to the metic banker Pasiōn (see Chapter XIX.2). Ariadne had at least the comfort of marriage to the god Dionysus.

III. *Pallakē*-Wife as Privileged Slave: Central Texts

The intention of the following citations and discussions is to demonstrate or to lay a foundation for the following conclusions. The Athenian *pallakē*: (1) has a special status due to her being designated for the production of free (*eleutheros*) children who qualify for citizenship; (2) is a purchased slave who manages a secondary household for her owner/husband (*kurios*); (3) might either be a foreigner or an Athenian woman; and (4) has the legal status of "wife." The first proposition that the grant of citizenship to the offspring of a *pallakē* by his father's deme was a matter of legal routine is fully argued in Chapter XV. The conclusion follows from the proposition that the Greeks recognized more than one type of marriage, which is supported at length in Chapters VI and VII.

Demosthenes (23.53, tr. Murray *LCL* modified; cf. Wyse 1904: 319):

> Read another statute. "Law. If a man kill another unintentionally in an athletic contest, or overcoming him in a fight on the highway, or unwittingly in battle, or in intercourse with his wife [*damar*], or mother, or sister, or daughter, or *pallakē* kept for procreation of free [*eleutheros*] children, he shall not go into exile as a manslayer on that account."

Demosthenes contrasts the legitimate wife (*gunē egguētē*) with the *pallakē*, whose role is to bear free children for the Athenian father. If the *pallakē* were a free woman then of course her children by a free man would be free. There is no need for a law about "keeping" a free woman for bearing free children.[1] My interpretation is that Demosthenes is *defining* the *pallakē*, as a slave woman whose children are free not, as would be expected for a slave, slaves.[2] Is it possible for a slave mother to provide "free"

1. Ogden (1996: 33) suggests that in Demosthenes 23.53, "the concubine is ... specified as 'for the production of [*eleutheroi*] free children' to make an implicit contrast with a very different type of concubine, one that, a slave herself, may only produce slave children." However, there is no "implicit contrast," as all *pallakē*-wives became slaves.
2. Demosthenes' formulation does not make entirely clear whether there might be other "*pallakai*" who were *not* kept (legally designated/registered) for the procreation of free (*eleutheros*) children (Sealey 1984: 118). Any undesignated *pallakē* would not (I think) qualify under the law as a "lawfully wedded wife" and her offspring would certainly be slaves, and certainly not eligible for Athenian citizenship. Presumably, a citizen woman who became the *pallakē* of a metic could not be "kept for the purpose of procreating free children."

   In Chariton's *Callirhoe*, written perhaps in the first century CE but set in classical Greece, Callirhoe having been kidnapped from Syracuse by pirates and then purchased in Miletus by Dionysius, finds she is pregnant by her Syracusan husband; she laments to Dionysius' maid Plangon: "But I am afraid that even if I yield to his passion, Dionysius may look down on my (*eleutheros*) children? Yes, if: (a) as in the present instance, the law states that children of a slave woman are free/freeborn when her owner has previously designated or "registered" her as his *pallakē*; or (b) the free owner had previously agreed/contracted to free his children by her. Note that the disguised Odysseus claimed to be the son of a "purchased *pallakē*" (*Odyssey* 14.199–205) but, as noted by Ogden (1996: 23), he was "unquestionably free" and also he was unquestionably respected.

Lysias (1.30–31, tr. Lamb *LCL* modified):

> Read out also, please, that law from the pillar in the Areopagus. "Law" You hear, sirs, how the Court of the Areopagus itself, to which has been assigned, in our own as in our fathers' time, the trial of suits for murder, has expressly stated that whoever takes this vengeance on an adulterer caught in the act with his spouse shall not be convicted of murder. And so strongly was the lawgiver [Draco in the seventh century BCE] convinced of the justice of this in the case of wedded wives, that he even applied the same penalty in the case of *pallakais*, who are of less account. Now surely it is clear that, if he had had any heavier punishment than this for the case of married women, he would have imposed

misfortune and, thinking me a *pallakē* rather than a wife [*gunaika*], refuse to rear another man's child" (2.115; tr. Gould *LCL*). As pointed out by Trzaskoma (2010), the text is corrupt and what Callirhoe really fears is that Dionysius will not wish to *raise his own child by a slave woman*. Later Callirhoe says, "So, if Dionysius merely wants me as a *pallakē* to satisfy his passion, I will hang myself rather than submit to being treated like a slave [*doulē*]. But if he wishes me as a legal wife [*gametēn kata nomous*], then I am willing to become a mother" (3.1.6; tr. Gould *LCL*). Finally, Dionysius assures Callirhoe that he intends to make her his "wife 'for the begetting of children' [*paidōn ep arotō*] [but not *gnēsion*] according to Greek law" (3.2.2; tr. Gould *LCL*). Callirhoe sees a pallakē as something like a sex slave but, more importantly, her children are slaves. She wishes to become a legal wife "for the begetting of children," which, it would seem, raises her unborn child from slave to free status and, hence, to eligibility for citizenship. There is no mention of "legitimacy" and in classical Athenian terms, Callirhoe's "legal marriage" is not a "legitimate marriage" and her children are certainly not legitimate. In classical Athenian terms, she can be seen only as seeking to become a designated *pallakē*. (Or taking PCL into consideration, she seeks to become a foreign woman granted designated *pallakē* status.) There is no other category in which to place her legal marriage.

Now consider much earlier evidence bearing on the "unkept" *pallakē*. In *Iliad* 19.295–99, Briseis laments: "But thou (Patroclus), when swift Achilles slew my husband, and laid waste the city of godlike Mynes, wouldst not even suffer me to weep, but saidest that thou wouldst make me the lawful wife [*kouridiēn alochon*] of Achilles, and that he would bear me in his ships to Phthia, and make me a marriage-feast among the Myrmidons" (tr. Murray *LCL* modified). How might Achilles have transformed Briseis into his *kouridios-alochos*, and why did this transformation have to wait until the couple's arrival the in Greece? My explanation is that only in Greece might Achilles have registered Briseis in his phratry (see e.g. *Iliad* 9.63–64) with the aim of legalizing (not legitimizing) her children by him. Similarly, in Apollonius Rhodius's *Argonautica* 4.98, Jason promises to make Medea his *kouridiēn akoitin* upon their arrival in Greece. Again, my hypothesis is that Medea extracted a promise that upon arrival in Greece Jason would legalize her children by him. In a classical Athenian perspective both Briseis and Medea sought to become designated *pallakai*. In the remainder of this study I will assume that classical Athens did not know undesignated or "other *pallakoi*." Obviously, this question requires additional research.

> it. But in fact, as he was unable to devise a severer one for this case, he ordained that it should be the same for that of *pallakais* also. Please read this law besides.

Lysias explains that, in view of their designation as bearers of free children, *pallakas* enjoyed in one respect the same status as legitimate wives (*egguētai*)—a non-husband who had sexual relations with her is an adulterer.[3] There is also the implication that a *pallakē* is a wife but of "lesser account."

Demosthenes (59.122, tr. DeWitt and DeWitt *LCL* modified):

> For this is what living with a woman as one's wife means—to have children by her and to introduce the sons to the members of the clan and of the deme, and to betroth the daughters to husbands as one's own. *Hetairai* [see below] we have for the sake of pleasure, *pallakas* for the daily care [*therapeia*] of our persons, but wives [*gunaikes*] to bear us legitimate [*gnēsiōs*] children and to be faithful guardians [*phulaka*] of our households.

"Daily care of our persons" does not mean only sexual care but it does mean *regular* care. Indeed, the care offered by the *pallakē* to her Athenian husband might have been as much or even more regular than the care offered by the legitimate wife. We know that their duties included procreating free children (Demosthenes 23.53). In addition, the term *gunaikes* is often used of women (reasonably understood to be *pallakai*) whose children could not have been legitimate (see Chapters IV and VI). Hence, as the context makes clear, by *gunaikes* Demosthenes must mean not simply "wife" but *gnēsiōs* wife. This passage, together with the protected status and designation for the bearing of free offspring, supports the view that the *pallakē* is a *wife* away from "home".

Antiphon (1.14, tr. Maidment *LCL* modified):

> There was an upper room in our house occupied by Philoneus, a highly respected friend of our father's, during his visits to Athens. Now Philoneus had a *pallakē* whom he proposed to place in a brothel [*porneion*[4]].

Philoneus's *pallakē* managed his household away from home. Apparently, Philoneus had become dissatisfied with the woman and, as her *kurios*[5] was planning to demote his *pallakē* from wifely status to her underlying slave status. The woman was unhappy

3. In Apollodorus (*Library* 3.13.8), Phoenix's father has him blinded for having sexual relations with his *pallakē.*
4. *Porneion* is uniformly translated in this study as "brothel". However, this word, like *pornē* (prostitute), is probably related to the verb *pernēmi*, meaning "to sell" or "to sell for export." I leave open the possibility that in the present context the *porneion* is a "place for selling" goods or services other than sexual services.
5. In a fragmentary comedy by Menander titled *Sikyonioi* ("The Man from Sikyon"), a woman named Philoumene is in the possession of Stratophanes who is infatuated with her. At several points (lines 191, 194, and 240; cf. Konstan 1987: 128, n. 23), Stratophanes is referred to as her *kurios*. In addition, at line 207, Stratophanes is her *despotēs*, a term typically used of slave owners. Although the term *pallakē* is not used, it seems clear that Stratophanes has either made

about her situation but there is no mention of any legal protections. Some time passed before the woman, still his *pallakē*, killed Philoneus, perhaps unintentionally.

In a fragment (583, tr. Lloyd-Jones *LCL*) of Sophocles's *Tereus*, Procne, wife of king Tereus, laments:

> But when we have understanding and have come to youthful vigour, we are pushed out and sold [*diempolōmetha*], away from our paternal gods and from our parents, some to foreign husbands, some to barbarians, some to joyless homes, and some to homes that are opprobrious. And this, once a single night has yoked us, we must approve and consider to be happiness.

LSJ (s.v.) renders the verb *diempolaō* "sell to different buyers" or "sell in lots" and Ormand (1999: 24) notes that the word "does not carry the limited sense of sale that the more legalistic *ekdidōmi* does. It is, in fact, commonly used for the sale of slaves." Further, the verb *zeugnumi* "to yoke" has also the meaning "to join in wedlock" (LSJ s.v. II.2; Aristotle *Politics* 1253b.10). Thus, *Tereus* shows us sold women who become slave-wives and, hence, although the term is not used in Athenian drama, they are *pallakē*-wives.

Euripides refers to the institution of "double marriage" and "sons from two mothers"; Andromache is the *aichmalōtos*—"taken by the spear captive,"—and *doulē*—"slave"—of Neoptolemus (*Andromache* 26 ff., 56 ff., 465 ff., 930 ff.; cf. Patterson 1990: 66; Torrance 2005).

Andromache manages a secondary household including her son. She is a privileged slave who owns at least one slave. In Roman terms, Andromache is an *ordinaria* and the Trojan slave who calls her "mistress" (56) and whom she calls "fellow slave" (64) is a *vicaria*. Her relationship to Neoptolemus is not termed *gamos*—"marriage"—and Neoptolemus is not called Andromache's *posis*—"husband". On the other hand, in line 403, Andromache says, "I was made the bride [*numpheuomai*] of Hector's slayer" (tr. Kovacs *LCL*). Also, she and Hermione, Neoptolemus's legitimate wife (explicit in 192), are "rivals in marriage" (*suggamoi*; 182, 836) and Neoptolemus has "two wives" (*duoin gunaikoin*; 178). Euripides makes it possible to understand Andromache as a *pallakē* and her son as a *nothos* (Torrance 2005: 55, 66).

A discordant note is struck, however, in lines 198–200, wherein Andromache suggests that were she to usurp Hermione's place, her children would be slaves. However, I believe that Andromache is referring not to her current status in Neoptolemus's *oikos* but to being torn away unwillingly, by force, from her married life and children in Troy.[6] Her children by Neoptolemus would be *nothoi*, as is later stated by Hermione:

Philoumene his *pallakē* or anticipates doing so (Sommerstein 2014: 13). What is striking is the interchangeable use of *kurios* and *despotēs*.

6. "Tell me, young woman, what was the reliable argument that persuaded me to deprive you of your lawful due as a wife? [Is it that Sparta is a lesser city than Troy and is surpassed in fortune by it, and that you see me a free woman?] Was it in order that I might bear children instead of you, slaves and a miserable appendage to myself?" (Euripides *Andromache* 194–198; tr. *Kovacs LCL* modified)

"I had great wealth, I was mistress in the house, and I would have borne legitimate [*gnēsia*] children, while she would have borne bastards [*nothagenēs*] with half-slave parentage to serve my children" (941–42; tr. Kovacs *LCL*). Andromache is a slave and a wife and the mother of a *nothos.*

Similarly to Euripides's Andromache, Sophocles's Tecmessa is *lechos dourialōton*—"spear-won bedmate"—(*Ajax* 211) and *homeunetin*—"bed-mate" (*Ajax* 501)—but Ajax calls her his *gunai*—"wife" (or "woman"),—the chorus refers to her as *talaiphrōn gunai*—"broken-hearted wife" (or "woman")—and Teucer speaks of Ajax's "son and his *gunē*" (*Ajax* 684, 903, 1169; cf. 894–95, 940).

Tecmessa is, at most, Ajax's slave-wife rather his legitimate wife (compare Ormand 1996). At a number of points (368, 485, 585) she addresses Ajax as *despota*—"master"/"owner"—but she also calls him *philos*—"friend"—(529) and refers his indebtedness (*charis*) to him (520–22). Synodinou (1987a: 104) believes that Tecmessa does not understand the meaning of *charis*:

> *Charis* presupposes exchange, a give and take, and understanding of mutuality of the parties involved. So *charis*, as Tecmessa herself conceives it, could exist only between "sharing" partners, which is not the case with them.

I understand her to mean that upon her husband's death she will revert to her basic legal status as a slave. However, If Tecmessa had been introduced to Ajax's phratry she would have *pallakē* status and her children by Ajax would be eligible for citizenship. Indeed, at one point, Tecmessa tells Ajax:

> On whatever day you die and widow me by your death, on that same day, be sure, I shall also be seized forcibly by the Greeks and, with your son, shall obtain a slave's portion [*doulion*] (*Ajax* 495 ff.; tr. Jebb *LCL*; cf. 944–45).

I understand her to mean that upon her husband's death she will revert to her basic legal status as a slave. The legal procedure for transforming enslaved women into slave-wives in Chapter IV. Suffice it to say that such women were freed by their owners and then consented to become their slave wives.

In Euripides *Electra*, Electra is explicitly Farmer's wife but she cannot be his legitimate wife (see Chapter VII). Electra refers to herself as "slave":

> And, mother [Clytemnestra]—for I live as a slave [*doulē*] in this miserable house, cast out from my father's home—may I not take that blessed hand of yours? (1005–06; tr. Coleridge *LCL*).

Electra must be a *pallakē*. The "happy ending" of the drama includes Electra's transfer, actually sale, by Farmer to Pylades. The husband of a legitimate wife was not her *kurios* and hence could not transfer her to a different husband/owner.

In Aristophanes's *Wasps* (1351 ff.), Philocleon tells the flute girl that if she behaves properly he will "purchase"/"redeem" (*luō*) her and make her his *pallakē.*

> And yet, if you would not be a naughty girl, I would redeem you, when my son is dead, and you should be my concubine [*pallakē*], my little one (tr. O'Neill *Perseus Project*).

Thus, the flute girl is currently a slave and Philocleon is proposing to shift her ownership to himself while elevating her to *pallakē* status.

In Menander's *Perikeiromene* ("The Girl with Her Hair Cut Short"), Polemon punishes Glycera, his *pallakē*-wife (see Chapter IV), by cropping her hair. A short-cropped hairstyle is not a fashion but rather signals slave status (Euripides *Electra* 105 ff.), although not all slaves are depicted in this way (Joyce 2011: 39–40 with n. 62; Lee 2015: 74). By cropping her hair, Polemon effectively demoted his wife from privileged slave status to her underlying legal position of ordinary slave. The intention of the punishment was to emphasize Glycera's subjugation.

In Menander's *Samia* ("The Girl from Samos") (508), Nikeratos says with Chrusis in mind that he would have sold his *pallakē* had she been unfaithful to him. Only slaves could be sold. Note that elsewhere Chrusis is said to be *eleutheran* "free"/"freeborn" (*Samia* 577). Arguably, the implication of this identification is that she voluntarily entered slavery/became a *pallakē*. In addition, she retained certain residual rights of citizenship (see the discussion of Archippe's status in Chapter XIX.2).

In the *Homeric Hymn to Aphrodite* (5.136–40; discussed in Chapter V.2), Aphrodite (as Otreus's daughter) may be removed from *pallakia* by the payment of a ransom (*apoina*) to her husband/owner Anchises.

A fragment of Hesychius (*alpha* 176) glosses *Habra*—"favorite female slave" (LSJ s.v.)—as *pallakē* (cited by Sommerstein 2014: 22, n. 7). *Suda* On Line (headword: *habra*; translated headword: "favorite") is more expansive:

> Not simply a maidservant nor even the pretty maidservant is called [favorite], but a daughter of one of the house slaves and an honored one, whether born in the house or not. Menander in False Heracles [writes] "the mother of these two sisters is dead. A *pallakē* who used to be their mother's favorite slave is to bring them up" [Menander fr. 520 Kock] In Sikyonian: "he bought a favorite slave instead and did not hand the slave over to his wife, but kept her apart, as is appropriate for a free woman" [Menander fr. 438 Kock]. In Faithless One. "I thought if the old man got the gold, he'd get himself a favorite slave right away" [Meander fr. 64 Kock] (tr. Anne Mahoney modified; cf. Photius Lexicon *alpha* 50).

The *pallakē* is a privileged slave who may have originated as a household slave or else as a purchased free woman.

In Plato's *Laws* (8.841 D, E), the "Athenian" suggests:

> That of godly fear, and that of love of honor, and that which is desirous of fair forms of soul, not fair bodies. The things I now mention are, perhaps, like the visionary ideals in a story; yet in very truth, if only they were realized, they would prove a great blessing in every State. Possibly, should God so grant, we might forcibly effect one of two things in this matter of sex-relations,—either that no one should venture to touch any of the noble and freeborn save his own wedded wife, nor sow any unholy and bastard seed in fornication [sowing the bastard seed (*notha spermata* in *pallakai*)], nor any unnatural

> and barren seed in sodomy,—or else we should entirely abolish love for males, and in regard to that for women, if we enact a law that any man who has intercourse with any women save those who have been brought to his house under the sanction of Heaven and holy marriage [*gunaikas pasas*], whether purchased [*ōnētais*] or otherwise acquired [as possessions; *ktētais*], if detected in such intercourse by any man or woman, shall be disqualified from any civic commendation, as being really an alien,— probably such a law would be approved as right. So let this law—whether we ought to call it one law or two—be laid down concerning sexual commerce and love affairs in general, as regards right and wrong conduct (tr. Bury *LCL* modified; Sommerstein 2014: 12).

While not stated explicitly, it is clear that the *pallakē*—whose children are referred to as *nothoi* (bastards)—is the property of her Athenian owner and, given Plato's formulation, she became so by purchase. The commercial connotation is unmistakable (Patterson 1991a: 283). In addition, this difficult passage seems to refer to both the legitimate wife (the wife acquired through ritual "sprinkling"?[7]) and the *pallakē* (the wife acquired by purchase) as women who are properly qualified for intercourse with the husband.

Plutarch (*Moralia* 753D) tells that (in the later sixth century BCE) Themistocles's father "took to wife"/"married" (*gamein*) the Thracian Habrotonon *ex agoras* "from the marketplace."[8] Perhaps Habrotonon was already a slave or perhaps she was a free woman who sold herself to better her life prospects. There is no implication that Habrotonon was a *pornē*—that is, a woman who earned income by selling sexual services in the public marketplace. Neither does Amphicrates's (*FGrH* iv 300 F 1) reference to Habrotonon mean that she was a "courtesan;" rather it means that she was a single woman living on her own (see Chapters VI, VII).

In the *Odyssey* (14.199–210), Odysseus fabricates the following story concerning his personal history:

> From broad Crete I declare that I am come by lineage, the son of a wealthy man. And many other sons too were born and bred in his halls, true [*gnēsioi*, "legitimate"] sons of a lawful wife [*alochos*]; but the mother that bore me was bought [*ōnētē*], a *pallakē*. Yet Castor, son of Hylax, of whom I declare that I am sprung, honored me even as his true-born sons. He was at that time honored as a god among the Cretans in the land for his good estate, and his wealth, and his glorious sons. But the fates of death bore him away to the house of Hades, and his proud sons divided among them his substance, and cast lots therefor. To me they gave a very small portion, and allotted a dwelling (tr. Murray *LCL* modified).

Heroic Greece was familiar with both the legitimate wife and the purchased *pallakē* who bore recognized (but not legitimate) sons (*nothoi*). The servile/commercial origin of *pallakē* status is unmistakable and, again, we are not told the previous legal status, slave or free, of the sold woman. However, that Odysseus's mother is not referred to

7. See Chapter V.1. on *katachysmata*.
8. Note similarly, Mesopotamian tablets mentioning wives acquired *ina sūqi*, "in the street"—that is, in the marketplace (Malul 1988: 109). This was not "sexually-oriented slander."

having been a *doulē* or an *aichmalōtos* makes it more likely that Odysseus meant her to be understood as a free woman sold into marriage either by her male *kurios* or by herself.

The speaker in Isaeus (3.39) argues:

> Do you think that Nicodemus is so disinterested in money matters, that, if the fact which he alleges were true, he would not have provided for his own interests with scrupulous care? By heaven, I am sure he would have done so; for even those who give [*didontes*] their womenkind to others as *pallakia* make stipulations in advance as to the benefits which such women are to enjoy [alternatively: as to what the women will be paid/the sum to be paid for the women]. And was Nicodemus, when, according to his own account, he was going to give [*egguaō*] his sister in marriage, content with simply securing the requirements of a legal marriage—a man who shows himself only too anxious to be dishonest for a paltry sum which he hopes to receive for speaking in court? (tr. Forster *LCL* modified by Edwards 2007).

The second quoted sentence refers to Nicodemus's claim that his sister was given in legitimate marriage (by *eggue*) to Pyrrhus. It is advanced solely to quality her children for an inheritance. Nicodemus must have been confident that the jurors would accept his sister as someone qualified for legitimate marriage. If not, he was wasting his time and money. Given the reference in the first sentence to "money matters" there can be no doubt that "giving their women" means "selling their women." Further, the reference is too broad to refer only to slaves, illegitimate daughters of citizens, and non-citizens. Citizen women are being sold into slavery as *pallakia*.[9] This pattern is verified by Timocrates's sale of his sister to a visiting diplomat (Demosthenes 24.202–03).

Patterson (1990: 60 n. 80) does not think, "'those giving their women [*epi pallakē*]' should be taken to indicate that this was a normal arrangement within the citizen class."[10] However, Isaeus's, reference to "those" indicates that the practice of selling daughters into *pallakia* was not a one-off practice and leaves open that it was "normal".

A damaged Attic grave stele (*SEG* 13.189 = *IG* ii^2 11152) dated to the mid-fourth century BCE is restored as follows: [Hom]onoia, [*pall*]*akis* of Diognet[os], daughter of Hermocr[ates]" (tr. Kennedy 2014: 116).

Kennedy (2014: 116) makes an important observation:

> It is also most frequent in Attic gravestones that the father's name is listed first before the husband's. This inscription does the opposite, which suggests perhaps a privileging of the *pallakia* relationship.

9. But see Ogden's (1996: 159) objections.

10. See also Carawan (2008: 401); Kamen (2013: 92); Kapparis (1999: 11); Lape (2004: 94 n. 81, 161); Mossē (1991); Wyse (1904: 319).

However, this kind of "privileging" is to be expected, as in *pallakia* the husband, not the father, owned the woman (was her *kurios*). Kennedy adduces to various considerations to support her view that Homonoia is a metic. Most importantly:

> The name Homonoia is only attested as a metic name, though her father's name, Hermokrates, is attested as both citizen and metic. The husband's name is also attested as both, but all attestations as a metic name (five of the total sixty-eight attestations) are from the second century CE or later (Kennedy 2014: 116).

This is rather weak evidence for metic status, especially when Kennedy adds:

> In the *Onomastikon*... this particular instance of Homonoia [the name of the *pallakē*] [is listed] as uncertain, although it would be the only certain attestation if one read that way (Kennedy 2014: 122 n. 54).

There is little suggesting that Homonoia was a metic rather than a citizen and her patronymic unbalances the scales in favor of citizen status. Kennedy (2014: 157 n. 63) also notes that Homonoia may have been a "housekeeper" but acknowledges that usually in grave stelai the placement between two men suggests one was a husband and the other a father. "Homoneia" kept a house but as a slave-wife not as a "housekeeper".

Antiphon (1.20, tr. Maidment *LCL*):

> So they poured their libation, and, grasping their own slayer, drained their last drink on earth. Philoneus expired instantly; and my father was seized with an illness, which resulted in his death twenty days later. In atonement, the subordinate who carried out the deed has been punished as she deserved, although the crime in no sense originated from her: she was broken on the wheel and handed over to the executioner; and the woman from whom it did originate, who was guilty of the design, shall receive her reward also, if you and heaven so will.

The "subordinate" is Philoneus's *pallakē*, who is referred to in Antiphon 1.14 ff. (see Chapter II). That she is judicially tortured attests that she is legally a slave (Demosthenes 22.55).[11] There is some evidence that a husband had the legal right to physically discipline his *pallakē*, like his child or slave, but not his legitimate wife. It is suggested in Chapter XVIII that Hera had to endure physical abuse by her husband Zeus because Homer understood her to be a *pallakē* (slave-wife).

The above citations attest that the *pallakē* is a purchased (but privileged) slave-wife whose official role is to produce free (but not legitimate) offspring for her husband. The following chapters provide additional supporting evidence that a *pallakē* is a purchased wife and considers the role of restrictive covenants in the contracts of sale.

---

11. A review of the evidence demonstrates that free persons could not be tortured by the state in cases of homicide (Carey 1988). Torture of a citizen was possible only in cases of religious defilement and treason (Andocides 1.43).

IV. Constructing the Greek Wife: Legal Aspects

1. Alternative Forms of the Greek Marriage Contract

Marriage by loan (*egguēsis*) of the bride and marriage by sale/alienation (*apedōn/apodidōmi*) of the bride may be conceptualized as alternative methods or, more specifically, as distinctive contractual forms by means of which a man lawfully acquired a wife. The first contractual form (*egguēsis*) produced the legitimate wife (Demosthenes 46.18) whose father remained her *kurios* and whose offspring possessed inheritance rights to their father's name, cult, and estate. The second produced the *pallakē* or slave-wife—that is, a wife whose husband became her *kurios* and whose children lacked inheritance rights in their father's name, cult, and estate. Marriage by loan typically involved a transfer of real wealth (although sometimes only a validating token) from the father of the bride to the groom. Marriage by sale involved a transfer of material wealth (or sometimes labor) from the groom to the father of the bride or to the bride herself.

The above nuptial framework is grounded in textual evidence from classical Athens. However, both marriage forms are visible in Ptolemaic Egypt and in Heroic Greece. In particular, Homer and Hesiod provide ample evidence of marriage by sale of the bride to the groom but also reveal legitimate offspring and, by inference at least, marriages in which wealth is transferred from father to groom. Each body of evidence from antiquity is subject to its own specific bias; each shows us a different tip of the iceberg. Scholars may be tempted to conclude that they are seeing distinct icebergs when pooling of the biased fragments of evidence would actually display only a single iceberg. I have seen no commanding reason to postulate significant changes in Greek nuptial law before the Roman era.

I suspect that in Athens under both forms of marriage an *archon* (or comparable official) registered the wife together with her husband. There would have been little point in requiring a wife to register her divorce with a magistrate (as in Plutarch *Alcibiades* 8.2–3; Andocides 4.14; Demosthenes 30.17; cf. Harrison 1968; 42) unless the original marriage had been registered. Registration of the divorce also was probably required for the wife to recover her *proix*—"dowry"—and or her *phernē*—"trousseau" (Harrison 1968: 55–60).[1] Thus, Isaeus 3.35 (tr. Forster *LCL*):

1. When incentives were adequate, the Athenians maintained reasonably accurate records. Aeschines (1.119) explains: "The eminent orator Demosthenes says that you must either wipe out your laws, or else no attention must be paid to my words. For he is amazed, he says, if you do not all remember that every single year the senate farms out the tax on prostitutes, and that the men who buy this tax do not guess, but know precisely, who they are that follow this

> For seeing that, if a man gives with a woman a sum not duly assessed in a contract, and if the wife leaves her husband or the husband puts away his wife, the man who gave the money cannot, as far as the law is concerned, demand back what he gave but did not assess in a contract.

Registration of the divorce would also serve to sort out the legal status of offspring and to facilitate remarriage.

That the Athenian state played a greater role in marriage than is generally recognized is indicated by the entry in the *Suda* On Line (translated headword phrase: "I was a bear at the Brauronia"): "And the Athenians decreed that no *parthenos* might be given in marriage (*sunoikizesthai*) to a man if she had not previously played the bear for the goddess" (tr. Jennifer Benedict). Even if, as is likely, this regulation applied only to a subset of "virgins" (the *parthenoi*), it nevertheless called for a significant bureaucratic role. Note that the *Arkteia* was under the jurisdiction of the *Hieropoioi*, the ten magistrates (*AthPol* 54.7).

2. Marriage by Loan: Male Kurios Lender

The much discussed verb *egguan* has the meanings, "to promise to hand over"/"to deposit (for someone)"/"to pledge"/"to guarantee." It is a key element in both ordinary lending and nuptial transactions (Wolff 1944: 52; Sealey 1984: 120; Ferrari 2003: 29–31; Demosthenes 33). In the nuptial context, *egguan* refers to the formation of a betrothal contract. A second term *ekdosis* whose literal meaning is "to give out"/"to hand over" denotes the fulfillment of a marriage contract, whether or not for a legitimate marriage. Discussion of the latter term is postponed until the conclusion of this section.[2]

Ferrari (2003: 31) makes clear the essentials of the nuptial transaction in a legitimate marriage:

> The fact that the female is "spoken for" is cast in the figure of capital withdrawn from circulation and placed in the vault, from which she will be taken out when the moment comes to hand her over to the groom.

---

profession" (tr. Adams *LCL*). For the registration of land sales and leases, see Zelnick-Abramovitz (2015: 43–44).

2. In the book to which he gave the title *On Dowries* Servius Sulpicius wrote that in the part of Italy known as Latium betrothals were regularly contracted according to the following customary and legal practice. "One who wished to take a wife", says he, "demanded of him from whom she was to be received a formal promise that she would be given in marriage. The man who was to take the woman to wife made a corresponding promise. That contract, based upon pledges given and received, was called *sponsalia*, or 'betrothal.' Thereafter, she who had been promised was called *sponsa*, and he who had asked her in marriage, *sponsus*. But if, after such an interchange of pledges, the bride to be was not given in marriage, or was not received, then he who had asked for her hand, or he who had promised her, brought suit on the ground of breach of contract..." (Gellius *Attic Nights* 4.3.4; tr. Rolfe *LCL*).

The orators Isaeus (8.19) and Demosthenes (57.54) make clear in the phrase *ex astēs egguētēs gunaikos* that the betrothal pledge is a requirement for a woman to be "duly/lawfully married"—that is, to be *legitimately* married.

That the legitimate or *egguētē*-wife remained the property of the (male) *kurios* who pledged her is implicit in the use of loan terminology. As Wolff (1944: 53) concludes that "[t]he aim of the *egguē* was to entrust rather than to alienate the object" (similarly Sealey 1984: 120–21). The features common to a (fulfilled) loan and (fulfilled) nuptial contract for a legitimate bride are as follows. A lender who "pledged" and then "handed over" his cash to a debtor did not thereby surrender ownership of the cash. On the contrary, he permitted the debtor to use his cash (for a stated period and/or until called in) subject to a guarantee of repayment. By analogy, a father (*kurios*) who "pledged" and then "handed over" his daughter to a groom in marriage did not thereby surrender ownership of the daughter.

In legitimate marriage, the husband received from the father (*kurios*) attenuated rights over the woman he had borrowed/married. This set of rights is encapsulated as the right to use her to produce legitimate offspring. Other fundamental rights over the daughter were reserved for her *kurios*. The position of the legitimate wife in her husband's *oikos* is comparable to that of the "resident alien" in the larger Greek community (Lyons 2012: 88, discussed further in Chapter V.1).

Hence, I must disagree with Wolff (1944: 46) when he says that in legitimate marriage the "husband became his wife's *kurios*" (also Sealey 1984: 120–21). Surely, the husband lacked the fundamental right to change her household gods, or give his wife to someone in marriage or to sell her as could be done by the women's father or, most probably, even to physically discipline her (see Chapters X.1 and XVIII). Of course, the husband had rights over the labor-power of his legitimate wife. However, so did an ordinary employer over the labor power of a hired worker. Neither husband nor employer, however, is the legal owner of the person employed. *Kurios*, as has already been stated, is best understood as "owner" not renter/borrower/employer.[3]

Obviously, the ancient Greeks knew well the legal concept and practice of sale/transfer of title but they chose to place legitimate marriage within the same legal framework as the loan. They did this precisely because they (or at least Greek parents) wished to facilitate maximally the rescue of beloved daughters from bad marriages. Since the daughter continued to belong to her original *oikos*, the latter entity could legally demand repayment (of the bride) from the borrowing *oikos* at any time for any reason.

> Marriage did not create a new community of husband and wife; it was a means to provide heirs to the bridegroom's estate by continuing his line. Accordingly, dissolution

3. It is of course true that "ownership" is a vector of rights, but not all rights are equal. The set of rights reserved for the father of the bride have profound effects on social psychology and behavior. Therefore, I see only disadvantages in applying the same technical term to both the father and the husband of a legitimate wife.

> of marriage was relatively easy and could be initiated by the woman's former *kurios* (Sealey 1984: 121).

> [The] bride's journey to her new home is not irreversible and ... far from abandoning her, her kin retains control over her (Ferrari 2003: 36).

This line of analysis finds support not only in the employment of the loan terminology but also by certain facts of practice. As Wolff (1944: 47) notes, "a divorced woman [if legitimately married] passed back into the *kureia* of her relatives without any legal act specifically aimed at that effect." Similarly, a legitimately married widow was automatically legally subject to her original *oikos*. In Demosthenes 41.3–4, Polyeuctus gave his younger daughter in marriage to Leocrates and later took her away (*aphelomenos*) and gave her to Spudias.[4] Also in a fragment (480 Kock) of Menander's *Men at Arbitration*, the father Smikrines seeing that Pamphile's husband was wasting the dowry proposed to remove his daughter from the marriage. Similarly, in Plautus's *Stichus* (1–145), a comedy adapted from a play by Menander, two daughters acknowledge that their father has the right to divorce them from their long-absent husbands.[5] That in the attested examples the right of *aphairesis* is exercised in the interest of the daughter (Urbanik 2016) is not surprising as the main rationale for marriage by loan of the bride is precisely to preserve the welfare of beloved daughters.

Returning to *ekdosis*, according to Wolff (1944: 48–49):

> *Ekdosis* ... always implies that someone gives up power over a person or thing for a specific purpose. But it is at the same time understood that no definite severance of the relationship between the transferor and the object will take place.

I agree with Wolff's first sentence, which I take to mean that the term *ekdosis* signals the transfer of title to an object (nuptial or otherwise) subject to restrictive covenants (for Greco-Roman Egypt see Arnaoutoglou 1995: 17–19). However, I disagree with Wolff's second sentence.

It is true that no definitive transfer of title to the bride occurs in a legitimate marriage. However, there are (non-Athenian) nuptial transactions wherein the technical term *ekdosis* is used independently—that is, without being linked to *egguan*. Some such transactions might perhaps be explained by postulating a change in Greek marriage law. However, there is no direct evidence of any such legal change prior to

4. *Aphairesis* is discussed at length by Harrison (1968: 30–32) and Urbanik (2016).

5. Strabo (11.9.1): "The Tapyri are said to live between the Derbices and the Hyrcanians. It is reported of the Tapyri that it was a custom of theirs to give their wives in marriage to other husbands as soon as they had had two or three children by them; just as in our times, in accordance with an ancient custom of the Romans, Cato gave Marcia in marriage to Hortensius at the request of the latter" (tr. H.L. Jones *LCL*). However, Cato did not directly transfer his wife Marcia to Hortensius; he must first have divorced her and then, we are told, Marcia's father Phillipus married her to Hortensius (Plutarch *Cato* 25.4–5).

Roman times and, as will be discussed further below, legitimate marriage seems to have continued into Ptolemaic Egypt (in *P.Eleph.* 1 dated to 311 BCE). The argument made here is that instances of bridal "giving" without a prior "betrothal" reflect a different (non-legitimate) form of marriage, not a change in marriage law. In such marriages, there is a definitive transfer of the bride to a new *kurios*. The alternative form of marriage, it is well to recall, is demonstrated in Isaeus 3.39 wherein classical Athenians give away (*didōmi*) their womankind by sale. Of course, there is obvious evidence of marriage by sale for pre-classical times, as is amply attested in Homer and Hesiod. In short, the appeal to a change in Greek marriage law in the Hellenistic period is unnecessary as well as being unsubstantiated.

In written nuptial contracts, the giving might be explicitly subject to restrictive covenants concerning the expected treatment of the wife. If the latter covenants are violated by the husband, the woman (or her former *kurios*) has legally enforceable grounds to take her property and withdraw from the marriage. However, instead of being automatic as in marriage by loan, divorce required a legal act specifically aimed at this result (see further Section 4 below).

3. Marriage by Sale: Male *Kurios* Seller

It merits repetition that in mentioning "those [Athenians] who give their womenkind to others as *pallakia*" the speaker in Isaeus (3.39) reveals that a classical Athenian *kurios* might sell his daughter or other female dependent into wifeship. At the same time, the speaker makes clear that the children of women given away into *pallakia* lacked inheritance rights in the father's estate.[6] The testimony in Isaeus is supplemented by the report that instead of giving his sister in legitimate marriage, as only a citizen could do, Timocrates "sold" her or "sold her for export" (*peprake*, *ekdounai peprake*) to a visiting diplomat from Corcyra (Demosthenes 24.202–03).

Plutarch (*Moralia* 753D) recalls that in the sixth century BCE, Themistocles's father acquired his Thracian (non-citizen) wife Habrotonon *ex agoras gamein* "from the marketplace." Greek marriage by purchase might fruitfully be compared to Rome's *coemptio matrimonia causa* (Buckland 1921: 119; Watson 1967: 24) in which a free woman was sold into wifeship and thereby became her husband's property.[7] In the case of sale, the buyer—the husband—became the woman's new *kurios*.

6. That marriage form is subject to choice is implicit in a fragment of Euripides' *Andromeda*, "I forbid you the conception [*labien*] of bastard sons [*nothioi*]. Though in no way inferior to legitimate ones [*gnēsioi*], they are handicapped by convention/law [*nomos*], and this is something you must beware of" (Fragment 141; tr. Collard and Cropp *LCL* modified).

7. In Roman marriage by *coemptio* (a sale by mancipation), the woman legally becomes the daughter of her husband and could be mancipated by him just as any other property (Gaius *Institutes* 1.113, 1.117–20). Gaius *Institutes* 1.122 states that the wife in *manus* was not legally a slave (*servus*): "If anyone should ask what is the difference between coemption and mancipation, the reply is that the first ceremony does not reduce the party to a servile condition; but persons of either sex mancipated by parents or others are reduced to the condition of slaves, to such

In addition, note Isocrates 9.50 (tr. Norlin *LCL*):

> At present, however, they [the Cypriots] have undergone so great a change that they strive with one another to see who shall be regarded as most friendly to the Greeks, and the majority of them take their wives [*lambanein gunaika*] from us and from them beget children, and they have greater pleasure in owning Greek possessions and observing Greek institutions than in their own, and more of those who occupy themselves with the liberal arts and with education in general now dwell in these regions than in the communities in which they formerly used to live. And for all these changes, no one could deny that Evagoras [king of Salamis] is responsible.

Taking/receiving Greek wives may or may not refer to the Cypriots purchasing them but it certainly does not refer to legitimately marrying them.

When the woman sold into marriage was an ordinary slave, the Greek practice of sale into *pallakia* arguably involved two steps. First, the buyer/husband freed his purchased slave and then the free woman sold herself to him in *pallakia*. This kind of two-step process is visible in Menander's "*Misumenos*" ("The Man She Hated") 38–40, 707, a comedy set in an unnamed city, wherein: (1) Thrasonides purchases the *aichmalōtos* Crateia and frees her (*peritheis eleutherian*) (38–40); (2) the latter act gives Crateia the status of single woman (*parthenos* "virgin"); and then (3) Crateia sells herself to him as a wife (*gunaika nomisas*). Sommerstein (2014: 23, n. 19; cf. Traill 2008: 27–28) rightly refers to a "conditional manumission." The second sale transforms Crateia into the mistress of Thrasonides's household, a status that is recognized/remunerated by her receipt of slaves, jewelry and clothes. Later on, Demeas, Crateia's father, offers to pay to redeem her from her obligations (*apolutroun*; 699, 715). This demonstrates that she had slave status (see e.g. Tucker 1982). It also appears that

an extent that they cannot take either an estate or a legacy under the will of the party by whom they have been mancipated, unless they have been ordered to be free by the terms of the same will; just as the law is with reference to the persons of slaves. The reason for this distinction is clear, as the words used by parents and so-called purchasers are the same as those employed in the mancipation of slaves, but in the coemption of women this is not the case" (tr. de Zulueta). On the other hand, Gaius *Institutes* 1.138 says, "As persons who have been sold in this way [apparently by coemption] are considered to occupy the position of slaves, if they should be manumitted either by the praetor, or by enrollment in the census, or by will, they become their own masters." Frier and McGinn (2004: 90) comment: "A wife in *manus* was protected by certain social conventions, which were transformed into legal norms at a very early time; thus, it was apparently illegal for a husband to sell his wife, to give her in adoption, or to execute her even for serious misconduct without first consulting a *consilium* of relatives ... Further, the wife acceded to the responsible and socially honored position of *mater familias*. Although there is no denying that her position was weak in law, it was not entirely abject." With all due respect, I think Frier and McGinn underestimate the prevalence of *manus*-marriage in the later Republic and Empire and underestimate the extent to which the wife entered into the *patria potestas* of her husband. There are, however, indications of "ameliorative" changes in the law. That is, the Roman state attempted to prevent individuals from choosing *manus*-marriage. Even so, the *legal* difference between the wife in *manus* and the *servus* remained only a matter of a few degrees and she was very much closer to slave than to free status.

Thrasonides freed Crateia so that Demeas could give her to him in legitimate marriage (Traill 2008: 32 citing verses 794 ff.).[8]

The two-step marriage process for ordinary slaves is also apparent in Chariton's *Callirhoe*, a Greek novel possibly written as early as the first century CE but whose setting is the later fifth century BCE. First, Dionysius speaks of marriage to a slave girl (*gamous doulēs*) (2.4–5). Later on, there is a legal clarification:

> Rather he [Dionysius] bought her [Callirhoe] when she was offered for sale, and the law which applies to adultery does not apply to slaves. Let him first read to you the certificate of her emancipation and then let him talk of marriage (5.7.3–4; tr. Gould *LCL*).[9]

A final point is that Aristotle (*Politics* 2.1268b.40) mentions "ancient laws" according to which the Hellenes "purchase (*eōnounto*) their wives (*gunaikas*) from one another" (tr. Rackham *LCL*). The implication may be that these laws had been revoked or substantially modified. The evidence makes clear, however, that sale of wives persisted in Classical and Hellenistic Greece.

4. Marriage by Self-Sale/Auto-*Ekdosis*

As already argued, *ekdosis* "handing over" of the bride is a necessary but not a sufficient act in constituting a legitimate marriage.[10] Evidence from temporally and geographically outside classical Greece, but still from a Greek milieu, reveals self-sale (or "auto-*ekdosis*") meaning that women "gave *themselves* over" (*ekdosis*) in marriage. Also, there are examples where women are handed over not by a male *kurios* but by their mothers or grandmothers (Yiftach-Firanko 2003: 25–26 with n. 13). It is argued

8. Under Roman law a female slave manumitted by her owner for the purpose of marriage (*matrimonii causa*) was subject to reenslavement if she failed to marry him and, accordingly, could not divorce him (*Digest* 23.2.51.pr. Licinnius Rufunus; 24.2.10,11 Modestinus, compare Buckland 1908: 540; Perry 2014: 55–56). That she could not divorce (Modestinus contested by Julian) suggests to me that the manumitted slave had been transformed into a slave-wife (like Menander's Glycera).

9. There are additional, more speculative, illustrations of the two-step process of sale into *pallakia*. In Sophocles' *Trachiniae* (367, 1219 ff.), Heracles says that he sends the captive slave woman Iole to Hyllus, "not to be his (female) slave (*oud hōste doulēn*);" he then instructs his son to take Iole as a wife (*prosthou damarta*) and to form with her a "marriage bond" (*kēdeuson lechos*; tr. Segal 1994: 59–60). The implication is that Iole must first be freed and then married. I think MacKinnon (1971: 35–37) is correct in concluding that Iole cannot be a legitimate wife. In answer to Segal's question "Bride or Concubine?", my answer is "Bride and *Pallakē*". In Demosthenes 59.31–32, Phrynion purchased the freedom of Neaira and she followed him from Corinth to Athens. I submit that as a condition of freedom she agreed to become Phrynion's *pallakē* (see Kamen 2014: 296).

10. In *P.Oxy.* 6.905.4–5 (170 CE) a father hands over (*ekdosis*) his daughter to form a marital association/partnership (*gamou koinōnian*). The bride (not the father?) brings a dowry of gold into the marital association. This is a surprising formulation for a legitimate marriage. For other examples and discussion, see Yiftach-Firanko (2005: 70–72 n. 18).

in Chapter V.2 that auto-*ekdosis* is attested in classical Greece by the iconographic gesture of handshake between groom and bride.

In Chariton's *Callirhoe* (3.2.8–9), reference is made to women resident in Miletus who "give" themselves in marriage. Dionysius of Miletus has married Callirhoe, a citizen of Syracuse, whom he had purchased from the tomb robber Theron. Now Dionysius must devise a better legal and moral claim to his beloved wife:

> Soon Syracusan warships will be here with the general Hermocrates demanding back his daughter. What am I going to say? Theron sold her to me? But where is Theron? Even if I am believed in this, do I tell them the truth, that I am a receiver of stolen goods from a pirate? Dionysius, you had better get your story ready. Possibly you will have to plead it before the Great King. If so, it will be best to say. "I somehow heard that a freeborn girl had taken up residence here. She gave herself [*ekdidōmi*] to be my wife and I married her in the city, openly and according to the law" (Chariton *Callirhoe* 3.2.8–9; tr. Gould *LCL*).

Dionysius's explanation would have lacked all credibility if single women who were their own *kuria* and hence able to give themselves in legal marriage were not at least somewhat familiar in Miletus, note the arrival there of Pieria from Myus (Callimachus *Aetia* Fragment 83b Pfeiffer) and, indeed, in the Greek world generally.

A strong example of auto-*ekdosis* is *P.Giss.* 2.8–12, a marriage contract dated 173 BCE from Crocodilopolis in Ptolemaic Egypt. Therein, a woman named Olympias with a living *kurios* named Dionysios *gives herself* in marriage to an Athenian named Antaios. Olympias takes with her into the marriage substantial property of her own (designated as *phernē*), "reckoned in bronze ninety-five talents and her slave-girl ... and her nursling child ... worth five bronze talents" (tr. Rowlandson 1998: 168 no. 126).[11] Another provision in the contract calls upon Olympias and Antaios to jointly manage their marital property. That is, there is a commingling of the assets of wife and husband.

It is probably relevant that both the father and the groom are cavalrymen. Perhaps, the father's military duties had taken him away from Crocodilopolis for an extended period making it necessary and (evidently) legal for Olympia to give herself away. Most likely, her father had emancipated Olympia. Indeed, the contract calls for Antaios to support his wife in the accustomed fashion "both when he is at home and when he is abroad" (tr. Rowlandson 1998: 168 no. 126). The point is that the mention of the *kurios*,

11. Contrary to what is sometimes claimed, there is no mention of "dowry" (*proix*) in the papyrus. *Proix* and *phernē* have different meanings and both terms are used in Ptolemaic marriage documents. As noted by Yiftach-Firanko (2003: 108; cf. 123–24), unlike the *proix*, the *phernē* is "designated as the wife's own [*phernē tēs heautēs*], and any wrongdoings on her part in the course of the marriage could incur its forfeiture. When the marriage was dissolved, the *phernē* would be recovered by the wife, rather than by her earlier *kyrios*." Of course, the so-called "earlier *kurios*" need not have been the one who provided the *phernē* to the woman or who gave her in marriage. Modrzejewski (2005: 349) maintains that "[t]he classical *proix* gives place to the *phernē*." This is not a useful statement as the two are different and not mutually exclusive. It is possible that groom-purchase became less prevalent but we have no data for earlier times.

it seems to me, means only that he had consented to his daughter's independence/ on her own status.

Even so, notwithstanding the reference to *ekdosis* and the egalitarian arrangements, there is no mention of a betrothal contract and, in fact, Olympia is designated as *gunaika gametēn* "married woman" not as *gnēsion* "legitimate married woman."[12] Note that in *P.Eleph.* 1, there is no mention of *egguēsis* but the bride is nevertheless designated "*gunaika gnēsian*." So, at the very least, the ideal of legitimate marriage lived on into Ptolemaic times. It may be that the omission of "legitimate" lacked significance in terms of a loss of some citizenship rights since, as noted by Yiftach-Firanko (2003: 45): "In Egypt, most Greeks no longer lived under the precepts of a polis." However, whatever the merits of this line of argument, under Greek law, attested as early as *Odyssey* 14.199–210, any children born to a non-legitimate union would not have the legal right to inherit their father's property (cf. Ogden 1996, 23).[13] The civil rights of the wife would also be adversely affected.

My proposal is that Olympias actually lived outside Dionysios's *oikos* and was legally a single woman—that is, she was her own *kuria*. This would explain why Dionysios, her *kurios*, did not provide a dowry and why Olympias was not handed over into legitimate marriage.[14]

---

12. In *P.Eleph.* 1 (311 BCE), an early Ptolemaic document, the bride Demetria is handed over by *ekdosis* (= *lambanō*) by her father Leptines (and her mother Philotis) to the groom Heracleides. There is no mention in the text of *egguēsis* but it must be assumed to have taken place as the bride is designated "*gunaika gnēsian*" (Yiftach-Firanko 2003: 41–43). The groom accepted the responsibility "to supply to Demetria all that is proper for a freeborn wife" (tr. Rowlandson 1998: 165 no. 123). Modrzejewski (2005: 349) says, "[S]ome formalities disappear, like *engyēsis*, in which the father 'placed' his daughter in the hands of the man who was about to become her husband." This is not an accurate statement of the betrothal practice and we have no evidence that the offspring of other (non-legitimate) forms of marriage had inheritance rights.
13. Modrzejewski (2005: 148–49) claims: "The new conditions in which the Greek immigrants' family life organized itself modified matrimonial law. In the Hellenistic world, heads of families no longer settle by themselves the question of concluding a marriage, as in classical Athens; it becomes a matter for the couples themselves." This is circular reasoning. Since we do not have the laws we cannot say whether they changed or not. Indeed, it is not even possible to say that matrimonial practice changed, as we have no documents reveaing the classical Athenian practice. We know what classical scholars believe but we do not know how common *auto-ekdosis* actually was. With respect to the constancy of Greek nuptial traditions, it is useful to quote the Greek historian Diodorus Siculus (5.73.2) who was active in the second half of the first century BCE: "To Aphroditê was entrusted the youth of maidens, the years in which they are expected to marry, and the supervision of such matters as are observed even yet in connection with weddings, together with the sacrifices and drink-offerings which men perform to this goddess" (tr. Oldfather *LCL*).
14. In a much later Greek text (*P.Oxy.* 2.137.7.12–13 dated to 128 CE), a daughter contests her father's right to remove her from her current marriage. The available evidence signals that under received Greek law, the father who gave his daughter in legitimate marriage had the right to divorce her; the only valid legal ground for contesting the divorce would be that, the father was *not* the woman's *kurios* or that he had *not* given his daughter in marriage. If I reconstruct

So Olympias was legally able to give herself in marriage but the question remains what was her final legal status? Olympias did retain the right to sue for divorce under a number of conditions:

> Let it not be allowed for him [to introduce] another woman into Olympias' presence or have a *pallakē* or a boy lover. [Nor let it be allowed for him to beget children] from another woman in Olympias' lifetime, or to inhabit another [house of which] Olympias shall not be mistress, or cast her out, or insult her], or injure her], or alienate any property to Olympias' [detriment]. If he should be proved to do any of these things or not to supply her with [furniture or clothing] or the rest [as written above, let Antaios immediately pay back to Olympias] the *phernē* [and a fifty percent fine...] (tr. Rowlandson 1998: 168 no. 126, modified).

The handing over (*ekdosis*) was subject to numerous legally enforceable restrictive covenants but Olympias did not possess the right to divorce without a magistrate's authorization, as could a legitimate wife. A transfer of title had unquestionably taken place. Olympias, I believe, found it in her interest to become a *pallakē*-wife and in doing so she came under Antaios's ownership.[15]

5. Menander's Glycera as *Pallakē*

The case of Glycera in Menander's "The Girl with Her Hair Cut Short" is both complex and reasonably well documented. We learn (130–31) that Glycera, an exposed citizen-girl (in Corinth?), was "raised as a daughter" by an "old woman" and then she was "given" (*didōsi*) "to possess" (*echein*) by the old woman to a man from Corinth named Polemon.

Two kinds of interpretations present themselves. First, Glycera was a *nothē* and hence arguably the property of the "old woman" who was her *pallakē*-mother (or grandmother). In Roman terms, the "old woman" was Glycera's *materfamilias* (see Section 5 below). Second, one may think of Glycera in terms of auto-*ekdosis*—that is, Glycera was her own *kuria* and gave herself in marriage to Polemon. In this second view, the "old woman" perhaps played the role of *promnestria* "(old woman?) matchmaker" (e.g. Aristophanes *Clouds* 41; Pollux 3.31).

The second interpretation is reinforced by Glycera's acting "as her own *kuria*" (*heautes kuria*) in giving herself (*autē*) to Polemon in marriage (487, 490, 497). Famously, when Pataikos asked Polemon who gave (*histēmi*: "put in place") Glycera to him (as wife), he says, "Who? To me? She did herself" to which Pataikos responds: "All right. Perhaps she liked you—now she doesn't any more. She's left you because you've treated her so badly!" (490 ff.; tr. Arnott *LCL*).

---

correctly, it was the woman herself (Dionysia), not her father (Chairemon), who had given her in marriage (see the remarks of Yiftach-Firanko 2003: 47–49, 52 with n. 34). In short, Dionysia was "given" but not in legitimate marriage.

15. I would suggest that Olympias did not receive a marriage gift (*dōra*) from Antaios because, as a wife, she continued to live in her previous locality (see below).

Additional support for the first interpretation that Glycera was the property of the "old woman" is that *echein* "to possess" is usually understood in the sense of property and given the stress on the desperate financial straits of the "old woman" (124–27) it is possible to understand that Glycera was sold as a slave to Polemon (Furley 2015: 9–10 with n. 39, 93). Polemon then agreed to free her on the understanding (probably by oath[16]) that she would marry him (see below).[17] This might help to explain why Sosias refers to Glycera, whom I understand to be a slave-wife, as *eleutheran* "free woman" (375). The line of interpretation in which the "old woman" is the bride's *kuria* is examined in the next section in which Demeter plays the "old woman" role and Persephone plays the sold/self-sold bride.

Near the end of the play, Pataikos, Glycera's true father (Furley 2015: 25–27), gives Glycera to Polemon in what looks very much like legitimate marriage: "This girl I give to you to harvest [legitimate] children" (1012–14; tr. Arnott *LCL*). Polemon accepts his offer and then Pataikos adds a generous dowry (1014–15). Thus, it is made clear that up to this point Glycera had not been a legitimate wife. Nevertheless, Polemon is referred to as Glycera's *andra* (husband; 186). Elsewhere, Polemon calls Glycera his *gunaika* (wife; 376) and says he "treated her as his *gametēn* [lawful wife]" (489). In referring to the cropping of her hair, Polemon's slave Sosias (172) refers to Glycera as "wife": Polemon is "the one who won't let wives (*gunaikas*) keep their hair." Sosias (357, 370, 390) calls Moischion (who kissed Glycera without being aware she was his sister) *moischos*—"adulterer". Recall that according to a law of Draco, cited in Lysias 1.30–31 (quoted in Chapter III), a man was guilty of adultery only if he had a sexual relationship with either a legitimate wife or a *pallakē*. Most

16. Roman law recognized that a slave might take an oath to perform services for his (former) master (*Digest* 38.1.7 Ulpian). With respect to marriage to a (former) slave: "A patron cannot marry his freedwoman against her will" (*Digest* 23.2.28 Ulpian); "Note, however, that this rule does not apply where the patron manumitted her in order to marry her" (*Digest* 23.2.29 Ulpian) (tr. Watson).

17. In real life, Glycera might have been the biological daughter or granddaughter of the "old woman." Similarly, in Plautus's *Mostellaria* ("*The Ghost*") which is set in Athens, a young man (Philomaches) purchases the freedom of a young girl (Philematium) who desires to *marry* him: "He freed me alone for himself alone at his own expense; I think I ought to please him alone" (204–05). She is counseled by an "old woman" (Scapha) as follows: "You're indeed making a mistake by waiting on him alone; showing him your special favor like this, and despising others. It's appropriate for a married woman, not for a *meretrix*, to be at the beck of a single lover" [*meretrix* "woman who earns" seems to correspond *in usage* to *hetaira* "single woman"] (188–89). However, the old woman continues, "If you feel assured you'll have food for good and that he'll be your own lover throughout life, I think you ought to humor only him and assume the matron's plaits" [at marriage a Roman girl's hair was divided into six braids]; to which Philematium responds: "As one's reputation is, so one usually finds money. If I preserve my good reputation, I shall be rich enough," drawing a response from Philomaches: "If my father has to be sold, he'll be sold much rather than I ever let you be poor or beg while I'm alive" (224–30; translations of *Mostellaria* are from de Melo *LCL*; cf. Williams 1958: 19–20, 23).

importantly, Pataikos calls Glycera Polemon's *gametēn gunaika*—"legally wedded wife" but not "legitimate wife" (487; cf. Konstan 1987: 128; Gomme and Sandbach 1973: 458, 477, 505–06).

It is also significant that Polemon is called the *kurios* of Glycera (376). As noted earlier, Polemon's cropping of his wife's hair served to emphasize her slave status. In response to Glycera's departure to Moschion's house, Polemon ventured the legal complaint (*egklēma*) that Moschion had "corrupted" (*diaphtheirō*) Glycera (496 ff.) This indicates that as a *pallakē*-wife Glycera had slave status. One cannot legally "corrupt" a free person.

Thus, whether one prefers the first or the second interpretation, the internal evidence confirms that Glycera had been a *pallakē* owned by her husband Polemon *and* lawfully wedded to him. It is possible to understand her leaving Polemon to mean that the marriage contract was not legally enforceable (see Section 7 below). I do not believe this is the case, however. The Roman precedents bearing on this problem seem relevant.[18]

I would rely on two explanations of Glycera's desertion of Polemon. First, my preferred theory, the abused wife Glycera simply ran away from her husband Polemon who, as the play makes very clear, was much more interested in rekindling Glycera's affection for him than in pursuing his available legal remedies. With respect to the availability of legal remedies against a runaway *pallakē*, note Demosthenes 59.40:

> Phrynion, however, learned that the woman [Neaira, arguably his runaway *pallakē*[19]] was in Athens, and was living with Stephanus, and taking some young men with him he came to the house of Stephanus and attempted to carry her off. When Stephanus took her away from him, as the law allowed, declaring her to be a free woman, Phrynion required her to post bonds with the polemarch (tr. DeWitt and DeWitt *LCL*).

My second theory is that when Polemon cropped Glycera's hair he breached his oath or reversed treatment clauses (restrictive covenants) in their nuptial contract, and

18. Gaius *Institutes* 1.137a states: "They also cease to be in the hand of their husbands by remancipation; and if emancipated after a single sale they become their own mistresses. A woman who has concluded a coemption with a stranger by way of trust can compel him to sell her again to anyone whom she may select; *but one who has been sold to her husband, in whose hand she is, cannot compel him to do so, any more than a daughter can compel her father, even though she may be an adopted daughter. A woman, however, can, by serving notice of repudiation, force her husband to release her, just as if she had never been married*: (tr. de Zulueta; emphasis added). There seems to be a contradiction between the last two sentences and it seems possible that the last sentence about the "notice of repudiation" is a later interpolation (cf. Frier and McGinn 2004: 94).

19. I am inclined to the view that after being freed by Eucrates and Timanoridas in Corinth, Neaira agreed to come to Athens with Phrynion as his *pallakē*—that is, as his slave-wife. In the event of a dispute over status, an owner had to sue for the return of his slave (Demosthenes 59: 40, 45; Silver 2013: 108).

effectively created legal grounds for divorce. Surely, the legal authorities under the conditions stated in *P.Giss* 2.8–12 would have freed Olympias. Other Ptolemaic marriage contracts state that the husband "is not to 'cast out' [*ekballein*] his wife, 'treat her spitefully' [*hybridzein*], or 'ill-treat her' [*kakouchein*]" (Yiftach-Firkanko 2003: 187). Again, Roman precedents are relevant.[20]

6. Marriage of Persephone to Hades[21]

In the *Homeric Hymn to Demeter* 2 (esp. 1–32, 72–89), Pesephone seems to be both inside and outside the *oikos* of her father Zeus.[22] While enjoying flowers, including the crocus, in a lush meadow, a "lamenting" and "screaming" Persephone is abducted by Hades who carries her away in his (nuptial) chariot. Persephone's participation in a wilderness occupation indicates single woman status as is attested in the cases of Stratonice, Atalanta, and the Protids (all discussed below). Zeus had given the unwilling bride Persephone, his daughter by Demeter, to his brother Hades "without the consent" of her mother Demeter (2.72 ff.). Demeter departed from Olympus and joined humans in the guise of a *palaigenei* (old woman; 2.92 ff.).

It might appear that Zeus gave away his unwilling daughter in legitimate marriage (see Foley 1999: 108). There are severe problems with this interpretation, however. First, as pointed out by Foley (1999: 107):

> [T]he inaccessibility of Hades makes it geographically impossible for the marriage to function endogenously. Thus Persephone is subjected to an extreme form of virilocal exogamy in which she is permanently denied access to her parents.

Given the vast distance between domiciles, my model predicts that Hades would have paid *hedna* "bride-price" to Zeus for Persephone (see Chapter IX). In fact, in lines 79–80 (also line 3), we learn that Zeus "gave her to Hades, her father's brother, to be called his buxom wife [*thalerēn akoitin*]." The verb is *didōmi*, whose meaning, as noted elsewhere, includes "sale." Thus, potentially, Zeus sold his daughter into *pallakia* as called for in my model. The second problem, however, is that Persephone was a single

20. In terms of Roman law, Polemon's physical and probably his accompanying verbal abuse constituted a *contrarius actus* that terminated *manus* (Nótári 2008: 335–36). There is some reason to believe that this kind of rule prevailed in Athens as well. By claiming that Myrrihine and Moschion were holding a free (freeborn?) woman (Glycera) against the will of her *kurios* (Menander, "The Girl with Her Hair Cut Short" 380 ff.), Polemon's slave Sosias was putting forward a legal justification for storming the house and carrying her off. In fact, Glycera suffered no legal consequences. Similarly, when Neaira was living in Athens, arguably as Phrynion's *pallakē*-wife, she left him when he abused her. Later, Neaira returned to Athens with Stephanus and Phrynion wished to take her by force. However, other than having to return some property, she did not suffer any visible consequences (Demosthenes 59.35, 40, 45 and below).
21. The reader is advised to return to this section after reading Chapters V and X.
22. Translations of the *Homeric Hymn to Demeter* 2 are from Everlyn-White *LCL*.

woman and, consequently, Zeus was not her *kurios* and lacked the legal right either to betroth her in legitimate marriage or to sell her into *pallakia*.

Adding to the interpretative difficulties there is a "happy ending" (443 ff.). Because of a negotiation concerning both distance and price, a nuanced compromise emerges. Persephone is to live with Hades for one-third of the year and with Demeter and the other gods of Mount Olympus for two-thirds of the year. Also, Demeter, as is appropriate for an "old woman" as *materfamilias*, is to be compensated with *timai*—"honors"—for being separated from her daughter (443–44). In line 462 Rhea reveals that Zeus also offers new "honors" to Persephone. The additional "honors" must refer to an increase in the wealth of the cults of Demeter and Persephone. Note in support of this "materialistic" understanding that in line 86 it is noted: "As for honor, he (Hades) got his one-third at the world's first division" (*Iliad* 15.187–93; Rudhardt 1999). The problem with the *dōra*—"gifts"—to Demeter and Persephone is that Zeus makes them, not Hades. This apparent problem is remedied in alternative versions.

In a second version" of Persephone's marriage, Zeus purchased Persephone (or to name her with a metronymic "Persephone, daughter of Demeter") from her *kuria* Demeter to give her as bride to his brother Hades.

In a third version, probably the original one, Persephone sells herself into *pallakia*. The payment is made directly to her and the payer, as expected, is her husband (*gambros*, 84) Hades (Suter 2002: 3, 34–35, 59, 129–30). Hades promises to his bride Persephone (364–69):

> And while you are here [in the Underworld], you shall rule all that lives and moves and shall have the greatest rights among the deathless gods: those who defraud you and do not appease your power with offerings (*timas*), reverently performing rites and paying fit gifts, shall be punished for evermore.

The understanding that Hades purchased Persephone from herself finds support in her designation as *thalerēn akoitin* (79–80) meaning not "buxom wife" but "*rich* wife" (see the discussion of Stratonice below).

Of course, it needs to be kept in mind in all of this that the Persephone myth as we have it has been "Olympianized" (Suter 2002: 129–30) and also that it is intended to explain not only nuptiality but also seasonality (Rudhardt 1999). The contradictions are therefore understandable.

7. Legal Enforceability of Self-Sale into *Pallakia*

The problem at hand is whether self-sale into *pallakia* was legally enforceable in classical Athens. A most relevant law is stated in Lysias 10.10: "For a minor is not allowed to make a will; for the law expressly forbids any child—or woman—to contract for the disposal of more than a bushel (*medimnos*) of barley" (tr. Forster *LCL*; discussed by de Ste. Croix 1970).[23] The specified quantity of barley is sufficient to feed a family for a week or so.

There is of course the unsettled question of whether this law applied to self-sale into slavery or to women who were their own *kuria*, including those who were freed slaves. I doubt it. Also, it is not clear and does not even seem reasonable to assume that law applied to the value received by a woman as well as to the value dispersed by her.

In any event, the absence of legal enforceability would have had the effect of deterring men from purchasing women who proposed to self themselves into wifeship but not to the point of making the practice uncommon. The main reason is that in the ancient world and specifically in classical Athens, the most important contractual binding force was good faith whose major building block was the oath. Contracts of self-sale into *pallakia* would be enforceable by the consciences of the contracting parties and by the gods, even if not by the courts. Another, previously noted, factor is that a dissatisfied husband might confiscate the *peculium* (purchase price) of the *pallakē*, which was legally his property. The threat of confiscation constituted a self-enforcing mechanism in the self-sale contract.[24]

E. Cohen (2015: ch. 4) notes that Athenian women formed legally enforceable commercial contracts to provide men with sexual companionship, a practice known as "whoring under contract." Unfortunately, it is not easy to find even one clear real world example of this practice.[25] De Brauw and Miner (2004: 308) make an important point: "The advantage of a contract for the customer (whether he was contracting a citizen or a slave) was the guarantee that the sex was consensual." The contract was important not so much to protect the buyer against a woman's non-performance as to protect him from being sued or charged with adultery.

Turning to more traditional contracts, Antigone, called a *hetaira* by the speaker, acted as a broker in a business transaction between Epicrates and Athenogenes in which role she "took the most solemn oaths" and pocketed a significant commission for her services (Hyperides 3.2–3; tr. Burtt LCL; Fletcher 2014: 167–69). There is

23. There is evidence for the commercial independence of women elsewhere in the Greek world as in Hellenistic Sicily (Souza 2016).

24. As a result of an arbitration proceeding, the runaway *pallakē* Neaira was allowed to keep some or all of her *peculium*: "she [Neaira] should give back to Phrynion all that she had taken with her from his house except the clothing and the jewels and the maid-servants; for these had been bought for the use of the woman herself." However, the relationship between Phrynion and Neaira was not terminated as it was also agreed that "she should live with each of the men on alternate days" (Demosthenes 59.46; tr. De Witt and De Witt *LCL*).

25. In Plautus's *Asinaria* ("*The Comedy of Asses*" 746 ff.), a comedy based on a Greek original, there is a written contract (*syngraphus*) calling for Philaenium to provide exclusive sexual services to Diabolus for a period of one year in return for a large payment in advance. There are many restrictive covenants including the phrase: "If she sets her eyes on another, she shall be blinded immediately" (770–71; tr. de Melo *LCL*). This clause surely reflects the contemporary reliance on the oath-curse mechanism (see e.g. Hesiod *Theogony* 231–32; Croon 1952: 118, 120).

no reason to believe that prostitutes/courtesans typically undertook this kind of commercial duty. Neither is there any reason to assume that Antigone was not a citizen. Phillips (2009: 99) asserts that Antigone could not have served as a court witness to the contract between the parties because she was a woman.[26] Perhaps not, but the reliance of the contractors on her "solemn oaths" made it possible for the contract to be formed and implemented. Further, the oaths taken by women could be introduced as evidence in trials (Demosthenes 29.26; 39; 40; Isaeus 12.9; Harrison 1968: 79; Blok 2017: 62 with n. 73). In addition, Phillips does not consider whether it was legally significant that, as a *hetaira* (single woman), Antigone did not have a male *kurios.*[27]

8. Restrictive Covenants Generally and in the Marriage Market

Wolff (1944: 51) theorized: "From a sociological point of view, however, marriage and purchase were never the same thing. It was never forgotten that in the former the acquisition was to serve a particular purpose, and early people distinguished well between the two transactions, in terminology as well as in practical details. It is therefore, by no means contradictory to assume that sooner or later the transfer effected in the case of marriage might lead to consequences different from a transfer effected by an ordinary purchase." Obviously, Wolff can provide no evidence about the attitudes of imagined "early people;" he is obliquely recognizing the possibility of ongoing sales into slavery with a restrictive covenant providing that the slave be employed as a wife (see usefully Corbett 1930: 11; Finley 1954: 15).

Roman law, including slave law, was of course familiar with restrictive covenants. Besides incorporating a legally recognized manumission clause (*ut manumittatur*), self-sellers might negotiate a sales clause calling for them to be exported (*ut exportetur*) or not to be exported, or a covenant which forbade the buyer to prostitute them (*ne serva prostituatur*) (*Digest* 18.7.0, 40.8.0, 37.14.7.pr Modestinus, 18.1.56 Paul; Perry 2014: 34–37; McGinn 1990; Buckland 1908: esp. 69–72, 628–40).

It might be justified to speak of marriage by purchase as a special kind of marriage ("morganatic" marriage) if Greek law (unlike Roman law) did not know restrictive

26. The "wife of Polyeuctus" left behind a sealed will ("papers"), which was respected by her family and referred to in a court case (Demosthenes 41.9, 21; Hunter 1989: 44 n. 25).

27. In Aristophanes' *Thesmophoriazusae* (839–45), the "mother of Hyperbolus" is said to make interest-bearing loans: "Oh! citizens! Is it just that the mother of Hyperbolus should sit dressed in white and with loosened tresses beside that of Lamachus and lend out money on usury? He, who may have made a deal of this nature with her, so far from paying her interest, should not even repay the capital, saying, What, pay you interest? After you have given us this delightful son?" (tr. O'Neill *LCL*). In Isaeus 10.23, a woman is spoken of as *kuria* of an estate (cf. Isaeus 6.30; Hunter 1989: 45–46). Kron (1996: 141), citing Demosthenes 59.115–17, suggests that a woman, an Athenian priestess, filed a lawsuit over the performance of a sacrifice by an unauthorized male: "As far as we can see, priestesses did not unconditionally need a *kyrios* ... to act legally for them".

covenants (compare Koschaker 1937: 79 f., 83 f.). This is not the case, however. As will be seen, Greek legal practice, like the Roman, was accustomed to restrictive covenants.

The general law of contract/contractual norm at Athens left ample room for writing and enforcing restrictive covenants, "Well, gentlemen of the jury, you have heard the facts in detail. But Athenogenes will presently tell you that in law whatever agreements one man makes with another are binding" (Hyperides 3.13; tr. Burtt *LCL*; cf. Demosthenes 47.77, 56.2; Phillips 2009; Carawan 2006: esp. 343; Avilés 2012; but compare Thür 2013: 8–9).

More specifically, a contract well attested in fourth-century Attica included a significant restriction on the rights of a purchaser of real estate/reservation of rights to his property by a seller (Fine 1951: 62, 69). The contract, called *prasis epi lysei* "sale on condition of release," is a *sale* of land (and/or structures) in which the seller reserves the option of repurchase (Fine 1951: 62, 69, 143, 156–60; cf. E.M. Harris 1988). The contract is found engraved on stone pillars and is mentioned by the orators (e.g. Isaeus 6.36; Demosthenes 37.4–5).

With respect to restrictive covenants in slave law, Athens knew the "sale [to a third party] for the purpose of [granting] freedom" (Kamen 2014; Glazebrook 2014). At Delphi, slaves were sold to Apollo for the purpose that they should be freed (Tucker 1982). In a much-discussed Athenian trial it is noted that Neaira was sold and freed by Eucrates and Timanoridas on the condition that she no longer work in Corinth (Demosthenes 59.31–32; Kamen 2014: 292, 295–96). Note also the sale of Midas and his sons for the purpose of freedom (Hyperides 5.5).

In the classical Athenian marriage market, sales contracts with restrictive covenants and contracts permitting unrestricted use of the purchased woman might coexist. Thus, in Antiphon 1.14, it appears that Philoneus had effectively unrestricted rights over his *pallakē*, whom he contemplated demoting from wife to prostitute (see Chapter III). On the other hand, the contract between Phrynion and Neaira arguably included covenants governing the husband's treatment of his purchased wife: note that an Athenian arbitration panel freed Neaira (placed her in her own hands) after she had deserted her abusive *kurios* Phrynion (Demosthenes 59:31–35, 40, 45–46). As already noted, the form of the contract binding Menander's Glycera to Polemon is unclear. The clearest and most direct evidence for restrictive covenants comes from Isaeus 3.39 wherein the speaker explains, "[E]ven those who give [*didontes*] their womenkind to others as *pallakia* make stipulations in advance as to the benefits which such women are to enjoy." Written or unwritten, "stipulations in advance" for a woman entering *pallakia* are restrictive covenants. Manifestly, the written Greco-Roman Egyptian nuptial contracts just discussed include numerous restrictive covenants.

To conclude, the evidence suggests that free women including former slaves, foreigners (before PCL), and citizens could be made into legally recognized (*pallakē*) wives by sale but once so transferred they were also slaves. Most sale contracts (especially self-sale contracts) probably included restrictive covenants requiring the sold woman to be treated as a wife. Many excellent studies have run into a wall because they recognized only legitimate marriage as legal marriage.[28]

Legitimate marriage or marriage by loan of the bride is made recognizable by a distinctive betrothal terminology involving cognates of the verbs *egguan* and *eggamizein* or the noun *egguē*: "to put into the hand." It is possible, even probable, that *pallakia* or marriage by sale of the bride is made recognizable by use of the verb *harmozein*—"to fit together"—in *gamos*—"marriage"—(as expressed in Pindar *Pythian* 9) and by such cognates as *harmostēs* meaning "husband" (see Chapter VI.2). "To fit together" is capable of expressing the outcome that the bride (a slave) merged into the household of the groom unlike in legitimate marriage wherein she continued to belong to her father's *oikos*. Indeed, *harmozein* has the meanings "to rule"/"to govern.

28. Rhodes (1981: 333), K.R. Walters (1983: 321, 332, 335), Ogden (1995: 227), Vérilhac and Vial (1998: 229–66), Yiftach-Firanko (2003, 2005: esp. 68–70), and Kamen (2013: 63–67).

V. Constructing the Greek-Wife: Ritual Aspects

1. Marriage Rituals: Fundamentals

A woman taken in lawful marriage (*gamein*) by means of one set of rituals, associated with a loan procedure, becomes an *egguētē* or *gnēsia*—"legitimate" wife (*gunē*, *damar*). Another woman taken by a different set of rituals associated with a legal sale becomes a *pallakē*-wife. The ritual forms employed should reveal the legal form of marriage.

Buermann (1877–78: esp. 569 ff., 638 ff.) supported his theory of legitimate concubinage by arguing that both the *pallakē* and *gunē*/*damar* were equally *egguēte*. Sealey (1984: 129–31), if I understand correctly, supports this theory of "legitimate concubinage" with somewhat different arguments. My position is that *pallakia*, which resembles the Roman marriage *cum manus*, was legally recognized, but not as legitimate marriage. The difference is made obvious by the fact that the children of the *pallakē*-wife and of the legitimate-wife were unequal in civic rights (Demosthenes 46.18). Thus, it was crucial for the accompanying rituals and *verba solemnia* to convey unambiguously to participants and to onlookers the precise nature of the change in status that had taken place (Tiersma 1988).

The rituals for legitimate marriage are, speaking relatively, well known. "Then Cleisthenes bade them all be silent and spoke to the company at large: 'Suitors for my daughter's hand, I thank you one and all; if it were possible I would grant each of you his wish, neither choosing out one to set him above another nor disparaging the rest. But since I have but one maiden to plan for and so cannot please all of you, to those of you whose suit is rejected I make a gift of a talent of silver to each, for his desire to take a wife from my house and for his sojourn away from his home; and to Megacles son of Alcmeon do I betroth (*egguō*) my daughter Agariste, by the laws of the Athenians.' Megacles accepted the betrothal (*phamenou de enguasthai Megakleos*), and Cleisthenes brought the marriage to pass" (Herodotus 6.130; tr. Godley *LCL*).

Similarly, in Menander's "Dyskolos" ("The Peevish Fellow," 842–44), Callippides announces publicly, "I make available (*egguō*) my daughter now, young man, to you to harvest [plough] legitimate (*gnēsiōn*) children. I add three talents dowry"[1] (tr. Arnott *LCL* modified; cf. Menander "The Girl with Her Hair Cut Short" 1013–15).

1. Sealey (1984: 117 with n. 10) suggests that in marriage by *egguēsis*, fathers and brothers were required to supply a dowry but, as he notes, Nicodemos says he gave his sister in marriage in *egguēsis* without a dowry (Isaeus 3.38). Nicodemus was lying, but he would have been laughed out of court if giving a dowry were required to make a marriage legitimate. On nuptial assigns, see Chapter X.

That the legitimate marriage betrothal ritual included the swearing of oaths is indicated in Pindar (*Nemean* 9.16) wherein the sons of Talaus take an oath (*horkos*) to give Eriphyle in marriage to Amphiaraus son of Oicles.

Van Wees (2005: 9) takes the account of the courtship of Cleisthenes's daughter Agariste as evidence that around 570 BCE the Greeks had ceased to sell brides to suitors: "Moreover, marriage-related gift-giving is all one way: the bride's family is expected to display generosity and above all to present a substantial 'dowry,' for which they receive no return and which is therefore called *proix*, 'free gift.'" The marriage of Agariste was a legitimate marriage in which the bride remained part of her father's *oikos*. However, this marriage form had a pre-classical history of its own. Van Wees (2005: 9) acknowledges this but maintains, "by the sixth century it had become the norm." This claim may be true but it is not supported by evidence. Indeed, as discussed below, it may be contradicted in Euripides's *Electra* (930–35) by Electra's remarks suggesting a relative increase over time in metronymics (discussed in Chapter VII). It is clear that marriage by sale continued in classical Athens.

Unfortunately, Herodotus does not reveal how Megacles accepted or ratified the betrothal. Perhaps, Cleisthenes and Megacles shook hands and/or Megacles pronounced a standard verbal formula. Oakley and Sinos (1993: 9 with n. 3; cf. Oakley 1995: 71) assert that a handshake between the father of the legitimate bride and the groom concluded the betrothal ritual. This claim cannot be confirmed by literary evidence. On the other hand, the handshake between groom and father of the bride is attested iconographically but an interpretative problem arises because the handshake would also be expected when the father concluded the *sale* of his daughter to a suitor. Thus, identifying the form of the marriage would require the interpretation of additional iconographic symbols. The interpretative problem is compounded by the very small size and obscure details of the sample in which the handshake is depicted. Examples include Side B, Boston, Museum of Fine Arts 03.802 (discussed below) and the much more complex Malibu, California, J. Paul Getty Museum 85.AE.102 (Oakley 1995: 71 with fig. 21).[2]

Of course, some ritual of incorporation into the household must have been employed for both the legitimate and the *pallakē*-wife. A scholion to Aristophanes's *Plutus* ("Wealth" 768) tells that newly purchased slaves as well as brides and bridegrooms were welcomed by being brought to the hearth of the house and showered/sprinkled (*katachysmata*) with dates, cakes, small coins and the like (also Demosthenes 45.74; cf. Sutton 1989: 353 with n. 63). The inclusion and indeed emphasis on the groom in

2. The image is available for download at: http://www.perseus.tufts.edu/hopper/artifact?name=Malibu+85.AE.102&object=vase). Based on Ovid *Metamorphoses* 4.691 ff., it might be concluded that Perseus contracted to acquire Andromeda from Cepheus by agreeing to save her from the sea monster; Cepheus accepted Perseus's labor as his payment of *hedna*. However, in *Metamorphoses* 4.705, Perseus is promised the kingdom as a dowry (*regnum dotale*). Later on, in *Metamorphoses* 4.755 ff., it is stated that Perseus "carried off" (*rapit*) Andromeda as a "prize" (*praemia*) and *indotata*—without receiving a dowry.

the sources leaves open the possibility that the ritual of "pouring-on" was a nuptial universal aimed at promoting the health and wealth of the *oikos* (Sutton 1989: 354–55).

However, as her father remained the *kurios* of a legitimate wife there would be a reason for a special ritual in which the groom himself recognized and mitigated her outsider status in his *oikos*. There is evidence from the Pythagoreans of a ritual in which the groom "led her [his wife] from the hearth with his right hand" as or as if she was a "suppliant" (*hiketēs*).[3] By means of such a ritual, the legitimate bride gained the status of guest (*xenē*) or "resident alien"—that is, she was elevated in a way that the *pallakē* and other slaves would not have been (see Belfiore 2000: 56–58).

Some confirming evidence for the practice of a ritual for raising the legitimate bride to suppliant status is provided in Euripides's *Alcestis* (917) by the mention that Admetus "raised/lifted (*bastazō*) the *cheir* (hand, hand and arm, arm)" of the nobly born Alcestis during the wedding procession (see further below). Was Alcestis a legitimate bride?[4] Euripides leaves several clues that he intends Alcestis to be understood as such.

First, when Heracles asks Admetus how Alcestis came to die in his house he answers: "After her father died, she spent her orphan years here" (*Alcestis* 534–35; tr. Kovacs *LCL*). A woman whose father sold her into marriage would not be called an orphan. Admetus's evasive answer is intended to conceal that Alcestis entered his house as a legitimate bride *before* her father died. Second, as noticed by Goldfarb (1992: 113 ff.), the relationship between Admetus and Alcestis is frequently characterized as one of *philia*" (17 f., 201., 231 ff., 279, 376, 432 ff., 460, 472, 599, 876 f., 917, 930, 991 f., 993 f). A *pallakē* would not be called a "friend". Moreover, *philia* is fundamentally a social rather than an emotional bond as is explained by Benveniste (1973: 273): "The social meaning [of *philos*] is prior and connected in particular with hospitality—the guest is *philos* and benefits from the specific treatment designated by *philein* 'to be hospitable'—but also with other forms of attachment and mutual gratitude" (quoted and discussed by Goldfarb 1992: 119). The point is that the legitimate wife (Alcestis), who continues to be owned by her original *oikos*, is her husband's (Admetus's) guest (*xenia*).

Most importantly, when Heracles asks Admetus whether the woman he is mourning (Alcestis his wife) is *othneios*—"strange, foreign"—or *suggenēs*—"a blood relative"—he answers that she is *othneios* but "closely connected/essential" to the *oikos* (*Alcestis* 532–33). A legitimate wife was essential because she perpetuated the *oikos* by providing it with legitimate heirs but she was not constitutive of the *oikos*. The *pallakē* was not essential to the *oikos* because she could not provide legitimate heirs but she was constitutive of the *oikos*. A legitimate wife was a foreigner/stranger in the oikos. A *pallakē*, a slave-wife, like an ordinary slave or a blood relative was intrinsic to the

3. Iamblichus, *De vita Pythagorica* 9.48, 18.84; cf. Aristotle *Economics* 1444a; discussed and translated by Belfiore 2000: 49 ff.

4. In Hyginus *Fabulae* 50, 51 and Apollodorus *Library* 1.9.15, with the help of Apollo, Admetus received Alcestis as a prize from her father Pelias. There is no mention of a dowry. It is difficult to see a legitimate marriage in these reports.

household and could not be categorized as "foreign" or as an "outsider."[5] Finally, Alkcestis says she was willing to die for her husband because she did not wish her children to be *orphanoi* (288). But "fatherlessness" is legally relevant only for legitimate offspring. Had Alcestis been a *pallakē*, her children would have been legally *nothoi* and hence legally fatherless.

Perhaps the supplication gesture for a legitimate bride is illustrated in an Attic vase painting. On Side B of Boston, Museum of Fine Arts 03.802,

> a bearded man, holding a scepter ... shakes the hand of a youth dressed as a traveler or ephebe [he has a broad-brimmed hat (*petassos*), tunic (*chitoniskos*), cloak (*chlamys*), sandals and carries a spear (Sutton 1989: 347).

The roles played by the two figures is not uncontroversial but they are connected with the nuptial scene on Side A and it is reasonable to understand them as representing the father of the bride and the groom. Although the groom holds a spear, it is clear that the marriage takes place by mutual consent, not by force. Indeed, there is reason to suspect that the spear actually symbolizes the exchange of the oaths that completed the nuptial transaction.[6] Sutton (1989: 351) concludes:

> [W]e find what is apparently a unique representation of the *engye* set in the mythological world, one that may serve as the founding act of the wedding on the other side. The free juxtaposition of images drawn from myth, allegory, and daily experience found on this vase makes it a good example of the Classical style in art (cf. Oakley and Sinos 1993: 9; Reeder 1995: 165–68).

On Side A of the Boston vase, the groom, having already shaken hands with the father, looks back at the willing bride (she is bracketed by flying erotes) as he leads her with his right hand grasping the top of her left hand to the door of the bedroom in the house. The bride's hand is open with fingers outstretched so the couple is definitely not clasping hands (about which gesture more shortly). It is also clear that the groom is grasping the bride's hand not her wrist (more about this shortly). This is also Sutton's (1989: 345 with pl. 33) reading, but he seems to equate the two gestures.[7]

5. In Roman law, the *uxor in manu* is legally the daughter of her husband (Gaius *Institutes* 1.114). Daughter status is attested by the marriage ritual described in Terence *Andria* 295–97, wherein it seems to have an emotional as well as a legal significance.

6. The spear may be a symbol of consensual transfer, see Alföldi (1979: 20–23), Nótári (2007: esp. 233). In pursuit scenes, the spear held by the youth may symbolize the intention to propose marriage. There is Roman evidence that self-sale into slavery was a sale *sub hasta* "under the spear" (Silver 2011b: 87 citing Juvenal *Satires* 3.33).

7. In another scene (Oxford, Ashmolean Museum 1966.888) with erotes (but lacking the handshake), the groom (again) holds the open hand of the bride or her wrist (Reeder 1995: 168—69). There is a similar possible ambiguity in a nuptial painting of the fourth century BCE in the Thracian Tomb of Kazanlak (Bulgaria). A beautifully dressed woman sits eyes downward with her open right hand resting on the wrist or lower arm of a seated man who has placed his open left

Given the proximity of the upper hand and wrist, it is quite possible that the artist had wrist-grasping in mind. Ambiguous scenes of this kind are not convincing depictions of a distinctive supplication ritual. Fortunately, a better candidate is available. An Etruscan vase of the fourth century BCE from Vulci (Plate 2) depicts two standing figures, a man and a woman. The woman Alcestis (inscribed as *Alcsti*) wraps her arms around the neck of Admetus (inscribed as *Atmite*). Admetus's right hand is placed under his wife's arm just below her right shoulder. That is, he holds or better lifts/supports Alcestis's arm. Both figures are crowned and richly dressed and gaze affectionately into each other's eyes (Bonfante 2010: 463–64 with fig. 1; Pieraccini and Del Chiaro 2014: fig. 1). The scene refers to the death (and resurrection) of Alcestis but, at the same time, it recalls her wedding to Admetus (Bonfante 2010). Admetus's raising of Alcestis's arm, recalling Euripides *Alcestis* 917, is non-functional and must be symbolic. Further, it cannot be confused with the groom-grasping bride's wrist or with their handshake. I submit that it symbolizes the legitimate bride taken as a suppliant into the home of her (borrower) husband.

Moving on to *pallakia*, Patterson (1991a: 286) maintains: "Concubinage also [like legitimate marriage] took place over time, but without the same socially recognizable, communally established signs." However, it is not possible to imagine that the negotiations over the legal sale of women alluded to in Isaeus 3.39 (quoted in Chapter III) were finalized without a solemn ritual.[8] *Pallakia*, not least because it involved the procreation of free offspring, could not be an "informal" marriage arrangement, as suggested by Harrison (1968: 17). Sealey (1984: 116) is surely correct in insisting that *pallakia* came into being as the result of an explicit contractual agreement.

The rituals of marriage into *pallakia* remain to be discovered, however. The following efforts at discovery raise important issues and provide important clues but the findings must be viewed as only provisional. Anything resembling proof is impossible given the present state of the evidence.

In Euripides *Alcestis*, having forcibly rescued Alcestis from death, Heracles clearly intends for her to be (re)married to Admetus. At first (1025–29, 1035–36), Heracles lies that he won the woman in an athletic contest and, consequently, he is her legal owner (*kurios*). Later he admits that he actually obtained the woman by "fighting with the divinity who controlled her" (line 1140; tr. Kovacs *LCL*). "Controlled" is the rendering for *koiranō*—"ruler"—for which most editors read *kurios* (Halleran 1988: 125–26 with n. 12). In sculptures of the fifth century BCE from Cyrene and the third century CE from Slovenia, Heracles leads Alcestis by her wrist (Blasone 2010: 5–7 with Figure 4). Heracles asks Admetus to reach out his right hand (1115, 1117) and "take"/"possess" (*echō*)

hand below the wrist or lower arm of the woman. Women bearing gifts and pomegranates flank the couple. Is the man about to grasp her wrist or is he raising/supporting her arm? The image is available for download at: http://www.lifebeyondtourism.org/img/puntidiinteresse/site_0044_0004.jpg.

8. Gaius (*Institutes* 1.113, 119) makes clear that *coemptio* is an act *per aes et libram* by which the woman/wife entered into his *manus*.

Plate 2. Etruscan Red-figure crater from Vulci, Italy of the fourth century BCE featuring Admetus and Allcestis. Paris, Musée Du Cabinet Des Medailles De La Bibliothèque National De France De Ridder.918 (De Agostini Picture Library/Bridgeman Images).

the woman (1118); Admetus confirms that he has "taken"/"possessed" her (1119). Halleran (1988: 126) understands that Admetus has grasped Alcestis's wrist (*karpō*). He may well be correct, although "wrist" is not explicit. In classical Athenian terms (and in Greek law generally), Heracles was not qualified to give Alcestis in legitimate marriage and, hence, in their second marriage Alcestis became Admetus's *pallakē*.

What can only be a ritual for *pallakia* is sketched in Menander's *Sikyonioi* ("*The Men from Sikyon*"), a comedy set in Attica. Sommerstein's (2014: 16) discussion is most helpful:

> Another case of a *hetaira* becoming a *pallakē* ... seems to appear in a sub-plot... involving Theron, a parasite who has attached himself to the soldier Stratophanes, and a woman named Malthake (a name which elsewhere, significantly, is normally that of a *hetaira*) ... There is a reference in Pollux (4.119) to a parasite in this play who "wears white when he is about to get married" ... and on the strength of this Arnott ... has suggested that the play ends with the marriage of Theron and Malthake. However, an actual wedding is impossible. There is no trace of the usual betrothal formula, and no evidence that anyone would have been in a position to pronounce it; *the only person who can be said to give Malthake to Theron is Malthake herself*, who first holds up proceedings by saying she has not yet agreed to Theron's request (419), and then declares "I will" [*drasō*, 420] after which she is asked by Theron to confirm her consent [*kataneuson*] ["with a nod"] ... That Theron dresses up as a bridegroom, and leaves the scene with Malthake in what is in appearance a wedding procession, does not prove that he is *in fact* marrying her... Theron is in reality leading Malthake not into matrimony but into *pallakia* unless, indeed, as I strongly suspect, Theron is a citizen of Sicyon rather than Athens, in which case he and Malthake might well have been entitled to call themselves man and wife (emphasis added; transliterations mine).

Sommerstein (2014: 23, n. 14) suspects that Theron is from Sicyon because the title of the play is often plural in the sources (*Sikyonioi* but *Sikyonios* is attested). Even so, Stratophanes discovered he really was an Athenian (124–25) so perhaps Theron did as well in one of the comedy's missing sections. The point of the plural title being that neither Sicyonian turns out to be Sicyonian. Alternatively, perhaps the title means merely that the Stratophanes and Theron came to Attica from Sicyon. The citizenship status of Malthake is not stated. Arnott (1997: 101, 99) reasons that she is "an Athenian citizen without living parents" and, if I understand him correctly, he deduces from verses 144–45 that Theron is also an Athenian. This much is clear: Menander portrays a *wedding* in Attica whose rituals, especially the call for the consent of the bride, are not known to be those for a legitimate marriage. As noted by Sommerstein, it appears that Malthake is a free woman who gives herself in marriage. She must have given herself into *pallakia*—that is, she consented to become a slave-wife. Ogden's (1996: 106) over-the-top suggestion that all of this was no more "than a night of bliss with the courtesan" cannot obscure that Menander has a single woman marry into *pallakia*.

2. Marriage Rituals: Oaths and Handshakes

As shown above, there is some evidence for verbal formulae in Greek legitimate marriage but little for marriage into *pallakia*. The bride in Roman *coemptio* seems to have consented to the sale by uttering the formula: *Ubi tu Gaius, ego Gaia* "Where you are Gaius, I am Gaia" (for Gaia, Cicero *For Murena* 12.27; Hersch 2010: 24). The meaning of the formula appears to be that the bride took the name of the groom (joined his family) as would be expected in a marriage with *manus* (Treggiari 1991: 27).

Similar marriage formulas are found in Old Babylonian (earlier second millennium BCE) literary texts. For example, in the myth of Nergal and Ereshkigal, queen of the netherworld, the latter says, "You be my husband, I will be thy wife ... Be thou master, I will be mistress" (Greengus 1969: 517). Greengus (1969: 522) suggests. "The literary texts suggest that they [the marriage formulas] were recited in conjunction to the groom coming to the bride's home and offering her a marriage gift." That is, the phrase was recited at the time of purchase. We may be confident that the *pallakē*-wife took a similar oath of loyalty to her owner/husband.

Perhaps a hint of a verbal marriage formula may be detected in Callimachus. As elucidated by Faraone (1990: 233 citing Callimachus fragments 67–75): "The myth of Acontius and Kydippe ... turns on a tossed apple. Acontius inscribes an apple with an oath ('I swear by Artemis I shall get married to Acontius's) and tosses it to Kydippe over the *temenos* wall, as she stands within the sanctuary of the goddess. The unsuspecting girl takes the fruit and reading aloud (as was customary in the ancient world) she utters the oath, which the goddess hears and demands be fulfilled." The story is obviously fictional but the woman's oath and the nuptial role of Artemis, I think, are not.

Examined next is a gesture that must have been accompanied by mutual oaths between the *pallakē* and her *kurios*. In Euripides's *Medea* (484) it is made clear that Medea had left her father's household prior to marrying Jason: "Of my own accord I abandoned my father and my home and came with you to Iolcus under Pelion, showing more love than sense" (tr. Kovacs *LCL*; Burnett 1973: 13). The speech of Medea's nurse (*Medea* 18–25; cf. 160–72) suggests a practice wherein women in their own hands (outside a male-headed household) sealed mutual oaths (*horkoi*) with their husbands to be by means of a handshake: "But now all is enmity, and love's bonds are diseased. For Jason, abandoning his own children and my mistress, is bedding down in a royal match, having married the daughter of Creon, ruler of this land. Poor Medea, finding herself thus cast aside, calls loudly on his oaths, invokes the mighty assurance of his sworn right hand (*dexias*), and calls the gods to witness the unjust return she is getting from Jason. She lies fasting, giving her body up to pain, wasting away in tears all the time ever since she learned that she was wronged by her husband, neither lifting her face nor taking her eyes from the ground" (tr. Kovacs *LCL*; cf. Pippin 1973; Flory 1978). *Dexias* "the right hand," means "pledge, promise" (LSJ s.v.; Ojennus 2006: 262–63). Medea (690) also refers to Jason as her *posis*—"husband." As noted by Williamson (1990: 18), "In contracting a marriage on this basis she [Medea] has already translated herself into the role of a male citizen, operating in the public sphere as Jason's equal."[9] Perhaps the Athenian audience saw the behavior of Medea

9. In Euripides's *Medea* 709 ff., Medea who is to be exiled from Corinth, apparently with the assent of Jason, requests suppliant status from Aigeus of Athens: "*Medea kneels before Aegeus in the*

as extreme, but the tragedy could not have worked if self-sale into *pallakia* was not familiar.

In Apollonius Rhodius (*Argonautica* 4.98–100), Jason swears to take Medea to Greece with him as his wife [*kouridios akoitin*] and then he "clasped her right hand in his [*cheira paraschedon ērape cheiri dexiterēn*]" (tr. Seaton *LCL*; Ojennus 2006: 260; see below). I would hypothesize that her objective in extracting this oath was for Jason to legalize her children by him. This option would have been precluded when Jason took the daughter of Creon in legitimate marriage thus requiring him to remain in Corinth. (It is understood that, like Xuthus in Athens, he was granted citizenship.) Medea's responded to her children's "darkness" (lack of free status) by killing them and hiding them in the temple of Hera Akraia.

The *Homeric Hymn to Aphrodite* 5 provides another, somewhat messy, example of the handshake between a single woman transformed into a bride and the groom.[10] In order to convince Anchises to marry her, Aphrodite must first convince him that she is a mortal woman not a goddess. She begins by telling him:

> Nay, I am but a mortal, and a woman was the mother that bare me. Otreus of famous name is my father, if so be you have heard of him, and he reigns over all Phrygia rich in fortresses. But I know your speech well beside my own, for a Trojan nurse brought me up at home: she took me from my dear mother and reared me thenceforth when I was a little child (5.110–15; tr. Evelyn-White *LCL*).

Then, Otreus's daughter goes on (5. 116–25) to explain that while at Artemis's dancing ground with other *alphesiboiai*—"cattle-fetching maidens"—she was abducted by Hermes and carried from Phrygia to Troy. Thus, from possibly residing with the nurse, to attending the nuptial dance of Artemis, to being carried away by Hermes from Phrygia to Troy, Otreus's daughter conveys that she is a single woman outside

---

posture of a suppliant. But I beg you by your beard and by your knees and I make myself your suppliant: have pity, have pity on an unfortunate woman, and do not allow me to be cast into exile without a friend, but receive me into your land and your house as a suppliant. If you do so, may your longing for children be brought to fulfillment by the gods, and may you yourself die happy! You do not know what a lucky find you have made in me. I will put an end to your childlessness and cause you to beget children, for I know the medicines to do it" (tr. Kovacs *LCL*). Medea had explained to Aegeus, "He [Jason] has put another woman [Creon's daughter] over me as mistress of the house" (694; tr. Kovacs *LCL*). In Medea's view, the devious Jason had effectively divorced her when he broke his marital oath. Thus, divorced and ordered to leave Corinth, Medea resells herself into *pallakia* in return for being given safety in Athens. As Williamson (1990: 19) explains, "The equivalence between this exchange and the contract of marriage is confirmed by the account Medea later gives of it to Jason: she tells Jason that she is going to 'live with Aegeus' [*sunoikēsousa* 1385]. This relationship too, like Medea's with Jason, is sealed by oaths, and the transaction can be seen as completing the translation from private to public of the marriage bond which her relationship with Jason had already initiated" (transliteration mine).

10. Translations of *Homeric Hymn to Aphrodite* by Evelyn-White *LCL* modified.

a male-headed household. Otreus's daughter proves that she is her own *kuria* by proposing marriage to Anchises:

> But I beseech you by Zeus and by your noble parents—for no base folk could get such a son as you—take me now, stainless and unproved in love, and show me to your father and careful mother and to your brothers sprung from the same stock (5.134–35).

Anchises accepts the proposition of Otreus's daughter:

> If you are a mortal and a woman was the mother who bare you, and Otreus of famous name is your father as you say, and if you are come here by the will of Hermes the immortal Guide, and are to be called my wife always, then neither god nor mortal man shall here restrain me till I have lain with you in love right now; no, not even if far-shooting Apollo himself should launch grievous shafts from his silver bow. Willingly would I go down into the house of Hades, O lady, beautiful as the goddesses, once I had gone up to your bed. So speaking, he caught her by the hand [*labe cheira*] (5.145–55).

The mutual hand grasping seals the marriage contract.

The problem with my interpretation is that instead of receiving (or being promised) the *dōra* due to a single woman who agreed to become a *pallakē* (see Chapter X), Otreus's daughter offers *apoinos* to Anchises:

> Moreover, send a messenger quickly to the swift-horsed Phrygians, to tell my father and my sorrowing mother; and they will send you gold in plenty and woven stuffs, many splendid gifts as *apoina* (5.136–40; cf. Van Wees 2005: 8).

Of course, the delivery of the *apoina* to Anchises would not make the marriage legitimate because Otreus had played no role in forming the contract.[11] This *apoina* is not legally a dowry or even a wedding gift (compare Olson 2012: 210–11; cf. Keaney 1986; van der Ben 1986: 16–18). Instead, it needs to be understood as a "ransom"/"price paid" (LSJ s.v.) to be paid by Otreus to Anchises personally for releasing his daughter from her status as his slave—that is, from *pallakia*. Here, we might compare the *apoina* offered by her father Chruses to redeem Chruseis from Agamemnon's hand (*Iliad* 1.112).[12] Such a release from slave-wife status would prepare the ground for a legitimate marriage between Anchises and Otreus's daughter. In any event, Aphrodite reveals her identity to Anchises before he can try to take advantage of her fraudulent offer. The fictional tale has become irregular but it has also ended.

In a vase painting (New York, Metropolitan Museum of Art 75.2.15; Plate 3), a woman reaches out to take the man's extended hand as winged female Erotes hover on each side of the groom (Sutton 1997/98: 40 with fig. 21). Sutton (1997/98: 40) comments:

11. Aphrodite asks Anchises to take her to his parents and brothers but no mention is made of her fictional parents (5.134–36).

12. In line of the *Homeric Hymn to Aprhodite*, Zeus pays an *apoina* of "high-stepping horses" to the father of Ganymedes for taking away his son (see Chapter X.5).

> The bride is not passively grasped but reaches out to take his [the groom's] extended hand in a motif familiar from the fourth-century grave reliefs and Roman weddings but very rare in Greek wedding scenes.

Rare, perhaps, but there are additional examples. A similar scene of bride and groom shaking hands is provided by Buffalo, Buffalo Museum of Science C23262 (Oakley and Sinos 1993: 39, 122). A hydria of the fourth century BCE from a tomb in Metaponto depicts a seated man shaking hands with a standing woman while Eros walks along their outstretched arms to place a wreath on the man's head (Propriety Iasi, tomb 250; Silvestrelli 2014: 105–06 fig. 4.5). In another scene (Warsaw, National Museum 147367), a man and woman grasp hands. In typical nuptial fashion, the woman (bride) inclines her head and gazes downward. To the right, an older man, possibly a witness, leans on a walking stick as he watches the couple.[13]

The handshake is familiar in Greek literature as a gesture of contract serving to solemnize unilateral or mutual pledges, promises and oaths (Torrance 2014: esp. 144–47). What makes the handshake between bride and groom so intriguing is that it might be seen as replacing the handshake (contract) between the groom and the father of the bride (her *kurios*) when the latter sold his daughter into *pallakia*. That is, the handshake between groom and bride occurs only when she, like Medea or "Aphrodite," acts as her own *kuria* and hence is able to swear oaths and make contracts. In this event, the handshake becomes a key indicator of the contractual transformation of a single woman into a *pallakē*-wife. Even if it were true that Greek (Athenian) women could not make legally binding contracts (Flory 1978: 70), they and their nuptial partners would remain bound by solemnly given oaths. Jason breaking his oath is exactly what Medea complains of so bitterly.

In "standard" descriptions of the Roman wedding, "the couple grasped each other's hands to show consent" and, significantly, I think, there was a (so-called) "mock abduction" in which the bride was "ritually torn from the embrace of her *mother*" (Festus s.v. *rapi simulatur*; Hersch 2013: 223; emphasis added). That she was not torn from the embrace of her father suggests the bride was not under *patria potestas*—that is, she was a single woman.

In Terence's *Andria*, a mother on her deathbed brought together her daughter Glycerium and the youth Pamphilus, and said:

> "You do I give to her as a husband, friend, protector, father. This property of mine do I intrust to you, and commit to your care." [Pamphilus recalls] She placed her in my hands; that instant, death came upon her. I accepted her; having accepted, I will protect her (295–97; tr. Riley *Perseus Project*).

Williams (1958: 21) comments:

13. In Reeder (1995: 156–58) the scene is understood not as a wedding but as representing the departure of groom from bride.

Plate 3. Athenian red-figure loutrophoros of ca. 400 BCE featuring a wedding scene in which bride and groom shake hands. New York, Metropolitan Museum of Art 75.2.15 (Metropolitan Museum of Art).

> Note especially (297) *hanc mi in manum dat*, which is rightly interpreted by [the Roman grammarian] Donatus [see http://hyperdonat.tge-adonis.fr], who says on (295) *ie isti virum do* "*apparet quod iungens dexteras haec dicebat*" ["It appears that she joined their right hands as she said these words"]. The words represent the climax of the Roman ceremony, the moment at which the *pronuba* performed the *dextrarum iunctio* ["joining of right hands"] by laying the bride's hand in that of the bridegroom.

What seems clear is that by clasping hands with the groom the bride agreed to become his property—that is, as implied by *in manu*, the handshake ritual creates a *manus*-marriage. Of course, as Williams (1958: 21) is careful to note, "Terence has portrayed the scene as a reflection of the Roman marriage ritual." However, it still needs to be explained why Terence would choose to portray a *manus*-marriage unless the ritual in Menander's original play made "Glycerium" into a *pallakē*. In Menander's "The Girl with Her Hair Cut Short," Glycera, an exposed citizen-child raised as a daughter by an independently living "old woman" (playing the *pronuba* role), acted "as her own *kuria*" in giving herself in marriage (see Chapter IV.4). Probably, her ritual handshake with Polemon was understood by the Greek audience.

The handshake between a man and a woman is in fact a frequent motif in classical Athenian funerary art, but not all scholars link the gesture with a previous marriage contract (Flory 1978: 70; G. Davies 1985). My explanation for the handshake gesture in a funerary context is that it simultaneously recalls the couple's nuptial gesture and their separation.[14] I suggest that the same explanation applies in the case of a scene in a Laconian ivory plaque from the sanctuary of Artemis Orthia (Athens, National Archaeological Museum M 15362). The plaque depicts a dignified woman standing on the gangplank(?) of a warship grasping the right hand of a naked man standing on the stern while she affectionately lays her left hand on his shoulder. After writing this sentence, I found reason to believe that the bride's "affectionate" placement of her left hand on the man's shoulder is a ritual gesture. A scene in the sarcophagus relief of Gorgonion in the Cathedral of Ancona, dating to perhaps the late fourth century CE, depicts a woman and a fully dressed man grasping right hands with the woman draping her left hand over the man's shoulder. The couple stands between two columns (Ricks 2006: 435 with fig. 6). A similar scene is depicted on a marble sarcophagus in the Museo delle Terme (Wilson 1929: pl. 18). The hand on shoulder motif confirmed the bride wished to become the groom's slave-wife.

14. In Roman funerary art, the depiction of the handshake is in several instances accompanied by an altar, see e.g. London, British Museum 1805.0703.143). However, G. Davies (1985: 635) sees "no reason to suppose, as some have done, that it refers to the marriage ritual rather than the funerary rites, nor indeed that the scroll often held by the man is to be seen specifically as the *tabulae nuptiales*: rather it is the usual attribute of a togate figure" Hersch (2013: 227) sees the problem differently: "In the end, we should probably interpret marital handshakes on sarcophagi as expressions of eternal domestic harmony: wedding, marriage and devotion, frozen for all time in one brief gesture." However, it is reasonable to understand the combination of handshake between a man and woman, scroll, altar and torch held by Hymenaeus as representing mutual contractual oaths taken in marriage rites.

It is argued below that both types of *pallakia* transactions, sale by the father or self-sale by the woman to the groom were consummated by handshakes. The handshakes were followed by a wedding procession in which the groom led the bride by holding her left wrist (or, more generally, lower arm) with his right hand, a gesture of domination or ownership known as *cheir' epi karpoi*.

3. Marriage Rituals: Lifting the Bride and Riding Together in a Chariot

A possible clue concerning form of marriage is provided by the appearance of apparently distinct ritual themes in Athenian depictions of the wedding procession. The themes are: (1) the groom lifts the bride; (2) the bride and groom ride together in the nuptial chariot (or mule-drawn cart; cf. Oakley and Sinos 1993: 29–30); and (3) a theme, called *chamaipous* by Pollux (3.40), in which a veiled (with *krēdemnon*?) bride stands motionless as the groom grasps her wrist (lower arm) and/or walks with the groom who leads her by the wrist. All three themes are found in black-figure and in the later red-figure pottery (Jenkins 1983).

With respect to the first ritual, Jenkins (1983: 140), writing in 1983, notes "little agreement among commentators over the meaning of the [bride-lifting] action." This uncertainty seems surprising as the lifting up/snatching of eligible women is found in reports of abduction including Aphrodite's fabrication in the *Homeric Hymn to Aphrodite* (5.107–15). Having surveyed the evidence, I am unable to link the lifting of the bride with a specific form of marriage, whether legitimate or *pallakia*. Indeed, I suspect that bride-lifting is a kind of universal nuptial custom that plays the same kind of role as the groom's carrying the bride "across the threshold"—that is, into his house (or possibly out of her own).[15]

The riding together of bride and groom, they may even hold the chariot reins together (New York, Metropolitan Museum of Art 17.230.14a, b), suggests an egalitarian marital relationship. It is appealing to understand this theme as representation of legitimate (or even "free" marriage[16]) in which the bride retained her roots in her

15. A practice of this kind was familiar in ancient Rome (Catullus Poem 61.159–60; Ogle 1911; Williams 1958: 16). Plutarch (*Roman Questions* 29) notes that in "Boeotia they burn the axle of the bridal carriage before the door, signifying that the bride must remain, since her means of departure has been destroyed" (tr. Babbitt *LCL*). In Plautus' farcical wedding in *Casina* (815 ff.), the bride is advised: "Raise your feet above the threshold gently, my new bride. Begin this journey safely, so you will always stand above your husband and you will have the upper hand over your husband and be victorious, and so that your voice and your command will be stronger. Your husband shall clothe you, you shall plunder him" (tr. de Melo *LCL*). The question is how much of this is Diphilus and how much Plautus? (Williams 1958: 17–19). Is Plautus for comic effect shifting a Greek threshold crossing ceremony from the end of to the beginning of the wedding celebration?

16. Wolff (1944: 43–48, 64–65) explains Roman "free marriage" well, but his discussion of Athens suffers because he assumes, with obvious hesitation, that the husband of a legitimate wife was her *kurios*.

father's household and was not the property of the groom. In fact, there is a major obstacle to interpreting chariot sharing as necessarily representing legitimate marriage: "Her (Eurythemiste) beside their father ... horse-taming Thestius ... he led off with his horses and closely joined chariots presenting countless wedding gifts (*hedna*)" (Hesiodic *Catalogue of Women* Fragment 26 = Fragment 23 lines 34 ff.; tr. Most *LCL*). The groom has paid for the bride sharing the chariot with him. This evidence disconfirms the hypothesis that nuptial chariot-sharing signals legitimate marriage. Rethinking, the theme of bride and groom in a chariot it may simply signal that the *oikos* of the groom is distant from the bride's ancestral oikos. This is certainly the case in the "abductions" of Aphrodite, Hippodameia, Persephone and others. It becomes probable that the chariot-riding bride has been sold to her husband—that is, she had become a *pallakē* (see Chapter X).[17] Gven the present state of the evidence, chariot sharing cannot be regarded as a reliable indicator of the form of marriage.

4. *Chamaipous* as a Symbol of Taking Ownership

On the most general level, I understand the grasping of the wrist/lower arm (*cheir' epi karpoi* gesture) to be an iconographic signal that the holder has taken mastery/ownership of the held individual. This meaning is most apparent in Paris, Musée du Louvre G 146 (side A at center) wherein Agamemnon walks to the left leading the captive Briseis by her right wrist while the herald Talthybius, who holds the *kerykeion* in his right hand, raises his left hand in an apparent gesture of approval or validation of the marriage (available for download at: http://www.perseus.tufts.edu/hopper/artifact?name=Louvre%20G%20146&object=Vase). One may of course argue that Briseis was not really Agamemnon's wife, but it is clear that she was his slave (*Iliad* 1.312 ff).

In an Attic red-figure hydra (St. Petersburg Hermitage B201: St. 1538), two chorusmen wearing masks and wreaths with nonsense words coming from their mouths are reluctantly (their weight is on the back foot) conveyed to Dionysus, god of theater, by Hermes, god of commerce. In his left hand, Dionysus carries his *kerykeion* and a writing tablet with stylus and with his right, he grasps the wrist of one of the reluctant artists and pulls him toward Dionysus. Dionysus leans forward and reaches out his right hand in a gesture of welcome to the chorusmen (Green 1995: 77–80 with pl. 1). The scene bears a remarkable resemblance to the depictions of marriage processions discussed earlier. My understanding is that Hermes plays the role of slave dealer and the (otherwise unexplained) tablets he holds are sale documents recording that the chorusmen have been sold/sold themselves into slavery to Dionysus. To say

17. Note that the bride-lifting theme may have a role independent from the chariot ride. This is suggested by its inclusion in scenes both with and without a nearby chariot. Thus, in Berlin, Staatliche Museen, Antikensammlung F 2175 and in London, British Museum 1843.1103.75, Theseus lifts Helen while his "friend" Perithous waits in a nearby chariot (Edmunds 2016: 71 Fig. 4; similarly A. Cohen 2007: Fig. 13.7). In Munich, Antikensammlungen 2309, Theseus lifts Helen (or it is Korone "Crow"?, all are labeled), off the ground; Perithous is nearby but there is no chariot in the scene.

that the chorusmen have become "servants" of the god Dionysus may serve to signal their privileged status relative to ordinary slaves but does not change that that they have ceased to be free men. This transformation in legal status into *doulos* or *hierodoulos* is signaled by the wrist-grasping gesture.

For me, it most difficult to imagine that a gesture suitable for the acquisition of slaves/slave-wives or of maenad wives by satyrs (Cambridge, Harvard Art Musuem 1925.30.129) would be practiced also for legitimate wives. At the very least, dual usage would invite grave misunderstandings among witnesses. Admittedly, however, there are examples in which the ownership meaning of *chamaipous* is not obvious. For example, in London, British Museum B424, Athena grasps Heracles by his left wrist with her right hand in conveying him/sponsoring him for immortality to an enthroned Zeus on Olympus. By "putting him into her hands," Athena assures Zeus (the creditor) that she has taken full responsibility for Heracles (the debtor). Given this assurance, Zeus granted Heracles entry into Olympus (advanced "capital" to him).[18] In the same way, when Poseidon "put Ares into his hands" (took responsibility for his debt), he convinced Hephaestus to release Ares from bondage (*Odyssey* 8.351). More obviously, in Würzburg, Martin von Wagner Museum L 508, Hector is led by his wrist from the battlefield by a herald (*Iliad 7.275* ff.*)*. There are, however, much more problematic examples in which it is difficult to identify *cheir' epi karpoi* with the act of taking ownership.[19]

A final question detail is whether the two nuptial motifs, chariot sharing and wrist grasping, are mutually exclusive or occur together in the same marriage procession. Unfortunately, the evidence does not provide a definitive answer to this question.[20]

18. There are Greek pottery paintings and an Etruscan mirror in which Athena leads by her wrist a young woman named Athanasia, which means "immortality" (Beazley 1947).

19. In a vase painting (London, British Museum 1842.0822.1) Aithra, mother of Theseus, is shown being returned from Troy by her grandsons Acamas and Demophon. Aithra, who is labeled, is represented as an old bent woman who walks with the aid of a crutched staff in her right hand; the right hand of Demophon who looks back at her holds her left wrist. This leading away is noted by Apollodorus (*Epitome* 5.22). Frazer's note on Apollodorus' report suggests that Aritha had been made a prisoner in Troy and that her grandsons went there to rescue or ransom her. Perhaps they succeeded in ransoming Aithra and in so doing became owners of their grandmother. In the *Iliou Persis* the Theseids took her back to the ships and later, when booty and prisoners were distributed, they were granted ownership of their grandmother (M.L. West 2013: 235). Another unclear example: in the *Iliad* 24.671–72, Achilles *promises* Priam that he will keep a truce by grasping Priam's wrist (Kozak 2014: 220). But see below for an interpretation.

20. A chariot procession from bride's door to groom's door is depicted in British Museum 1920.12-12.1 (cf. Bérard 1989: 99–100). In this scene, the *chamaipous* motif is not represented. However, there are vase paintings that show or at least suggest both motifs. First, a wedding depiction (Athens, Athens Archaeological Museum 2388) shows on one side a procession in which the groom walks holding the wrist of the bride but also on the other side *erotes* and women are making ready a nuptial chariot with pillows (Sutton 1997/98: 40 with fig. 22). Apparently, the chariot is intended for the couple on the other side of the krater. Second, on a bowl (Bonn, Akademischen Kunstmuseum 994; A. Smith 2016: 145 fig. 7.1) a groom holds the wrist of the

5. Marriage Rituals: Linking *Chamaipous* with *Pallakia*

The Greek and Roman "mock abduction" did not evolve from a pre-historic practice of abducting women to generate marriage (alleged by Nótári 2008: 322) or from some intrinsic unwillingness on the part of the bride (Hersch 2010: 144–48). The "rape" (*harpazō, rapio*) —that is, the seizure and carrying off of the bride—is more accurately described as a "mock purchase," as it was a ritualized purchase staged to demonstrate that legal title to the bride had been fully transferred to the groom. It proved that the groom had taken possession of the bride. Consent to the marriage had previously been given by the bride's father (the seller) or, I believe, by the bride herself (in auto-*ekdosis*). It is well to remember that in Greek law a consensual sexual act might be classified as rape (cf. Plutarch *Solon* 23.1).

The proper distinction is not abduction vs. marriage, but between two forms of marriage (compare Oakley and Sinos 1993: 13). The use of bridal imagery in abduction scenes is not intended to suggest slyly that the wedding is legitimate but to demonstrate unambiguously that is not legitimate. The interpretative problem remains a hesitation to recognize as marriage marriage by purchase of the bride.[21]

My hypothesis is that the wrist-grasping gesture was made after a betrothal ceremony wherein either the father of the bride or the bride herself completed the sale contract for the bride by shaking hands with the groom. Hence, it is important to note the implication that the wrist-grasping gesture would be inappropriate when the marriage was legitimate and, consequently, is not an obligatory element in ancient Greek weddings. The evidence, literary and iconographic, demonstrates that wrist grasping was common in wedding processions but, although this remains possible, the evidence does not demonstrate that it was a nuptial universal. There is, indeed, some complicated evidence that it was not. Up to now, I have not found an example of a legitimate marriage in which the gesture is attested.

What might a *pallakē* look like? Like a bride being led by the wrist into the home of the groom who makes eye contact with her "abductor" (Boston, Museum of Fine Arts 03.802). Or, like a bride who passively resists being led by the groom.[22] Or, as

---

bride as the procession approaches a donkey cart. Third, a vase depicting a wedding procession in which bride and groom ride in a donkey cart includes a subsidiary theme of wrist-grasping female dancers (New York, Metropolitan Museum of Art 56.11.1).

21. Flory (1978: 70 with n. 3) maintains, "Both the handclasp between Jason and Medea and the agreement it represents are extraordinary according to the *mores* of fifth century Athens. No Athenian woman could enter into such a contract on her own behalf ... In a Roman wedding the handclasp was 'the most solemn moment in the ceremony' [reference omitted], but I find no evidence of it for a Greek wedding, where it would be inconsistent with the passive status of the bride." Thus, direct evidence that Greek brides were not necessarily passive is dismissed on the ground that brides were passive in Greek weddings.

22. Daughters were not always pleased by the marital choices made by fathers or, for that matter, by their own choices. In Euripides's *Ion* (885 ff.), Creusa laments that when she was gathering crocus flowers in the meadow the attractive Apollo gently led her with his hand on her wrist (*karpos*) and then impregnated her in a cave. Burnett (1970: 86) comments: "In fact, however, the

depicted in Boston, Museum of Fine Arts 13.186, like Helen when she was "abducted" by Paris: "We might think that the aggressive gesture of the groom seizing her wrist is intended ... to indicate a violent abduction, but standing behind Aphrodite is Peitho (Persuasion), whose presence indicates the bride has been persuaded, through divine intersession, to go willingly" (Oakley and Sinos 1993: 33; Boston, Museum of Fine Arts 13.186).[23]

Most interestingly and perhaps most significantly, in Munich, Antikensammlungen 2309, Theseus lifts Helen off the ground while she grasps his right wrist with her right hand and touches his hair with her left hand. Meanwhile, Theseus's left arm encircles Helen's waist and his left hand clasps his own right hand. Thus, the wrist-clasp and hand-clasp are represented in the same abduction—that is marriage into *pallakia*. Of course, the artist has reversed the nuptial expectations: Theseus should grasp Helen's wrist (not her his) and he should clasp her hand (not his own). The scene is available for download at http://www.perseus.tufts.edu/hopper/image?img=Perseus:image:1993.01.0229.

The groom's grasping of the bride's wrist may have signaled not only his taking ownership, but also that he would honor the commitments made to her or to her father at the time of nuptial contracting.[24] This line of interpretation of wrist-grasping as symbolizing a solemn assurance would clarify why Achilles grasped the wrist of Priam in *Iliad* 24.671–72 (noted above; see similarly Avagianou 1991: 57–58).

6. Linking *Chamaipous* with *Pallakia*: Additional Considerations

Further to the nuptial significance of wrist-grasping, Gaius (*Institutes* 1.113, 121) tells that in Roman marriage by coemption (marriage by purchase) the ritual required the

---

verb of touching which Creusa employs to depict the god's coercion is as gentle as any in the language. *Emphuein* represents most frequently the touch of a friend, especially an affectionate handclasp; in *The Iliad* it often means the touch of a suppliant who begs a favor." There is no mention of a handshake or of a father but it is seems that the marriage was consensual (but contrast Zacharia 2003: 93). In addition, the "rape" of Creusa Is not portrayed as being violent. In her story about what happened to her "friend" says merely that she "had intercourse (*migēnai*) with Apollo" (*Ion* 338; tr. Potter *Perseus* Project). See below for an alternative meaning of this intercourse.

23. I grant that there is merit in Edmunds's (2016: 252) conclusion that wrist grasping "has no single, particular, fixed significance."

24. Possibly, the bride confirmed her promise of loyal wifely behavior by grasping the wrist of her husband. That is, the wrist grasping by the groom was reciprocated by the bride. Thus, in Munich, Antikensammlungen 2309, Helen grasps the right wrist of her abductor Theseus who lifts her off the ground. In addition, in a shield band (Olympia Museum B 696; Edmunds 2016: 113 fig. 11) a woman holds a spindle in her right hand, a wreath encircles her left forearm and her left hand grasps the right wrist of a departing warrior who raises a sword. In another shield band (Olympia Museum B 1803; Edmunds 2016: 114 fig 12) the departing warrior holding up his sword grasps the right wrist of a woman who holds a wreath in her left hand.

husband to grasp in his hand (*manus*) his new wife which act signaled to witnesses that the woman/bride had come under his ownership. The anatomical form assumed by the groom's taking hold of his bride is not stated. Indeed, despite Roman usage of the phrase *uxorem ducers* (literally "leading a wife into her husband's house") to signify marriage, "there are no recorded instances of a groom actually leading his bride anywhere during a wedding procession" (Hersch 2010: 142).[25] Nevertheless, the fact that Roman ritual called for grooms to seize purchased brides makes credible my hypothesis that the Greek *cheir' epi karpoi* nuptial seizure signals not only a change in the bride's ownership but also that this change took place by sale.[26]

Thus far, I have not been able to find direct Greek examples wherein grasping of the wrist/lower arm is accompanied by a payment for the bride. However, there is circumstantial evidence linking wrist grasping with payment. First, is a scene depicted on the Shield of Achilles (*Iliad* 18.574):

> There were youths dancing and maidens [single women] of the price of many cattle [*parthenoi alphesiboiai* "cattle-earning maidens"[27]], holding their hands upon the wrists one of the other [*allēlōn epi karpōi cheiras echontes*] (tr. Murray *LCL* modified).

Two caveats are in order: (1) If wrist-grasping were a standard feature in dance intended to provide the dancers with a strong grip (Oakley and Sinos 1993: 32), there

25. In Plautus's *Cistellaria* ("The Casket Comedy" 98–99), based on Menander's "Synaristosai" ("Women Lunching Together"), a young man takes an oath before Selenium's mother to "lead her to his home" (*uxorem ductorum*). A wooden relief from the Heraion at Samos dated to the end of the seventh century BCE depicts Zeus grasping Hera's right breast while Hera grasps Zeus's right wrist with her left hand (Avagionou 1991: 56–57, 77–78 with fig. 3).

26. Gaius *Institutes* 1.113, 121: "In marriage by coemption, women become subject to their husbands by mancipation, that is to say by a kind of fictitious sale; for the man purchases the woman who comes into his hand in the presence of not less than five witnesses, who must be Roman citizens over the age of puberty, and also of a balance-holder... The sale of land differs from the mancipation of other things, in that both slaves and free persons, as well as animals subject to mancipation cannot be disposed of in this way unless they are present; as it is necessary for him who acquires the object by mancipation to be able to grasp it with his hands, and the ceremony is designated mancipation because the property is seized with the hands. Lands, however, are usually mancipated at a distance" (tr. de Zulueta).

    Note Gaius' use of the present tense in describing coemptio (Corbett 1930: 84; Treggiari 1991: 31). Also, with respect to the prevalence of *manus*-marriage in late Republican times, note that the so-called *Laudatio Turiae* (I.13–26): (1) includes the claim that the father of "Turia" had contracted a marriage by *coemptio*; and (2) affirms that "Turia's sister had been transferred (meaning "married") into the *potestas* of her husband Cluvius (*CIL* 6.1527, 31670, 37053 [= *ILS* 8393]; tr. Wistrand 1976). In addition, with respect to the vitality of marriage with *manus*, it appears that Turia's (half-)sister although legitimate—that is, her mother was married *sine manu*—chose to be married *cum manu*. Turia herself was illegitimate—that is, her mother was married *cum manu*—and she married *cum manu*.

27. Finley's (1954: 20 n. 44) objection that the term appears "exactly once in the poems (and once in *HAphr* 119)" cannot salvage his argument that brides were not sold.

would be no particular reason for Homer to mention it; (2) Homer employs a variety of expressions to convey the beauty/desirability of young women and there is no particular reason to cite their market price to make this point unless such women might be sold. Thus, the scene provides circumstantial evidence that wrist grasping accompanied payment for the bride.

The scene on the Shield suggests the known phenomenon of the community courtship dance (*Iliad* 16.179–84; Plato *Laws* 771e–72a; Lonsdale 1993: 10, 210–18). Dillon (2002: 68) has described a fragment of a Samothrace frieze dated to the mid-fourth century BCE in the following terms:

> [T]he maidens are arranged in facing pairs, each dancer holding the right-hand wrist of the dancer in front of her, forming a continuous line. The dancers wear a short-sleeved chiton of Ionic style over which they wear a mantle. Every second dancer, the ones turning backwards to face their immediate dancing companion, wears a shawl-like (or scarf-like) garment draped over the shoulders and billowing out at the elbows.

One gets the sense of a nuptial pursuit of the "fleeing woman." Note also Boston, Museum of Fine Arts 65.908 as described on the website of the Boston Museum of Fine Arts:

> The interior of this libation bowl, used for liquid sacrifices, depicts what appears to be a religious ritual, in which girls dance around an altar. The girls are identically dressed in flowing dresses (*chitones*) and pink mantles (*himatia*). Seven of them grasp each other by the wrist, but do not join at the ends, so it is unclear whether they are simply meant to be in a row, or a circle. One other girl faces the altar, playing the double pipes to facilitate the dance. Upon the altar is a burnt offering, evidenced by the high flames. To the right of the altar is a wool basket (*kalathos*) and a ribbon hanging above (http://www.mfa.org/collections/object/libation-bowl-phiale-154010).[28]

The *kalathos* may be understood as a nuptial symbol (see Chapter XI).

Additional evidence linking wrist grasping with *pallakia* is provided in Chapter XVIII by the etymology of Hera ("She who is seized/grasped") and by an analysis of the marital status of Penelope (Chapter XVII). Evidence is presented that Penelope was Odysseus's *pallakē*. It is then suggested that when Odysseus grasped Penelope's wrist before departing for Troy (*Odyssey* 18.250 ff.) he was recalling having years earlier made her his *pallakē*. Pausanias (3.12.2), who reveals that Odysseus would have had to pay to marry Penelope if her father Icarius had not waived the expected payment (*hedna*), supplies the element of payment. In short,

28. The Boston Museum phiale 65.908 is believed to have been found together with a pyxis (Boston, Boston Museum of Fine Arts 65.1166) that shows young women engaged in wool working and casual activities in an interior quarters or courtyard. An inscription scratched inside the lid tells that one woman (Lysandra) gave it to another (Lysimachus) (Truitt 1969; http://www.mfa.org/collections/object/container-pyxis-with-lid-154011.

wrist-grasping is again circumstantially linked with payment for the bride and *pallakia*.

The Roman evidence for *coemptio*, the scene on the Shield of Achilles, the (yet to be presented) evidence for the etymology of Hera and for the marriage of Penelope with Odysseus and, finally, the forceful nature of the gesture itself are offered in support of the hypotheses that the wrist-grasping gesture signals the sale of the bride into *pallakia*.

7. Marital Rituals: Torch and *Pallakia*

That torches were held aloft only in legitimate marriages is possibly indicated by the scholiast on Euripides *Alcestis* 989 who says about *Iliad* 6.121–26 that Boucolion (see below) was *skotio* ("dark") because he was "born from a marriage [*gamōn*] unlit by torches" (Wright 2006: 77; see similarly Eustathius 622.43 and Euripides *Ion* 1475; Ebbott 2003: e.g. 24).

On the other hand, somewhat unclear remarks of Hecuba to Cassandra (Euripides *Trojan Women* 343–52) seemingly refer to the holding of torches to celebrate her illegitimate marriage to Agamemnon: "Take in those torches, Trojan friends, and for her wedding madrigals weep your tears instead" (tr. Coleridge *Perseus Project*). More decisively, as noted earlier, in "The Men from Sikyon," Menander incorporates the deployment of torches in the marriage of Theron and Malthake, a marriage that certainly is not legitimate. During the wedding ceremony, Theron shouts for torches and garlands and a slave brings them for the procession (416–20).

A main piece of iconographic evidence is the inclusion of a torch in a nuptial scene wherein the bride and groom shake hands. As described by G. Davies (1985: 628),

> A red-figure loutrophoros [London, British Museum GR 1923.1–18.1] of ca. 440–420 B.C. has a representation of a handshake between a man and a woman in the presence of two other women, one with a torch, the other adjusting the woman's hair, surely a reference to the marriage ceremony.[29]

I argued above that marriages in which bride and groom shake hands are not legitimate but are marriages into *pallakia*. Torches also appear in wedding scenes together with the *cheir' epi karpoi* gesture (e.g. Toronto, Royal Ontario Museum 929.22.3; Athens, National Museum 1388; Bonn, Akademisches Kunstmuseum 994). Again, I argued above that marriage in which the groom grasps the bride's wrist are not legitimate but are marriages into *pallakia*.

In Euripides *Ion* 1475, Creusa tells Ion: "My wedding rites had no torches or dances, child, when I bore you" (tr. Potter *Perseus Project*). In the same drama (line 73), Hermes says the *gamos*—"marriage"—was *kruptoi*—"secret." Also, Hermes (*Ion* 11) speaks of a

29. The torch, it may be added, is included in handshake scenes not only in Greek but also in Roman art wherein the marriage god Hymenaeus (London, British Museum 1805.0703.143) holds it.

gamos bia—"marriage by force". Do these lines in *Ion* mean that Creusa married Apollo or that she did not? Ebbott (2003: 24) says that each time Hermes mentions marriage, the term is qualified, but this answer leaves unexplained the decision to mention the term in the first place. Is Ion a *nothos* or a *parthenios* or both (line 1474)? In *Ion*, we see a deliberate blurring of the nomenclature that previously had distinguished between the offspring of *pallakia* and those of unmarried mothers.

Boucolion, the eldest son of Laomedon, king of Troy, was *skotios* (*Iliad* 6.23–24). Ebbott (2003: 21) observes, "there is little doubt that Boukolion is illegitimate (and, perhaps, since he was the eldest son of Laomedon, this status is mentioned as a reason why he was not king of Troy)." Thus, it is possible to understand that *skotioi* are *nothoi*[30] who stand outside the light cast by inheritance rights.

To return to the original point, I accept that clandestine sexual relationships initiated without torches are not marriages. Indeed, it seems that women participating in such affairs remain "virgins" (*parthenoi*; discussed by Sissa 2013: 74–76). This fits the sexual relationship between Hermes and Polymele and, uncomfortably, between Apollo and Creusa. I agree that those born in such sexual relationships are without inheritance rights and might loosely be called *nothoi* or *nothon me partheneuma*—"bastard of an unmarried woman" (Euripides *Ion* 1472). This designation fits uncomfortably on the son of Apollo by Creusa. However, I believe the lifting of torches is a nuptial universal and for this reason cannot signal the form of marriage, legitimate or *pallakia*.

Lycaon of Troy is the *kasignētos* of Paris (*Iliad* 3.333) who was born to Hecuba. Lycaon is not called *nothos* (which he is) but neither is the relationship between Priam and his mother depicted as being formed without torches. Again, note that Homer's much-esteemed archer Teucer is described (by Agamemnon) as a *nothos* who was reared as a beloved son by his father Telamon (*Iliad* 8.284); elsewhere, Teucer is said to "have the same father" as Ajax (*kasignētos* in *Odyssey* 8.585; *opatros* in Iliad 12.371). Teucer's mother is the Trojan Hesione (*Iliad* 13.173), whom Agamemnon calls an *aichmalōtos* (*Iliad* 8.1228–307). There is no reason to assume that the the sexual relationship between Hesione and Telamon was "torchless"—that is, not established in a legal marriage. Teucer is not, for example, a *parthenios* (the son of an unwed mother) like Eudorus, but rather he is a *nothos*, the son of a slave-wife (*pallakē*). I see no reason to dismiss the idea that the Greeks would have celebrated such marriages including by the raising of torches.

30. Hesychius (s.v. *skotios*) equates *skotios* with *nothos*. Ferrari (2008: 65) explains, "[T]he fact they [*nothoi*] cannot attain adult status and perform their fathers' functions reveals the inadequacy of their claims. Accordingly, the *nothos* is cast back into the secrecy that surrounded his birth becoming in Phaethon's case, hidden and *mukhios* (*Theogony* 991), a creature of interior spaces, out of the sunlight." Ogden (1996: 17) cites Erdmann's (1934: 365 n. 3) suggestion that *nothos* "might be related to the word *nython*, which Hesychius glosses 'without speech, dark' (*aphōnon*, *skoteinon*) ... But a connection between *nothos* and *nythos* is very hard to justify in philological terms."

Much more evidence and much more analysis is required before we can be truly confident about the relationship between marriage rituals and marriage form in the ancient Greek world. Meanwhile, I have carried my discussion as far as might be considered profitable. The handshake between bride and groom is indicative of auto-*ekdosis* into *pallakia* and there is evidence of a distinctive supplication ritual gesture for legitimate brides. Musée du Louvre G 146 demonstrably links *chamaipous* with the groom's ownership of the bride, who, in this case, is clearly his slave. On the other hand, it has not proved possible to find examples explicitly linking *chamaipous* with bride-purchase.

VI. "Wife" as a Multidimensional Status in Ancient Greece: Supplementary Evidence

According to Ogden (1996: 73), "A woman's rights to be called a 'wife' [*gunē*] and to be mother of legitimate children were inseparable...." The body of evidence reviewed below collects additional evidence that the ancient Greeks recognized two forms of marriage, hence the right to be a Greek wife and her right to bear legitimate children were, in fact, separable.

1. Forms of Marriage: Classical Athens

Classical Athens lacked a compact definition and terminology of legal marriage (Leão and Rhodes 2015: 77). As Aristotle (*Politics* 1.1253b) put it: "I mean that of mastership, that of marriage (there is no exact term denoting the relation uniting wife and husband), and thirdly the progenitive relationship (this too has not been designated by a special name)" (tr. Rackham *LCL*). However, the reason for the omission is not that the definition was self-evident and "in the singular," as Patterson (2012: 382) believes. It is that Athenian law recognized two forms of legal marriage as is indicated by evidence of various kinds.[1]

First, basing himself on a distinction between *gnēsion* and *gametēs* in an oath relating to the Demotionidai and the Dekeleieis (*IG* II^2, 1237 lines 109–11), Sealey (1984: 122; cf. Wolff 1944: 68) hypothesizes that the term used "*gametē*-woman," unlike

---

1. I should admit that I found Homer's nuptial terminology intractable—*alochos, kouridiēn alochon, kouridiēn akoitin, opuiomenē* and the others. However, as we see in this and the following chapter, Athenian drama provides significant nuptial insights.

2. Patterson (1990: 49 n. 38), adds the example of Isaeus 12.10, but goes on to conclude, "I do not agree with Sealey ... that *gametē* in these contexts is significantly different from *egguētē*" (my transliterations). She provides no further explanation. However, in Sophocles *Trachiniae* 460, Heracles is said to have taken many "brides" where the term used is *egguē*. If taken literally, the implication would be that all Heracles's marriages were legitimate or even that all marriages are legitimate. However, not all of Heracles's "*egguē*" are portrayed as having been acquired in legitimate marriages. Line 360 reveals that Heracles had intended Iole for his "dark bedmate" (*krupthion* lechos). As noted by Patterson (1990: 49 n. 38), in *Trachiniae*, Deianeira is said to forsee new *gamoi* in her house (843) and both Iole and Deianeira are called *damar* (406, 428). If bigamy is excluded, the implications are that *gamoi*—"married women" ("marriages"; cf. 545–46)—need not mean "legitimately married women" and *damar* need not mean "legitimate wife." Again, the point is that the Greeks recognized more than one form of marriage, a point that Patterson, despite her brilliant analysis, seems determined not to recognize.

"*egguētē*-woman," did not only refer to legitimately married woman with the result that "the children of *gametai* were a larger class, comprising the children of *engyētai* and some others."

Along the same line, Aristotle's *Athenaion politeia* (*AthPol* 4.2), referring to Draco's constitution, mandates that holders of certain offices have children over ten years old born to *gametēs gunaikos gnēsious*. Such detail would be pointless unless the referent is to a *subset* of legally recognized "married women" (*gametai*) that includes legitimate wives but excludes other recognized forms.[2]

More directly, as discussed in Chapter XIX.1, a number of sources attribute to Socrates (and to other notables) two "women/wives" (*gunaikes*), Myrto and Xanthippe, both of whom were legally recognized wives (*gametai*). One approach is to understand that Socrates (and others) had *two* legitimate wives. The other is to recognize that the sources attribute a lower status to Xanthippe, who may be understood to be a secondary or *pallakē*-wife (discussed by Woodbury 1973: 21–25). The implication is that the *pallakē*, as much as the legitimate wife, is a legally recognized wife (*gametē*-woman).

In addition, in Athenian social practice, as revealed in Menander's plays, the *pallakē* is represented as a wife. For example, Glycera who can only be a *pallakē* is referred to as "wedded wife" (*gametēn gunaika*) by Pataikos in "The Girl with Her Hair Cur Short" (487). There is no reason to dismiss this characterization as delusional.

Additional evidence for dual forms of legal marriage in classical Athens is provided by use of the term *sunoikein*—"to dwell in a common household" (Wolff 1944: 65–6). In Demosthenes 59 (esp. 61, 119, 121), Stephanus is prosecuted for violating a law banning a male citizen from "dwelling with" (*sunoikein*) an allegedly alien woman named Neaira. Based primarily on an arbitration freeing her, my position is that Neaira had been dwelling with Stephanus as his legally recognized slave-wife (*pallakē*). Thus, in this case, *sunoikein* would refer to marriage but not to legitimate marriage.[3]

---

3. Compare Wolff 1944: 66–68; Just 1989: 43–45. Fortunately, drama provides reasonably clear evidence that "dwelling with" has the meaning "legally married." In Euripides' *Andromache* (15 ff.), Andromache tells: "I live now in the lands that border on Phthia here and the city of Pharsalia, lands where the sea-goddess Thetis, far from the haunts of men and fleeing their company, dwelt as wife (*sunoikizō*) with Peleus. The people of Thessaly call it Thetideion in honor of the goddess's marriage (*numpheumatōn*)" (tr. Kovacs *LCL*). However, in Apollodorus's (*Library* 3.13.5) telling, the shape-shifting Thetis was married as a result of "seizure" by Peleus: "Chiron, therefore, having advised Peleus to seize her and hold her fast in spite of her shape-shifting, he watched his chance and carried her off (*sunarpazō*), and though she turned, now into fire, now into water, and now into a beast, he did not let her go till he saw that she had resumed her former shape. And he married her on Pelion, and there the gods celebrated the marriage with feast and song" (tr. Frazer *LCL*). Thetis is clearly a wife but her previous residence "far from the haunts of men" (sometimes indicated by background trees) and her "seizure" by Peleus argue that she had been a single woman and, therefore, was not a legitimate bride. Vase paintings show the "seizure" of Thetis by Peleus but not the grasping of Thetis' wrist (Barringer 1995: 90–94) or the handshake, as I would expect in self-sale. However, an unusually shaped vase (Baltimore, Walters Art Museum 48.198) with unnamed figures may show Peleus grasping the wrist of Thetis.

Further, support for this conclusion is provided by the reference to "Phano, daughter of Neaira"—rather, "Phano, property of the wife Neaira" (discussed below)—not of Stephanus. Contrary to Ogden, Neaira is married to Stephanus but her daughter Phano has no legal right to Stepanus's property.

2. Pindar *Pythian* 9 and Dual Marriage Forms

Perhaps the most explicit evidence for dual forms of marriage is provided by Pindar's use of the verb *harmozein* "to fit/join together" meaning "to legally bond" (see *Iliad* 22.255[4]) in the context of a marriage between Apollo and Cyrene, a marriage that clearly is not set in the legitimate format. The reference occurs in Pindar *Pythian* 9.1–14:

> With the help of the deep-waisted Graces I want to shout aloud proclaiming the Pythian victory with the bronze shield of Telesicrates, a prosperous man, the crowning glory of chariot-driving Cyrene; the long-haired son of Leto once snatched her from the wind-echoing glens of Mt. Pelion, and carried the girl of the wilds in his golden chariot to a place where he made her mistress of a land rich in flocks and most rich in fruits, to live and flourish on the root of the third continent. Silver-footed Aphrodite welcomed the Delian guest from his chariot, touching him with a light hand, and she cast lovely modesty on their sweet union, joining together [*harmozoisa*] in a common bond of marriage [*gamon*] the god and the daughter of wide-ruling Hypseus (tr. Svarlien *Perseus Project*; Carson 1982: 122).

Note the absence of a betrothal by a male *kurios*, the joining together of Apollo and Cyrene by Aphrodite and the mention of *gamon*, which is the usual word for marriage.

Pindar also uses the verb *harmozein* in connection with the Libyan Antaios marrying his daughter to a Greek man named Alexidamos as the prize for winning a footrace (*Pythian* 9.117). As pointed out by Carson (1982: 125), "for Alexidamos and for the Danaids, a footrace is also a bride-race and is called *gamos* (111, 114)".[5] Unlike the

The François Vase (Florence, Muse Archaeologic National 4209) shows Peleus standing in front of his house greeting a procession of gods while Thetis sits in the open doorway. At the head of this procession is the centaur Chiron who clasps hands with Peleus. Whether the married couple arrived by foot or by chariot is not depicted. T. Smith (2014: 36) argues from continuity with her understanding of the theme on the other side of the same vase (University of Virginia, Fralin Museum of Art 1988.62) that Peleus and Thetis are the unnamed couple depicted in a wedding procession in which they ride in a chariot pulled by four horses accompanied by an unnamed lyre player. There appears to be an Eretrian vase in which Peleus and Thetis are said to stand in a chariot.

4. "But come hither, let us call the gods to witness, for they shall be the best witnesses and guardians of our covenant [*harmoniaōn*]: I [Hector] will do unto thee no foul despite, if Zeus grant me strength to outstay thee, and I take thy life; but when I have stripped from thee thy glorious armour, Achilles, I will give thy dead body back to the Achaeans; and so too do thou." (*Iliad* 22.254–59; tr. Murray *LCL*).

5. Pausanias 3.12:2: "In my opinion, Icarius [father of Penelope] was imitating Danaus when he held the running-race. For Danaus contrived the following plan to solve the difficulty about his daughters. Nobody would take a wife from among them because of their pollution so Danaus

marriage of Cyrene with Apollo, which is found in the Hesiodic *Catalogue of Women* (see below), the tale of Antaios is probably innovated by Pindar (Woodbury 1982: 255–58 with n. 42). More importantly, being a marriage between a Greek and a Libyan, it cannot refer to a legitimate marriage. Accordingly, there is no trace of the betrothal by a (Greek) father that characterizes marriage by loan of the bride.

Admittedly, the use of *harmozein* by Herodotus (6.65.2) raises difficulties:

> Leotychides had already become strongly hostile to Demaratus for the following reason: Leotychides was betrothed to [*harmosamenou*: "joined together with"] Percalus, daughter of Demarmenus, but Demaratus plotted and robbed him of his marriage, stealing [*harpazein*: a better translation would be "seizing"] Percalus and marrying her [*schon gunaika*] first (tr. Godley *LCL*; for Sparta's peculiar "seizure" ritual, see Plutarch *Lycurgus* 15.4–9).

Demaratus somehow invalidated her marriage and then married Percalus himself. Perhaps, he argued that Percalus was not in her own hands and could not legally give herself in marriage. On the other hand, Kulesza (2008: 138) suggests that *harmozein* is "probably the Spartan equivalent of *engyan*." However, Pindar's usage suggests that even if *harmozein* refers to a "betrothal" or "promise" (rather than to a consummated marriage), it does not refer to legitimate marriage. Indeed, Leotychides seems to have contracted with Percalus, not with her father.[6]

It is tempting to conclude from the analysis of *Pythian* 9 that the terminology "fitting together in marriage" is specific to marriage by sale of the bride. Moreover, this proposition finds support outside Pindar in the second century CE *Onomasticon* of the Greek grammarian Pollux, who tells that a bridegroom might be called either the *egguētēs* (3.34–35)—a clear reference to legitimate marriage—or the *harmostēs* (3.39). The latter name is cognate to *harmozein* (Carson 1982: 121–22). Two very different Greek names for the groom would of course be needed to distinguish between two very different sets of legal powers and two very different sets of marriage rituals. Note that in the Spartan Constitution the *harmostēs* is a governor (Xenophon *Constitution*

---

sent round a notice that he would give away his daughters without bride-gifts (*hedna*), and that each suitor could choose the one whose beauty pleased him most. A few men came, among whom he held a foot-race the first comer was allowed to choose before all the others, after him the second, and so on to the last. The daughters that were left had to wait until other suitors arrived and competed in another foot-race." (tr. Jones and Ormerod *LCL*) There is no obvious reference to the betrothal characterizing legitimate marriage.

6. Herodotus 9.108 also uses *harmozō* in a matrimonial context but the reference is to the Persian court (cf.3.137.5; 5.32.1). The reference seems to be consummated marriage, not betrothal: "So he [Xerxes] betrothed [*harmosas*] them [his son Darius with the daughter of his brother Masistes] with all due ceremony and rode away to Susa. But when he had come and had taken Darius' bride into his house, he thought no more of Masistes' wife, but changed his mind and wooed and won this girl Artaynte, Darius' wife and Masistes' daughter" (tr. Godley *LCL*). Another difficult example is Euripides' *Phoenician Women* 411, wherein Adrastus is given an oracle by Apollo to *harmosai* his daughters to a boar and a lion.

of the Lacedaimonians 14.2). It has been argued at length that in marriage by sale, but not in marriage by loan, the husband is the bride's *kurios* or "governor."

Analysis of the status of Harmonia, the wife in myth of Cadmus ("Easterner"), provides supporting evidence on the matrimonial significance of *harmozein*. The term *harmonia* is cognate to *harmozein*. Harmonia literally means "legally fitted/joined" wife and, according to our theory, she should be a *pallakē*. Is she?

To begin with, there is no indication that Harmonia's father Ares betrothed her to Cadmus. Hesiod (*Theogony* 935–37) says simply that Cadmus made Harmonia his wife (*akoitin*). According to Ilievski (1993: 29):

> Judging from the names of Cadmus and Harmonia one can conclude that their wedding represents a union of two cultures: Mediterranean with Semitic elements and IE [Indo European]. The name Cadmus is from a Semitic stem *qdm*, Hebrew *qedem*, *qddim*, "east," *qadmeni*, "men from the east" ... Harmony, as we have already seen, has an IE etymology.

As argued in Chapter X.3, increases in distance, including in cultural distance, favor marriage by sale (self-sale) of the bride to the groom/disfavor legitimate marriage. Apollodorus (*Library* 3.4.2), indeed, testifies that Cadmus *purchased* Harmonia:

> But Cadmus, to atone for the slaughter [of the armed men called "Sparti"], served Ares for an eternal year; and the year was then equivalent to eight years of our reckoning. After his servitude Athena procured for him the kingdom, and Zeus gave him to wife Harmonia, daughter of Aphrodite and Ares. And all the gods quitted the sky, and feasting in the Cadmea celebrated the marriage with hymns. Cadmus gave ⌊*didōmi*⌋ her a robe and the necklace wrought by Hephaestus, which some say was given to Cadmus by Hephaestus, but Pherecydes says that it was given by Europa, who had received it from Zeus (tr. Frazer *LCL*).

Harmonia was sold, or, better, sold herself into *pallakia* (see Chapter XI).

3. The *Pallakē* as Understood by a Roman Legal Scholar

Granius Flaccus, a legal scholar of the late Republic-early Empire, compared the Roman *pellex* with the Greek *pallakē*:

> *Granius Flaccus in libro de iure Papiriano scribit pellicem nuch volgo vocari, quae cum eo, cui uxor sit, corpus misceat: quosdam eam, quae uxoris loco sine nuptiis in domo sit, quam* pallakēn *Graeci vocant* (*Digest* 50.16.144 Paul).
>
> Granius Flaccus writes in his book about the *jus Papirianum* that a *pellex* is now the usual name for someone who sleeps with someone *who has a wife*, but once upon a time someone who was in a household in place of a wife, but without being married, whom the Greeks call *pallakē* (tr. Watson; emphasis added).

Flaccus's explanation is, in effect, that the *pellex* (*pallakē*) was regarded as an unmarried wife. On the other hand, a good deal of evidence cited throughout this study supports that *pallakia* was a legally recognized status, that it was created by distinct nuptial rituals and also that in Greek society generally the *pallakē* was viewed as a wife. In addition, Flaccus says that the *pellex* only cohabited with a married man. So perhaps, contrary to Flaccus, the Roman *pellex* differed in important ways from the Greek *pallakē*.

An additional line of interpretation is that by "*sine nuptiis*," Flaccus did not mean "without being married," and that by "*uxoris loco*," he did not mean "in place of a wife."[7] Flaccus is perhaps explaining that in old times the *pellex* was a wife but not a "legitimate" wife—that is, she was woman whose marriage was not confirmed by a distinctive set of rituals. This two-tracked solution finds possible support from within the classical Greek world. A difficult fragment tells that Euripides, in his *Phoenix*, described (defined) a *pallakē* with the phrase *amnēsteutos gunē*, meaning "wife without a wooing", i.e. without the proper preliminaries of marriage (Euripides fr. 815; Fitton 1970: 63; LSJ s.v.). However, this is a rather uninformative translation. *Mnēstē*, a building block of *amnēsteutos*, has meanings such as "fame" (LSJ s.v.), which raises new questions. In ancient Greek terms, "fame", like "honor", has a material dimension. In *Iliad* 11.240 ff., Agamemnon kills Iphidamas:

> So there he fell, and slept a sleep of bronze, unhappy youth, far from his wedded wife (*mnēstēs alouchou ... kouridēs*), bearing aid to his townsfolk—far from the bride of whom he had known no joy, yet much had he given for her; first he gave an hundred kine, and thereafter promised a thousand, goats and sheep together, which were herded for him in flocks past counting (tr. Murray *LCL*).

In this case, the remembered or famous or wooed wife is a *purchased* wife. Perhaps, the underlying meaning is that a *pallakē* is not a wife purchased from her father. This is not quite true, however.

As the discussion stands, it appears that Granius Flaccus's position opposes my interpretation of the Greek *pallakē*. Specifically, he does not appear to identify her, or more directly the *pellex*, with the Roman wife *cum manus*. On the other hand, a variety of Greek evidence presented in this chapter and the next offers support for a two-tiered Greek marriage system. Moreover, the testimony of Granius Flaccus stands in sharp contrast to the secondary wife status of Caenis, the *pallakē* of Vespasian (see Chapter X.1).

---

7. I note that McGinn (1991: 344) who analyzes the Flaccus passage writes "an unmarried woman *uxoris* loco" but leaves the passage untranslated. Similarly, Adams (1983: 355) quotes the Latin but offers no translation.

VII. "Wife" as a Multidimensional Status in Ancient Greece: Testimony of Euripides's *Electra*

Evidence from the *Electra* of Euripides confirms and casts new light on the coexistence of dual forms of marriage in ancient Greece.

Electra's speech in lines 930–35 concerning the marriage of her mother Clytemnestra with Aegisthus is complicated but revealing:

> Among all the Argives you would hear this: "That woman's husband (*anēr*)," not "that man's wife (*gunē*)." [In all of Argos you used to hear this: "The husband is the wife's, and the wife is not the husband's"] Although this is a shameful thing, for the wife to rule the house (*dōmatōn gunaika*) and not the husband; and I hate those children who are called in the city not the sons of the man, their father, but of their mother. For when a man makes a remarkable marriage, one above his rank, there is no talk of the husband but only of the wife. (tr. Coleridge *Perseus Project*; bracketed translation Ormand 2009: 262)

To extract historical information from this intentionally negative speech, it is helpful to begin at its ending.

At the end, Electra explicitly has in mind the subset of marriages wherein children bear their mother's name, not the name of their father. As in the Roman *cum manus*-marriage, the children bear a metronymic, not a patronymic. This practice is also attested at Athens. Such marriages are not legitimate marriages and must be marriages by sale/self-sale of the wife to the husband, in which offspring lack inheritance rights to the father's property.[1]

This conclusion of course applies whether the husband/wife is marrying up or down in the socioeconomic scale. Specifically, the basic point remains the same whether or not Electra means that Aegisthus had a metronymic, not a patronymic.

Electra refers to the ("shameful") marriage of Clytemnestra with the social climber Aegisthus (a *nothos*?). Given the following reference to children who bear their mother's name, my understanding of this most difficult passage is that Electra is referring to the type of marriage in which the wife belonged to her husband ("that man's wife") as opposed to the type in which the wife belonged to her father but not to her husband ("that woman's husband"). Thus, Clytemnestra became the *pallakē* of Aegisthus.

1. Metronymics are also alluded to by Electra in Sophocles *Electra* 365–67, but in this case, the sense is unclear.

In support of this interpretation of what Euripides had in mind, note that in line 929, Electra observes that, "Both being wicked, she [Cytemnestra] took up [*anēreiothon*] your [Aegisthus'] fortune, you [Aegisthus] her evil" (tr. Coleridge *Perseus Project* modified). In addition, in lines 1086 ff., Electra confronts Clytemnestra as follows:

> But if, as you say, my father killed your daughter, what is the wrong I and my brother have done you? How was it that after you had killed your husband, you did not assign to us our father's home, but *you brought the goods belonging to another to bed* [*lechee*], buying your marriage [*gamous*] with wages [*misthos*]? (tr. Coleridge *Perseus Project*; emphasis added).

Clytemnestra bought the goods of Aegisthus with her wifeship. One might say equally that Clytemnestra sold her wifeship for Aegisthus's goods. That wealth and wifeship moved in opposite directions seems clear: Electra says that Aegisthus received the wife and Clytemnestra received the/his wealth. Clytemnestra's *misthos*—"price"—must be *dōra*, a form of "bride-price" and certainly not *proix*—"groom-price" (terms discussed in Chapter X).

There are crosscurrents and ambiguities in Electra's speech but it is clear that Euripides gave his audience ample grounds to understand that the widow Clytemnestra contracted to become Aegisthus's *pallakē*—that is, his slave-wife. It follows from the logic of my argument that, in line 930, when Electra speaks of wives who do not belong to their husbands ("that woman's husband"), she must be referring to the (allegedly) historically typical Argive (also Athenian) marriage, as a marriage by loan of the bride to the husband (legitimate marriage).

Clytemnestra's (assumedly) legitimate children by Agamemnon, Electra and Orestes, being their (dead) father's property, became *parerga domōn*—"outsiders to the house (of Aegisthus)" (line 63; discussed by Ormand 2009: 252); Aegisthus was not their *kurios*. If Euripides had intended merely to have Electra insult Clytemnestra, he could have chosen a better tool than *parerga domōn*. An Athenian audience would not understand this uncommon phrase as an insult but rather would appreciate it as a technical term meaning something like "belonging to an independent household," or "without legal standing in the new household."[2]

One interpretation of her marriage to Farmer is that Electra had been a single woman outside any male-headed household. The assumption finds support in line 209 wherein Electra calls herself *phugas*—"runaway" or "exile"—from her father's *oikos*. In addition, in 1008–10, Electra says she is *orphanos*—"fatherless". In line 312, if *emnēsteuon* is understood as first-person singular, then Electra "before he joined

2. Roisman and Luschnig (2011: 100) comment on *parerga domōn*: "By giving Aegisthus heirs, Clytemnestra deprives Electra and Orestes of their right to succession." However, Aegisthus' heirs had no right to the estate of Agamemnon. Euripides is necessarily reticent about this point but realistically if Clytemnestra could murder Agamemnon, the returning conqueror of Troy, without protest then he could not have been wealthy. Clytemnestra had to be the wealthy partner in this fictionalized marriage.

the gods, betrothed herself to Castor." Kovacs (1985: 306) counters: "To take the verb as first-person singular is a manifest impossibility. Greek girls do not betroth themselves." However, the fact is that they do betroth themselves. Thus, there are several grounds for concluding that Electra is presented as outside the household of Agamemnon even before his death at the hands of Clytemnestra. After his death, she sold herself to Farmer.

In line 1004–05 Electra says, "I live as a slave [*doulē*] in this miserable house [Farmer's house], cast out from my father's home" (tr. Coleridge *Perseus Project*; bracketed tr. Kovacs *LCL*; cf. 60–3). (Electra also refers to herself as a slave in Aeschylus *Libation Bearers* 135.) Electra's self-description as "slave" is correct both emotionally and legally.

As a woman left under her own power, Electra had the right to transfer herself to Farmer as his slave-wife. At line 259, Electra makes the ambiguous claim that Farmer "thinks the person [*kurion*] who gave me did not have that right" (tr. Coleridge *LCL*). However, it would seem that if Farmer thought this he would not have accepted the virtually unrelieved burden of having Electra as his wife (69–70). As a single woman, Electra was the sole *kuria* who had the right to give her in marriage.

Electra is consumed by hatred because, having become an endangered outsider, her best available course of action was to sell herself into *pallakia* to a nobody and to reside nowhere—that is, far from the city of Argos (169–74, 297–99). As Electra admits, Farmer was for her "a healer for ill fortune" (69–70). She chose a *thanasimos gamous*—"deadly marriage" (247)—because neither her mother nor Aegisthus offered her a preferred alternative. One might add that Electra contracted into a fraudulent marriage, as she refused to have sexual relations with her husband. She used Farmer in much the way that Cassandra used Apollo when, in return for the gift of prophecy, she gave herself in marriage to the god and then broke her oath (Aeschylus *Agamemnon* 1178 ff.; Apollodorus *Library* 3.12.5; Debnar 2010: 132–33).

Up to the point of Electra's marriage to Farmer, the *Electra* of Euripides has much in common with the Electra of Sophocles. Sophocles's version of the myth also indicates that Electra was the property of her father. As Ierulli (1993) points out the chorus initially identifies Electra with her mother (122–26) but Electra insists on identifying herself with her father Agamemnon and by the end of the drama, her peers are converted to this position (1070 ff.). Tellingly, while her sister Chrysothemis lives with her mother Clytemnestra in the house of Aegisthus in relative luxury, the (unmarried) Electra laments:

> But the best part of life has passed away leaving me in hopelessness, and I have no strength left. I waste away without children and have no loving husband to champion me, but like some despised foreign slave (*oikonomos*), I serve in the halls of my father (*thalamos patros*), wrapped in shabby garments and standing to eat scanty meals (Sophocles *Electra* 185 ff.; tr. Jebb *Perseus Project*).

Clearly, Sophocles's Electra lives outside a male-headed household. That she is a single woman is underlined by Electra's reference to herself in line 165 as *anumpheutos* "unmarried" or, more accurately I believe, "woman not eligible for legitimate marriage."[3]

A second, much different, explanation of Electra's marriage to Farmer made available by Euripides is that Clytemnestra was Electra's *kuria*. This understanding finds support in lines 1008–10, wherein Electra complains to Clytemnestra,

> What? You sent me away from home, a captive (*aichmalōtos*); I was taken when my home was taken, like these, all of us orphaned of a father (tr. Coleridge *LCL*).

The implication is that Clytemnestra was Agamemnon's *pallakē* and, hence, upon Agamemnon's death she became Electra's legal *kuria*.[4] That Clytemnestra was not a legitimate wife finds support in her revelation in Euripides's *Iphigenia in Aulis* (1148–56):

> Well, now listen; for I will unfold my meaning and no longer employ dark riddles. In the first place—to reproach you first with this—it was not of my own free will but by force that you took and wed me, after slaying Tantalus, my former husband, and dashing my baby on the ground when you had torn him from my breast with brutal violence. Then those two sons of Zeus, who were my brothers, came flashing on horseback to war with you; but Tyndareus, my old father, rescued you because of your suppliant prayers, and you in turn had me to wife" (tr. Coleridge *LCL*).

It very much appears from this that Clytemnestra was never betrothed by Tyndareus to Agamemnon.[5] Another clue to Clytemnestra's *pallakē* status is in Euripides's *Andromache* 1115, wherein Electra's brother Orestes has a metronymic: "son of Clytemnestra".

However, both the above explanations of Electra's marriage are contradicted by Farmer's direct statement that it was *Aegisthus* who transferred Electra to him in marriage (34–35; cf. 39–42), a statement apparently endorsed by Electra (267–69). The solution that emerges is that the *nothē* Electra, she is the daughter of Agamemnon's *pallakē* Clytemnestra, was placed under Aegisthus's ownership when he purchased

3. Note that in Sophocles's *Antigone*, a woman (Cleopatra) who matured in a distant cave—outside a male-headed household (983–4)—and is called *agrios damar* "savage wife," and who bore children to Phineus (970–9), is nevertheless termed *anumpheutos* (866–68, 980) (compare Ormand 1999: 100–01).

4. Clytemnestra's sister Helen was the *pallakē* of Agamemnon's brother Menelaus. Helen married Menelaus because he outbid her other suitors (Hesiodic *Catalogue of Women* [Fragments 154, 155 Most *LCL*]). Perhaps their father also sold Clytemnestra. In *Iliad* 1.110–14, Agamemnon makes an interesting comparison: "I would not accept the glorious ransom for the girl, the daughter of Chryses, since I much prefer to keep her in my home. For certainly I prefer her to Clytemnestra, my wedded wife [*kouridiēn alochou*], since she is not inferior to her, either in form or in stature, or in mind, or in any handiwork" (tr. Murray *LCL*). Helen is also termed *kouridiēn alochou* and is not a legitimate wife. It is quite possible, then, that Agamemnon is comparing like-for-like—that is, Clytemnestra is not a legitimate wife but, like Chruseis, a slave-wife.

5. In Aeschylus *Agamemnon* 914, Agamemnon refers to Clytemnestra by the metronymic "daughter of Leda," apparently indicating her own *nothē* status.

Clytemnestra to be his *pallakē*. Perhaps, this would explain Farmer's reported doubt about whether the person who gave Electra to him had the right to transfer her. It must be added that it is unlikely that Aegisthus would alienate Clytemnestra's property ("peculium") without her permission.

I prefer the first explanation, which offers an explanation of *parerga domōn*. What is made very clear by all the explanations is that Electra is not a legitimate wife. It becomes clear that she is legally owned by Farmer at the end of the drama, when Castor tells Orestes to give Electra in legitimate marriage to Pylades (1249 cf. 1340; *katēggués* in *Orestes* 1079, 1645) but goes on to add:

> Now let Pylades, having one who is both a virgin and a married woman, go home from the Achaean land, and let him conduct the one called your brother-in-law to the land of Phocis, and give him a weight of riches (1284 ff.; tr. Coleridge *Perseus Project*).

Electra is the slave-wife of Farmer and hence he must be paid to release her. Electra's *virgo intacta* status (43–53) helps to explain the willingness of her owner-husband to sell her to Pylades. One might also say that Farmer purchased Electra as his slave-wife and shrewdly stored her in a vault, for which act of abstention from current consumption he expected to earn interest.[6]

Thus, the Electra provides important evidence attesting to: (1) the existence of two coexisting forms of marriage; (2) an (alleged) trend in the relative prevalence of the two forms; (3) sale or self-sale into *pallakia*; (4) the slave status of the *pallakē*; and (5) a structural difference in inheritance rights as revealed by the nomenclature of offspring.

6. Similarly, In the *Homeric Hymn to Aphrodite* (5.136–40; discussed in Chapter V.2), Anchises may profit by selling/ransoming Aphrodite (as Otreus's daughter) back to her parents.

VIII. Path to *Pallakia*

1. From Male-Headed Citizen Household to *Pallakia* in Isaeus 3

It is most difficult to find concrete, real world examples in which the head of an *oikos* sells a female relative into *pallakia*. It is argued below that Isaeus 3 provides such an example, and that supported by the verdict of an Athenian jury that the woman in question had not been betrothed in legitimate marriage. Thanks to Isaeus's convoluted presentation, the analysis is difficult and even tedious, but it provides new understanding of several important questions.

The speaker in Isaeus 3.28 says:

> Another matter which surprises me is that there was no agreement about a dowry for the woman on the part either of him who gave her [Nicodemus] or of him who took her in marriage [Pyrrhus]. For, on the one hand, if Nicodemus gave a dowry, it would have been only natural that the amount of the dowry should be mentioned in the evidence of those who allege that they were present; on the other hand, if our uncle, under the influence of his passion, contracted a marriage with a woman of this character, clearly he who gave her in marriage would have been all the more careful to procure an agreement from the other party stating that he received money with her, so that it might not be in the latter's power easily to get rid of the woman whenever he wished (tr. Forster *LCL*).

I find the speaker's line of reasoning convincing. Indeed, I would add that if Pyrrhus (the uncle) had been "under the influence of his passion" for "a woman of this character", then Nicodemus would not have paid but rather received money for giving his sister away in *pallakia*. Wyse (1904: 313) proposes this understanding:

> If Isaeus could have proved that under the fiction of a dowry paid and received money had been settled on the woman by Pyrrhus, he would have nimbly turned round and argued that she must have been a concubine, not a lawful wife.

Recall that marriage by sale of the bride is attested in Isaeus 3.39.

The speaker (the son of Pyrrhus's sister) does not believe Pyrrhus's maternal uncles who say they were present and that the couple was married in "due legal form" (3.26–27, 70; tr. Forster *LCL*). In ancient Greece, maternal uncles were expected to play a special role on such occasions (Bremmer 1983: esp. 178–81). The speaker reasons that Pyrrhus would not have invited his uncles to witness his discreditable marriage and, more importantly, their deposition did not mention that Nicodemus had given a dowry as was usual in legitimate marriages. The speaker mentions only one independent (non-related) witness, one Pyretides, lacking either patronymic or demotic (Hatzilambrou 2010: 26 n. 24), who had been brought to the wedding by Nicodemus but whom later (the speaker asserts) denied he had knowledge of the facts (3.18, 26). Dionysus of Erchia and Aristolochus of Aethalidae, both of whom are dismissed as "untrustworthy", had witnessed Pyretides's absentee deposition. More importantly, no honest person, the speaker argues, would have had only two witnesses at the deposition.

My understanding, in agreement with the speaker (3.27), is that Nicodemus colluded with the passionate Pyrrhus not to make public the financial details of the marriage. Pyrrhus was motivated by his love for the woman. Nicodemus's motivation for concealment of the sale transaction was that the bride's children would otherwise be known as *nothoi* and consequently without inheritance rights (compare Kapparis 1999: 9 with n. 18; see further below). What stands out as a motivating factor in this concealed marriage by sale is not the poverty of Nicodemus's family but the incentive provided by the wealth of Pyrrhus.

The jury in the "former trial" (3.5, 22) agreed with the speaker's numerous arguments by probability that the marriage had not been legitimate:

> At the same time we convicted Nicodemus, the present defendant, before the same judges, of the most shameless lying in the evidence which he then gave, since he had the impudence to bear witness that he had given his sister in marriage to our uncle in the proper legal manner (3.4; tr. Forster *LCL*).

That Pyrrhus's wife was really a *pallakē* finds strong support in the verdict of a presumably unbiased jury that had access to all the evidence, considered the arguments of both sides and was familiar with Athenian social practices.

The speaker seeks to disorient the jury by telescoping the two trials: He pretends that the earlier trial took place after the death of Endius and that in both actions the issue was the legitimacy of Pyrrhus's marriage. His presentation makes no sense. The conviction of Nicodemus for falsely claiming the marriage was legitimate probably took place not very long after the death of Pyrrhus. To raise a different but hidden issue the speaker initiated the second, much later action. Sealey (1984: 125) explains:

> It would have been foolish for a litigant to initiate a second action in an issue he had already won with the first action. For if he loses the second action, he will be in a weaker position than he was before he initiated it ... One may suspect that this singularly skillful speech suppresses some important point.

The speaker's strategy was to bolster weak arguments relevant to the second action by repeating strong but irrelevant arguments from the first action.

Despite the speaker's efforts at suppression, it emerges that additional evidence supported Philē's claim to Pyrrhus's wealth. This evidence became actionable only after the death of Pyrrhus's adopted son Endius. It was strong enough that Xenocles was emboldened to evict the speaker's family from their factory at the mines near Laurium (3.22). It was that the "same uncles" who deposed that Pyrrhus's marriage had been "according to the law" also deposed that they

> were present by invitation of their nephew at the tenth-day ceremony [the child-naming ritual] in honor of the child who was declared his [Pyrrhus's] daughter. Here I note with the utmost indignation that the husband, in claiming her paternal inheritance on behalf of his wife, has put down her name as Phile, while Pyrrhus's uncles, alleging that they were present, deposed that her father called her Cleitarete, after her grandmother ["the name of your own sister"] (3.30; cf. 3.71; tr. Forster *LCL*).

Unless we completely disbelieve the uncles, this was a real marriage. It is most improbable that maternal uncles would be called to officiate at the birth of a child whose father "once had an affair with her mother" (Hatzilambrou 2010: 19). Second, if Pyrrhus had not been married to her mother, it is difficult to believe that Endius would have kept her in his house and then portioned her in legitimate marriage (see below).

Finally, the uncles deposed that that the child was named Cleitarete after Pyrrhus's mother, as would be expected for a legitimate daughter (Ogden 1996: 96). However, a newborn *nothē* would be named after her maternal grandmother, and be identified as "Cleitarete daughter of X [her never-named mother]". Perhaps this is overly conspiratorial, but I suspect that the name Cleitarete was chosen by Nicodemus and Pyrrhus to trick the uncles into believing that the marriage had been legitimate. However, what turned out to matter most about the name of Pyrrhus's daughter is that it was changed.

I propose that Cleitarete, as a very young child (Wyse 1904: 310–11), was adopted by her loving father (3.71) Pyrrhus and renamed Philē. The adoption of women is attested in Isaeus (7.9, 11.8 f., 41, 45) and in epigraphical sources (Rubinstein 1993: 20–21 with n. 15). Name change in adoption is attested in Isaeus 7.17 (cf. Demosthenes 39.27, Isaeus 2.36; M. Smith 1967: 309). By means of this (hypothetical) adoption, Philē would have become Pyrrhus's legitimate daughter and potentially an heir (3.58–59, 66). The adoption was probably *inter vivos*, or perhaps she was adopted by testament together with Endius (3.60).

In either instance, Pyrrhus satisfied the law of inheritance requiring that a man "may not either adopt a son or leave any of his possessions to anyone without also disposing of his legitimate daughters" (3.68, cf. 3.42; tr. Forster *LCL*). If Cleitarete/Philē had been Pyrrhus's natural (*gnēsios*) daughter then Endius, as the adopted son, would have been legally required to marry her (3.69, 73; Phillips 2013: 252–53; cf. Hatzilambrou 2010: 28–29). He did not marry her but the will was judged vaild. (Endius owned Pyrrhus's estate for some 23 years.) Instead of marrying Cleitarete/Philē, Endius (as "our opponents allege") legally disposed of Pyrrhus's daughter by giving her in marriage to Xenocles "as his legitimate sister (*adelphē*)" (3.58; tr. Forster

LCL; emphasis added). Cleitarete/Philē had to wait until Endius died to adjudicate (*epidikos*) his estate precisely because she was Pyrrhus's adopted legitimate daughter, not his *epiklēros* ("property" daughter). As the speaker explains (3.59), naturally born legitimate children (*gonō gegonasi gnēsioi*) succeeded to the property of their father without needing the consent of a court.

It is now time to tie some loose ends together. If Philē had been adopted by Pyrrhus why, in the earlier trial, did Nicodemus try (unsuccessfully) to prove that her mother was the legitimate wife of Pyrrhus? What did he hope to gain? To the best of my knowledge, this question is not answered by surviving Athenian law (compare Rubinstein 1993: 90–97). The fifth-century BCE Gortynian Code (Column X.41, 48 to Column XI.9) does provide an answer (Willetts 1967; Patterson 1990: 54 with n. 57). My understanding of the Code is that as a legitimate wife's daughter (*gnēsia tekna*), Philē would have been eligible to receive half the estate of Pyrrhus. The entire estate would have been received if the challenge to Endius's adoption (3.56, 61) had been successful. On the other hand, as the adopted daughter of a *pallakē*, Philē would receive an inheritance only after the death of Endius, the adopted son of Pyrrhus, and then only if Endius died without leaving legitimate children—that is, children born to Endius by a legitimate wife. In matters of inheritance, one's illegitimate adopted/made son/daughter was less legitimate than one's son/daughter naturally born to a legitimate wife (see Ogden 1996: 17–18). The daughter of a *pallakē* could not become an *epiklēros* even when adopted by her father.

To summarize: The adoption scenario explains why the woman had, or was alleged to have, a second name, why Endius gave her in marriage as his sister instead of having to marry her himself, why, Philē was required to adjudicate the estate as a sister after the death of Endius (Hatzilambrou 2010; 31) and, in the end, why there was a second trial after the death of Endius to decide the proper disposition of Pyrrhus's wealth. However, I cannot explain why Pyrrhus chose in particular the name "Philē".[1]

Isaeus was certainly aware of the adoption opening and he sought to prevent the jurors from taking it seriously. First, he questioned whether Pyrrhus's daughter had even been named Cleitarete:

> Is it not obvious, gentlemen, that the events which they deposed to have happened long ago were invented by them much later for the purpose of claiming the estate? For otherwise it would have been impossible that the uncles, who were summoned, according to their own account, to the tenth-day ceremony in honor of Pyrrhus's daughter, the defendant's

1. The speaker does not reveal the name of Pyrrhus's paternal grandmother. Patterson (1990: 72 n. 111; cf. Wyse 1904: 310) suggests that Philē—"beloved girl"—was merely a "familiar or childhood name". Even so, this does not prove that it was Cleitarete's pet name. In addition, Philē is known as a given name. Hatzilambrou (2010: 27 n. 42) suggests that name change was an indicator of *hetaira* status. If so, then Xenocles would not have changed Cleitarete's name. It is clear that Cleitarete/Philē was not a *hetaira*.

> niece, could ever have come into court with so accurate a recollection from that distant date, whenever it was, that her father at that ceremony named her Cleitarete" (3.34; tr. Fortster *LCL*).

Xenocles and Nicodemus must have told the name to them. This amounts to saying the uncles of Pyrrhus were senile or colluding (even bribed) or both. The speaker fails to substantiate the aspersions he makes against the uncles. Perhaps Pyrrhus implored the uncles to say the marriage they witnessed was legitimate or, or more probably, Nicodemus and Pyrrhus tricked the uncles into believing it was legitimate. With respect to Cleitarete, how accurate does one's memory have to be to remember a birth name (compare Isaeus 8.14)?

With respect to possible collusion, I find it difficult to believe the uncles would risk perjuring themselves about something as basic as the child's birth name. Other family members and slaves must have known the name and some of them may have been present at the ceremony (Isaeus 6.64–65, 8.9–12). Finally, I believe that the uncles were deposed only once, at which time they testified to both the nuptial formalities and the naming ceremony.

Second, the speaker makes light of the name change. He asks the jury whether Xenocles is so incompetent that he cannot even keep track of the name of this own wife:

> I am amazed that the man who had lived with her for more than eight years did not know the name of his own wife. Could he not have found it out before from his own witnesses? Did his wife's mother never in all that long period tell him her daughter's name? Did his uncle, Nicodemus himself, never do so? (3.30–31 tr. Forster *LCL*).

However, the speaker nowhere denies that the woman was known as Philē. Further, it is most improbable that Xenocles would have referred to Pyrrhus's daughter as "Philē" (instead of the legitimizing "Cleitarete") unless the renaming helped his case. This is an *eikota* that surely would have impressed the jury.

The speaker says,

> My brother having died last year, Phile, ignoring the existence of the last tenant, came forward, claiming to be the legitimate daughter of our uncle, and Xenocles of Coprus, as her legal representative, demanded to be given possession of the estate of Pyrrhus, who had died more than twenty years before, having fixed the value of the estate at three talents" (3.2; tr. Forster *LCL*).

Two points in response: (1) Xenocles could hardly have ignored Endius's ownership; (2) in this context, "legitimate daughter" arguably means "adopted daughter," as Xenocles would hardly need to wait until a few days after Endius's death to assert that Philē's mother was legitimately married to Pyrrhus. If this were Xenocles's claim, it could and should have been made as soon as possible while Endius was alive. Indeed, it very much seems that this claim had already been made and rejected by an Athenian court.

All this being said, it remains unclear to me what the speaker means by (repeatedly) suggesting that if Philē's mother had been a legitimate wife, then Nicodemus would not have allowed Endius to give Philē "to be married [to Xenocles] in the quality of a *hetaira*" (45, 48, 52, 55. 70, 71; tr. Forster LCL; see Patterson 1990). Patterson (1990: 72) understands: "Phile was given [*egguasthai*] to Xenocles *as the child of a hetaira* [*hos ex hetairas*]" (emphasis added). The underlying reality of the betrothal is that it transformed the daughter of a slave-wife (*pallakē*) into a legitimate wife (3.58). In any event, the speaker's line of argument is very weak not least because Nicodemus was not Philē's *kurios*.

To return to our central theme, Patterson (1991: 284) suggests:

> [I]f a man did give a daughter into *pallakia*, he thereby deprived her of her citizenship status ... Athenian families may have been pushed to this extreme by poverty, but it would have been indeed an extreme situation and, I think, a highly undesirable one.

If becoming a *pallakē* removed a woman from citizenship then *pallakia* must have had a legally recognized status. The woman lost her citizenship (or better, some citizenship rights) because she had become a slave. Moreover, there are neither persuasive arguments nor evidence that in classical times the *pallakia* institution had become obsolete or little used within the citizen class, except in cases of extreme poverty.

2. From Single Woman Status to *Pallakia*

A more basic response to Patterson is that Athens knew a large class of citizen women in the childbearing ages lacking anyone legally qualified to give them in *eggue*. "Unless she was an *epikleros*, a woman could only be given in marriage by her father, her paternal grandfather, her brother (if they had the same father) or by a (male) guardian designated by her father [Demosthenes] 46.18–19); and it is all too credible that some girls had no one entitled to give them away" (Sommerstein 2014: 12). Possibly, even probably, some citizen women *necessarily* lacked a male *kurios* who could give them in legitimate marriage. This group would include women released/ emancipated from the control of a male *kurios*. It appears also that some Athenian women were too poor to be given in legitimate marriage (Sealey 1984: 117). "Thete-ess is the name the Attic writers used to give to the impoverished girl. It was compulsory for the nearest male relatives either to take her in marriage or to pay [her] five mnai" (The *Suda* On Line headword phrase, *thēteus kai thētikon*, tr. Whitehead). Obviously, such marriages could not be legitimate.

In addition, Boethius (in *Cicero Topics* 3.14) cites Ulpian to the effect that during marriage by sale (*coemptio*), "the man asked the woman if she was willing to be *materfamilias* to him. She replied that she was willing. She then asked if he was willing to be *paterfamilias* to her and he replied that he was willing" (cited by Treggiari 1991: 27; Latin in Corbett 1930: 78–9). According to Cicero (*Topics* 3.14), only the wife *in manus* became materfamilias. If one identifies the Roman wife *cum manus* with the

Greek *pallakē*, as I do, then one may be willing to extrapolate from this identification to conclude that the *nothē* fell legally under the *kuria* of her *pallakē*-mother. That is, she necessarily had no legal *kurios* and so was necessarily a single woman.

This theory would explain the presence of households headed by "old women" who give away or advise young women in plays by Menander, Plautus and Terence (see Chapter IV.5, 6). The hypothesis may also explain why Phano, the daughter of Neaira who arguably was Stephanus's *pallakē*-wife, is referred to by a metronymic: "Phano, daughter of Neaira" (Demosthenes 59.51, 55, 59, 63, 67, 72; cf. McClure 2003: 76–77; cf. Chapter VII on Euripides *Electra* 930–35).

IX. Single Woman as *Hetaira* as Suppliant

1. Single Women Status in Classical and Hellenistic Greece

Hunter (1989: 44) raises the question "whether it was possible that some women in Athens might have lived alone and been *kyriai* of themselves. For a time, it appears, both Kleoboulē [widow of Demosthenes the elder] and Archippe [widow of Pasiōn the banker] were in this category." That such women comprised a legally recognized class is proven by Demosthenes 59.46:

> These men (Stephanus and Phrynion) came together in the temple, and after hearing the facts from both parties and from the woman (Neaira) herself gave their decision, and these men acceded to it. The terms were: that the woman should be *free (eleutheron) and her own master (autē hautēs kuria)* [the status is validated by the polemarch], but that she should give back to Phrynion all that she had taken with her from his house except the clothing and the jewels and the maid-servants; for these had been bought for the use of the woman herself; and that she should live with each of the men on alternate days, and if they should mutually agree upon any other arrangement, that arrangement should be binding; that she should be maintained by the one who for the time had her in his keeping; and that for the future the men should be friends with one another and bear no malice (tr. DeWitt and DeWitt *LCL* modified; emphasis added).

There is no reason to assume that the legal status *autē hautēs kuria* was created *de novo* for Neaira by an arbitration panel. She was simply placed within an existing class of women.

Athenian women might be "on their own" not only because of circumstances beyond their control, but also by choice. Note, for example, the young woman Herotime in a poem by Anacreon dating to the sixth century BCE (see below). For classical Athens, Demosthenes (29.26) says it was for the sake of her children that "she [his mother Kleoboulē] gave herself up to a life of widowhood." Hunter (1989: 40) notes the implication that Kleoboulē "*chose* to be a widow" (emphasis added). Although her children had come under the *kurioi* of Aphobus, Kleoboulē chose to remain in her own hands, a choice leaving her (not Aphobus) in control of substantial wealth (cf. Aeschines 1.170).

However, while some single women like Kleoboulē were wealthy and prominent most were workers, mainly in the textile industry (as in Terence *The Woman from Andros* 69 ff.) and socially insignificant. Some were young and others were old. Infamously, most of the women who sold sexual services for a living were probably drawn from the ranks of the single women.[1] In Hellenistic poetry (the *Anthologia Palatina*) we find references to the widow Bitto (6.48) and to Nicarete (6.285) both of whom left textile production to become prostitutes (see McKechnie 2005: 70–1; Neils 2000: 203–6):

> Bitto dedicated to Athene her industrious loom-comb, the implement of her scanty livelihood, for then she conceived a hatred for all toil among workfolk, and for the weaver's wretched cares. To Athene she said, "I will take to the works of Cypris [Aphrodite], voting like Paris against you" (anonymous; tr. Paton *LCL*).

> Nicarete, who formerly was in the service of Athene's shuttle, and stretched out many a warp on the loom, made in honour of Cypris a bonfire in front of her house of her work- basket and bobbins and her other gear, crying, "Away with you, starving work of wretched women, that have power to waste away the bloom of youth." Instead the girl chose garlands and the lyre, and a gay life spent in revel and festivity. "Cypris," she said, "I will pay you tithe of all my gains. Give me work and take from it your due" (Nicarchus; tr. Paton *LCL*).

Also drawn from the ranks of the single women were the respectable women who, like their male partners, sought to attract sexual partners and enjoy (not sell) sex outside marriage.

2. Meaning of *Hetaira*

The hypothesis put forward and gradually supported with evidence in this Section and the next is that, at least in everyday language, Athenian single woman—that is, women outside male-headed households—were called *hetairai*. It follows that *pornai*, sellers of sexual services, are accurately called *hetairai* (Plutarch *Solon* 15.3) because they continued to belong to the broader sociolegal class of single women. Sexually active single women who did not sell sexual services are accurately termed *hetairai* but not *pornai*.

The basic meaning of the term *hetaira* is clarified in Apollodorus's *On the Gods*:

Aphrodite *Hetaira*, who brings together male and female companions (*hetairai*), that is to say female friends (*philia*). Even today, at any rate, free women and girls (*eleutherai gunaikes*) refer to their friends and associates as *hetairai* (13.28 p. 571c; tr. Olson *LCL*).

Schlesier (2013: 216, 217) notes that *hetaira* is used in a technical sense in the works of Sappho, a later seventh-early sixth century BCE poet from Lesbos, where it "appears as an exclusively positive, non-contemptuous term, a synonym for a

1. In Terence's *Andria* ("*The Woman from Andros*" 69 ff.), which is based on a comedy by Menander, we see the transition: "Meanwhile, about three years ago, a woman moved into the neighborhood from Andros, driven here by poverty and the indifference of her family, a most beautiful woman in the prime of life ... At first, she lived a virtuous life, sparing and thrifty, earning her living by spinning wool. But when a lover approached her offering money, first one and then another, human nature being always inclined to prefer pleasure to toil, she accepted the offers and took up the profession" (tr. Barsby *LCL*).

female friend and associate..."; she suggests that the aristocratic poet was herself a *hetaira*. *Hetairai*, we detect, are "female companions of females". We may derive from the basic meaning that single women who "owned themselves" (*autē hautēs kuria*) or perhaps were owned by an "old woman" who are referred to or characterized as *hetairai* are actually "companions to each other."[2] They are not, as usually assumed in the scholarly literature, courtesans.

Thus, to begin with, when we read in Menander's *The Girl from Samos* (21–22) that a man fell in love with a *hetaera*, it does not mean that he fell in love with a call-girl. Similarly, when Clement of Alexandria (*The Schoolmaster*) cites the sixth-century poet Anacreon's (fr. 138; tr. Henderson *LCL*) description of "going along with hips swaying" as being "thoroughly hetairic," it does not mean the swaying women were selling their sexual favors. Anacreon (fr. 78; tr. Henderson *LCL*) found hetairic the "Thracian filly" who plays the field, but this "filly" was not selling to the field (cf. Kurke 1997: 113–14).

Again, Anacreon (fr. 358):

> Once again golden-haired Eros, striking me with a purple ball, challenges me to play with a girl with embroidered sandals. But she, for she is from well-built Lesbos, blames my hair, because it is white, and she is gaping at another (tr. Yatromanolakis 2008: 12).

Yatromanolakis (2008: 12) explains:

> That the word "another" (feminine) refers to an object of interest or desire seems beyond doubt, since the young girl *chaskei* [gaping] and the amatory tone of the song is conspicuous—at least in its opening phrasing. Similarly central is the emphasis placed on the marked agency of the girl, who can strongly blame (*katamemphetai*) the singing voice's "white hair" and prefers to gape at other seductive personae (my transliteration).

The "other seductive personae" are clearly younger than and most probably not as rich as the singer is. The "girl" in question is strikingly unlike a wealth-seeking prostitute or courtesan. Plato (*The Republic* 3.404d) says that a man seeking to remain in good shape would not choose a *Korinthian korēn philēn* "young Corinthian girl friend." Classical Corinth was noted for its prostitutes but this does not mean the sexually active girl friend was after money, not pleasure. Sexually liberated women, as Plato is testifying, would be relatively common in affluent cities such as Corinth. In these passages Anacreon and Plato do not refer to prostitutes/courtesans but to single women especially to sexually active single women. The question remains whether the contemporary men of Corinth and Lesbos thought, with ancient Athenians and modern readers, that local women were much more sexually liberated than Athenian natives.

2. McClure (2003: 139) sees the understanding "companion of women" as an attempt to cleanse the term *hetaira* of its negative implications. I see it as an attempt to probe below the sexual connotations to the basic meaning and social significance of the term.

3. *Hetaira* as Single Woman in the Greek World

In a fragmentary poem by Anacreon (*PMG* 446), a poet popular in Athens, a young girl named Herotime leaves the house of her mother and settles in Aphrodite's meadow. This woman, possibly a *nothē*, has chosen the life of a single woman (*hetaira*). However, instead of waiting in the meadow to be married, she, as Rosenmeyer (2004: 173) explains, "darts into the midst of a crowd, presumably in a town, and citizens respond to her erotically, as their hearts and wits begin to flutter." The poem ends: "O much-trafficked, much-trafficked Herotime" (tr. Rosenmeyer 2004: 174). "Much-trafficked" renders *leōphoros* (LSJ s.v. *laophoros* "bearing people"). Kurke (1999: 192–94) takes the final line to mean that Herotime has become a prostitute (a "public thoroughfare"). However, it may mean that she has become popular and sexually active but not necessarily a purveyor of sexual services.

Already in the mid-seventh century BCE, the poet Archilochus of Paros (*P.Colon.* 7511) refers in a fragmentary poem to a male narrator's relationship with two free, unmarried young women who "exist in a house/household" (*estin en hēmeterou*). The two women are single women who are sexually active but their participation in sex is for the sake of gratification, not for cash or gifts. One of the young girls is willingly "seduced" in a meadow-like location, like a mythical *numphē* (see below). During the preceding negotiation, the seduced girl had teasingly offered to her lover, as a substitute for herself, her very sexually active housemate Neoboulē. The male narrator refers to the seduced girl by a metronymic "daughter of Amphimedo". The mother is deceased and the father goes unmentioned.[3] James (2012: 83) finds that the poem

> proposes, very surprisingly, that premarital sexual activity might not destroy the reputation and life of a citizen girl. How we are to interpret that suggestion remains a matter of debate, and keeps scholars returning to this disconcerting fragmentary poem.

My interpretation is that the young women mentioned by Archilochus are unrelated members of a larger household of respectable single women. In short, they are members of a pack of *hetairai* (see Chapter XII). A reference to Archilochus's poetry by Synesius of Cyrene in the 4th–5th century CE suggests that he was familiar with the *hetaira* as a respectable single woman:

> And so everyone thinks and says that hair is a natural sunshade. And the best of poets, Archilochus, praises it on a *hetaira*'s body, and says the following: "and her hair shaded her shoulders and back" (Fragment 31; tr. Swift 2016; 254 modified).[4]

3. Sources for the Archilochus fragment: Eckerman (2011); Swift (2015).

4. Swift (2016: 256) comments: "Yet Synesius's description of the girl in fr. 31 as a *hetaira* suggests that Archilochus's use of imagery differs from its typical use to describe the defloration of a chaste *parthenos*. Whoever the girl is, we can infer that Archilochus described her or her behavior in a way, which suggests promiscuity, if not professional prostitution. Thus, while the image of a young girl with long hair holding flowers might normally suggest her desirability (as found commonly in archaic *kouroi*), here we find a wry mismatch between what the girl

The sexually aggressive single woman is already visible in the story of Tyro whom Odysseus saw in Hades:

> Then verily the first that I saw was high-born Tyro, who said that she was the daughter of noble Salmoneus, and declared herself to be the wife of Cretheus, son of Aeolus. She became enamoured of the river, divine Enipeus, who is far the fairest of rivers that send forth their streams upon the earth, and she was wont to resort to the fair waters of Enipeus. But the Enfolder and Shaker of the earth took his form, and lay with her at the mouths of the eddying river. And the dark wave stood about them like a mountain, vaulted-over, and hid the god and the mortal woman. And he loosed her maiden girdle, and shed sleep upon her. But when the god had ended his work of love, he clasped her hand, and spoke, and addressed her: "'Be glad, woman, in our love, and as the year goes on its course thou shalt bear glorious children, for not weak are the embraces of a god. These do thou tend and rear. But now go to thy house, and hold thy peace, and tell no man; but know that I am Poseidon, the shaker of the earth." So saying, he plunged beneath the surging sea. But she conceived and bore Pelias and Neleus (*Odyssey* 11. 235 ff.; tr. Murray *LCL*).

Tyro is portrayed as having been on her own and her previous sexual relationships did not prohibit her from marrying Cretheus.

Even more striking are the sexually liberated themes voiced by Nausicaa to Odysseus in the *Odyssey* 6.270–88:

> For the Phaeacians care not for bow or quiver, but for masts and oars of ships, and for the shapely ships, rejoicing in which they cross over the grey sea. It is their ungentle speech that I shun, lest hereafter some man should taunt me, for indeed there are insolent folk in the land, and thus might some baser fellow say, shall he meet us: "Who is this that follows Nausicaa, a comely man and tall, a stranger? Where did she find him? He will doubtless be a husband for her. Haply she has brought from his ship some wanderer of a folk that dwell afar—for none are near us— or some god, long prayed-for, has come down from heaven in answer to her prayers, and she will have him as her husband all her days. Better so, *even if she has herself gone forth and found a husband from another people*; for of a truth she scorns the Phaeacians here in the land, where she has wooers many and noble!" So will they say, and this would become a reproach to me. *Yea, I would myself blame another maiden who should do such thing, and in despite of her dear father and mother, while yet they live, should consort with men before the day of open [public] marriage [amphadion gamon]*. (tr. Murray *LCL*; emphasis added)

Homer makes Nausicaa, the young daughter of a king, familiar with the single woman who, outside the control of parents, chooses her own husband and plays the sexual field—but certainly not for pay. The implications for the sexual and geographic mobility of single women are striking to say the least. It appears that auto-*ekdosis* is not a late innovation but was already practiced in "Homeric times" among the mysterious Phaeacians.

---

appears to be and what she actually is." There is no mismatch in Archilochus, however: his *hetaira* is simply an attractive single woman who may or may not be sexually active. In fact, the *parthenos* is a *hetaira* (single woman).

Hesiod (*Theogony* 205–06) mentions the seductive "whisperings of maidens (*parthenoi*)" (tr. Evelyn-White LCL). However, why go on belaboring the obvious, the sale of sexual services is old but not older than sexual display and courtship. In her concluding remarks Neils (2000: 226) is impressed by *hetairai*:

> They are "heroic" in the sense that they do, and apparently do well, what men admire, but because they are female, this activity must be controlled through safeguards such as religious ritual, price-fixing, and the law.[5]

If single women/*hetairai* typically dressed more showily than married women, this hardly means they were call girls whose clothing was purchased by pimps (Dalby 2002: 114, 121). Indeed, in Menander's comedy "The Girl from Samos," Chrusis—meaning "[made] of gold," a popular hetairic name—acquired expensive clothes after she had given up single woman status to become a *pallakē*. The more general point is that many, if not most, *pallakē*-wives must have come from the single woman class. The importance of this contribution may be reflected in the expression "woman married in the quality of [as] a *hetaira*" (*hos ex hetairas*) (Isaeus 3.45, 48, 52, 55. 70, 71; tr. Forster LCL). I suspect the expression identifies the married *hetaira* with a *pallakē*; it means that the *pallakē* formerly was a *hetaira*. I agree with Ogden (1996: 105) on the "absoluteness of the disjunction between the roles of the *hetaira* and the wife." There was no such disjunction in the case of the slave-wife, however.

The citizen single woman is explicitly identified with the *hetaera*. In a fragment of Antiphanes, a writer of the fourth century BCE:

> And Antiphanes says in his *Hydra*: But he the man of whom I was speaking, seeing a woman who lived near his house, a *hetaira*, did fall at once in love with her; she was an Athenian [a citizen not a foreigner], without a guardian or any near relations, and her manners pure, and on virtue's strictest formed. A genuine companion (*hetaira*); for the rest of the crew bring into disrepute, by their vile manners, a name which in itself has nothing wrong (Athenaeus 13.19. p. 572a; tr. Yonge *Perseus Project* modified).[6]

The woman (probably named Chrusis) is called *hetaira* because she was a citizen single woman.

Antiphanes's description of an "honest woman" fits Menander's Glycera (in "The Girl with Her Hair Cut Short"), an exposed citizen-child raised as a daughter by an independently living "old woman" (124–27). Acting "as her own *kurios*" (*heautes kuria*)

5. "What an enormous difference between spending the night with a free girl (*koriskēs*) and with a prostitute ... The fact that everything is not too much ready for you, and you have to wrestle a little, and get slapped and punched by her soft hands. That's nice, by Zeus the greatest" (Athenaeus 13.27 pp. 570f–571a citing Timocles's *Men from Marathon*; tr. Olson *LCL*). This *koru* is surely not a married woman and was very likely a single woman.

6. Ogden (1996: 161) arbitrarily dismisses this woman as "almost certainly a 'pseudo-*hetaira*', the victim of an unfortunate paradox awaiting monogamous marriage with her lover."

Glycera gave herself (*autē*) in marriage (487, 490, 497; Sommerstein 2014: 12, 17). The description "honest woman" also fits Menander's Chrusis in "The Girl from Samos," who is called *hetaira* (20–21), *pallakē* (508), and *gunaikas* (561). That is, Chrusis had been a *hetaira*, but she was now a slave-wife.

More evidence is available. Athenaeus (13.6 p. 572b) tells that Anaxilas, a writer of the fourth century BCE, in his *Neottis* ("*The Chick*"), says: "But if a woman does at all times use fair, moderate language [But if a woman who has a reasonable amount of money], giving her services favourable (*pros charin* "gratis") to all who stand in need of her, she from her prompt companionship (*hetareias*) earns the title of companion (*hetaira*); and you, As you say rightly, have not fallen in love with a vile prostitute (*pornē*), but with a companion (*hetaira*). Is she not one of pure and simple manners [a person of integrity]? At all events, by Zeus, she's beautiful [she's a lady]" (tr. Yonge *Perseus Project* modified by McKechnie 2005: 72). The reference seems to be to a wealthy and open-handed single woman; a *hetaira*. I see no indication that she gained her wealth by trading in sexual services.[7]

Additional examples demonstrate the presence in Greek antiquity of a class of respectable, socially and sexually active single women. Theocritus (*Idylls* 2) tells the story of Simaetha, a Coan young woman who lived on her own and chose to enter a sexual affair. Theocritus does not explain to his audience why Simaetha was living outside a male-headed household; an oversight perhaps suggesting that single women were not extremely rare in the real world (Dover 1971: 96). Simaetha mentions several girl friends and they are not obviously prostitutes. Dover (1971: 95–6), whose focus is on slave vs. free status, comments:

> Among the women who figure as her friends one, the "Thracian nurse of Theumaridas" (70) is probably a slave; "Anaxo, daughter of Eubulus" (66) is surely not so, for she went as "basket-carrier", normally a function of girls of honourable citizen families, to take part in a cult of Artemis; and the status of the "mother of Philisto, our flute girl, and of Melixo" (146) turns on a point which admits no clear answer.

The "Thracian nurse" and "Anaxo" seem respectable, which leaves only a doubt about "Philisto our flute girl." This much is clear: the reference to *our* flute girl is indicative of a continuous rather than a one-off relationship. Indeed, the reference is consistent with the named women belonging to a formal organization, perhaps even with corporate status.

Theophrastus (*Characters* 19) tells of the person who,

> [w]hen he is listening to a flute performance, he is the only one of the group to clap his hands, and he hums along and asks the flute girl accusingly why she stopped so quickly (tr. Rusten *LCL*).

Apparently, the flute girl did not hurry to end the concert to engage in sex for pay. In Menander's *Epitrepontes* ("*Men at Arbitration*" 451–85) the harp-girl Habrotonon, as

7. McKechnie (2005: 72) interprets Anaxilas's character as a covert "courtesan."

Dalby (1993: 171) points out, "attended the Tauropolia, a women's all-night festival, with a party of respectable women, and played to accompany the girls' dancing." An Attic vase (Vienna, Kunsthistoriche Museum 1.6788) depicts a perfectly respectable (fully clothed) seated "flute girl" playing, probably before an audience (Bérard 1989: 91–92 with fig. 125; cf. J.N. Davidson 2006: 37 ff. on *mousourgoi*, "workers of the Muses"). In fact, despite the overheated rhetoric, there is no evidence that flute girls, whether free or slave, engaged in sex for pay within the symposium or elsewhere in classical Athens (Goldman 2015; Starr 1978). Again, "our flute girl" was a regular performer at the social gatherings held by Simaetha and her set of single friends, a group of *hetairai*.

Written at about the same time, the epigrams of Asclepiades of Samos attest to sexual activity by unmarried young women. Thus, a woman laments,

> In the past Archeades was chafed by me, but now he doesn't visit me even in fun. Honeyed Eros is not always sweet, but after [or "in"] causing pain the god often becomes sweeter for lovers (Asclepiades *Epigrams* 19; tr. Sens 2011: 125).

Some of Asclepiades's sexually active single women are explicitly called *hetairai*, but the context is unclear. However, there is little or no evidence that the women were motivated to participate sexually by a desire to increase their wealth (Cameron 1995: Appendix C; Cairns 1998).[8] The same holds for the Alexandrian Hedylus's single women who lose their virginity or participate in beauty contests (*Anthologia Palatina* 5.199; 6.192; McKechnie 2005: 77–79).

Note the explicit reference to Athenian citizen *hetairai* in Plutarch *Alcibiades* 8.3:

> Hipparete was a decorous and affectionate wife, but being distressed because her husband (Alcibiades) would consort with *heterais*, foreign and native (*xenais kai astais*), she left his house and went to live with her brother (tr. Perrin *LCL*).

Pallakai and *hetairai* were distinct statuses as is attested in Demosthenes 59.122. The transformation of a *hetaira* (apparently) of the disreputable sort into a *pallakē*-wife is directly attested:

> But Hermippus in his Essay on Isocrates, says that Isocrates, when he was advancing in years, took the *hetaira* Lagisca into his house, and had a daughter with her. And Strattis speaks of her in these lines: "And while she was still in her bed, I saw Isocrates *pallakēn*, Lagisca playing her tricks; and with her the flute-maker" (13.51 p. 592d; tr. Yonge *LCL*).

In the *Anthologia Palatina* (6.208 Antipater), three "citizen [*astai*] *hetairai*" make a joint dedication to "the Paphian" (Aphrodite) on their marriages. The women do not dedicate tools of the prostitution trade but rather a portrait [of Aphrodite] by

8. In Homer (*Odyssey* 5.194–225), the *numphē* Calypso enjoyed a fine dinner with Odysseus and then the "two went into the innermost recess of the hollow cave, and took their joy of love, abiding each by the other's side" (tr. Murray *LCL*; cf. *Odyssey* 1.14–15, 5.154–57).

"Aristomachus the Strymonian" (McClure 2003: 164; cf. *Anthologia Palatina* 6.207 Archias). There is no reason to suppose that transformations of single women into *pallakai* via self-sales were rare or undesirable. Contrary to Ogden (1996: 157), their children were legally recognized *nothoi* (Chapter XV). Finally, as the transformation into a kind of slave status was voluntary, it must have been viewed as an improvement relative to remaining an unmarried citizen woman.[9]

A final piece of evidence indicates that a *hetaira* is a single woman. In Hyperides 3.2.3, the speaker refers to the woman Antigone, a *hetaira*, who acted as a broker in a large business transaction and received a commission for her services. I see no reason to believe that Antigone normally earned her living as a purveyor of sexual services. Instead, I see Antigone as a citizen single woman who earned income by participating in real estate transactions.

To conclude, J.N. Davidson (2004: 170) thinks

> *hetaira* is used for any woman from *mousourgos* [musician] to mistress who regularly consorts with strange men outside the confines of the brothel or family.

My position is that a *hetaira* is legally a woman outside a male-headed household—that is, she is a woman who is "in her own hands"/"owns herself" (*autē hautēs kuria*)—whether or not she consorts with "strange men" regularly, irregularly or not at all.[10] She is, in Roman legal terms, *sui iuris*. The provision about *hetairai* consorting with strange men is in part based on contemporary Athenian denigration of single women and in part based on valid historical observation of their behavior. It is not, however, part of the legal definition. A woman can be both a *hetaira* and a prostitute or a business agent or a textile worker; she cannot be both *hetaira* and wife.

But then, can she be both? Consider a marvelously devious statement by the speaker in Isaeus 3:

> That the woman, whom the defendant [her brother, the citizen Nicodemus] has deposed that he gave in legal marriage to our uncle [Pyrrhus], was a *hetaira* who gave herself to anyone and not his wife, has been testified to you by the other acquaintances and by the neighbors of Pyrrhus, who have given evidence of quarrels, serenades, and frequent scenes of disorder which the defendant's sister occasioned whenever she was at Pyrrhus's house (3.13; tr. Forster *LCL*).

9. The acquisition of wives by purchase was no relic among the Romans when Gaius wrote in the affluent high empire (c. 170 CE) (cf. Buckand 1921: 119). Looper-Friedman (1987: 284) comments: "What is significant is that some marriages were *cum manus* [hand] and other equally valid marriages were not."

10. The ancient Near Eastern myth of the god Erra usually takes note of three categories of women including *harīmtum*, whom the goddess Ishtar deprived of husbands and put under their own authority, literally "in their own hands" (Silver 1992: 186–88, 194 with references). Many prostitutes were drawn from the ranks of these self-owned women but they were not only prostitutes (Silver 2006). The ancient Near East also knew a kind of female companion called "*lukur* of the road" (Diakonoff 1986: 234).

Was the unnamed citizen woman a single woman with an active sexual life? Did the woman's brother who claimed to be her *kurios* permit her to date? Did the "scenes of disorder" take place before or during the alleged marriage? Did the alleged wife reside only part-time in the home of her husband or only part-time in the home of her *kurios*? Incidentally, the "*hetaira*" is never named in the trial, and this omission suggests she was regarded to be respectable (Schaps 1977). Without question, this statement before a jury of Athenian citizens contradicts our received model of Athenian/Greek family life. The latter model takes the "courtesan" to be an aberration or special case with the normal woman living in seclusion in the house of her *kurios*. As it stands, this model is false.

4. Aetiological Myth and Legal Status of the Single Woman/*Hetaira*: Danaids and Amazons

Unquestionably, Athenian law promoted the social interest when it recognized the status "woman in her own hands." There are questions, however, about how this recognition was incorporated in the legal structure. Some women were outside a male-headed *oikos* for reasons outside anyone's control but others because their fathers had chosen to *emancipate* them. The legalities of the emancipation process are somewhat familiar for the Roman *familia* but not for the Greek oikos. This section deals only with the question of how single women might have been accommodated in *polis* law.

No direct evidence answers our question. However, Aeschylus's *Suppliant Women* arguably knows the answer and utilizes it as a dramatic building block. The Danaids come from Egypt to Argos and request suppliant status. They reveal that they are implacably opposed to having husbands imposed on them. For the Danaids, this would be a fate worse than death (455–67). They wish never "to be subject to" (*hupocheirios*, literally, "under the hands of") men (392–93). Accordingly, they ask the Argives to protect their freedom to choose to be single. Zeitlin (1992: 217) explains:

> The king [Pelasgos of Argos] is not accustomed to women insisting on their *eleutheria* ("freedom", 221, 609). For him, as for all Greeks, women are legally defined in terms of their male guardians (*kurios*, 387–91). Nevertheless, it is morally required that democratic Argos, devoted to the concept of *eleutheria* (948), support those who flee despotism and enslavement, even in the domestic sphere.

One may conclude that the Danaids were not so much opposed to marriage as they were to having a male *kurios* choose their husbands. They wished the choice to be in their own hands. This suspicion is reinforced by Bakewell's (2013: 66) observation,

> The Danaids' approach to marriage clearly implies a great deal of independence from their nominal *kyrios*. At one level, this is exemplified by Danaus's [the father of the Danaids] many absences from the stage.

Danaus cautions his daughters:

> The tender ripeness of summer fruit is in no way easy to protect; beasts despoil it—and men, why not?—and brutes that fly and those that walk the earth. Love's goddess spreads news abroad of fruit bursting ripe ... So all men, as they pass, mastered by desire, shoot an alluring arrow of the eye at the delicate beauty of virgins (1000–5; tr. Smyth LCL).

The Danaids have placed themselves outside the household of Danaus—they are positioned where passing men (silens) can "give them the eye"—and he can only hope they will properly conduct themselves (1006–09).

The underlying lesson is that *hiketeia* "suppliant status" provided the legal basis for recognizing the right of citizen women to be "in their own hands." The status "single woman" is a permanent legal class but not necessarily for its current members. Murnaghan (2005: 190) notices,

> By the end of the *Suppliants* we see increasingly that marriages of some sort lie in the future for these women ... And of course the chorus contains within it, unacknowledged but known to the audience, the figure of Hypermestra [who did not murder her husband].

As some women marry leaving behind the single woman class, other women are departing from male-headed households and entering single status. Aeschylus's *Suppliant Women* stand for a self-renewing class of women who, by choice or circumstance, are *anumpheutos* "unwedded," or better, "removed from marriage."

A further implication of the derivation of the right to be single from suppliant status is that an Athenian woman who was her own *kuria* did not necessarily possess all the legal rights and immunities of other citizens. As Zeitlin (1992: 217) points out, the Danaids in *Suppliant Women* were granted only the intermediate status of *astoxenos* (356, 618) with the political rights of metics (609). Aeschylus does not lead us beyond this point. It may be added, however, that the legal status of suppliants/single women in a *polis* was very much like that of legitimate wives in a husband's *oikos* (Gödde 2000: 244). Both groups were regarded as outsiders having citizenship rights elsewhere.

The outcome of the mythical invasion of Attica by the Amazons (Aeschylus *Eumenides* 685–89) has arguably similar implications for the place of single women in the legal structure of Athens. Interestingly, Aeschylus has Pelasgos consider that the Suppliants might, among other things, be Amazons (*Suppliants* 287–89). The Amazons, who "were naturally friendly to men" and even "man-loving" invaded Attica in response to the abduction of Queen Antiope by Theseus (Plutarch *Theseus* 26.2; tr. Perrin *LCL*; Hellanicos *FGrH* 323a F 17c; compare "man-hating" in Aeschylus *Prometheus Bound* 724). However, after several months of fighting they were badly defeated and had to sign a peace treaty with Athens (Plutarch *Theseus* 27.1–4). After their surrender, none of the invading Amazons returned to their homeland:

> [W]e are told regarding the Amazons that of all who came not one returned again, while those who had remained at home were expelled from power because of the disaster here (Isocrates 4.70: tr. Norlin *LCL*).

Of course, dead Amazons could not return home. However, why would Athens make peace with the corpses of Amazons? Indeed, even the abducted queen of the Amazons who lived to make peace apparently did not return home. My understanding of the "tradition" (what "we are told") cited (actually exploited) by Isocrates is that some Amazons remained in Athens. Indeed, the myth of an invasion served to "explain" the presence of (surrendered) "Amazons" in Athens. Kennedy (2014: 46) puts it this way:

> But to be of use, the Amazon had to accept her place and practice the woman's appropriate type of *sophrosynē*, much like Hippolytē (Antiope) is said to have yielded to Theseus and fought beside him against her sisters and sacrificed herself for the city by dying in the battle.

The contemporary understanding of an Amazon as a single woman (*hetaira*) is consistent with Aeschylus *Suppliant Women* 287 where they are termed *anandroi*—"husbandless." The same point is well illustrated by an Attic vase painting (Vatican 632) in which an axe-bearing Amazon flees not from a silen, like a nymph (see Chapter X), but from a young man carrying a spear. As described by Kennedy (2014: 64 n. 62), the Amazon

> is running forward with her head turned back, sharing a desirous gaze with her pursuer. They both reach out towards the other with their unweaponed hands. Both pursuer and pursued have slight smiles on their faces and bear labels; above the man is *kalos* ["handsome"] and above the woman is *kalē* ["beautiful"].

The spear carried by the young man in this and other pursuit scenes arguably represents that he intends to propose marriage.

Herodotus portrays the Amazons are women outside male-headed households who live in packs and give themselves in marriage to men of their choosing (auto-*ekdosis*).

> At midday the Amazons would scatter and go apart from each other singly or in pairs, roaming apart for greater comfort. The Scythians noticed this and did likewise; and as the women wandered alone, a young man laid hold of one of them, and the woman did not resist but let him do his will; and since they did not understand each other's speech and she could not speak to him, she signed with her hand that he should come the next day to the same place and bring another youth with him (showing by signs that there should be two), and she would bring another woman with her. The youth went away and told his comrades; and the next day he came himself with another to the place, where he found the Amazon and another with her awaiting them. When the rest of the young men learned of this, they had intercourse with the rest of the Amazons [*ektilōsanto* "tamed the Amazons as wives"]. Now the men could not learn the women's language, but the women mastered the speech of the men; and when they understood each other, the men said to the Amazons, "We have parents and possessions; therefore, let us no longer live as we do, but return to our people and be with them; and we will still have you, and no others, for our wives." To this the women replied: We could not live with your women; for we and they do not have the same customs. We shoot the bow and throw the javelin and ride, but have never learned women's work; and your women do none of the things of which we speak, but stay in their wagons and do women's work, and do not go out hunting or anywhere else. So we could never agree with them. If you want to keep us for

> wives and to have the name of fair men, go to your parents and let them give you the allotted share of their possessions, and after that let us go and live by ourselves." The young men agreed and did this. (Herodotus 4.113.1–4.114.4; tr, Godley *LCL*; modified by Brown and Tyrrell 1985: 297–98)

The "Scythian women" in male-headed households live in seclusion. The Amazons, however, are portrayed as untamed nymphs/*parthenoi* wandering alone in the wilderness wherein they consent to be raped by and married to their abductors. The sole discordant note is that they do not differentiate between one satyr/silen and another. The "manly" behavioral traits of the Amazons persist (in the succeeding Sauromatian nation, Herodotus 4.116) but in Herodotus's telling the unusual gender roles are required to explain why a pack of single women, the Amazons, chose to become *pallakai* managing independent *oikoi* distant from the homeland of their Scythian *kurioi*. After the transformation, the women were no longer Amazons. Brown and Tyrrell (1985: 299) are correct is observing that the outcome described, "is not patriarchal marriage but its reversal," but they are mistaken, I suggest, in claiming that Herodotus was not describing "Greek marriage." Obviously, Herodotus did not originate the rape in the meadow theme.

That the historical Greeks identified Amazons as single women is revealed by their designation as *parthenoi* (Aeschylus *Prometheus Bound* 416; Herodotus 4.114, 117; cf. Stewart 1995: 578). On the other hand, Herodotus (4.110) tells:

> About the Sauromatae, the story is as follows. When the Greeks were at war with the Amazons (whom the Scythians call *Oiorpata*, a name signifying in our tongue killers of men, for in Scythian a man is "oior" and to kill is "pata"), the story runs that after their victory on the Thermodon they sailed away carrying in three ships as many Amazons as they had been able to take alive; and out at sea the Amazons attacked the crews and killed them" (tr. Godley *LCL*).

Thus, the Amazons are "man-killers". However, Elderkin 1935: 344–6) concluded that *oiropata* (as "man-killers") is cognate to Greek *parthenos* (Latin *virginus*). This appears to be a case in which etymological meaning facilitates the construction of strange fiction but not the understanding of contemporary usage. The English expression "lady-killer" means "a man who is very attractive to woman" not "a man who kills women". Not surprisingly, in the battle scenes, the man-killing Amazons "are always sexually mature" (Steward 1995: 584). This is a polite way of saying they are sexy. The Amazon's inhabiting the ancient Greek real world were both man-killers and man-lovers.

The Athenians needed pacified Amazons because they needed a proper place for the city's single women. Tombs of defeated Amazons, in Athens and elsewhere (Dowden 1997: 118 ff.), testified to their normalization and permanent place in the Athenian *polis* and in Greek society generally. The invasion myth taught that contemporary single women—the "descendants" of the surrendered Amazons—had the legal status granted to foreign adversaries who had surrendered (unconditionally) to the Athenians. Again, it appears that Greek and specifically Athenian single woman were legally accommodated to supplicants.

My argument has been that Amazons are a reflection in myth of the "untamed" single women present not only in Athens but also throughout the Greek world (see Stewart 1995: 580).[11] It follows that, throughout the Greek world, single women might be viewed as Amazons and, hence, would have had the legal status of suppliants. Therefore, it is of great interest, I think, that Amazons were suppliants at the temple of Artemis in Ephesus.

> Pindar, however, it seems to me, did not learn everything about the goddess, for he says that this sanctuary was founded by the Amazons during their campaign against Athens and Theseus. It is a fact that the women from the Thermodon, as they knew the sanctuary from of old, sacrificed to the Ephesian goddess both on this occasion and when they had fled from Heracles; some of them earlier still, when they had fled from Dionysus, having come to the sanctuary as suppliants (Pausanias 7.2.7; tr. Jones and Omerod *LCL* cf. Penrose 2016: 90 ff.).

Penrose (2016: 91) wonders, "Could it be possible that the Amazon served as more than an 'other' for the classical Greek girl, and rather might have been a figure with whom she could identify?" My answer is that Amazons "lived on" in Athens as single women: *hetairai.*

11. The conflation of Amazons, Danaids, and nymphs is indicated by an overlap of personal names (Bachvarova 2009: 293 n. 20).

X. Wealth Transfers in the Greek Marriage Market with Emphasis on the Roles of Distance and Single Woman Status

Why was wealth typically transferred *to* the groom in the case of legitimate marriage and transferred *from* the groom in the case of *pallakia*? This Chapter aims to answer this basic question as well as subsidiary ones dealing with the meaning of the Greek terminology of nuptial wealth transfers (*hedna* vs. *dōra*, *proix* vs. *phernē*) and whether the *pallakē*-wife acquired a *peculium*.

We begin by proposing that the main motives for the father of the bride to offer a dowry/pay a bride-price (in legitimate marriage) are to compensate the groom for settling away from his ancestral home and for agreeing to receive only attenuated rights over his bride. The main motive for the groom to offer a bride-price (in *pallakia*) is to compensate the father for surrendering all rights over his daughter when he (the groom) carries the bride to his ancestral home. These propositions are developed below. First, however, it is well to emphasize that the nuptial transaction is a real negotiation to determine the bride's residence, which should not be characterized as "gift exchange."

1. Relative Value of the *Pallakē*-Wife: Demand

For the "demand for brides" side of the marriage market, the most obvious consideration is that by paying a bride-price a husband acquired far more extensive property rights over his *pallakē*-wife than over his legitimate wife. In purely materialistic terms, the *pallakē*, other things being equal, was for the husband the more valuable commodity (Koschaker 1937: 99 f.). This may explain why, "In New Comedy it is considered paradoxical that a concubine be given a dowry" (Ogden 1996: 159 with n. 45). Thus, in Plautus's *Stichus* 562: "Really that young man was certainly clever, since he didn't want to give that old man a concubine with a dowry" (tr. de Melo *LCL*). *Stichus* is based on Menander's *Adelphoe*—"*The Brothers*".

The husband borrowed his legitimate wife from her father for conceiving legitimate children. It is intuitively plausible therefore that the borrower (husband) did not possess the legal or socially accepted right to use physical force to discipline her. Intuition finds support in a papyrus letter from Alexandria dated to 10 BCE.

> To Protarchos. From Tryphaine, daughter of Dioskourides. Asklepiades, to whom I am married, persuaded my parents, although I, Tryphaine, was unwilling, to give me to him as my caretaker, and ... (Asklepiades) entered into the marriage, [receiving?] also on my

> behalf a down payment on my dowry consisting of clothing worth forty drachmas and twenty drachmas of coined silver. but my accuser, Asklepiades, since he kept going off(?) throughout the marriage for no reason, squandered the aforementioned goods, abused me and insulted me, and, laying his hands on me, he used me as if I were his bought slave (*BGU* iv 1106; tr. Rowlandson 1998: 324 # 257)

Tryphaine argues to the official Protarchos, who is handling the return of the dowry, that a husband could not abuse a legitimate wife like a "bought slave."

However, the *pallakē* is a "bought slave." Unless excluded by specific clauses inserted by the father (or the bride) into the nuptial contract, the husband of a purchased wife had the same right to discipline her physically as he did over his child and ordinary slave. Homer provides supporting evidence of a surprising nature. It is argued in Chapter XVIII that Hera whom her husband Zeus physically disciplined was meant to be understood as his *pallakē*-wife.

Obviously, in real life a husband's resort to physical force, whether legal or not, would operate to undermine his emotional relationship with his wife. Thus, as noted elsewhere, the abused Neaira ran away from Phrynion, and Menander's Glycera deserted the utterly dismayed Polemon after he falsely accused her of adultery and cut off her hair. Nevertheless, the legal right to use physical force must have been of value to some husbands/owners just as it was for some parents.

A less obnoxious advantage to husbands/owners is that the *pallakē*, as a slave, could serve as his business agent. Evidence for agency by slaves is slim for Greece[1] but it is available for Rome and to ordinary Roman slaves we may add the agency of Roman sons (Kirschenbaum 1987). More to the present point, we should add Roman wives or, more accurately, wives in *manus*. According to Gaius, property may be acquired through those subject to our *potestas, mancipio* and *manus* (*Institutes* 2.86, 3.114, 3.163; but see also 2.96, 4.80).

Note that Caenis, to whom we turn next, is explicitly called the *pallakē* of Vespasian and the same Greek source explains,

> And not only for this reason [her faithfulness and memory] does she seem to me to have been a remarkable woman, but also because Vespasian took such excessive delight in her. This gave her the greatest influence and she amassed untold wealth, so that it was even thought that he made money through Caenis herself as his intermediary. For she received vast sums from many sources, sometimes selling governorships, sometimes procuratorships, generalships and priesthoods, and in some instance even imperial decisions. For although Vespasian killed no one on account of his money, he did spare the lives of many who gave it; and while it was Caenis who received the money, people suspected that Vespasian willingly allowed her to do as she did (Cassius Dio 65.14; tr. Cary *LCL*).

1. However, the evidence for Greek agency is not as slim as E.M. Harris 2013) wishes to suggest. For example, in his discussion of a lead letter (*SEG* 26.845), Harris (2013: 115) fails to explain (or raise the question) of why Matasys claimed that Archilodorus was the slave of Anaxagoras unless he had seen that he was acting for him "like a slave."

Clearly, Caenis, a non-owner, not only acquired but also validly alienated property for its owner Vespasian. The Roman jurists spoke in this connection of *potestas alienandi*.

Important insight into the status of Caenis is provided in Suetonius 3:

> After the death of his wife (*uxor*) he [Vespasian] renewed his union (*revocavit in contubernium*[2]) with his former concubine (*uxor*), Caenis, the freedwoman of Antonia, and also her amanuensis, and treated her, even after he was emperor, almost as if she had been his lawful wife (*paene iustae uxoris loco*) (tr. Thomson *Perseus Project*).

Obviously, Caenis the *pallakē* is a slave-wife, not a *concubina*[3] or, with Granius Flaccus, a *pellex* (see Chapter VI.3).

What I am suggesting is that slave-wives of Athenian businessmen acted as business agents for their husbands. In the case of agency by slave-wives, there would be no disputes due to commingling of assets as all the wealth of the *oikos* was legally owned by the husband. The legitimate wife, on the other hand, kept property of her own: inheritances, *phernē*, and market earnings.[4] Thus, in Euripides's *Andromache* (210–11), Andromache attacks Neoptolemus's legitimate wife Hermione saying "you are a rich woman living in the midst of the poor" (tr. Kovacs *Perseus Project*). Roman law excludes gifts between spouses but the supporting argument

2. *Concubina* and *contubernalis* are different words with different nuptial significance. "In literature, *contubernalis* is *vox propria* for a slave 'wife' or 'husband' in Columella and Petronius; this is also the usual sense in the jurists and the commonest sense in inscriptions. *But contubernium is also a quasi-marital relationship involving one slave partner rather than two.* The Elder Seneca has this sense, as do the jurists: *Inter servos et liberos matrimonium contrahi non potest, contubernium potest*. It was unnecessary for lawyers to point out that valid Roman marriage was impossible between slave and slave. The word *contubernalis* is used in the *Digest*, however, in the context of *contubernium* of slave with slave, rather than of a slave with a free person" (Treggiari 1981: 43 referemces ommited; emphasis added). See further the excellent discussion in Jeppesen-Wigelsworth (2010: 311–30). The *conturbernalis* is a wife (or husband) *and* a slave.

3. Similarly, Drusilla (Suetonius *Caligula* 24), Marcella (Herodian 1.16.9), Galeria Lysistrate (*Historia Augusta Pius* 8.9; *CIL* 6.8972) and the daughter of his deceased wife's procurator (name unknownl *Historia Augusta Marcus* 29.10) were, respectively, the secondary *wives* of Caligula, Commodus, Antoninus Pius and Marcus Aurelius. Interestingly, little is heard about the children of secondary wives (see McGinn 1991: 337 n. 11).

4. The position of the Roman wife *sine manus* was stated by Cato in 169 BCE and interpreted by Aulus Gellius *Attic Nights* 17.6.1); "Cato himself too, wishing to describe the woman as rich, says: 'The woman brings a great dowry and holds back a large sum of money'; that is, she gives a great dowry and retains possession of a large sum of money. From that property then which she kept for herself after giving her dowry, she lent money to her husband. When she happened to be vexed with her husband and determined to demand the money back, she appoints to demand it from him a *servus recepticius*, that is, a slave of her very own, whom she had held back with the rest of the money and had not given as part of her dowry, but had retained; for it was not right for the woman to give such an order to a slave of her husband, but only to one of her very own" (tr. Rolfe *LCL*). The control of the Athenian legitimate wife over her estate is not made very clear in the sources.

is flimsy and leaves room for suspicion that gifts had been permitted in marriages *cum manus*.[5]

The hypothesis that a Greek wife might act as her husband's financial or business agent gains substance from a large loan made by the wife of Polyeuctus to her son-in-law Spudias (Demosthenes 41.9). The loan was for 1800 drachma, which exceeds the estimated value of the maximum financial transaction permitted to a woman under Attic law (Isaeus 10.10 ff.; Kuenen-Janssens 1941; Brock 1994: 341). Hence, the woman's brothers, who served as witnesses (*martures*), could have vetoed the loan had it been drawn from her personal wealth.[6] In fact, as noted by E.M. Harris (2014: 199) citing Demosthenes 41.8, the funds loaned out by the wife to Spudias belonged to her husband or rather to his estate, since he was already dead at the time of the lawsuit. This applies also to the (interest-bearing) loans taken by the speaker from his mother-in-law (Demosthenes 41.9). The important point regarding the wife's agency is that the loan of her husband's money to Spudias is not obviously a one-off transaction. The wife of Polyeuctus not only kept records (*grammata*) of her affairs but also authenticated these with her personal seal (Demosthenes 41.9, 10, 21, 24; D. Cohen 1998: 55). Demosthenes 41.9 refers to the wife of Polyeuctus as *gunaikos*, not as *pallakē*, but a legitimate wife could not lend out her husband's money.

A final thought is that rather than being only a useful by-product of *pallakia*, the right of wives to act as agents for an *oikos* may for some individuals have been the motivating force in choosing this marriage form. By becoming in legal practise the slave of her husband, the woman became in business practise his partner/companion (*koinōnos/hetairos*).

2. Relative Value of the Legitimate Wife: Supply

On the "supply of brides" side of the marriage market, the obvious consideration for the father is that by offering a groom-price—that is, a dowry—he is better able to marry his daughter legitimately and thereby able to retain ownership rights. This includes enhanced access to a beloved child and, as a last resort, the

5. (*Digest* 24.1.3 pr Ulpian): "The explanation is also drawn from an oration of our Emperor Antoninus Augustus, for it says: 'Our ancestors prohibited gifts between husband and wife in the belief that true affection was based on the heart alone. They also took into account the reputation of the parties to the marriage in order to prevent the agreement appearing to have been made for money and to stop the more generous partner becoming poorer and the less generous richer'" (tr. Watson). Commingled assets and purchased wives are negated in the same sentence.

6. The question of legality would arise only if the woman defaulted on her promise to make the loan, as she could not be sued for nonperformance of an illegal contract. On the other hand, the recipient could not refuse to repay the loan on the ground that it was illegally large.

legal right to reclaim the dowry and to rescue his daughter from a bad marriage (Blundell 1995: 68).

3. Role of Distance in the Direction of Nuptial Wealth Transfers: Theory and Evidence

The value of his ownership right to the father would depend on a number of variables, most obviously the distance of the married daughter's residence from his *oikos*. Distance increases costs of information and movement and often is accompanied by cost-raising political/legal barriers. Consequently, other things remaining equal, the greater the geographic distance of the bride's nuptial residence from his *oikos* the higher the cost to the father of exercising his ownership right and, hence, the lower its net value (value of benefit from ownership minus cost of exercising ownership).

On the other hand, the groom typically has a definite preference, economic and emotional, to form his new household in his own ancestral community. As noticed by Pache (2011: 99), this preference is clearly reflected by Homer, wherein

> divine offers in marriage are ... contrasted to the hero's longing for home: for Odysseus, there is no place sweeter on earth than country and parents (Odyssey 9.28 and 34), not even immortality in the company of a beautiful goddess [Circe].

Consequently, other things remaining equal, the greater the geographic distance of the groom's nuptial residence from his ancestral home the lower the net value to him of the marriage (value of his benefit from the marriage minus the cost of communicating with his ancestral home).

The distance-generated conflict in the interests of groom and father sets the stage for a negotiation whose outcome will vary from case to case. It is possible, however, to theorize about the central tendency in negotiation outcomes. Predictably, the greater the distance between the *oikos* of the father and the ancestral *oikos* of the groom: (1) the more likely it is that a groom whose *ex post* residence is near his father-in-law's will have been compensated with a dowry (groom-price); and (2) the greater the likelihood that a father whose daughter's *ex post* residence is near the groom's ancestral home will have been compensated with a bride-price.

Put in another way, fathers who agree to permit their married daughters to depart for distant places are likely to have been compensated by their grooms (in *pallakia*); fathers who do not agree to permit their married daughters to depart for distant places are likely to have compensated their grooms (in legitimate marriage).

Clearly, distance of the groom's birth residence from the bride's birth residence should be a major factor in determining the direction of wealth transfers and, consequently, of the form of marriage, legitimate or *pallakia* (compare Sealey 1990: 117). Greater distance between the marriage partners discourages legitimate marriage and encourages *pallakia*. Lesser distance discourages *pallakia* and encourages legitimate marriage. It should also be understood that geographic distance is actually a proxy variable for communication cost, which would, of course, be influenced by cultural factors—that is, by "cultural distance."[7]

It is not possible to test rigorously the prediction about the effect of distance on marriage form but it is broadly in accord with available evidence, which often explicitly notices the importance of distance in determining marriage form.

To begin with, Finley (1954: 9, 12 with n. 20), in studying the sale of brides in Homer,[8] concludes:

> Not once in either the *Iliad* or the *Odyssey* is there a sale transaction ... in which we can be sure that two Greeks were involved, or two Trojans. Either one of the parties is clearly identified as a foreigner, usually a Phoenician or a Taphian, or the poet fails to indicate the *ethnos* of the second party. I use the word "foreigners" instead of "outsiders" here because I mean not merely men from another community, but men from outside the Graeco-Trojan world altogether.[9]

Finley seems to be suggesting that bride purchase is an aberration, something exotic, but this is not what his finding means. Mixed nationality in marriage may be assimilated to increased distance/communication cost between ancestral residences.[10]

---

7. Ours is a "partial equilibrium" analysis, in which the preferences and wealth of the father of the bride and the groom are taken as given and the only variable is distance between the household of the father and the ancestral household of the groom. Distance is not the only variable determining the direction of wealth assigns and the form of marriage but it is the variable whose effect is most clearly visible in the ancient Greek data. Other prominent theories of marriage payments include Goody and Tambiah (1973), Becker (1991) and Botticini and Siow (2003). Blundell (1995: 69) notes Hesiod's (*Works and Days* 700) advice to "marry one [a woman] who lives near you" (tr. Evelyn-White *LCL*) and she suggests, "Changes in marriage customs associated with the emergence of the *polis* presumably affected the lower classes much less than the aristocracy, since the former were already in the habit of marrying women from their own communities." Blundell predicts that wealth transfers from groom to father would be less prevalent among the lower socioeconomic classes and more vaguely, that the change from stateless to stated community (the *polis*) caused an increase in the relative prevalence of dotal marriage.
8. As Finley (1954: 13) points out, the Homeric world is familiar with the sale of persons/slaves.
9. Here, I cite a few examples not mentioned by Finley that seem to involve marriages by sale of Greeks to Greeks. Laertes and his wife sent their daughter Ctimene to Samos, a Greek island, to wed an unnamed person and "got themselves countless bridal gifts [*hedna*]" (*Odyssey* 15.387; tr. Murray *LCL*). Odysseus reports: "And I saw beauteous Chloris, whom once Neleus wedded because of her beauty, when he had brought countless gifts of wooing [*hedna*]. Youngest daughter was she of Amphion, son of Iasus, who once ruled mightily in Orchomenus of the Minyae. And she was queen of Pylos, and bore to her husband glorious children, Nestor, and Chromius, and lordly Periclymenus, and besides these she bore noble Pero, a wonder to men" (*Odyssey* 11.280 ff.; tr. Murray *LCL*). It appears that Neleus purchased Chloris in Boeotia and carried her to Pylos in the Peloponnese.
10. There are possible deviations from the predicted pattern. For example, in *Odyssey* 15.231 Neleus, king of Pylos, sells his daughter to Melampus for the cattle of Phylacos (Phylace is in Thessaly)

That is, the finding that a party to the bridal transaction is a foreigner typically signals a significant distance between the father's *oikos* and the *oikos* of the groom. Therefore, as already noted, it is only to be expected that the daughters transferred to foreign grooms will be transferred by sale (Into *pallakia*).[11] Common nationality in marriage, on the other hand, signals decreased distance which operates to increase the likelihood that daughters transferred to native grooms will be transferred by loan (into legitimate marriage). The predicted pattern, as will be demonstrated below, is supported by a variety of specific evidence.

Consider first within this framework a fragment of Euripides's *Danae*:

> When a woman has left her ancestral home she is not her parents', but belongs to her marriage-bed; but male children stand always in a house to protect ancestral gods and tombs (Fragment 318; tr. Collard and Cropp *LCL*).

Euripides (actually a character) might only be suggesting that wives identified more with their newly formed households than did husbands. There is perhaps something to be said in favor of such a generalization but not very much. Euripides is not advocating the demonstrably false position that the Greek bride necessarily became the legal property of her *lechos* "marriage-bed" meaning "husband" (Euripides *Electra* 481 pointed out by Funke 2013: 53 n. 130). Neither is Euripides sponsoring the demonstrably false proposition that foreign grooms necessarily returned to their ancestral homes. I am convinced that Euripides (through a character) has nuptial legalities in mind when he refers to the *patrōōn domōn*—"ancestral home"—instead of to the much more narrowly defined *oikos*—"household". He is suggesting that those brides who traveled far away from their ancestral homes were, as a rule, married by sale rather than by loan. That is, they were not legitimately married. Further, Euripides is saying that foreign grooms as a rule returned to their distant ancestral homes with their (typically purchased) brides. Euripides is acknowledging a form of marriage in which wives belonged to husbands although he is not necessarily proposing that marriages were typically (geographically) exogamous.

Before turning to evidence confirming the role of distance in determining marriage form, note that an implication of the reasoning about the role of distance is that we do not necessarily have to postulate a difference in socioeconomic structure among societies mostly practicing dowry and those mostly practicing bride-sale (compare Snodgrass 1974 on the introduction of "complex" agriculture). Whether a society had mostly dowry or mostly bride purchase would largely be explained, other things equal, by whether its native women were mostly marrying native men (distance relatively

but Melampus "brought the maiden home to be his own brother's wife" (tr. Murray *LCL*). The brother's "home" may be in Pylos. See also some examples provided by Snodgrass's (1974: 118, n. 24).

11. The form taken by a mixed marriage may be viewed as an equilibrium position determined by the values placed on distance by the father and the husband.

small) or mostly marrying foreign men (distance relatively large). The latter pattern would itself be determined by a number of variables determined largely outside our model of the marriage market.[12] Let us now turn to concrete examples.

In Fragment 583 of Sophocles's *Tereus* (quoted in Chapter III), Procne is stressing the negative role of distance when she complains of brides being

> *sold* [*diempolōmetha*], away from our ancestral gods and our parents, some of us to foreign husbands, some to barbarians, some to joyless homes, and some to abusive ones. And, when a single night has yoked us, this is what we must approve of and think of as a good life (emphasis added).

After the giver and take of negotiation settles down to a new equilibrium, the average sold wife will reside more distantly from her original *oikos* than the average legitimate wife. The sold woman was sold into *pallakia* precisely because, as a foreigner or barbarian, the chosen husband placed a relatively high value on distance from the father's *oikos* (he very much wished to "go home"). The woman cannot "go back" because she has been transferred into the ownership of her husband's *oikos*.[13]

12. Osborne (1985: 130–31) collected data from Attic grave stelai casting light on inter-and intra-deme marriages (mainly) in the fourth century. There are 163 marriages wherein the deme of origin (demotic) is stated for both partners. Of these, 80.4% (131) are inter-deme marriages. However, the demotic is not stated in 80 more marriages. If we understand the omission to mean that the marriage partners had the *same* deme origin, then the percentage of inter-deme marriages declines to a—still substantial—53.9% (131 out of 243). Even more interestingly, consider the subset of 97 marriages in which the demotics of both partners are stated and the deme of burial is known. It is found that 73.2% of the wives were buried outside their deme of origin indicating, *with all due caveats*, that upon becoming brides many/most women departed from their ancestral homes. Hence, our theory stressing the economic importance of distance predicts that the proportion of purchased wives would have been higher among wives buried outside their demes of origin than for the stay-at-home wives. The predicted direction of wealth transfers might be quite different in other times and places.
13. Compare Medea's important speech in Euripides's *Medea* 230 ff: "Of all creatures that have breath and sensation, we women are the most unfortunate. First at an exorbitant price we must buy a husband and master of our bodies. [This misfortune is more painful than misfortune.] And the outcome of our life's striving hangs on this, whether we take a bad or a good husband. For divorce is discreditable for women and it is not possible to refuse wedlock. And when a woman comes into the new customs and practices of her husband's house, she must somehow divine, since she has not learned it at home, how she shall best deal with her husband. If after we have spent great efforts on these tasks our husbands live with us without resenting the marriage-yoke, our life is enviable. Otherwise, death is preferable. A man, whenever he is annoyed with the company of those in the house goes elsewhere and thus rids his soul of its boredom [turning to some male friend or age-mate]. But we must fix our gaze on one person only. Men say that we live a life free from danger at home while they fight with the spear. How wrong they are! I would rather stand three times with a shield in battle than give birth once" (tr. Kovacs *LCL*; cf. Williamson 1990: 18–19). Medea's reference to the woman "buying a husband" is difficult to understand except as a reference the *phernē* she brought with her into *pallakia* (*P.Giss.* 2.8–12 discussed in Chapter IV.5) and, possibly, to the payment of the groom-price

Homeric Greece is familiar with bride-sale, but Alcinous, father of Nausicaa, offers Odysseus a handsome dowry (groom price) should he choose to remain in Phaeacia:

> Better is due measure in all things. I would, O father Zeus, and Athena and Apollo, that thou, so goodly a man, and like-minded with me, wouldst have my daughter to wife, and be called my son, and abide here; a house and possessions would I give thee, if thou shouldst choose to remain, but against thy will shall no one of the Phaeacians keep thee; let not that be the will of father Zeus (*Odyssey* 7.314 ff.; tr. Murray *LCL*).

If Odysseus chooses to leave for distant Ithaca, he must leave Nausicaa behind or perhaps pay handsomely for her. He left without her.

Cepheus, king of the Ethiopians, in Ovid's *Metamorphoses* 4.705, offers Perseus the kingship as a dowry (*dos)* for saving his daughter Andromeda from the sea-monster. When instead Perseus prefers to return from Ethiopia to Seriphus, one of the islands in the Cyclades, he carries off (*rapit*) Andromeda as a "prize" (*praemia*)—that is, without having to pay Cepheus for her—but also "without a dowry" (*indotata*) (4.755 ff.). Thus, Perseus's preference to depart for distant parts denies to Andromeda the status of dowered legitimate wife and makes her into a *pallakē* purchased by labor service instead of by cash/material wealth.

In Euripides's *Ion*, Creusa, the daughter of the King of Athens, is given in legitimate marriage to the foreign-born (*xenos*) warrior Xuthus; Creusa explains that Xuthus took me "as the dowry [*proix*] of war and the prize of his spear" (298; tr. Potter *Perseus Project*). As well noted by Leão (2012: 148), "What is striking in this situation is not the carrying out of a marriage under such circumstances, but the fact that Xuthus had decided to remain in Athens." Typically, the foreigner decides to go home and if the bride goes along she, like Andromeda, does so in the status of paid for *pallakē*. As compensation for remaining, Xuthus received Creusa and the status king-consort of Athens. It is understood that Xuthus, like Jason in Corinth, also received citizenship.

The ancient Greeks were aware of the importance of distance in determining the direction of wealth transfers and the form of marriage. Such awareness is suggested in the story of Erysichthon (or Aithlōn) and his shape-shifting daughter Mestra (Hesiodic *Catalogue of Women*: Fr. 43a, 43b, 69–71; Most *LCL*). To feed his "hunger," Erysichton sold Mesta into marriage "every day."[14] He was able to do this because she always transformed herself into an animal and returned to her father to be resold/remarried. In the meantime, the *gunē*—legally "wife" but now "unmarried" woman

(dowry) in legitimate marriage. Medea seems to credit the legitimate wife with much more input into the nuptial process than is usually assumed. The legitimate wife, it appears, made sacrifices in order to accumulate resources for acquiring a husband. If Medea comes close to speaking truth a new look at the classical Greek household is required.

14. "In the *Ehoiai* [*Catalogue of Women*], according to Philodemus, Erysichthon sells his daughter (cf. *diaprasthēnai*) in order to feed his hunger. Also, [*gepern*], a form of *pernēmi* ('to sell') seems to be attested in her *ehoie* fr. 431.10]" (Ziogas 2013: 144–45 with n. 92; my transliteration). Clearly, Erysichthon receives material compensation for giving Mestra in marriage.

(Fr. 69.32)—worked at the "great loom" beside her mother (Ormand 2004: 311–12). In this way, father and daughter defrauded even the clever Sisyphus, who had paid a substantial bride-price (*hedna*) on behalf of his son, Glaukos. The details of the following lawsuit and of Athena's role as arbitrator are unfortunately fragmentary but it is clear that it involved the "purchase price" and that the case supports the conclusion that purchasers of slave-wives received a warranty just as did purchasers of ordinary slaves.[15]

At a later stage,

> Poseidon [sexually] overpowered (*damazō*) her (Mestra) far from her father, carrying her over the wine-dark sea in sea-girt Cos, clever though she was, there she bore Eurypylus, commander of many people..." (tr. Most LCL; *damazō* has the meaning "of maidens" to "make subject to a husband" (LSJ s.v. II).[16]

There is no mention of the payment of bride-price (*hedna*) by Poseidon to Mestra's father Erysichthon. Hence, the question arises did the Greeks really worship gods who confiscated the property of mortals or weaker gods? I will return to this question very shortly but the quick answer is that even gods paid for their brides. In any event, a god of Poseidon's caliber should have had no trouble in holding Mestra as his *pallakē*-wife even if he had settled her next door to her father. Nevertheless, the emphasis on distance and natural barriers to travel is neither redundant nor inserted purely for dramatic effect. It reflects instead a contemporary understanding that marriage by purchase generally becomes the preferred marriage form when father and daughter will live far apart. Otherwise, legitimate marriage tends to be more prevalent.

The lesson taught by the myth of Mestra is that sale into marriage does not "stick" (= is not the preferred form of marriage) when the bride resides close enough to return from her husband to her father. We are told that Mestra was taken a very great distance from her father only in the case of Poseidon and only in this case does the marriage last. It is quite true that no evidence shows that Poseidon paid Erysicthon for carrying his daughter Mestra to distant shores, as did other gods, but also Poseidon's marriage to Mestra is surely not portrayed as legitimate.

---

15. For classical Athens, see Hypereides 3.15. Warrantied slaves are very well attested in Rome by the *Edict of the Curule Aediles* (*Digest* 21.1). On the other hand, Osborne (2005: 19–20) suggests "we seem to have a ruling that, once paid, purchase price cannot be recovered: bride-price is not provisional, as dowry historically was, to be recalled if the marriage breaks down, but absolute" (similarly Rutherford 2005: 107). I think that Osborne would be correct only if the market, and hence the law, viewed the married woman as "spoiled goods" and hence as not returnable. However, this is not the case. Compare also Hephaestus vs. Zeus in connection with the adultery of Aphrodite.

16. Ormand (2004: 312; cf. 2014: 95–96) notes the use of the verb *damao,* which is related to *damar*—"wife".

4. Two Test Cases: Hephaestus's *Hedna* and *P.Eleph.* 1

It was noted in Chapter IV that Hephaestus paid *hedna* (bride-price) to Zeus for Aphrodite. Is this payment consistent with our argument concerning the role of distance? That is, would *hedna* be expected given the distance between Hephaestus's *oikos* and Zeus's on Mount Olympus? Foley (1999: 106) argues,

> But epic frequently treats these residences largely as a place for sleeping (see *Iliad* 1.605–11), and the regular presence of Olympian goddesses at the assembly of Zeus indicates that a separate residence in no way isolates them from the divine community or inevitably subordinates them to their husbands. Hence Aphrodite, for example, arrives home *from the presence of Zeus* to find Ares awaiting her (8.289–91).

It may be objected to Foley's argument that,

> Ares came into the house and clasped her [Aphrodite's] hand and spoke and addressed her: "Come, love, let us to bed and take our joy, couched together. For *Hephaestus is no longer here in the land, but has now gone, I ween, to Lemnos, to visit the Sintians of savage speech*" (*Odyssey* 8.191 ff; tr. Murray LCL; emphasis added).

Actually, Homer (*Odyssey* 1.590–93; 18.395–97) tells that on separate occasions Zeus and Hera cast down Hephaestus the entire long and painful way from Olympus to earth. In one case, it is said that he sojourned on earth for many years (*Iliad* 18.400–04). Hephaestus, it appears, alternated his domicile between Lemnos and Mount Olympus. More generally, Hephaestus was a god of earthbound circulating artisan and traders, hence his lameness, and arguably, like Hercules, he was promoted to Olympian status relatively late in his cultic "career" (Silver 1992: 135–44). Hephaestus did not fall from Mount Olympus—he rose to it. Rinon (2006: 16) considers Hephaestus to be "an exceptional god who hovers between the divine and human realms". His divided residence, between Lemnos and Mount Olympus, explains why, like a traveling human merchant or landowner, he needed several wives: Cabeiro on Lemnos and Charis, whose status is not clear, on Mount Olympus (see Chapter XI). To conclude, there is something to be said for Hephaestus being a cultural and geographic outsider at Olympus and hence having to pay *hedna* for his bride Aphrodite.

The second test case, *P.Eleph.* 1, dated to 311 BCE, the earliest dated Greek papyrus from Egypt, represents a different kind of test case for my hypothesis concerning the role of distance in determining the form of marriage. The groom Heracleides is from Temnos, on the coast of Asia Minor, and the bride Demetria is from the island of Cos. As noted earlier, the father Leptines does not sell Demetria to Heracleides but rather gives her to be his legitimate wife. Demetria takes into the marriage "clothing and ornaments to the value of 1000 drachmas" (tr. Rowlandson 1998: 165 no. 123). The contract designates these items to be *phernē*. Thus, Leptines does not collect wealth (*hedna*) from Heracleides but neither does he provide him with wealth in the form of a *proix* "dowry." Significantly, I think, the marriage contract specifies that the couple "shall live together wherever it seems best to Leptines and Heracleides consulting in common" (tr. Rowlandson 1998: 165 no. 123). Therefore, we have explicit reference to the importance of the couple's final distance from the father and to the role of negotiation in the determination of this distance. Under certain conditions, the contract might be modified or re-opened: if the groom agreed to live nearby, the father might agree to provide a dowry; if the groom insisted on living far away, he might have to purchase the bride and take her away as his *pallakē*. Alternatively, as possibly in the present case, the negotiated distance from the father might fall into an intermediate geographic range calling for neither dowry nor bride-price.

5. Additional Factors Determining the Price Paid for a *Pallakē*

Focusing on the "demand for wives" side of the marriage market, there is the thought that the price offered for a *pallakē* depended not only on her beauty and social status (providing the buyer with sexual and reputation value; Ormand 2014a: 76–78) but also on her economic productivity, especially in textile work. In the *Odyssey* (13.289), Athena takes "the form of a woman, comely and tall, and skilled in glorious handiwork [*aglaa erga iduiē*]" (tr. Murray *LCL* cf. 16.158). Strikingly, it appears that especially skilled women were recognizable by their demeanor or dress, or some other standardized attribute. When Calchas priest of Apollo, offers "ransom (*apoina*) past counting" to free his daughter Chruseis, Agamemnon turns him down:

> Let me not find you, old man, by the hollow ships, either tarrying now or coming back later, lest your staff and the wreath of the god not protect you. Her I will not set free. Sooner shall old age come upon her in our house, in Argos, far from her native land, as she walks to and fro before the loom and serves my bed" (*Iliad* 1.10 ff.; tr. Murray *LCL*).

Most directly, when Penelope offered herself for sale to the highest bidding suitor (*Odyssey* 16.76–77) she was marketing not only her sex appeal and fame but also her marvelous weaving skills. In *Iliad* 23 the first prize in the Funeral Games for Patroclus is a "woman to lead away, one skilled in goodly handiwork, and an eared tripod of two and twenty measures" (263) and the second prize in the wrestling contest is a "a woman of manifold skill in handiwork, and they prized her at the worth of four oxen" (705; tr. Murray *LCL*).

6. Did Greek Gods Pay for their Mortal Brides?

We are not told that Poseidon gave *hedna* for Mestra. However, there are other cases to consider. The myth of Zeus and Europa is relevant to the question of whether gods paid for their *pallakē*-wives. Zeus "overpowered/married" Europa, the daughter of Phoenix, while she was picking flowers in a meadow. This wilderness occupation signals single woman status, as is attested in the myths of Stratonice, Atalanta, the Protids and perhaps Persephone (all discussed below). Europa was carried over to

Crete where at some point Zeus transferred his *pallakē* to Asterion, the king of the Cretans (Hesiodic *Catalogue of Women* Fr. 89 Most *LCL*). In a different fragment in the Hesiodic *Catalogue of Women* (Fr. 141 = Fr. 90 Most *LCL*), Zeus makes compensation for marrying Europa in the form of a golden necklace made by Hephaestus. In Most's rendering, the necklace is a gift (*dōron*) to Europa. However, In Ormand's (2014a: 71) rendering, Zeus compensates the father Phoenix for the loss of his daughter. However, although this is not reflected in his translation of the Fragment, Ormand (2014a: 72) suggests the necklace gift "must surely be for the bride. Line 6, however, has the father receiving his own gift."[17] Thus, Zeus was understood as having paid Europa, and possibly Phoenix as well. The payment to a single woman is expected but a payment to her father is not.

Europa was intended to be viewed as Zeus's bride (Heldmann 2016; 56 ff.). The "Europa as slave-wife" perspective has strong iconographic support. For example, depictions on fishplates found near the Black Sea include a seated Zeus together with Europa who is arriving from the sea together with the bull, Nereids and Erotes. Nereids have connections to weddings and Erotes are a nuptial symbol (McPhee and Trendall 1987: 29; Barringer 1995: 95–100; Stafford 2012: 201–06; and at length below). One of the Erotes in the scene holds a chest, which might have held Zeus's marriage gift for the single woman Europa. Again, in a painting by Asteas (Malibu, California, Getty Museum 81.AE.78; available for download at: http://www.perseus.tufts.edu/hopper/image?img=Perseus:image:1990.05.0469), a labeled Europa, fully and indeed spectacularly dressed and ornamented, sits calmly on the bull; the pair are accompanied (guided?) by the winged "Desire" as Zeus awaits. Jentoft-Nilsen (1983; 139), comments, "In view of Zeus's lust for Europa, Pothos personifying passion, is a far more appropriate figure than Eros would have been." Arguably, Pothos also signified Europa's desire for Zeus and Hermes, depicted with his caduceus, might have arranged the nuptial transaction. Note that the scene also includes a bust of Eros.[18]

Pindar (*Pythian Ode* 9.1–14) tells of Apollo's marriage to Cyrene:

> With the help of the deep-waisted Graces I want to shout aloud proclaiming the Pythian victory with the bronze shield of Telesicrates, a prosperous man, the crowning glory of chariot-driving Cyrene; the long-haired son of Leto [Apollo] once snatched her from the wind-echoing glens of Mt. Pelion, and carried the girl of the wilds in his golden chariot to a place where he made her mistress of a land rich in flocks and most rich in fruits, to live and flourish on the root of the third continent. Silver-footed Aphrodite welcomed the Delian guest from his chariot, touching him with a light hand, and she cast lovely modesty on their sweet union, joining together in a common bond of marriage the god

17. Ormand's (2014a: 72) translation of line 6: "...bearing to [her] father. And he received the gift."
18. The Europa myth is depicted on vase shapes associated with weddings (Barringer 1995: 98–9). Deacy (2013: 401–03) comments, "Europa's experiences lend themselves to an interpretation of the heroine as a victim but also as a desiring subject who goes so far as to display agency" and, further, scenes of Europa at play with her companions include "an erotic dimension to this play" via the inclusion of Eros.

> and the daughter of wide-ruling Hypseus. He was at that time king of the proud Lapiths, a hero of the second generation from Oceanus (tr. Svarlien *Perseus Project*).

Cyrene, living in the wilds, was a single woman at the time she was taken as a wife by Apollo (Section 7 below). As such, she was owed *dōra* "payment/gift" by Apollo. Pindar does not use this term but the poet nevertheless makes it very clear that Cyrene was richly rewarded by Apollo for becoming his *pallakē*: Apollo "made her mistress of a land rich in flocks and most rich in fruits."

Two points are clear. First, like mortals, both Zeus and Apollo paid compensation, probably in the form of *dōra*, for their brides Europa and Cyrene who were single women outside the *oikos* of their fathers (but compare Ion's discussion of the problem in Euripides *Ion* 430–51). Second, at the same time, Zeus and Apollo cannot be allowed to marry Europa and Cyrene legitimately because the myth requires them to carry their brides far away. Thus, Zeus carried his *pallakē* Europa across the sea, from Boeotia or Phoenicia to Crete (West 1985: 146–47, 151), and the *pallakē* Cyrene is carried in Apollo's chariot from Central Greece to North Africa.

According to Fragment 654 of Corinna of Tanagra, Zeus, Poseidon, Apollo and Hermes took the nine daughters of the river god Asopos as wives. So begins the fragment which goes on to explain: "For so did Eros and the Cyprian prevail, that the Gods go in secret to your house, and take for themselves your daughters nine" (18–19; tr. Page 1953: 82–83). "At the end of his prophecy," Lardinois (2011: 188) explains, "Acraephen [a seer] addresses Asopos as 'father-in-law to the gods' ... after which Asopos renounces his grief. In column iv, line 16, 'wedding gifts for the bride' (*hedna*) [actually a payment to the father] are mentioned and, although too little of the context survives to determine who is giving these gifts to whom, it is perhaps not too far-fetched to assume that gods are giving these gifts to Asopos in recompense for the rape of his daughters" (Lardinois 2011: 188; cf. Kousoulini 2016: 84–88). Again, it appears that the gods paid the rightful owner of the bride.

Because of an admixture of references to the virgin priestess institution any interpretation of the Danaē myth must leave loose ends. However, it is possible to fit Danaē into the model developed here. Zeus impregnated Danaē against the wishes of her father Acrisius king of Argos. Acrisios had consigned his daughter to an underground bronze *thalamos* "treasury," "bedroom," or "bridal chamber." His intention in placing Danaē in a guarded vault was not to pledge her in legitimate marriage but the complete opposite, to prevent her from being married at all (compare Ebbott 2003: 12–14). Nevertheless, Zeus presented to Danaē, not to her father Acrisius, a stream of gold that he placed in her lap (Pherecydes of Athens scholion on Apollonius Rhodius *Argonautica* 4.1091 and, more compactly, Apollodorus *Library* 2.4.1;) or, as Sophocles (*Antigone* 950 ff.) has it, with the *gonē* "seed" (understood as "money" or "capital") that he left in her keeping (cf. Kenens 2012; Silver 1992: esp. 217–18). Pherecydes of Athens, our oldest source, makes clear that only after making the required payment did Zeus consummate the marriage by having consensual sexual intercourse with Danaē. That Zeus and Danaē were married is implied by Sophocles

(*Antigone* 944 ff.: "So too endured Danaē in her beauty to change the light of the sky for brass-bound walls, and in that chamber, both burial and bridal, she was held in strict confinement" (tr. Jebb *Perseus Project*).

Seaford (1990: 77) notes, "She [Danaē] was, says our chorus, hidden and yoked in a sepulchral chamber ... The association of 'yoking' (*katezeuchthē*) with marriage implies that the chamber (*thalamos*) is a *bridal thalamos*" and, indeed, Danaē had a "kind of wedding". Of what kind? Zeus's prior payment to Danaē is understood by Apollodorus to be *phtheirō*—"corruption"/"seduction"—meaning, I believe, that she thereby became a *pallakē*. The view that Danaē sold herself for gold is expressed by Acrisius in Euripides's *Danae* (*Fragment* 7) and Karamanou (2006: 78–79) adds that this perspective is shared by many authors after Euripides including, most famously, by Eustathius in commenting on the "Golden Aphrodite" in *Iliad* 3.64. In the *Anthologia Palatina* (5.3), Anitpater, writing in the first century BCE, imagined that Zeus came to Danae with a hundred gold coins.

Zeus's "rape" of Danaē was consensual not forcible as is well attested her bared body in Plate 4.

Arguably, Acrisius had originally excluded Danaē from his *oikos* and ceased to be her *kurios* (he emancipated her) when, as stated by Pherecydes, he confined her and her *trophē*—"nurse"—in a dwelling place located in an *aulē*—"courtyard." In the aftermath of the marriage, Danaē and her *nothos* Perseus are put to sea in a *larnax*—"chest" (also "ark")—destined to arrive at the distant island Seriphus where Danaē supplicates Dictys, son of Peristhenes, to bring them into his house. Thus, the myth requires Danaē to travel far away, which is inconsistent with Acrisius having given her to anyone in legitimate marriage.

In conclusion, there is weak evidence that gods compensated mortal fathers for their daughters and there is strong evidence that gods compensated daughters taken from outside the *oikos* of their fathers. Apparently, the gods created by the Greeks were law-abiding with respect to nuptial transactions. It appears that they created these gods in their own image.

7. Behind the Terminology: *Dōra* vs. *Hedna*

As already seen, the payment made by the groom for his bride was sometimes called *hedna* and sometimes *dōra*. Is this difference in terminology significant?[19] The scholium to the *Odyssey* 1.276 explains:

19. Osborne (2005: 17–18) observes: "In narrative terms, there is some reason to think that 'bride-price' is a marked signifier, a feature of foreign or otherwise odd unions. But in the *Catalogue*, there is no dowry: there is a single uniform practice without any disruption, for whenever we meet the exchange of gifts on marriage it is from the man to the woman ... This is a world in which women are bought by men, though not in the same way by gods, and where among mortals the greater gift takes the trick ... Given the likelihood that the poem was performed in a world where dowry was universal and bride-price unknown, the choice of a uniform narrative of

Plate 4. Boeotian red-figure crater of the mid-fifth century BCE featuring Danaē receiving Zeus as a shower of gold. Paris, Musée du Louvre CA 925 (RMN-Grand Palais/Art Resource, New York).

> *Hedna* means the things given by the bridegrooms, from the words *hedran kai paramonēn proxenein*, to the bride. But the gifts from the fathers are *keimēlia*. *Hedna* are the gifts (*dōra*) given by the one marrying to the wife. *Phernai* are the things [given] by the wife, from the words "to carry into bed" (*pherein eis eunēn*) (tr. Ormand 2014a: 52 modified).[20]

This explanation of the terminology is, however, both obscure and incomplete.

Ormand (2014a: 52–53) notes that, in post-classical texts, the term *hedna* usually refers to gifts given by the groom to the bride's father, and further,

> the term virtually disappears from public discourse in the literature of the fifth century *polis* (though it reappears in Hellenistic and later literature) and to date no sufficient explanation has been given for this disappearance.

In the classical period, as already seen, the selling/purchase of brides, not necessarily "elite" brides, demonstrably continued but the price paid by the groom is rarely called *hedna* (as it is, however, in Pindar *Olympian* 9.5–10, *Pythian* 3.92–97).

The apparent change in terminology deserves an explanation but it is not correct to equate, with Ormand (2014a: 57–58), absence of the word with absence of the deed of selling women into marriage (see similarly Van Wees 2005: 8). Who it was that received (in the sense of owned) the tendered payment would depend on whether the bride sold herself to the groom or whether she was sold to him by her father. That is, it is a question of whether the sold bride was or was not her own *kuria*. That is, the payment was owned by the owner of the transferred woman. Of course, even if the father received (owned) the *hedna* he might in perfect legality transfer all or part of it to his departing daughter.[21]

Europa clearly received a substantial bridal payment (*dōra*: "gift") from Zeus but the evidence does not make clear that her father Phoenix received any form of compensation (*dōra* or *hedna*). The circumstances discussed above suggest that Europa might be understood as being outside the household of her father Phoenix. This supposition is supported by the information that at the very time she was abducted by Zeus, Europa was "plucking flowers with *numphai* in a meadow" (Hesiodic *Catalogue of Women*, Fr. 89; tr. Most *LCL*). Thus, it is reasonable to hypothesize that the term *hedna* applies when brides are sold to grooms by their fathers and the term *dōra* applies

---

bride-price can only further emphasize the plot in which women have something irresistible to men, and which men will pay out to acquire." A few responses: (1) the cases in which purchase of the woman is not mentioned may be cases of groom-purchase (dowry); (2) Medea (quoted above) claims that women purchased men; (3) women had "something irresistible to men" even when men received a dowry; and (4) there is no evidence that Hesiod's world was one of universal dowry. In addition, Osborne's analysis is not interested in whether the "bride-price" paid for the woman was paid to her father (*hedna*) or to the woman herself (*dōra*).

20. On *proix* vs. *phernē*, see at length Vérilhac and Vial (1998: Chapter II) and, earlier, Häge (1968).
21. A transfer of her father Icarius's *hedna* to Penelope is anticipated in *Odyssey* 1.277–78, 2.196–97 (see Chapter XVII).

when self-owned women sell themselves into marriage. Further, it would be expected that distance would play a role in the payment of *dōra* just as in the payment of *hedna*. That is, other things being equal, brides being taken far from their ancestral homes would be more likely to demand and receive *dōra* and certainly larger *dōra* than those who would reside with new husbands in closer proximity to their birth-families.

The hypothesis that *dōra* was paid to self-owned women may be subjected to testing by examining cases in which brides are explicitly stated to be acquired *anaednos* "without *hedna*". Firstly, in the Hesiodic *Catalogue of Women* (Fr. 26 = Fr. 23 Most *LCL*), Apollo carried off Stratonice "without *hedna*." Elsewhere in the same Fragment, we learn that Stratonice was a companion of the nymphs and muses in the high mountains wherein she was "[leaving] their [father's] mansions and their dear [mother]" (line 17; tr. Most *LCL*). Stratonice is clearly her own *kuria*.[22] Hence, my theory predicts correctly that her father Porthaon would not collect *hedna* for her (compare Osborne 2005: 18–19). Stratonice agreed to accompany Apollo and to be married to his son Melaneus. However, there is no mention of Stratonice being given a "gift" (*dōra*), as predicted by my theory. Perhaps the reference to the payment of *dōra* is indirect. In line 24 we are told that Apollo gave Stranonice to his son "to be called his *thalerēn* wife." The Greek term *thaleros* has been translated as "buxom," "blossoming," "luxuriant," "vigorous" and "fertile," but "rich" also seems possible and, in this case, meaningful (LSJ s.v. *thaleros* citing *Odyssey* 8.476 "'rich' meat"). In support of "rich", note that Persephone, who is also a *thalerēn akoitin*, is richly rewarded by Hades for marrying him (*Homeric Hymn to Demeter* 2.79–80, 364–69; discussed above).

In the *Iliad*, there are three references to *anaednos*, but unfortunately, they are not helpful in testing our hypothesis, because in each case the father had received alternative compensation from the groom for his daughter. In *Iliad* 9.146 and 9.288 Agamemnon offers a daughter to Achilles to compensate him for having taken Briseis from him; in *Iliad* 13.366, Othreoneus received Cassandra for having rendered military assistance to Priam (Ormand 2014a: 79). One might suggest that these examples are not truly *anaednos*.

Important evidence is available in Apollodorus's telling of the Atalanta myth. Apollodorus, like Theognis (1283–94) much before him in the sixth century BCE, makes clear that Atalanta was outside her father's household in the wilderness and hence was her own *kuria*:

> This Atalanta was exposed by her father, because he desired male children; and a she bear came often and gave her suck, until hunters found her and brought her up among themselves. Grown to womanhood, Atlanta kept herself a virgin, and hunting in the wilderness, she remained always under arms. The centaurs Rhesus and Hyles tried to force her, but were shot down and killed by her. She went moreover with the chiefs to hunt the Calydonian boar, and at the games held in honor of Peleus she wrestled with Peleus and won. Afterwards she discovered her parents, but when her father would have

22. That "nymphs" lived outside male-headed households and represent real world single women is argued at in Chapter XII.

persuaded her to wed, she went away to a place that might serve as a racecourse, and, having planted a stake three cubits high in the middle of it, she caused her wooers to race before her from there, and ran herself in arms; and if the wooer was caught up, his due was death on the spot, and if he was not caught up, his due was marriage. When many had already perished, Melanion came to run for love of her, bringing golden apples from Aphrodite, and being pursued he threw them down, and she, picking up the dropped fruit, was beaten in the race. So Melanion married her (*Library* 3.9.2; tr. Frazier *LCL*; emphasis added; cf. Sourvinou-Inwood 1987:152–53 with n. 139).

It should be added that Aphrodite handed the apples to Eros (or vice versa) who passed them on the suitor (Bologna, Museo Civico Archeologico 300). In Plate 5, a veiled Atalanta, wearing a transparent gown, is pursued by three winged Erotes (all figures are labeled) one of whom holds up a golden apple with tendrils that she gazes back at as she runs.

Justifiably, attention has been given to the sexual, cultic, civic, initiatory, spatial and athletic dimensions of the myth. The focus here is on its economic core. Atalanta who was living outside a male-headed household *offered herself in marriage* to the suitor who could defeat her in a race/chase (see Ormand 2014a: 134, 2014b; Barringer 1996: 71–72). No mention is made of payment of *hedna* to her father. Instead, Atalanta chose to be "defeated" by "picking-up the dropped apples"—that is she sold her consent to the suitor who transferred wealth directly to her (the latter wealth being expressly termed *dōra* in the Hesiodic *Catalogue of Women;* Fr. 73 = Fr. 48 Most *LCL*). I would weaken my economic determinism to note that in *choosing* to race all challengers, Atalanta must have had romantic as well as monetary objectives in mind.

If Aphrodite's *mēla* came from the dragon-guarded gardens of the Hesperides then probably they should be understood as lumps of gold or perhaps golden fleeces. "Apples" of this kind would be capable of infusing marital desire in many recipients. Atalanta is portrayed as having sold herself into *pallakia*. My hypothesis well explains the evidence provided in the Atalanta myth.

A final point, consistent with Atalanta's single woman status, is that the name of her son by Melanion "Parthenopeus" (Euripides *Phoenician Women* 150; Apollodorus *Library* 3.9.2), meaning "son of a *parthenos*" (J. Smith 2013: 11–12), is like a metronymic in that it refers back to herself as the parent/owner.

Taken together, the examples of Stratonice, Atalanta, and perhaps Andromache (discussed below) argue for the following propositions: (1) Both *hedna* and *dōra* are technical terms in the context of marriage by purchase (*pallakia*); (2) Grooms paid *hedna* to the father only when the bride lived within his household[23] and (3) Grooms

23. Van Wees (2005: 5 n. 22) asserts: "There is no evidence for bridewealth [*hedna*] going to the bride herself rather than her family." Actually, as Van Wees is aware, there is evidence for the family acting as an intermediary between groom and bride. In *Odyssey* 1.277–78, the disguised Athena advises Telemachus, "And for thy mother, if her heart bids her marry, let her go back to the hall of her mighty father, and there they will prepare a wedding feast, and make ready the gifts [*eedna*] full many—aye, all that should follow after a well-loved daughter" (tr. Murray

Plate 5. Athenian red-figure lekythos of the early fifth century BCE featuring Atalanta being pursued by three Erotes. Cleveland, Cleveland Museum of Art 66.114 (reproduced with permission of the Cleveland Museum of Art).

paid *dōra* to the bride only when the bride was her own *kuria*.[24] It is discussed below whether these conclusions apply to Penelope and to the usage of the terms *poluednos* and *poludōros*.

Unfortunately, the term *dōra* might be used in two different but related senses: *dōra* is the final payment given by a suitor to a woman in her own hands but also it is a *bid* for the bride that might be kept by the father of the bride. As Ormand (2014a: 71) explains, *dōra* sometimes refers to contributions made by suitors that "must be sent in advance of a marriage agreement and are not returnable." My understanding is that the "contributions" constituted an "admission fee" to an exclusive club and/or "earnest money"—that is, they served to demonstrate that a suitor was serious about purchasing the bride. Presumably, some lower limit was set for a qualifying "gift." The suitor submitting the highest deposit/bid/gift won the bride. Alternatively, there ensued a bidding process in which members of the "suitor's club" augmented their qualifying deposits/gifts. The losing depositors/bidders probably forfeited their qualifying gifts. Even if the gifts were ultimately refundable, however, the seller, whether the father or the bride herself, benefited from the temporary use of the gifts and also from pledges which had value because they increased the seller's creditworthiness (see Lacey 1966: 58, n. 21, 60 for bride-gifts as promises). If the bride sold herself, the winning bid was called dōra, but if the father sold his daughter the winning bid was called *hedna*—"bride-price." That is, the winning bid might be either *dōra* or *hedna* depending on the recipient.[25] This understanding finds support in Hesychius's equation of *poluednos* with *poludōros* (see below).

The reasons for the adoption of this terminological system are unclear but it obviously did matter whether the bride or her father was the owner and hence the recipient of the final payment. In the example of the shape-shifting Mestra in the Hesiodic *Catalogue of Women* (discussed above), the importance of ownership is

LCL; cf. *Odyssey* 2.196–97). It seems clear, however, that Penelope's father is expected to give her *some* of *his hedna*. Van Wees (2005: 6) puts it: "Marriage gifts from the bride's family are called by the same name as gifts from the groom's family: *hedna* or *eedna*." Finley (1954: 22) maintains, "the fact that the same word [*hedna*] could have two opposite meanings has been a stumbling block to commentators ever since the ancient scholiasts. If the *hedna* are understood as purchase-money, there is no satisfactory way out." Finley is overreacting; the meaning is that some purchase money was transferred from father or brother to the bride.

24. Alcmene was her own *kuria* prior to marrying Amphitryon: "or like her, leaving behind her houses and her father's land, she came to Thebes following warlike Amphityron" (Hesiod *Shield* 1–2; tr. Most *LCL*). A scholion to the *Argonautica* 1.747 makes this status clearer and less interesting. It tells that after her father Electryon and her brothers had been killed: "Alkmene stood forth and announced her marriage with whoever should avenge the murder of her father" (tr. Ormand 2014a: 160). In terms of my argument, Alcmene, as a single woman, took vengeance as her *dōra*.

25. Van Wees (2005: 5) says, "Unlike courting gifts, *hedna* are offered conditionally and actually given only by the chosen suitor." However, this leaves unexplained the relationship between the courting gifts and the bride-price.

demonstrated by the lawsuit filed by her husband Sisyphus to recover his bridal payment from Mestra's father. Similarly, when Hephaestus found his wife Aphrodite having an affair with Ares, he demanded that her father Zeus return his payment: "Soon shall both lose their desire to sleep; but the snare and the bonds shall hold them until her father pays back to me all the gifts of wooing [*eedna*] that I gave him for the sake of his shameless girl; for his daughter is fair but bridles not her passion" (*Odyssey* 8. 316–20; tr. Murray *LCL*). Evidently, Zeus had warrantied his daughter's good behavior. Aphrodite is the purchased wife of Hephaestus and, hence, not his legitimate wife. The sources do not reveal how Hephaestus acquired Charis, his wife in his palace on Mount Olympus (*Iliad* 18.382; *Theogony* 945; cf. Rinon 2006: 16). Hephaestus also had another wife on Lemnos named Cabeiro (Strabo 10.3.210) who, according to Nonnus *Dionysiaca* 14.7 ff., "had borne to the heavenly smith, Alcon and Eurymedon well skilled at the forge, who bore their mother's tribal name [*ounoma meteros*]" (tr. Rouse *LCL*). Given that Caberoi's sons bore a metronymic we may predict that she was a *pallakē*.[26]

In the *Odyssey* (18.285–304) when Penelope presents herself for sale to the suitors, *dōra* are given but no mention is made of *hedna* (cf. 16.76–77). However, *hedna*, but not *dōra*, is mentioned in *Odyssey* 15.16, 16.389–92, and 21.161–62. Elsewhere, Athena advises Telemachus:

> On the morrow call to an assembly the Achaean lords, and speak out thy word to all, and let the gods be thy witnesses. As for the wooers, bid them scatter, each to his own; and for thy mother, if her heart bids her marry, let her go back to the hall of her mighty father, and there they will prepare a wedding feast, and make ready [*artuneousin*; better "fit together" or "contrive"] the gifts [*eedna*] full many—aye, all that should follow after a well-loved daughter (*Odyssey* 1.274–78 = 2.196–97; tr. Murray LCL modified).

That is, if Penelope were to reenter the household of her father, they (Icarius and his sons) will fit together/contrive *hedna*, meaning they will arrange to collect a great deal of it (see Sealey 1990: 114). This interpretation is supported by *Odyssey* 2.50–53:

> My mother have wooers beset against her will, the sons of those men who are here the noblest. They shrink from going to the house of her father, Icarius, that he may himself exact the bride-gifts for his daughter, and give [clearly "sell"] her to whom he will, even to him who meets his favour (tr. Murray *LCL*).

My somewhat convoluted solution is as follows: (1) the *dōra* actually given by the suitors in *Odyssey* (18.285–304) are simultaneously "earnest money" and bids; (2) when

26. Ogden (1996: 94, 96) argues cogently against identifying individuals with metronymics as bastards by noting that in the historical record "metronymy is an overwhelmingly female phenomenon" for which finding he offers the explanation that "in their own private social spheres women understandably connected themselves together with metronymics (only), just as men connected themselves together with patronymics (only, for the most part) in theirs." I agree that bastardy is not the only explanation of metronymy but it is the most reliable explanation.

Athena says (*Odyssey* 15.16; tr. Murray *LCL*): "For now [Penelope's] father and her brothers bid her wed Eurymachus, for he surpasses all the wooers in his presents, and has increased his gifts of wooing," the goddess actually refers to the giving of *dōra*, the highest of which may become *hedna*; and (3) *hedna* will actually be paid for Penelope only if she reenters the household of her father Icarius, if not she receives *dōra*.

As things turn out, Penelope remains outside the household of her father, Penelope and Odysseus are left in possession of the "earnest money" (*dōra*) and the suitors are rendered incapable of requesting a refund. A final point, taken up later, is that Penelope having been sold to Odysseus was not a member of Icarius's household but of Odysseus's.

8. Behind the Terminology: *Poludōros* vs. *Poluednos* plus *Proix* vs. *Phernē*

Another problem is the final disposition of the purchase price of a *pallakē* (Harrison 1968: 14). When the bride was purchased from her father the latter may have turned some of the proceeds (his *hedna*) over to the bride for her personal use.

Thus, when Penelope is referred to as *alochos poludōros* "wife having many gifts" (*Odyssey* 24.294; also used of Andromache in *Iliad* 6.394 and 22.88) one is not required to infer that Penelope (Andromache) *sold herself* to Odysseus (to Hector).[27] Instead, I understand Homer to mean that Penelope (Andromache) was *poluednos*, a term Hesychius defines as *poludōros* (cited by Lacey 1966: 58 n. 19). In Andromache's case, there is explicit testimony that she was sold by her father into *pallakia*:

> Far from off her head she cast the bright attiring thereof, the frontlet and coif and kerchief and woven band, and the veil that golden Aphrodite had given her on the day when Hector of the flashing helm led (*ēgageth*) her as his bride forth from the house of Eetion, after he had brought bride-gifts (*hedna*) past counting (*Iliad* 22: 469–72; tr. Murray *LCL*; similarly in Euripides *Andromache* 2).

Neither Homer not Euripides (*Andromache* 1–5) report that Andromache was betrothed to Hector by her father. In addition, Homer's reference to Hector "leading" Andromache suggests *pallakia* (see above). Add to these indicators of *pallakia* the reasons for believing that the elaborate headdress worn by Andromache was specific to purchased wives (see the discussion of Hera in Chapter XVIII).[28]

27. There are, however, versions in which self-sale may be indicated. Pausanias 3.20.10–11 (discussed below) gives reason to believe that Penelope was outside her father's household when she married Odysseus. In the *Iliad* 6.414 ff., Andromache reports that Achilles had killed her father Eetion and his seven sons in a raid raising the possibility that she was outside a male-headed household at the time she married Hector. On the other hand, *Iliad* 17.575 ff. mentions a son of Eetion named Podes as having been killed by Menelaus at Troy and *Iliad* 22:469–72 has Hector taking Andromache from Eeetion after giving *hedna*.

28. Vester (2009: 296 n. 14), argues reasonably that in Euripides *Andromache* lines 1–4, the marriage of Andromache is portrayed as if it were legitimate. However, most importantly for her argument, Vester translates *paidopoieō* in line 4 as "to make legitimate children" citing:

Using later Greek terminology, the "gifts" from fathers received by Penelope and Andromache are *phernē*, not *proix* (dowry; Westbrook 2005: esp. 7–11; similarly Penelope's *eedna* in *Odyssey* 1.277–78, 2.196–97).[29] Penelope had received slaves from her father (*Odyssey* 4.736, 23.227–28) and the precious brooch she presented to Odysseus when he departed belonged to her personal property (*Odyssey* 19.256–57). Although, the term *peculium* is Latin, it is clear that heroic and classical Greece knew slaves with significant personal assets. Eumaeus, the purchased swineherd himself purchased a slave with his own property (*kteatessin*; *Odyssey* 14.115, 14.452). In classical Greece, the best attested example is, of course, Neaira (Demosthenes 59.30–31, 45–46, 49) but also the slave-wife Archippe (Chapter XIX.2).[30] However, a fragment of Euripides's *Andromeda* explicitly refers to a wealthy slave:

> Gold is what I most desire to have in my house. A man who is rich gets respect even if he is a slave [*doulos*], while a free man who is needy has no power. You better believe that gold is what makes you successful (Fragment 142; tr. Collard and Cropp *LCL*).

The same practice would apply when the bride sold herself directly to her husband. Thus, when Chrusis, Demeas's *pallakē*-wife (she is his *gunē* and *gameton hetairan*), first came to him she had only a "plain dress" but when he drove her out (divorced her), she left with all her possessions, two servants, and gold(?) (Menander, "The Girl from Samos" 129–30, 379–82, 561). Sommerstein (2014: 20) adds that the "Mytilene mosaic, depicting the scene of her expulsion ... depicts her sumptuously dressed and bejeweled." Further, Demeas's dire forecast of Chrusis's future life shows that he freed her—that is, Chrusis became once gain her own *kuria* (*Samia* 390 ff.; cf. Fantham 1975: 65–66). It does seem that Demeas turned over to Chrusis her purchase price (*peculium*) and apparently added some interest (380 ff.; Demosthenes 27.17, 59.52).[31]26,27 In an example from the orators, Neaira was permitted to keep

(1) Demosthenes 59.17 whereas, in the context of the Athenian marriage law, it must mean "to make any child, legitimate or not"; and (2) Diogenes Laertius 2.5.26 whereas, in the context of Socrates "bigamous" marriage to Xanthippe, it arguably means "to make a lawful son (a *nothos*)" (Chapter XIX.1).

29. For evidence of the practice of dowry in Homer, see *Iliad* 22.46–51 and Ormand's (2014a: 240–41) discussion.

30. For classical Athens, note the *skytotomos* "leather worker" Aristarchus, the confiscated (arguably living apart) slave of Adeimantus, whose property is listed below his name in the Attic Stelai of 415 BCE (*IG* I^2 426.24–39).

31. Based solely on her being called *hetaira* (20–21), E. Cohen (2015: 100–01) uses the Demeas/Chrusis divorce settlement as an illustration of proceeds from "whoring under contract." A possible problem is that Chrusis is also called *gunaikos* (561) and *pallakē* **(508).**

In discussing the examples of Archippe and Kleoboulē, Hunter (1989: 43) notes, "in both cases ... women alone and widows are in possession of money or property as long as they are on their own, but lose full control of it when they take a husband who is their *kyrios*." However, when they emerge from *pallakia* the women resume control of this money and property plus additional money from their former *kurios*. The additional money, perhaps a contractual "the clothing and the jewels and the maid-servants; for these had been bought [by Phrynion] for the use of the woman herself" (Demosthenes 59.46; tr. DeWitt and DeWitt *LCL*). Although legally a slave, a *pallakē* was viewed by the Athenian authorities as having a rightful claim on wealth given/paid to her by her owner-husband.[32]

There is some tantalizing evidence that the *pallakē*'s purse may have had a specific Greek name. In a fragment of a play by Menander (*Fabula Incerta* 5 Arnott), as Sommerstein (2014: 16) reports:

> [A] woman gives some clothes and jewelry to Moschion and Parmenon, to be pawned for 1,000 drachmae which can then be used for the benefit of another woman, Dorkion, as a "contribution to her *sōtēria*."

A *sōtēria* appears to be a personal fund or purse of "savings"/"deliverance" (LSJ s.v.). The most obvious, but not the only use of such a fund, would be for a slave (including a slave-wife) to purchase her freedom. Sommerstein (2014: 62) suggests that as the two men enter the house of Dorkion and speak to her, "she can hardly be a slave (else where is her owner?)" However, Dorkion can be a privileged or autonomous slave, a class to which the *pallakē* belongs.

There is an explicit reference to self-sale into marriage in Plautus's *Casina* (80 ff.):

> The girl (Casina) whom the slaves seek as their wife ... will turn out to be both chaste and free, a freeborn Athenian, and indeed she won't commit anything in the way of fornication, at least not in this comedy. But soon, when the play has reached its end, I suspect that if anyone gives her money (*argentum*) she'll marry (*nuptum*) him willingly and won't wait for the augurs (tr. de Melo *LCL*).

The slaves wanted her in marriage when she was a slave and then as a free citizen, she finds it to her advantage and consents to becoming a slave-wife. The Greek original of the comedy is said to be by Diphilus and the fact is that Plautus refers to the way things happened in Athens or at least in Athenian plays. The chaste Athenian Casina may be identified, I submit, with Athens's "Spinning *Hetaira*" (see Chapter XI).

---

requirement, might be referred to as "indirect dowry" but "indirect bride-price [*dōra*]" seems more accurate.

32. According to Cicero (*Topics* 23), when a woman became a *manus*-wife, all her property became her husband's dowry (but compare Gaius *Institutes* 2.98, 3.83). As Frier and McGinn (2004: 91) note, this should mean the wife could recover her property when the marriage ended by one means or another.

XI. Wealth Transfers in the Greek Marriage Market: The Spinning *Hetaira*

In mentioning "those who give their womenkind to others as *pallakia*," Isaeus 3.39 reveals that classical Athens was familiar with bride-sale/purchase. At the same time, however, evidence has been presented that classical Athens and the ancient Greek world generally were familiar with women living outside male-headed households (single women) who, being in their own hands, might legally sell themselves into marriage (auto-*ekdosis*). It is argued below that a much-discussed classical Athenian "genre scene" (Ferrari 2002: 26 ff.; Keuls 1983: 227) in Greek pottery paintings depicts the practice of self-sale into *pallakia*.

The reference is to scenes in which men offer a money pouch with a drooping top (*ballantion*) to a respectably clad young woman who is spinning. For example, a now-lost alabastron [formerly Berlin, Staatliche Museen F2254] "on which three figures appear: a seated and diligently spinning veiled woman (her head is covered but hair shows through the shoulder-length veil), a young man draped in a himation who holds a purse out to her, and a standing woman holding a *kalathos* [wool basket]. A second *kalathos* rests behind the spinning woman's chair, while a lekythos and mirror hang in the field" (Bundrick 2008: 299; cf. Ferrari 2002: pls. 3–4).[1] Similarly, Plate 6 depicts a youth leaning on a staff while holding out a money pouch to a fully clad woman who is seated on a chair spinning.

Such scenes "brought into existence the 'spinning hetaira,' who has cast her shadow since over every nameless spinster on the vases" (Ferrari 2002: 12–13 with references

1. "Traditionally, it [the *kalathos*] has been seen as the sign of an industrious wife ... The scene on an amphora by the Providence Painter [Cambridge, Massachusetts, Harvard University, Sackler Museum 1972.45] ... [shows] a woman wearing a headdress ... admiring a wreath given to her as a gift by the man facing her, a *kalathos* is placed between them and the red wool is overflowing out of the basket. In this vein, a *kalathos* appears as an ambiguous symbol of female sexuality" (Fischer 2013: 243–44). Must a respectable married woman be sexually restrained? As Lacey (1968: 113) points out, Demosthenes 59.122 (quoted in Chapter III) "does not state that we cannot have either pleasure or care of our persons from our wives—quite the reverse; the services to a man of the three classes of woman are intended cumulatively, and it is the purpose of the argument merely to stress that you can beget legitimate children only from a properly married wife." McClure (2015: 58) refers in this connection to "domesticated eroticism." Already in the seventh century BCE, Semonides of Amorgos (*Poem* 7) contrasted the ideal wife (Bee-woman) who doesn't enjoy sitting with other wives "discussing sex" (92–93) and also referred to the "sex-crazed" (53) wife (tr. Svarlien *Diotima* available for download at http://www.stoa.org/diotima/anthology/sem_7.shtml).

Plate 6. Athenian hydra of mid-fifth century BCE featuring a seated spinning woman being offered a purse by a standing youth (once Horsfall, 1918.355). Manchester, Manchester Art Gallery amphora 1918.346 (Manchester Art Gallery, UK/Bridgeman Images).

to the literature).[2] What do such scenes actually depict? To begin the analysis, note a number of scenes in which a money pouch may reasonably be understood as being offered by a customer (male or female) to a vendor (male or female) in payment for a commodity (an albastron, an eel, wreaths, olive oil, pottery) or, possibly, for the services of musicians (Harvard 1977.216.2236; S. Lewis 2002: 93–95, 196; Fischer 2013: 240–41). Thus, the simplest explanation for the spinning scene would be that the man is offering to purchase the woman's textiles.

One difficulty with this kind of explanation is that while the scene depicts the act of spinning, finished textiles are not displayed. That the man is trying to hire the woman to work in his textile firm is possible but seems to be a stretch. In another scene, a seated fully clad woman who holds up a large *kalathos* is accompanied by a man holding a money pouch and Eros who holds a handloom and an aulos "flute" (once Stettin, now lost Vogell Collection; cf. Bundrick 2008: 323–24 with fig. 15). In this example, one may suppose that textiles are being offered for sale. However, it is most difficult to explain why a marital/romantic and celebratory interest (in the forms of Eros and the flute) should be injected if the woman is marketing textiles or textile-making labor services.[3] Textiles are part of the answer but what is being negotiated is more personal and intimate. Presently, there are two main lines of interpretation of the Spinning *Hetaira*.

Fischer (2013) has accentuated the unrespectable aspects of the spinning woman scenes: they depict men hiring the services of prostitutes. To make this perspective credible Fischer (2013: 219–29) constructs an economic model of textile work carried out within the prostitution industry and/or a model of prostitution work carried out within the textile industry:

> Prostitutes spun yarn and made small textiles, such as headdresses, on portable frames while they waited for customers, and these particular wool-working tasks were purposely chosen for their simplicity, cost-effectiveness, and the maneuverability of the paraphernalia on which they labored. The free courtesans may have sought an appearance of respectability, while their lower-class equivalents worked between customers to provide for their own clothing needs and to supplement their earnings. The brothel slaves, on the other hand, were forced to labor both as prostitutes and as wool workers, and seemed to have worked wool on a greater scale than smaller establishments or independent free prostitutes because of their larger numbers and better organization.

2. "Another *example of a spinning prostitute* is a Heidelberg Red figure hydra [Heidelberg inv. 64.5], which portrays a [bareheaded] seated woman at task ... In front of her is another woman wearing a headdress and holding a yarn of wool and behind her is a portable braiding frame. To the left is a man with a moneybag and behind him a servant girl balancing a hydra on her head" (Fischer 2013: 240 with fig. 4; emphasis added). Both textile-working women are fully clad.
3. Fischer (2013: 235) sees the flute and Eros as evidence that the woman is a prostitute: the flute produced "lewd music and deformed the face in the process." This argument goes nowhere.

Fischer's sinuous model does not make clear why "brothel slaves" could not have been profitably employed full-time in textile work/in prostitution work. It is also possible to wonder whether subjecting "brothel slaves" to textile work on a commercial scale would have tired them and, hence, made the women less capable of commanding the fees expected for professional sex objects. In the *Anthologia Palatina*, quoted earlier, there are references to women, Bitto (6.47, 48) and Nicarete (6.285), who left full-time textile production to become full-time prostitutes.[4] Bitto and Nicarete are probably fictional but even so, they are more convincing than Fischer's prostitutes who are also textile workers.

More basically, while Fischer's prostitution theory can explain the money pouch held by a man it struggles to explain the depiction of the woman being "propositioned" with a money pouch. That the depicted woman is respectable is signaled by a strong combination of features: she spins (Beazley 1931: 121), wears a veil (Llewellyn-Jones 2007: 256) and, most importantly, is fully and modestly dressed.

Fischer's (2013: 219–20) suggestion is that "free *courtesans* may have sought an appearance of respectability" (emphasis added; cf. Jenkins and Williams 1985: 416). However, it is most doubtful that, whatever the pretensions of their subjects, Greek artists would have chosen to give prostitutes in a brothel (or "courtesans") the appearance of respectability. As pointed out by S. Lewis (2002: 102), the profession of prostitution called for display of the prostitute's body so that customers could see what they were buying. Eubulus (cited by Athenaeus 13.24f p. 568) describes:

> Thrifty decoys, who gather in the money, well-trained fillies of Aphrodite, standing naked in line, clad in transparent robes of thinnest web, like the fair damsels whom Eridanus waters with his holy stream; from whom, with safety and frugality, you may buy pleasure at a moderate cost (tr. Yonge *Perseus Project*).

Similarly, Philemon in *The Brothers* (cited by Athenaeus 13.24g p. 569) cites a law of Solon that set up brothels around Athens in which customers could

> see in the light of the sun a willing row of naked damsels, standing all arrayed In robes transparent, like the damsels whom Eridanus waters with his holy stream, and buy some pleasure at a trifling rate (tr. Yonge *Perseus Project*).

Of course, the point being made here is not whether Solon really set up brothels (how did his brothels differ from the others?) but rather of how contemporary brothels marketed their merchandise. Horace (*Satires* 2.7.48) also describes the advantage of the

4. E. Cohen's (2015: 51) believes, "substantial evidence suggests that numerous female slaves functioned as wool workers and as brothel prostitutes" There is no substantial evidence. In discussing prostitution at Corinth, Strabo 8.6.2 reports, "a certain courtesan said to the woman who reproached her with the charge that she did not like to work or touch wool: 'Yet, such as I am, in this short time I have taken down three webs'" (tr. Jones *LCL*). The point is surely that prostitutes/courtesans did not typically participate in cloth production.

brothel wherein women are exposed naked in bright light so that the client must know exactly what he is purchasing (Griffin 1986: 104). Indeed, Fischer (2013: 223) elsewhere notes, "[i]n vase painting, prostitutes were easily recognizable due to their nudity, which was not the social norm, and when depicted usually implied sexual activity."[5]

For some scholars "spinning and textile activity have become synonymous with prostitution" (see E. Cohen 2015: 52). Nevertheless, the prostitution explanation of the spinning *hetaira* is difficult to accept not least because it cannot explain why a prostitute would be depicted as fully clad, wearing a veil and spinning. Juggling the words "prostitute" and "courtesan" merely avoids this interpretative problem.

That a man offers a money pouch to a woman doing textile work does not make her a seller of sexual favors. Of course, as already noted, some single women were tempted to become prostitutes. This transformation is illustrated In Terence's *The Woman from Andros* (69 ff.):

> At first she lived a virtuous life, sparing and thrifty, earning her living by spinning wool. But when a lover approached her offering money, first one and then another, human nature being always inclined to prefer pleasure to toil, she accepted the offers and took up the profession (tr. Barsby *LCL*).

Bundrick (2008: 299–300) has accentuated the respectable features of the spinning woman scenes: They depict, she suggests, a married household in which

5. Fischer (2013: 241) provides more convincing depictions of prostitution: "The Makron cup portrays six courting couples: on side A, a woman is climbing on top of a seated man and on Side B a couple is kissing, a mirror and a flute-case are visible on the wall and a few of the men are holding purses. Finally, a lost tondo on a Munich vase pictured a nude couple copulating ... with a purse hanging on the wall behind them..." More subtly, note San Antonio Texas, San Antonio Museum of Art 86.134.59 (Reeder 1995: 181–82). The textile working theme is absent from these scenes. There is also a more questionable example. Fischer (2013: 238) cites a hydria by the Washing Painter (Copenhagen, National Museum VIII.520) which depicts "a woman nude but for a thigh amulet, and spinning in the presence of another [clothed] woman, most likely a madam. What identifies her as a prostitute, besides her nudity, is the thigh amulet, which was used in the practice of aggressive erotic magic" (cf. E. Cohen 2015: 52, Reeder 1995: 216–17; compare S. Lewis 2002: 104). if thigh amulets were use for "aggressive erotic magic" then ordinary women practiced it as well (Aristophanes *Thesmophoriazousa* 256). Female nudity, however, deserves respect as an iconographic symbol. Still, I find the scene puzzling. Is the madam instructing the prostitute in spinning? Why does the madam allows her prostitute to keep her clothes on the chair behind her? The obvious implication is that the clothes were removed to do the weaving and will be put back on when this task is completed. Is this a fetish peculiar to this madam? Note that females were depicted nude washing themselves at a fountain house or at a portable basin, at the nuptial bath, in the gymnasium, and in initiations into certain cults, for example of Artemis. However, why weave in the nude? In Callimachus's *Aetia* 66 there is a description of an "Argive practice where women wove a robe for Hera, but only after they sit down on a rock in the fountain of the water nymph Anymone and pour water over their heads" (MacLachlan 2004). It seems possible (even reasonable) that the women would remove their clothes before bathing and then perform symbolic weaving before getting dressed again. In this case, the seated figure is either Hera or Anymone.

> [T]he husband makes his contribution to the household (money) and the wife makes hers (textiles) ... The scenes also recall the fact that many women would have had charge of the family's finances, looking after money and household expenses even though their capacity to engage in public transactions was limited ... The men's gesture on the vases, handing over control of the money pouches to the women, demonstrates respect and trust in their wives' managerial abilities.

Bundrick makes a coherent and reasonable argument but the man and woman do not look like husband and wife. Indeed, it is possible to wonder whether an artist would depict a wife working in her home and seen only by her husband wearing a veil or otherwise formally dressed.[6] Further, some related scenes clearly represent courtship (e.g. the presentation of a flower to the spinning woman), not the familial division of labor between husband and wife. Also, as will be seen shortly, some of the relevant scenes better fit a textile workshop or a single woman's home than a married woman's home. Simpler, more direct explanations are available which are recommended by Occam's razor.

My hypothesis is that the Spinning *Hetaira* scenes depict men in the act of bidding for the wifeship of explicitly respectable unmarried women. As S. Lewis (2002: 196–97) puts it, the scenes refer to courtship, persuasion, and negotiation. The women being "courted" with money pouches represent themselves, no other males are present. The spinning hetairai are in fact *hetairai*—by which I mean that they are single women who are in their own hands, like those portrayed in Menander's comedies or the one spoken of in the fragment of Antiphanes's *Hydra* (see Chapter IX). Upon the completion of a successful purchase the spinning woman = single woman in her own hands, became a *pallakē*. The money pouch is the *dōra* presented to the self-selling bride (see Chapter X). It represents her *peculium*. The propositioned women have much more in common with Homer's Penelope who offered to sell herself to the highest bidding suitor than with prostitutes/courtesans (compare Ferrari 2002: 20).

In what appears to be a variation on the Spinning *Hetaira* theme, a youth leaning on a walking stick offers a pomegranate (or a pomegranate-shaped pot) to a fully clad seated woman whose head is veiled (Athens, National Archaeological Museum TE1623; Sutton 2004: 342 with fig. 17.12a). In Greek myth (Hera/Persephone), the pomegranate serves as a wedding gift and eating it (taking it) represents acceptance of the marriage contract (Foster 1899: 45 ff.) In Cambridge, Massachusetts, Harvard

6. With respect to how wives dressed in the privacy of their homes, note McClure's (2015: 58) comments on the depiction of a family group (Cambridge, Massachusetts, Harvard University, Sackler Museum 1960.342): "To the right a young husband stands dressed in a cloak and carrying a walking stick. He looks on as a seated woman passes a male infant to another woman at left ... The wreath draws attention to the seated woman and perhaps alludes to her wedding or the birth of her son ... Note that the drapery of the seated woman is semi-transparent, showing the outline of her left arm ... This is the *chitōn* (long tunic). A generic term for the finely woven undergarment worn by women at home and almost completely covered by a mantle when outdoors ..." On the significance of the passing of the male child in weddings, see Reilly (1989: 426–27).

University Art Museum 1972.45 a fully dressed woman sits in front of a *kalathos* admiring a garland or ribbon given to her by a man with a long walking stick who seems to be extolling his gift to her. I see courtship, not prostitution (compare Reeder 1995: 182–83). A scene of the fifth century BCE from Pisticci in southern Italy shows a young man who leans on his walking stick while offering a necklace drawn from a small casket to a respectably clad young woman; the latter turns away from work on her loom to appraise the offering; the transaction is witnessed by a young man holding a spear who stands behind the apparent suitor (Meo 2019: 81 fig. 1; Barber 1991: 110 with fig. 3.28). The scene may be identified as referring to the purchase of Harmonia by Cadmus the Phoenician founder of Thebes, although none of the figures bear a label. The suitor wears the fine pilos favored by upper class travelers such as Odysseus (Pipili 2000: 174) and Cadmus when he confronts the snake (dragon) at the spring (Paris, Musée du Louvre N 3157; cf. Boston, Museum of Fine Arts 69.1142). The spear held by the man behind the suitor signals the transactional nature of the scene. Of course, other interpretations of the "Necklace of Harmonia/Eriphyle" are possible.[7]

In another variation on the Spinning *Hetaira* theme, a young man leaning on a staff offers a scarf to a fully dressed woman who sits before a *kalathos* looking down at a wreath she is making as a small female figure (a "maid") looks on holding an albastron (Paris, Cabinet des Médailles 508; Reilly 1989: 425 with pl. 80a; Sutton 1997/98: 31; Bundrick 2008: 31). An inscription refers to the man as "handsome Timodemos" and the seated female is *numphē kalē*, which might mean "pretty bride," but since the woman is being courted (not yet married) the better translation is "pretty young woman."

Sutton (1981: 280) might object that there is no literary evidence of courtship gifts leading to marriage. However, this would ignore the ample literary evidence (cited above) of citizen women being given in marriage in return for a gift/payment from the suitor. Indeed, it is possible to understand the offer of the money pouch as a display of the suitor's affection for the woman. He must have met her at least once previously. Why, after all, proposition this woman and not another.[8]

7. Lyons (2016: 93) says, "Eriphyle is bribed with a necklace to betray her husband," citing *Osyssey* 11.521. However, *Odyssey* 11.521 says, "the prince Eurypylus! Aye, and many of his comrades, the Ceteians, were slain about him, because of gifts (*dōron*) a woman craved" and *Odyssey* 11.326–27 is more explicit: "And Maera and Clymene I saw, and hateful Eriphyle, who took precious gold (*chruson*) as the price of the life of her own lord" (tr. Forster *LCL*). Perhaps Homer had a necklace in mind, perhaps not (Duffy 2013: 42). (Homer mentions gold necklaces in *Odyssey* 15.459–60 and 18.295–96.) Pausanias (9.41.3) renders *Odyssey* 11.327: "She received precious gold in exchange for a precious husband" (tr. Duffy 2013: 40) which fits very well the sale of Eriphyle into *pallakia*. In Malibu, California, Getty Museum 78.AE.256 a pursuing satryr offers a jewelry box to an interested maenad.

8. In yet another variation on the theme of the Spinning *Hetaira*, a youth approaches a seated respectably clad spinning woman carrying a hare and a wreath (Athens, Acropolis Museum 2713). In this case, we may understand that the hare is a symbol of the hunt or better of pursuit including sexual pursuit (Schnapp 1989). Unfortunately, Schnapp (1989: 82) who documents well the connection of the hare with Eros misunderstands the pursuit of the woman: "The

The *pallakē*-wife interpretation of the spinning scenes is reinforced by a column-krater of the Harrow painter (Museo Nazionale Etrusco di Villa Giulia 1054, ca. 480) depicting a young man leaning on a walking stick who holds a money pouch and faces a young woman holding a lotus flower. Both individuals are fully clothed and they are flanked by two floating erotes who adorn them with fillets that are known to have played a role in a ritual welcoming couples to their new home (Sutton 1997/1998: 34). The erotes, like the lotus flower, are familiar in nuptial scenes (S. Lewis 2002: 196 with fig. 5.18; Bundrick 2012: 22–23; Sutton 1997/98: 32). The scene also includes a *kalathos* (wool basket) and a hunting dog, perhaps a reference to the cult of Artemis (Chapter XIV.4) or to a location in the countryside or to both. A similar scene, but without erotes and *kalathos* (but with an albastron), is depicted on an Attic funerary urn (British Museum 1914.5–12.1; S. Lewis 2002: 194 with fig. 5.15).

Another scene (Chicago, Art Institute 1911.456) deserves full description:

> More brazen behavior appears on a hydria by the Leningrad Painter, dating to ca. 460–450: a wreathed, beardless man bending to kiss and fondle a peplos-clad young woman forms the compositional focus ... The gesture, certainly unusual in a domestic setting, seems at first glance more characteristic of a sympotic or komastic scene. At left stand another draped young man with staff and a draped woman, both watching the couple at center. At right appears a second draped woman, holding up the edge of her himation as though she has just walked into the scene. In her left hand she holds a hand loom or textile frame; these objects appear more frequently than standing warp-weighted looms in textile production scenes and may have been used for smaller embroidered textiles or even sprang hairnets (Bundrick 2008: 298–99 with fig. 7).

Fischer (2013: 236), observes that the breasts of the woman carrying the handloom are fully drawn. The money pouch is missing but not the symbols of textile production. It occurs to me that the depiction is of a, possibly impromptu, gathering of unrelated individuals to celebrate the engagement of the purchaser and his chosen *pallakē*. The

---

woman spinning in her chair is the very symbol of the mistress of the house, the woman of the interior. This is not, however, a scene of married life, as the archaeologists of the nineteenth century imagined. The woman spinning in this modest pose is a hetaira who, by identifying herself with the wife, adds grater worth and distinction to her seduction." This is informed delusion.

Sutton (1981: 356) notes the "voice of a woman herself, Sappho, who has left a fragment in which a girl laments to her mother that she cannot weave because Aphrodite and desire for a boy have distracted her." Therefore, we take it that respectable Greek girls did see boys. Men and women attended weddings and other events together (Oakley and Sinos 1993: 22: Burton 1998). In addition, both utilized the public fountain houses (Keuls 1983: 210 ff.; Bérard 1989: 95–96 with Figure 130). Theophrastus (*Characters* 22) tells of the man who "Even though his wife brought him a dowry, he doesn't buy her a slave-girl, but rents from the women's market a slave to go along when she leaves the house" (tr. Rusten *LCL*). Apparently, legitimate wives went outdoors even if in the company of rented slaves.

woman performing the *anakalypsis* or "wedding gesture" plays the role of spectator or protective bridesmaid.

Fischer (2013: 242) refers to a hydria by the Orpheus Painter (New York, Metropolitan Museum 17.230.15) that shows a "brothel scene" wherein

> a woman is busy spinning. Eros holds her slippers and is watching another woman interacting with her client, who is intimately grabbing her shoulder. It appears that Eros is about to hand her the slippers so that she can leave the residence with her client. A headdress is hanging on the wall and an empty wool basket is about to be refilled by a third woman.

I see unrelated individuals and textile work but no "brothel" and no "clients." The Metropolitan Museum provides the following label for the scene: "Eros presenting shoes to bride, surrounded by the groom, two other men, and four women." Eros is sometimes depicted in the act of fastening the bride's sandals (Boston, Museum of Fine Arts 95.1402).

There is perhaps additional pictorial evidence for men bidding successfully for *pallakē*-wives. An Attic red-figure *kylix* (Toledo, Ohio, Toledo Museum of Art 72.55) on the outside shows two fully clad women, one standing one seated, being offered money pouches by two men. The interior shows an elegantly and fully clad woman pouring wine over a flaming altar. Reeder (1995: 185–86) provides additional details of the scene:

> As the woman pours wine on the altar, she clasps the *kanoun* or ritual basket ... The *kanoun* contained the tools of sacrifice ... In religious processions, the *kanoun* was carried only by girls of marriageable age, with whom these baskets were closely identified ... If the tondo depicts an unmarried Athenian maiden of good birth, her counterparts on the underside provide a sharp social contrast, although the painter has intentionally adorned them in a similar fashion. Two hetairai share the hairstyle of the *kanephoros* and all of the hetairai are dressed comparably to her, even to the gathered neckline of their chitons. Absent, however, on the underside is the stylish striping of the tondo figure's mantle, as well its elegant and probably ritualistic draping on both shoulders.

Beard (1991: 30 with figs. 7, 8) comments:

> This intrusion of the wife into the world of the hetaira necessarily raises the question of whether the division can so easily be maintained. Simply to see the wife where you expect to see the hetaira is to begin to question the validity (or reality) of the stereotype.

Neils (2000: 218) sees the libating woman as a courtesan

> making a thank offering to Aphrodite for past commercial success, and perhaps praying for more to come. An offering to Aphrodite Pandemos would not be amiss after the attentions of the rich men on the exterior of the cup, and, if this were the case, all three scenes would relate to a common theme.

Again, what needs explanation is why the artist has chosen to depict the propositioned women on the exterior as fully dressed instead of nude. Proper analysis requires iconographic symbols to have stable meanings. Elsewhere, Neils (2000: 224) recognizes that "without nudity as a guide it becomes difficult to recognize hetairai," by which she means "courtesans," but she believes that "close reading" will discern the intentions of the artist. What I see in the scene is a *hetaira*, who is a respectable single woman, transformed by self-sale into an expensively dressed *pallakē*-wife who dutifully honors a deity, even Aphrodite as would be expected for a bride (Rozenzweig 2004: 75–77).[9] Alternatively, the bride honors the gods of her new *oikos*.

Next, we come to the possible significance of the *krēdemnon* ("literally head-binder") worn by the Spinning *Hetaira*. This type of veil is worn over the hair and hangs down on both sides covering the cheeks. Such a veil was worn by Andromache in the *Iliad* (22.468–72):

> Far from off her head she [Andromache] cast the bright attiring thereof, the frontlet and coif and kerchief and woven band, and the veil [*krēdemnon*] that golden Aphrodite had given her on the day when Hector of the flashing helm led her as his bride forth from the house of [her father] Eetion, after he had brought bride-gifts [*hedna*] past counting (tr. Murray *LCL*).

Significantly, when Penelope presents herself for sale to the suitors for *dōra* she wears the *krēdemnon* (*Odyssey* 18.206–310). Homer links the *krēdemnon* with Aphrodite and marriage and with wealth transfers.

It is a leap from "heroic Greece" to classical Athens but one may entertain the hypothesis that the depictions of the Spinning *Hetaira* show simultaneously the man's proposition (represented by the money pouch or other offering) and that the *hetaira* has offered herself on the marriage market (represented by her wearing of the *krēdemnon*). The scenes reveal both the demand and the supply. With respect to spinning, the production of textiles is the quintessential occupation of the married woman. Hence, skill in textile production would be an important factor in determining the *dōra* offered by suitors. It is in Chapter XIV that the connection of textile work to the respectable single woman living on her own was of a more basic and immediate nature: *hetairai* had to earn their living and many/most accomplished this by producing textiles for the market.

9. As in Chapter IX, in the *Anthologia Palatina* (6.208 Antipater) three "citizen (*astai*) *hetairai*" jointly dedicate a portrait of Aphrodite to celebrate their marriages.

XII. Companionship as an Adaptation to the Dangerous Life of the Single Woman

A law of Solon, cited in Demosthenes 59.67, affirms that a man cannot be convicted of *moicheia*—"adultery"—for having sexual relations with women who either "sit" or "reside" (*kathēmi*) in a "workshop" or "place of work" (*ergastērion*) or "who walk to and fro in the open" (*pōlōntai* [or *pōlōsi ti*] *apopephasmenōs*; tr. DeWitt and DeWitt modified; cf. J.N. Davidson 1997: 328 with n. 13; Johnstone 2002). Even as slanted by the speaker,[1] it is apparent that both clauses of the law concern much more significant matters then whether a purchaser of sexual acts may be found guilty of having an adulterous relationship with his provider.[2]

The second clause of the cited law refers to women who "wander around" (Lysias 10.19), which must refer to circulating female vendors/peddlers (Johnstone 2002: 236, 247, 253; Silver 1992: ch. 6). The first clause may refer to female shopkeepers (Johnstone 2002: 253–54) but also it may refer to working women who literally resided in a workplace (*ergastērion*). Of course, Solon's law would pertain to the prostitute (*pornē*, male form *pornos*) who resided in a *porneion* "brothel" (Kapparis 2011: 255), a distinct kind of workplace, or who solicited on the streets. The intent of "Solon's law" is that a man cannot be punished for "adultery" for having sexual relations with any woman, whether prostitute or not, who makes a living on her own and in so doing

1. "Sitting" brings to mind the prostitute who openly solicits by sitting in a chair in front of the brothel (Adams 1983: 329).
2. Kapparis (2011: 226) considers *ergastērion* to be "the oldest attested Greek word for brothel." However, Johnstone (2002: 248), notes, "there are no known parallels from the classical period for using *ergasterion* to mean brothel." Kapparis (2011: 226) supports his position by noting that the Greeks regarded prostitution as "work": "However, it is remarkable that all terminology referring to prostitution or 'work' applies to female prostitution exclusively: there is no equivalent terminology for male prostitutes." Of course, female prostitutes worked, of course male prostitutes worked, and of course, some workplaces were places where sex-workers worked. However, when Apollodorus (Demosthenes 59.113) warns that citizen women might earn their living as prostitutes he says *pornōn ergasia*—"prostitute work"—not simply *ergasia*—"work." We also know that the women who annually lived together and wove the figured *peplos* (dress, more generally, rectangular woolen cloth) for Athena at the Panathenaia are called *Ergastini*. Such Athenian archaeological evidence as we have suggests a pattern (not a fixed rule) in which buildings combine workshops with residences (Kakavoyannis 2001: 376; Tsakirgis 2005: esp. 79; J.E. Jones 2007; Demosthenes 37.4; cf. Jameson 1977–78: 135–36). Larger facilities of this kind were typically referred to as *ergasteria*.

willingly interacts with strange men (cf. Plutarch *Solon* 23.1). The latter group would potentially include the majority of single women/*hetairai*.

This is significant because *moicheia* apparently includes forcible as well as consensual sexual relations (Gomme and Sandbach 1973: 612 on Menander "The Girl from Samos" 717) and, further, that the penalty was more severe than for "simple" rape of a free woman (Cole 1984a: esp. 100–01). According to Plutarch, Solon's laws had permitted

> an adulterer caught in the act to be killed; but if a man committed rape (*harpazō*) upon a free woman, he was merely to be fined a hundred drachmas; and if he gained his end by persuasion, twenty drachmas (*Solon* 23.1; tr. Perrin *LCL*).

Moreover, in the absence of corroborating evidence of forcible rape, the authorities might routinely assume that a single woman was a willing partner. Dismissal of rape charges would be automatic in cases of "date rape"—that is, when the single woman was socially acquainted with the rapist.

The implication of these considerations is that the legal system provided all single women, not only prostitutes, with much less protection against sexual assault than women within male-headed households. This relative leniency would become an even greater problem when the prevailing ideology was prone to equate single women with prostitutes. That this was the case is attested in Plutarch (*Solon* 15.2–3), who explains the term *hetaira* as a euphemism: "Now *later writers* observe that the ancient Athenians used to cover up the ugliness of things with auspicious and kindly terms, giving them polite and endearing names," for example, "they called harlots (*pornas*) 'companions' (*hetairas*)" (tr. Perrin *LCL*; emphasis added). In addition, Demosthenes (59.122) may be equating the single woman with the prostitute when he says, "we keep *hetairai* for the sake of pleasure" but omits mention of *pornai*—"prostitutes".

The life of a young woman (or, indeed, of any woman) who lived alone must have been rather difficult. The dangers are illustrated on an Attic red-figure pot (New York, Metropolitan Museum 37.11.19) depicting a rowdy man pounding at night on the exterior door of a house behind which is an obviously frightened woman who does not know how to respond (Sutton 2004: 331–33 with Fig. 17.3). Theophrastus (*Characters* 28) has the "Slanderer" tell that,

> These women snatch men passing from the street ... This house practically has its legs in the air ... They'll always talk to men ... These women answer their own front door (tr. Rusten *LCL*).

One caveat ignored in the "Slanderer's" testimony is that not every respectable Athenian woman could afford a slave, much less a burly male doorkeeper, capable of dealing with dangerous situations (compare Neils 2000: 210–11).[3] Theophrastus

3. Presumably, a brothel would employ a burly doorkeeper or "bouncer". In the *Iliad* (18.495 ff.) the women of the city all stand in front of their doors to behold a wedding procession.

(*Characters* 27) tells of the man who "becomes infatuated with a prostitute, uses a battering ram on her door" but he then adds "and gets a beating from her other lover" (tr. Rusten *LCL*).

In Menander's "The Girl with Her Hair Cut Short" (154–56), Glycera, a respectable *pallakē*-wife, is sexually accosted when she is observed in her doorway while sending a slave on an errand. In Menander's "The Peevish Fellow" (58–68), Sostratos tells his friend Chaireas that he is in love with a *hetaira* and the latter proposes to burn down her door and seize her (*harpazō*) for him. Apparently, he fears no legal consequences for undertaking such an assault. The plot thickens, however, when Chaireas explains that if a friend talks about marriage (*gamon*) with a free (*eleuthera*) girl he inquires about her family, character and financial situation. Glazebrook (2015: 91) reasons, "the mention of *eleuthera* (free) in the second circumstance suggests a *hetaira* of slave status" It is hard to believe, however, that Chaireas would face no penalty for damaging the slave-owner's premises and stealing his property (the "slave," *hetaira*). One might understand *eleuthera* to mean citizen and suggest that the *hetaira* is a foreigner. Alternatively, one might suggest that the two circumstances are independent which leaves open the possibility that the *hetaira* is a citizen but vulnerable as a single woman living alone. For what it is worth, I see a clear reference to legitimate marriage and a comically distorted reference to *pallakē*-marriage complete with seizure of the bride's wrist.

The dangers to single women are illustrated further in Plutarch's *De mulierum virtutibus* ("On the Bravery of Women," 249E–F):

> When the despots in Phocis had seized Delphi, and the Thebans were waging war against them in what has been called the Sacred War, the women devotees of Dionysus, to whom they give the name of Thyads, in Bacchic frenzy wandering at night unwittingly arrived at Amphissa. As they were tired out, and sober reason had not yet returned to them, they flung themselves down in the market-place, and were lying asleep, some here, some there. The wives of the men of Amphissa, fearing, because their city had become allied with the Phocians, and numerous soldiers of the despots were present there, that the Thyads might be treated with indignity, all ran out into the market-place, and, taking their stand round in silence, did not go up to them while they were sleeping, but when they arose from their slumber, one devoted herself to one of the strangers and another to another, bestowing attentions on them and offering them food. Finally, the women of Amphissa, after winning the consent of their husbands, accompanied the strangers, who were safely escorted as far as the frontier (tr. Babbitt *LCL*).

Apparently, unlike single women, women known to have a male *kurios* were reasonably safe even when he was not physically present.[4]

Real life respectable single women find iconographic reflection in the *numphai* "nymphs" or "naiads" or maenads (*mainades*) who are depicted being chased/stalked

4. The theme of the molestation of sleeping nymphs by silens is a common one in Attic vase paintings (discussed below). One may suspect that Plutarch's story about the women of Amphissa is a fiction inspired by vase paintings.

by or fraternizing with satyrs/silens in Attic vase paintings.[5] In the first place, as Larson (2001: 4) notices, the nymphs are typically unencumbered by family ties. For their part, the satyrs with their simian faces, bald masks and animal's tails and ears, are creatures of an entirely different ilk from their maenad companions. "They are theatrical impersonations of what anthropologists call 'man's basal primate urges': hunger, sex and self preservation" (Keuls 1984: 290). Nymphs are depicted protecting themselves from the unwanted advances of silens, by running away or, less frequently, by jabbing their characteristic *thrysoi*—staffs topped with pine cones—at the pursuer's sex organs (Hedreen 1994: 60–63; Lindblom 2007). As noted by Lindblom (2007: 246–47), the conduct of the silens

> does not differ from that of civilized male figures when they are trying to satisfy their sexual passions. But since they are satyrs, they are naturally bound to be exaggeratedly excited and tactless.

However, while all "silens" looked the same they were not regarded as being equal. Single women/*numphai* did their best to be "caught" by those "silens" whom they saw as desirable lovers and husbands. Lindblom (2007: 245) observes:

> Actually, there are examples in the repertoire showing females who seem to have an ambiguous attitude to the harassment of the satyrs. In these representations, the conflicting attitude of the females is expressed by the way in which they are trying to escape and at the same time signaling an approving stance towards the satyr. On some occasions, when the satyr is still at a distance, the ambivalent stance of the woman is marked by an approving look, as if she was just teasing the satyr by trying to resist him. A voluntary approach of the females is also apparent in the scenes in which, without any noticeable resistance, they allow themselves to be carried away by their male escort. Or, in the pictures, the woman meets the eyes of the satyr with a close and tender gaze, which in every respect seems to invite the satyr to closer acquaintance, rather than rejecting him.

In one painting (Harvard Art Museum 1925.30.129), the maenad and the satyr gaze lovingly into each other's eyes while the satyr grasps the maenad's wrist indicating they have agreed to marry. Sometimes women with *thrysoi* are shown with small satyr-like children. Friendly relations between satyrs and nymphs are also depicted on the Siphnian Treasury and the coins of Thasos (Knoblauch 2007: 54–56).

Numphai both with and without Dionsysian attributes[6] have been identified as *hetairai* (Lindblom 2007: 242–43). Nymphs and real single women might be willing to have sexual relations but, unlike prostitutes, only with the *right* silen/satyr or man,

5. For respectable status, Lindblom (2007: 239–40).

6. Nymphs associated with Dionysus are a sub-group of a larger group; there is no evidence demonstrating that the pursuit theme must be linked solely to Dionysus's maenads (Lindblom 2007: 233–34; Hedreen (1992: 72–73). Nevertheless, the nuptial practices of mythical and historical nymphs might differ in significant details from those of maenads.

not with the wrong ones. In myth, as Sourvinou-Inwood (1987: 153) puts it, Atalanta is "the mirror image, a consistent reversal, of the nexus 'erotic pursuit,'" yet the fact remains that she chased her final suitor until he caught and married her.

Nymphs coped with the dangers posed by the wrong silens by living in a geographically isolated "pack/herd/band" (*agelē, choros*).[7] Members of these mythical "packs" were called *hetairai* because they were "companions" to one another.[8] Thus, in a restoration of the text of Bacchylides (13.83 ff.), the young women who sang for the nymph Aegina are called *hetairai*. Significantly, as noted by Calame (1997: 33), in Virgil's *Aeneid* (13.83) the young women accompanying Artemis are *ex virginbus sociis*—that is, they are "companions" (cf. Aristophanes *Knights* 589).

In myth, *admētos*—"untamed"—*parthenoi* under the auspices of Artemis "Mistress of Animals" roam outside normal society in the wild where male "rapists" pursue them. Sometimes they are the pursuers instead of the prey. Often the pursued women or their companions are depicted carrying flowers (Sourvinou-Inwood 1987: 117). Their real-world counterparts are not unmarried women generally, but rather single women. Single woman, as outsiders, are visualized as *captured* by their husbands. Unmarried women in male-headed households are *delivered* to their husbands. Two betrothal roads, one individualistic the other deterministic, converge in *gamos*.[9] The initial step in the nuptial transaction (auto-*ekdosis)* is depicted in Malibu, California, Getty Museum 78.AE.256, wherein a pursuing satyr offers a jewelry box to a fleeing but clearly interested maenad who gazes back and stretches out her hand to meet the satyr's outstretched arm.

"Packs" of single women, like "packs" of young unmarried men had of course religious and educational roles. However, in the case of single women there is also a most realistic protective role. The grouping of nymphs is associated with textile work.

7. Larson (2001: 4) explains: "Surprisingly often, the Greek sources take the trouble to identify nymphs. The clues are easy to miss if, for example, one passes over the formula 'daughter of Aesop's' without realizing that the father mentioned is a river god. More often, the terms naiad and nymph are juxtaposed in order to make the sense unmistakable. This practice begins in Homer and continues as a habit of diction through late authors. Similarly, certain names are typical of nymphs, particularly names containing the element *naïs* (naiad) or those ending in the suffix *-rhoê*, so that they describe the flowing movement of water. Such etymologies are suggestive, but not infallible, indicators ... Nymphs are described with great frequency as the daughters of Zeus, of Ge, or of various river gods. Acheloōs, to some degree a generalized river god, often figures as the father, but many others are also invoked, depending on the region."

8. Neils (2000: 219–26) perceptively associates "maenads" with prostitutes, whom she refers to as *hetairai*. She does not recognize, however, the existence of a broader class of single women (*hetairai*) who were respectable (not prostitutes) *and* sexually active. Neither, does she focus on packs of nymphs as a reflection in myth of the kinds of measures necessary to keep these women safe in ancient Greece.

9. Persephone might be an exception: while on her own in the wild, Hades abducts her with the apparent approval of her father Zeus (*Homeric Hymn to Demeter* 1–32).

> In Greek myth, girls come in packs: the Nereids, the Minyads, the Proetids, and the Danaids to name only a few ... Calame has shown that in myth the paradigm for the band of maidens is Artemis with her nymphs, but in the poetic descriptions cited above another term of comparison is given: Aphrodite and the Graces. In literature the relationship of the goddess is to the Graces and the Horae... The Graces dance with Aphrodite and, together with Horae, bathe and dress her, they weave for her ... This is the key to a better reading of the pictures of the toilet of Aphrodite in a wool-working environment (Ferrari 2002: 45–46).

The association of *hetairai* with live-in textile work is made explicit in the sixth/fifth century by Pindar (*Pythian Ode* 9:15 ff.) when he writes about the naiad Creusa: "She loved not the path walked to and fro before the looms, nor the pleasures of dining with her *oikoriai hetairai* (female housemates)" (tr. Kennedy 2015: 65).[10]

Like nymphs (and Daniads and Amazons), real life single women gravitated to protected group living. Thus,

> On a stele [*CEG* 1.97 and 92 Hansen], a number of *hetairai* declare—as a group!—that they are laying a wreath upon the funerary monument of a certain Anthemis, to celebrate the memory of her virtue (*aretē*) and her fidelity (*philia*) (Calame 1999: 115).

The grouping of single women/*hetairai* manifested itself primarily in live-in workplaces. The latter being found in Athens but also in more isolated locations with good sources of water such as Brauron (discussed in Chapter XIV.4). In such places, away from urban turmoil and confusion, they were protected by Artemis's threats of horrible punishment against those who molested her self-dedicated *parthenoi* (Cole 1998 with references).

10. Elsewhere, Pindar (*Nemean* 5.34–36) refers to Nereids with "golden spindles."

XIII. Role of Cults in the Marriage of Single Women

None of the earlier discussion is to say, however, that marriage in the wild was necessarily completely unstructured. Zeus, after all, assigned to Aphrodite "works of *gamos*" (*Iliad* 5.426).

In Euripides's *Hippolytus* 616–24, Hippolytus complains,

> O Zeus, why have you settled women in the light of the sun, women, this bane mankind find counterfeit? If you wished to propagate the human race, it was not from women that you should have given us this. Rather, men should have put down in the temples either bronze or iron or a mass of gold and have bought offspring, each man for a price corresponding to his means, and then dwelt in houses free from the female sex (tr. Kovacs *LCL*).

Beneath the outer layer of misogyny, I detect a clever reference to the actual role of cults as sellers of babies.

A hint of organized activity in the marriage market in Euripides's *Hippolytus* 1139–40 is provided by the Chorus's reference to "a contest among girls (*kourais*) to be your (Hippolytuss) bride" (tr. Kovacs *Perseus Project* modified). The "contest" must have had a sponsoring agency.

Hippolytus provides explicit evidence that single women belonging to packs were given in marriage by a sponsoring goddess—that is, by her cult.

> That filly in Oechalia [Iole], unjoined as yet to marriage-bed, unhusbanded, unwed, Aphrodite took from the house of her father Eurytus and yoked her *like a footloose [running] Naiad or a Bacchant* and gave her [*exedōken*]—to the accompaniment of bloodshed and smoke, with bloody bridal—to Alcmene's son [Heracles]. O unhappy in her marriage [*numaios*]! (Euripides *Hippolytus* 545–54; tr. Kovacs *Perseus Project*; emphasis added).

The use of *ekdidōmi* indicates that Aphrodite was understood to be the women's *kurios*. That is, in giving them in marriage she acted as legal owner, not merely as an agent (matchmaker) for their consenting fathers (the *kurioi*). Further, since neither their fathers nor Aphrodite first betrothed the women to their future husbands the marriages could not have been legitimate (marriages by loan of the bride). Finally, Iole (explicitly) like a "footloose Naiad or a Bacchant," was outside a male-headed household (Halleran 1991: 113–14) and a good deal of evidence suggests that in the real world the "footloose Naiad" and the "Bacchant" were sold into *pallakia* (marriage by sale of the bride).

Lines 555–64 of *Hippolytus* confirm that Euripides means what he said about Aphrodite's role as *kurios* by having her give Semele in marriage to Zeus:

> Again, Cypris is directly involved in the action, and again, although less extensively, the imagery echoes wedding rituals. Cypris gave Semele as a bride (*numpheusamena*) to the thunder. This word is used here to describe Aphrodite's role in this union (Halleran 1991: 115 with nn. 37, 38; cf. Lloyd-Jones 1971: 342–43).

The evidence does not demonstrate that Semele belonged to a "pack" of single citizen-women. However, it is clear that Aphrodite gave Semele into *pallakia*, not into legitimate marriage. That her mother Harmonia is a *pallakē* has already been argued for in Chapter VI and also Chapter XI).

There is additional suggestive evidence of cultic participation in marriage. In Euripides's fragmentary tragedy *Phaethon* 230–32, the Chorus says, "Hymen. Hymen! We sing to the heavenly daughter of Zeus, the mistress of loves, Aphrodite. Who brings nuptials [*gamēlion*] to *parthenoi*" (tr. Ferrari 2008: 61 slightly modified). Also, Diggle (1970: 152) in his commentary on line 237 in *Phaethon* (citing *Hippolytus* 559–62) confirms that Aphrodite gave Phaethon in marriage. Phaethon had previously rejected his father Merops's "greedy" marriage plan saying, "A free man becomes slave of the marriage-bed who sells his person for a dowry" (158–59) (tr. Reckford 1972: 409). Aphrodite's role as *kurios* is significant because Phaethon's insubordination arguably led to his ejection from his father's *oikos*, as Reckford (1972: 409) explains. Aphrodite dealt with Phaethon as if he, like a meadow-dwelling *numphē* or *parthenos*, were outside a male-headed household. Indeed, Aphrodite arranges Phaethon's marriage in the context of his rejection of legitimate marriage.

Outside Euripides, Fragment 654 of Corinna of Tanagra dated perhaps to the fifth century BCE (Larson 2002), tells that Zeus, Poseidon, Apollo and Hermes took the nine daughters of the river god Asopos as wives. As is attested in lines 18–19, the nine women were assigned explicitly to the gods by Aphrodite: "For so did Eros and the Cyprian prevail, that the Gods go in secret to your house, and take for themselves your daughters nine" (tr. Page 1953: 82–83).

In Pindar's *Ninth Pythian* 1–14, Aphrodite "joins" in "marriage" Cyrene and Apollo (Carson 1982: 122 with citations; discussed in Chapter VI). And, of course, in the *Illiad* 5.427–29, Zeus acknowledges that Aphrodite's specialization within the divine division of labor is not war but *erga gamoio*—"works of marriage" (tr. Murray *LCL*). Diodorus Siculus 5.73.2 is more specific concerning Aphrodite's *erga*:

> To Aphroditê was entrusted the youth of maidens, the years in which they are expected to marry, and the supervision of such matters as are observed even yet in connection with weddings, together with the sacrifices and drink-offerings which men perform to this goddess (tr. Oldfather *LCL*).

A final and significant point is that Aphrodite provides the groom with the "golden apples" for purchasing Atalanta (Apollodorus's *Library* 3.9.2)

In the *Iliad* (3.386 ff.), Aphrodite assigns Helen to Paris:

> Then with her hand the goddess laid hold of her fragrant robe, and plucked it, and spake to her in the likeness of an ancient dame, a wool-comber, who had been wont to card the

> fair wool for her when she dwelt in Lacedaemon, and who was well loved of her; in her likeness fair Aphrodite spake: 'Come hither; Alexander calleth thee to go to thy home. There is he in his chamber and on his inlaid couch, gleaming with beauty and fair raiment. Thou wouldest not deem that he had come thither from warring with a foe, but rather that he was going to the dance, or sat there as one that had but newly ceased from the dance' (tr. Murray *LCL*).

The legal basis of Aphrodite's control (*kuria*) over Helen is arguably revealed in an Attic Red Figure amphora (Berlin, Antikensammlung, 30036; available for download at: http://www.perseus.tufts.edu/hopper/artifact?name=Berlin+inv.+30036&object=Vase). This depiction of the first meeting of Paris and Helen in Sparta has Helen, veiled as a bride, sitting on Aphrodite's lap and thereby signaling that she is Aphrodite's adopted daughter. That is, Aphrodite by mutual agreement has become, to use the Latin term, the *materfamilias* of Helen.[1] Placing on the knees is of course a well-attested Near Eastern adoption ritual[2] and references to it are not uncommon in ancient Greece. The most explicit reference is *Odyssey* 19.401 ff. wherein Odysseus is placed on his grandfather Autolycus's knees and promised rich *dōra*—"gifts."[3]

At this point, we face a question perhaps more central than at other points in our study: To what extent do marriage practices set by the tragedians and poets in a mythical age reflect the experiences of mortal women? Is there historical evidence that women outside male-headed households and, hence, unqualified for legitimate marriage, were married under cultic auspices?

There is some evidence for the presence of Aphrodite cults interested in marriage. Thus, Plutarch *Amatorius* ("Dialogue on Love" 23) mentions that Delos had a temple of Aphrodite *Harma* "Fitted Together" that was clearly concerned with marriage. At Sparta, there was Aphrodite *Harenta* (Lycophron *Alecandra* 832; cf. Carson 1982: 122

1. There are also scenes in which Aphrodite sits on the lap of Helen (Stafford 1997: 200 with n. 6). In what is unequivocally a wedding preparation context, a woman holds the bride on her lap as she crowns her with the bridal *stephane*, while Eros hovers above" (Stafford 1997: 200; Athens, National Museum 1454 CC1228). One question is whether the woman is Aphrodite or a mortal woman. A second question is whether the adoption is mutual.
2. In Genesis 48.6, Jacob informs Joseph that his sons, Ephraim and Manasseh, "shall be mine no less than [my own sons] Reuben and Simeon; the episode concludes in Genesis 48.12 with Joseph removing his sons from Jacob's knees. It is clear that Jacob adopted the sons of Joseph (de Vaux 1978: 586).
3. Adoption explains the sewing of Dionysus into Zeus's thigh (Apollodorus *Library* 3.4.3) and his depiction sitting on Zeus's lap (Taranto, Museo Nazionale Archeologico di Taranto IG 8264; Bonn, Akademisches Kunstmuseum der Universitàt, Inv. 1216/19). Note also the coming forth of Hercules from between Hera's knees when the goddess adopted him (Diodorus Siculus 4.39.2). Additional sources: Hoffner 1968: 201 with n. 27; Silver 1992: 124–25, 240–41. For real life adoption, I would suggest that in Demosthenes 28.15–16 the "taking on the knees" of Demosthenes by Aphobus refers to an adoption ritual. Mention should also be made of the portrait of Alcibiades sitting on the goddess Nemea's lap (Plutarch *Alcibiades* 16.5). Most importantly, in a cult of Persephone in South Italy a dead person was visualized as achieving rebirth by sitting in the lap (*kolpos*) of the goddess (Petridou 2004).

n. 4). Also, on the road from Troezen to Hermione there was a temple of Ahrodite *Numphias*—"Bridal" (Pausanias 2.32.7). A boundary inscription attests to an old shrine of *Numphe*—"Bride"—at Athens that in later times may have been associated with Aphrodite (Dillon 1999: 70–71). In the *Anthologia Palatina* (6.208 Antipater), three citizen (*astai*) *hetairai* make a joint dedication to "the Paphian" (Aphrodite) on the occasion of their marriages.

In addition, there is evidence for Artemis cults that would have played an intermediary role in the nuptial process by conveying eligible *parthenoi* to Aphrodite (or Hera) to be married. The *Suda* On Line (translated headword phrase: "I was a bear at the Brauronia") provides a more concrete indication that cults played a role in the real-life marriage of *parthenoi*:

> And the Athenians decreed that no *parthenos* might be given in marriage (*sunoikizesthai*) to a man if she had not previously played the bear for the goddess (tr. Jennifer Benedict).

Still, this entry does not answer the question about whether participating *parthenoi* were given in marriage *by* the cult of Artemis. It is easy to imagine that brides, having completed their legal duty to Artemis, were given by their fathers or by themselves.

The question is whether "no *parthenos*" actually refers to a subset of *parthenoi* who voluntarily became *hierodoulē*—that is, became slaves of Artemis—with the objective of later on being placed in good marriages.[4] It has been suggested that there is evidence of such dedications of women to cults of Artemis in inscriptions from northern Greece dating to the third and second centuries BCE.

Note first, a dedication to Artemis of Pagasai made by one Dynatis recording that she performed the *nebreuo*, "did the fawn ritual," which perhaps is comparable to Brauron's *arkteuo*—"do the bear ritual" (Graninger 2007: 152 n. 14, 154–57; Mili 2015: 203–04). Among several inscriptions to Artemis Throsia there is one (McD 360) that records:

> To Artemis Throsia Hippolochos son of Hippolochos, on behalf of Eubioteia, daughter of Alexippos, who served as *nebeuousa*. [dedicated] *lutra* (tr. Graninger 2007: 157).

This inscription becomes significant because another inscription (McD 370) commemorates that,

4. The scholium to Aristophanes's *Lysistrata* 644–45 says that *every parthenos* should imitate the bear before her wedding (*gamos*) but at another point it says that only *selected parthenoi* (aged five to ten) participated (Faraone 2003: 51–52). Probably, "every *parthenos*" refers not to every citizen young woman but only to those designated as *parthenoi*, meaning that they had been chosen to "play the bear" for the Artemis cult (cf. Dillon 1999: 74–75).

> The demos of the Larisans [dedicated a statue of] Eubioteia, daughter of Eubiotos, wife of Hippolochus son of Kephalos birth child of Alexippos son of Alexsippos, after serving as priestess (tr. Graninger 2007: 157).

Years ago, Clément (1934: 404–05) struggled to bring the two inscriptions into relationship with one another.

> [In the cult of Artemis Throsia there] existed a ritual in which the worshipper identified herself with the goddess's sacred animal whose name she assumed. During the period of the identification, the maiden was considered intimately the property of the goddess and there is evidence that this period was observed before marriage. For Hippolochos the son of Hippolochos, who pays to Artemis Throsia the ransom [*lutra*] in behalf of the *nebros* ["fawn"] Eubioteia the daughter of Alexsippos, would seem to have later married this Euboteia, if one is right in identifying these two people with the husband and wife mentioned in another inscription from Larisa, in which an Euboteia is honored by the people of Larisa as a priestess (of what goddess is not mentioned, but perhaps of Artemis Throsia).

The problem, as Graninger (2007: 157–58) has explained, is that identifying the Euboteia and Hippolochos in the dedication to Artemis Throsia with the wife and husband in the statue inscription requires the assumption of *three* adoptions. Hence, it is "difficult and methodologically unsound to argue that the Hipplochos and Euboteia mentioned in [A] and [B] are the same people" (Graninger 2007: 158). Agreed, but on the other hand, unless the Larisa region possessed an unusually limited stock of names, the probability that the same pair of names would appear by chance alone on the (presumably) later statue inscription is very small (cf. Clément 1934: 405 n. 2).

Unfortunately, we must leave the question of cultic nuptial intermediaries in a most uncertain state.

XIV: *Hetaira* as Textile Worker

Hetairai worked as prostitutes and courtesans but not exclusively or even primarily. Textile work was a main occupational interest.

1. Iconographic Evidence

One side of a red-figured cup from Munich depicts two men and four women:

> In the center, a bearded man sits with knobbed stick and watches a seated woman to his left who is putting a skein of wool into a basket already filled with wool, which a maid holds out for her. The woman's figure is only partially preserved ... To the right of this group a seated girl is playing the double flute for a standing man ... who is offering her a flower. Behind him a girl, who has risen from her stool is still spinning. Her dress shows that she is not a servant. Again, two flute cases hang from the wall (Immerwahr 1984: 10).

Sutton (2004: 334 with fig. 17.6) adds,

> Both sides of the exterior are united as a single courting scene showing men visiting women in their quarters ... [The] two men ... wait patiently for the women to complete their tasks before they leave for the evening. This is clear from the cup's principal side [which includes an inscription and a woman fastening her sandal] ... The flute cases hanging on both sides of the cup indicate that the women are professional entertainers who also spin either for income or simply to clothe themselves.

Sutton's interpretation of the scene is not convincing. If the depicted women were prostitutes or professional entertainers the men would not wait for them to finish their textile work. The explanation is that the women are contractually obligated to complete the work. The hanging flute cases on both indicate that they and their male friends will party *after* the women quit work.[1] The men are waiting for their dates. The offer of the flower, a frequent feature in nuptial pursuits, symbolizes a marriage proposal. My understanding of the two dogs under the handles is that gainful/for profit textile work is being performed in a place that is under the auspices of Artemis, a goddess with manifold connections to dogs (Silver 1992: 160; Trantalidou 2006: 109–10, 114–15) and with weaving. The women are fully clad and no cash is changing hands. There is no brothel and no prostitution.

1. On a grander, celebrated scale, Penelope's suitors must restrain their ardor for her until she finishes her weaving work (*Odyssey* 2.87 ff.).

Kosmopoulou (2001: 302) discusses classical period Attic gravestones depicting unaccompanied women in various acts of woolworking:

> [W]e are unable to determine with certainty whether gravestones of single woolworkers are idealistic portraits of women in their oikos or portrayals of working women celebrating the means for earning their life.

However, there is an important clue pointing to professional status/work outside an *oikos*, namely that the deceased women are identified only by their names with no mention of a *kurios*. With respect to possible citizen status, Kosmopoulou (2001: 302) suggests, "even *astai* were occasionally characterized on their gravestones by their own name only, not followed by their patronymic or demotic." Perhaps these citizen women were *hetairai* like the unaccompanied spinners. The latter were certainly not prostitutes. The thought occurs that wool working became a marker of *hetaira* status because single women typically earned their living doing it.

Wrenhaven (2009: 375) calls attention to an Attic red figure kylix (London, British Museum E71) depicting a female flute-player entertaining men in a setting with three *kalathoi* hanging on the walls. *Kalathoi* also hang on walls in several more sexually explicit scenes (Wrenhaven 2009: 375–77). As Wrenhaven (2009: 375–76) assumes, the women shown in the scenes may be prostitutes, but no money pouches are visible. That *kalathoi* hang on walls rather than being in use may indicate that the interactions with men are to be understood as taking place at night (J.N. Davidson 1997: 89). If so, then these *ergastula* were not full-time "brothels," which certainly existed in a large city, and the women (literally) moonlighted as prostitutes (compare Wrenhaven 2009: 378; cf. J.N. Davidson 1997: 84, 87). What seems clear is that the women are partying with men in the same buildings (*ergasteria*) in which they lived and produced textiles (Building Z discussed below comes to mind.) I understand the women as woolworkers enjoying their time off, not prostitutes (compare Fischer 2013: 245).[2]

2. Single Women as Live-in Textile Workers

A number of Babylonian cities possessed large workshops employing hundreds of women in spinning and weaving (see, for example, Delougaz 1967: 196–98).[3] Also, in

2. In the interior of a red-figure cup (London, The British Museum E44) a woman unties her belt as a man watches. The scene includes a lyre and a basket on the wall. Blundell (2002: 158 with fig. 7) explains: "[T]he image's position on the inside of a wine-cup informs us with some certainty that the woman fiddling with her belt is not a bride but a prostitute ... But in its essential meaning the scene differs little from those which show bridal adornment." The woman may also be a sexually active single woman.
3. One may wonder whether Babylonia's "woman's house" had anything in common with New Kingdom Egypt's *gereb wab hemewet net*—"pure foundation of women" or "all-women settlement"—in the temple of the craftsman god Ptah in Memphis (see Papyrus Harris I 47.8–9; Loprieno 1997: 208–09). The reference in the text to the dispersal of the *mesew* "children" of the

Babylonia, for a woman to enter the *gagūm* "cloister" [from Sumerian *ga.gi-a*—"locked house"] seems to have meant that she joined the household of the sponsoring god.[4] The Old Babylonian (earlier second millennium) version of the Atrahasis myth links these "cloistered" women with a "Flood" (Lambert and Millard 1969: 101–03).

As already noted, Pindar (*Pythian Ode* 9:15 ff.) writes of the Naiad Creusa: "She loved not the path walked to and fro before the looms, nor the pleasures of dining with her *oikoriai hetairai* (female house-mates)" (tr. Kennedy 2015: 65). Where did the nymphs place their looms? Homer (*Odyssey* 13.104 ff.) tells that in Ithaca:

> At the head of the harbor is a long-leafed olive tree, and near it a pleasant, shadowy cave sacred to the nymphs that are called Naiads. Therein are mixing bowls and jars of stone, and there too the bees store honey. And in the cave are long looms of stone, at which the nymphs weave webs of purple dye, a wonder to behold; and therein are also ever-flowing springs (tr. Murray *LCL*).

That the "cave" (*antron*, *speos*) in which the nymphs produced textiles and store "honey" is a temple is confirmed by its neat double-entrance system, one for gods and the other for mortals (13.109–10)[5] and by Athena's advice to Odysseus (*Odyssey* 13. 360 ff.) that he should "set his goods [the treasure given to him by the Phaeacians] in the innermost recess (*muchō* also meaning "store chamber") of the wondrous cave, where they may abide for you in safety" (tr. Murray LCL; but compare *Odyssey* 5.194–225). Inside the cave, Athena and Odysseus sought out a good *keuthmōn*—"hiding place" or "hole"—and then Athena set a *lithos*—"stone"—in the doorway (366 ff.). Clearly, Athena did not seal the entrance to the cave of the nymphs, as this would not only have made the cave unusable by mortals but also would have made pointless her search inside the cave for a good "hiding place." The "stone" must have been placed in/at the entrance of the depository. Odysseus stored his valuables ("honey"?) in a temple vault.

Merchants and traders were surely inclined to visit nymphs who set up textile enterprises in temple precincts located close to excellent harbors (*Odyssey* 13.96–101) outside major urban centers. Temples of Artemis in particular were known for the

---

foundation may refer to agents or employees. A comparable institution existed in Mycenaean Greece at, for example, Pylos (Olsen 2014: ch. 3).

4. This appears to be the situation of the *nadītu* of the god Shamash who were known especially for making interest-bearing loans (R. Harris 1964; Stone 1982). It should be noted, however, that not all the *nadītu* women resided in "cloisters."

5. Sophocles (*Philocetes* 16, 19, 159–60, 952) stresses the useful double-entrance feature in the "cave" of Philocetes although, as noted by J. Davidson (2002: 49), it "plays no significant role in the dramatic action." An inscription of the fifth century BCE in Vari, located on a road between Attica and Sounion, explains: "Archedemon of Thera, the *nymphlēphtos*, at the instructions of the nymphs worked out (*exoikodomeō*) this *antron*" (*IG* 1^2 788; tr. Pache 2011; 46). Thus, the "cave" is to some extent man-made as was certainly the case in Kafizin (Pache 2011: 46 with n. 24, 57). Also, Archedemon acted on the "instructions" of the nymphs.

presence of *adyta* or inner chambers that were "architectural caves" for the storage of valuables (see below). It is no accident that in Homer, as Malkin (2001: 11) notes, "Nymphs seem to mediate between the traveler's debarkation and actual 'arrival'" The real-world interest of businesspersons in nymphs is demonstrated by some 310 later third century BCE dedications in a cave of the Nymph near Kafizin four miles from Nicosia in Cyprus. Many of these dedications were inscribed by one Onesagoras son of Philounius who managed a firm (*koinonia*) involved with flax and linseed (Mitford 1980: 92; Nosch 2014: 24–29).[6] Although this is not explicit in the dedications, it very much appears that Onesagoras was a *numpholept*—that is, a mortal who had been "seized by the nymphs" (Connor 1988).

Textile work done by young females living in an isolated area with a water source is, I believe, indicated iconographically. The lid of an Attic *pyxis* (London, British Museum 1907.5–19.1; H.B. Walters 1921: 145–46 with pl. 3), a box for jewelry or cosmetics, depicts two running women, one of whom holds out an embroidery frame in proximity to a *kalathos*. Two more women are seated, one of whom holds out a long spotted sash while the other tosses five balls into the air. The scene also includes a large chest, a caged bird and a heron that walks freely. I understand the caged bird to reference an indoor, or more specifically a regimented location and the heron to locate the entire scene in the wild and, more specifically, near a body of water (see Siron 2014).

Larsen (2001: 8) explains that the

> term naiad (*naïs* is related to the Greek verb *naô*, "flow") is used from the time of Homer forward as a substitute or qualifier for *numphê* [e.g. "naiad nymph" in *Iliad*. 6.21–22, 14.444, 20.384; *Odyssey*. 13.348, 356; *Anthologia Palatina* 9.328, 814]. From Homer to the late epigrams in the *Greek Anthology*, nymphs are consistently the inhabitants of water sources ... Their cultural significance ... stretches far beyond the spring itself to all the symbolic and practical uses of water.

Perhaps it is not by mere coincidence that the origin of nymphs is traced back to the period of the "Great Flood" (Larson 2001: 4).

According to Hesychius (s.v. *ergastini*), the women who annually wove the figured *peplos* ("dress," more generally, rectangular woolen cloth) for Athena at the Panathenaia are called *Ergastini* "the female workers." According to the Scholia Vetara, Euripides's *Hecabe* 467, the team of workers included *parthenoi* (unmarried women, or better single women?) as well as *teleai gunaikes* (married women?) (Mansfield 1985: 266–67; Aleshire and Lambert 2003: 76–77). Other sources indicate that the (nine?) *Ergastini* lived on the Acropolis for a year where, with the assistance of two *Arrhephoroi*, they produced Athena's *peplos* (Pausanias 1.27.3; Barber 1992: 113 with n. 23; Neils 1996: 186–89; Mansfield 1985: 278–81). A possible implication is that *Ergastini* means

6. That the "pointy mountain," as it was called, was a site for the production of flax is suggested by the drawing of flax plants on some of the pottery used for inscribing dedications (Nosch 2014: 25; compare Jim 2012).

"the *live-in* women workers." Since it is difficult to believe that married woman lived away from their families for a year, a further implication is that *Ergastini* means "the live-in *unmarried* woman workers."

It is explored below whether classical Attica knew "houses of women" (*ergasteria*) employing live-in single women in the production of textiles for the market. The single women/*hetairai* would be the commercial world's counterparts of the nymphs/naiads who lived and wove textiles by streams and in caves and of the *ergastini* who wove Athena's *peplos*. The first step in this difficult identification process is to establish that Athens/Attica knew significant numbers of women who earned their keep by producing textiles for the market. This discussion is prefaced by noting that Bitto, Nicarete, and the "Woman from Andros" before turning to prostitution had earned their living from weaving.

Who are the *talasiourgoi*? The importance of textile production in the Athenian market economy is indicated in the "Attic Manumission" texts (*IG* 2^2 1553–78) (dating from the 320s BCE) by the official identification of many women as *talasiourgoi* "wool workers." The texts record the verdict in suits by Athenian slave owners against "deserting" slaves (*dikē apostasiou*). As reported by Rosivach (1989: 366–67), "of the sixty-three females with occupational labels recognizable in the surviving fragments, fifty-one, or 81%, are *talasiourgoi*."

This finding suggests the presence of a market-oriented textile industry in Athens. However, Rosivach (1989: 388; cf. Wrenhaven 2009: 379) asserts that the wool market "was certainly not large enough to require so many wool workers as our inscriptions seem to imply" and he concludes, "they were, by and large, typical Athenian housewives." Yet the wool market was large enough to support wool vendors, whether male or female, who were suspected of wetting their merchandise (Aristophanes *Frogs* 1386). Moreover, even if we ignore Aristophanes and other, soon to be cited concrete evidences for a market, the problem remains that Rosivach does not consider what "so many wool workers" were doing while still slaves under the control of their owners. The most obvious answer is that they had all along been *talasiourgoi*—that is, their owners found it profitable to own female slaves who produced textiles for the market (E. Cohen 2015: 58–59). Certainly, there was little profit to be made from owning "typical Athenian housewives."

It makes sense that some free single women must also have supported themselves by selling textiles or selling their labor-power to textile producers (cf. Wrenhaven 2009: 369–70). We may assume that Bitto and Nicarete were free, based on their being able to make the *choice* to leave textile work and become prostitutes. A gravestone inscription from Athens dated to the fourth century BCE commemorates Elephantis as a cloak-seller (*IGIP* 11254) and the accounts from Eleusis mention Thettale as a seller of felt caps to the building workers (*IGIP* 1672.70–71) (Stears 2001: 114 n. 25). In addition, in Demosthenes 57.45, Euxitheos claims:

> For, as I am informed, many women have become nurses and laborers at the loom or in the vineyards owing to the misfortunes of the city in those days, women of civic birth, too; and many who were poor then are now rich (tr. DeWitt and DeWitt *LCL*).

We may understand that "many" Athenians were motivated to raise their economic status by becoming "laborers at the loom".[7]

Also, in Xenophon's story of Aristarchus, when fourteen women moved in with him the desperate Aristarchus, on the advice of Socrates, went to the loan market and borrowed money for purchasing wool, and then had the women produce textiles for the market.

> The women worked during dinner and only stopped at the supper hour. There were happy instead of gloomy faces: suspicious glances were exchanged for pleasant smiles. They loved him as a guardian and he liked them because they were useful. Finally, Aristarchus came to Socrates and told him this with delight. "One objection they have to me," he added, "I am the only member of the household who eats the bread of idleness" (Xenophon *Memorabilia* 2.7.7–12; tr. Marchant *LCL*).

It may have been unusual for women of higher status to participate in textile production for the market but the market itself, Xenophon's story shows, was ongoing and open to new entrants and profitable.

If, as has been alleged, the "wool-workers" were actually prostitutes, why did the Athenian authorities designate them *talasiourgoi* instead of *pornai*? Wrenhaven (2009: 381) answers that these women were labeled *talasiourgoi* in order to avoid the stigma associated with the sex trade.[8] However, no evidence is provided in support of an empathetic public policy and, moreover, many/most of the freed slaves would have been expected to keep working at their (allegedly) stigmatized (but profitable) trade (compare Wrenhaven 2009: 383). No one would be fooled or comforted by the designation *talasiourgoi*. Neither could the women be officially designated as *hetairai* as this is a sociopolitical status ("single woman"), not an occupation. Again, the most obvious answer is that the (former) slave-women were designated "wool workers" because that is what they did.[9] They were neither "housekeepers" nor "prostitutes," though they were probably sexually active.

3. What Happened in Building Z?

Perhaps some Athenian single women labored outside the home in such structures as Building Z, located in a corner of the city wall west of the Sacred Gate, which,

7. Perry (2014: 47) notes, "Gaius [*Digest* 15.1.27.pr] implicitly categorizes a female slave in the textile industry as a familiar figure when he cites such an individual as an exemplary type of a woman with a *peculium*."

8. LSJ (s.v.) suggests that *pornē is "probably" from pernēmi*—"sale" or "export for sale" (cf. J.N. Davidson 1997: 117).

9. 7a. Timarchus owned "nine or ten slaves who were skilled shoemakers, each of whom paid him a fee of two obols a day, and the superintendent of the shop three obols. *Besides these there was a woman skilled in flax-working, who produced fine goods for the market*, and there was a man skilled in embroidery" (Aeschines 1.97; tr. Adams *LCL*; emphasis added).

between 350–300 BCE, held more than twenty rooms of various sizes, two courtyards, a number of large cisterns and drains and had two main entrances (Glazebrook 2011: esp. 39–42). The finds included more than one hundred loom-weights for weaving together with lamps and hundreds of drinking cups and plates. Some scholars classify Building Z as a brothel (Younger 2001) but others see it as a banqueting building (Ault 2016: 88, 92–93) or a factory for cloth production (Knigge and Tancke 2005: 49, 78).

On the former view, customers went from the central courtyard to one of the ten smaller (vestibular) rooms after viewing the sexual "merchandise" and paying the manager/madam. On the latter view, textile production took place in the central courts and the smaller rooms housed the textile workers (Knigge 1991: 93; Glazebrook 2011: 50). The street entrances in the rooms would seem to have made it most difficult for the manager of a brothel to monitor the entry and exit of paying customers. It becomes difficult to understand the function of the courtyards with the areas for meals (and a garden?) and, indeed, to view Building Z as a centrally organized establishment. If the building was intended for the use of prostitutes, why was it designed in this way? On the other hand, resident textile workers could have used their outside entrances to come and go and the inside entrances of their rooms could have been locked during non-working hours to prevent theft. If Building Z is a textile factory, it hardly resembles a sweatshop. It looks more like a structure in which *hetairai* lived and earned their living in "honest" labor.[10]

4. Brauron as a House of Textile Work

Another candidate for the role of "house of textile work" is the sanctuary of Artemis at Brauron near the mouth of the Erasinos River. Cole (2004: 192, 202) explains:

> At Brauron in Attica, Artemis's sanctuary ... presided over an especially lush spring, and her sanctuary overlooked a small harbor where the river joins the sea. Similarity between the natural features of this site and those of other coastal sites of Artemis suggest that managers of the Artemis cult deliberately chose such sites. The site at Brauron replicated the site of Artemis across the straits at Amarynthos, which was also located where a river flowed into the sea ... The sanctuary of Artemis at Brauron—situated as it was on the east coast of Attika, at an important harbor—was a stepping-off place to Delos and Ionia.

Moreover, Cole (2004: chap. 6) demonstrates in detail that temples of Artemis were typically placed on major highways at regional boundaries, at places of narrow passage and, in towns, at street intersections. In a word, Artemis sat on the commercial routes.

The epigraphic record proves that Artemis Brauronia was the recipient of dedications by women of various kinds of woven textiles, clothing, implements used in spinning and weaving, and pottery bearing depictions of women engaged in spinning

10. Ault (2016: 79) finds the vestibular rooms "unusual." Rotroff (2013) notes that the "saucer pyres" found in large numbers in Building Z are typically associated with industrial and commercial activity.

and weaving (Brøns 2017: 46–54). The textile theme, Cole (1984b: 239–40) explains, is "far more prominent in the pottery decoration at Brauron than elsewhere [and this theme] is repeated in sculpture." Also, while

> inventories of dedicated clothing are well documented elsewhere ... Artemis seems to be the only divinity to receive so many varieties and sizes ... [T]hey clearly were not made for the goddess to wear (Cole 2004: 214, 216).

With respect to the dedications of textiles, one may recall that in Mycenaean Pylos women were engaged in producing textiles and dedicated cloth to deities (Hooker 1990: 164).

The sanctuary possessed *hippōnes* "stables" and several stoas—that is, covered walkways in which textiles could have been stored, displayed and sold (Osborne 1985: 160). Cole (1984b: 239; cf. 2004: 214) adds:

> A long narrow stoa behind the main stoa seems to have been the place where at least some of the textiles were displayed. The foundations for the racks on which these textiles probably hung have been excavated.

Hollinshead (1985: 438–39) maintains that the security of valuables was the reason for the presence of "cave-like" inner rooms (*aduta*) at Aulis, Brauron and Haliai: "A bank vault is as good a parallel for the inner room as a sacristy." That Artemis's *aduta* actually functioned as bank vaults cannot be proven. However, Ekroth (2003: 93–94) argues,

> This interpretation of the *adyton* at Brauron is supported by a number of offerings found to the north and north-west of the temple terrace. Though most of these objects seem to have been intentionally deposited at the spring, some of this material may be taken to represent the remains of the dedications once kept in the *aduton*, which ended up north and north-west of the temple terrace when the temple was plundered and destroyed by the Persians in 480 BC or were dumped there during the subsequent cleaning up of the temple site.

This is only very weak evidence for the storage of valuables. Hollinshead's proposal about the function of *aduta* finds stronger support in Athena's advice to Odysseus upon his arrival in Ithaca that he should set his valuable goods in the innermost recess of the cave of the nymphs (*Odyssey* 13. 360 ff; discussed earlier. In addition, it was indeed "clever" for a fellow named Embaros to hide his precious daughter, together with other valuables in the *aduton* of the temple of Artemis in Mounychia to save her from being sacrificed (see Perlman 1989: 125–26 with n. 61).

It is important to note that an *aduton* is a vault for valuables *and* consequently a focus of cultic activity. The goods placed in the vault were under the protection of Artemis and protection was provided not only by physical means (guards, doors and locks) but also, more importantly, by spiritual means—that is, by potent myths and rituals. Perlman (1989: 126) who sees in the *aduton* only a "cave" for hibernating bears does not consider this factor. Brauron's myths and rituals arguably centered on Iphigenia who having become a "chthonian divinity" at Brauron served as Artemis's sacred *kleidouchos* "key-holder" and was herself served by devoted mortal *hierodoulē* "temple slaves" (Euripides *Iphigeneia in Tauris* 131, 1463; cf. McClure 2017: 119–20).

Commercial potency of the facility at Brauron would have been enhanced by its possession of a satellite or branch in Athens, the Brauronian, which was located on the south side of the Acropolis (Pausanias 1.23.7). Artemis Brauronia is the only divinity based in a rural sanctuary that had also a sanctuary on the Acropolis that, among other functions, may have served as a treasury (Hollinshead 1985: 443–45; Osborne 1985: 154–56, 160). Artemis's treasury might have served as a branch bank that helped finance textile traders. The inclusion of a stoa in the Brauronian indicates a commercial role. Artemis also had sanctuaries (branches?) in Mounichia (Piraeus) and such Mediterranean places as, for example, Cyrene in Libya where she had the epithet Katagōgis, Aulis in Boeotia where she was Aulideia and in Attica at Halai Araphenides (Loutsa) where she was Tauropolos.

The preoccupation with textiles provides a major clue attesting the central economic role of Artemis Brauronia. A second major clue is her connection with dogs. As noted earlier, dogs are depicted in scenes of women (*hetairai*) doing textile work in what appears to be a commercial context. Artemis received many dogs (Callimachus *Hymn to Artemis* 3.87–97) and was *skylakitis* "protectress of dogs" (LSJ s.v.; Pausanias 8.37.4–5).

Traders are explicitly identified as dogs by Cassandra in Lycophron *Alexandra* 1291–95 and by Diogenes Laertius (6.99–100) who tells, as I understand him, that Menippus who as an unbridled lender on bottomry earned the nickname "Cretan/Lying(?) Dog" (*Krētikon Kuna;* see Relihan 1990: esp. 219). The dogs that "parted Actaeon among them" (Euripides *Bacchae* 1291) included the Telchines, a corporation of multinational artisan-traders who were depicted as amphibious flipper-handed creatures with the heads of dogs and who bore the epithet "dogs of Artemis" (Silver 1992: 149–50). There was a marvelous sanctuary of Artemis on the Adriatic Sea in which deer coexisted with wolves (Pindar *Olympian Ode* 3.28–29). Strabo (5.1.19) tells that within this Artemis sanctuary: "Any that are being pursued (*diōkomena*) by dogs (*kunōn*) are no longer pursued when they have taken refuge there" (tr. Jones *LCL*). According to LSJ, *diōkō* has a meaning: "IV. as a law term 'prosecute', pursue (one's rights at law)". It appears that Strabo's "dogs" are creditors and that *diōkō*—"pursue"—is being used in the sense of "dun". One may suggest that Artemis's marvelous sanctuary was a free port and that those given sanctuary there were themselves "dogs"—that is, traders.[11]

11. The evidence for the commercial role of dogs is explored at length by Silver (1992: ch. 7). Later scholars writing on the significance of dogs have ignored this work and not considered the economic dimension. For a near exception, see Burnett's (1994: 160–61) discussion of Kynossema but compare Silver (1992: 157–58). Franco (2014: 43) explains: "In any case, a dog's collaboration is gained only by means of exchange. One persuades it to cooperate by forging a pact: in return for food, the dog is obliged to render its services to man. Force is neither

Brauron celebrated a "festival of the dog establishment (*kunēgesion*)" which apparently was controlled by Artemis's priestesses and seems to have coincided with the removal of dedicated textiles from the sanctuary (Osborne 1985: 161, 167; Libanius *Hypotheses to the Orations of Demosthenes* 24.1). We may imagine a temple building with a dog posted on its roof as in Crete.

Besides dogs, Artemis was also associated with nymphs who, as noted earlier, were concerned with weaving. In Callimachus's *Hymn to Artemis*, nymphs are depicted circling the goddess in dance (3.170) and otherwise closely tied to her (3.185 ff.).

Would textiles produced and/or finished at Brauron have any special features that might make them attractive to consumers elsewhere around the Mediterranean and in neighboring societies? It is known that Artemis was connected with yellow-dyed garments: the Athenian girls who "acted the she-bear" for the goddess wore yellow "saffron" dresses (Aristophanes *Lysistrata* 645); Iphigenia wore (shed) a yellow dress when her father "sacrificed" her at Aulis; and there are some 15 references to *krokōtos* (saffron) garments in the Brauron inventories (cf. Aeschylus *Agamemnon* 239; Osborne 1985: 156, 164; Brøns 2015: 68–69).

The yellow dye was produced from the *Crocus sativus*, a cultivated plant long familiar in the Greek world. One may suspect that there was a Mediterranean market for luxurious, colorfast yellow-dyed garments.[12] Note the implication of *Iliad* 8.1, wherein "Dawn the saffron-robed was spreading over the face of all the earth" (tr. Murray *LCL*; cf. *Iliad* 19.1, 24.695). That saffron-colored garments were popular in classical Athens is made clear by that the fact that they are "donned or doffed accordingly as the actor wants to be taken for a woman or not" (Perlman 1983: 125, citing Aristophanes's *Ecclesiazusae* 331–40 and *Thesmophoriazusae* 939–42, 945–46). Indeed, according to the Chorus in Euripides's *Hecuba* (466–74), Athena's dress (*peplos*) was dyed saffron-yellow. Homer and Hesiod also refer to "saffron-robed" women (Håland 2004: 158–59; Mansfield 1985: 266). Also, in Fragment 4 (Bernabé) of the *Cypria*, the Horai and the Charities dress Aphrodite in a flower-dyed dress; the same kind worn by the Horai themselves. Festivals such as the *Arkteia* would have promoted Artemis's textile "brand."

Fragments of miniature vases (*krateriskoi*) found at Brauron depict young girls racing or being chased. Among the running girls, there are "at least two age levels" but there are also "older women preparing the girls for the race" (Hamilton 1989: 461; cf. 465). The older women have their hair up in buns and wear floor-length dresses (Kilker 2008: 96 with figs. 3.6, 3.7). The latter group may have included permanent,

necessary nor possible. The dog's duties require a freedom of action not found with any other animal helper." Obviously, exchange/the evolutionary foundation of the relationship is not the whole story of man's best friend.

12. This market is reflected in mythology. Europe was "abducted" and carried away across the sea to Crete by Zeus. At the time Europe was "plucking flowers with *numphai* in a meadow and he [Zeus] was seized by desire for her. He came down and changed himself into a bull whose breath was saffron-scented" (Hesiodic *Catalogue of Women*, Fragment 89; tr. Most *LCL*).

full-time employees in a cultic textile enterprise. As will be seen shortly, Brauron had facilities capable of housing and feeding workers.

What did it mean to "play the bear"? Saffron-yellow dresses might easily be taken to represent honey, a food much beloved by bears (Silver 1992: 203). Thus, the "bear" game might have involved girls posing as bears (naked and/or wearing masks) who chased/"raced" after honey—that is, after younger girls wearing yellow dresses (as referenced in *Lysistrata* 645). The problem with this explanation is that the *krateriskoi* do not depict racing girls in yellow dresses.[13] The (Ravenna) scholiast on *Lysistrata* says "to tend/honor the shrine [*periepein to hieron*] ... wearing the crocus himation was called 'playing the bear'." (tr. Hamilton 1989: 461). The Leiden scholium adds, "Imitating (*misoumenai*) the bear, they executed the secret rite (*musterion*). The girls who played the bear for the goddess wore the *krokoton* and performed the sacrifice to Artemis Brauronia and Artemis Munichia" (tr. Ferrari 2002: 171). "Playing the bear" involves something significant in addition to wearing a yellow dress. The girls who played the bear for the goddess wore the *krokoton* and performed the sacrifice to Artemis Brauronia and Artemis Munichia" (tr. Ferrari 2002: 171). "Playing the bear" involves something significant in addition to wearing a yellow dress. However, I will focus on the yellow dress as a possible indicator that the Brauron cult participated in the production of saffron for dying textiles.

A crocus-gathering role played by young girls, not wearing yellow dresses, is demonstrated by the Bronze Age "Saffron Gatherers" fresco in Xeste 3, a building of some 30 rooms, in Akrotiri (Thera/Santorini). I quote the late Paul Rehak's (2007: 207–08) description:

> Two walls of an upper-story room show a goddess and four girls in a rocky landscape with clumps of blossoming crocus plants [Figure 11.1] ... The east wall shows two girls picking crocus flowers with stigmas, which they deposit in wicker baskets ... The adjacent north wall of the room ... continues the narrative sequence of activities depicted on the east ... A girl with red hair and a blue eye balances a filled basket on her shoulder and carries it to the left, in the direction of an architectural platform ... At the far left, on the lowest stage of the platform, a girl empties her basket into a large pannier. On the next higher stage to her right is another smaller pannier, from which a blue monkey has selected just the crocus stigmas culled from the blossoms, the animal offers these stigmas to an enthroned woman at the highest level.[14] [It is the styles that are made into saffron.] Behind her to the right is a griffin ... The association of this goddess with crocus and saffron ... seems undeniable: she has a crocus blossom painted (or tattooed) on her cheek, and her loose, diaphanous blue blouse is decorated with these flowers ... The seat of the goddess is not a conventional throne or chair but rather a stack of yellow cushions, which could represent bales of saffron-dyed cloth or even a pile of yellow-dyed garments. The cushions

13. Keuls (1985: 316) suggests that on a red-figured vase from Brauron the yellow dress is represented as a spotted diaphanous robe.

14. I am not sure how to understand the role of the monkey. In the south Pacific, I witnessed monkeys trained to climb the trees and turn cocoanuts from side to side and by the sound to pick out and harvest ripe ones.

> most represent the folded textiles in some Archaic vase paintings and in marble relief on the east frieze of the Classical Parthenon.

Based on "the shallow curve of her exposed breast" and the control of an animal, Rehak (2007: 208) sees a resemblance with "the later Artemis and other goddesses." The grounds for identifying the seated goddess with classical Artemis are slight but reasonable.

There are two important points. First, the scene in the Thera fresco would be pointless if the cult of the seated goddess were not actually producing saffron-dyed textiles or medicine or both. The production objective explains the extraction of stigmas from the flowers. Second, three adolescent girls are unmistakably participating in the production process.[15] Of course, the participation of a handful of elegant girls may have been largely symbolic with the main work of producing dye in commercial quantities[16] being left to older women depicted in other Xeste 3 frescoes and, more importantly, attested in the Linear B texts. Rehak (1999: 13) suggested,

> In Xeste 3 ... we seem to have a building that was intended to be used by women at all stages of their lives, and not just for rites of passage at puberty.[17]

That a production scenario applies at Brauron cannot be proven but it fits the available evidence.[18] In *Lysistrata* (641–47) we are informed by the chorus of older women:

> I bore the holy vessels at seven, then I pounded barley at the age of ten, and clad in yellow robes, soon after this, I was Little Bear to Brauronian Artemis; then neckletted with figs. Grown tall and pretty, I was a basket-bearer [*kanēphoreō*] (tr. Lindsay *LCL*).

This "basket bearing" is not explicitly linked with Brauron and Artemis and basket carriers played a role in several cults (e.g. Aglauros, Zeus *Sotēr* and Athena *Sotēria*). However, Wallbank (1981: 277) argues that *all* the services listed in *Lysistrata* might

15. As Rehak (1999: 12) notes, the intimate connection of the crocus-gathering girls to the goddess is underlined by the fact that "all wear a forehead band which no other woman in Xeste 3 possesses." Saying that the girls were participating in an "initiation ritual" or "rite of passage" is likely true but it does not explain why the ritual/rite took the specific form it did. In the Hesiodic *Catalogue of Women* (Fragment 23 Most *LCL*), Stratonice and her sister Sterope who were companions of the nymphs in the mountains "around the fountain of the silver-eddying Euneus, early in the morning they walked ... the dew seeking flowers, a sweet smelling ornament for their heads" (reconstructed text, tr. Most *LCL*).

16. Commercial quantities of saffron dye are indicated in the Linear B texts from Mycenae (Nosch 2004: 34).

17. Numerous loom-weights have been found in various buildings in Akrotiri but not in Xeste 3 (Tzachili 2003: 190–91).

18. The goddess Artemis is attested several times in Linear B texts and there is archaeological evidence of Mycenaean activity at Brauron (Nosch 2009).

be "services performed at Brauron by female votaries of Artemis, more likely quite few in number, rather than by the total, free population of Athens."

Specifically, with respect to basket bearers for Artemis, Wallbank (1981: 280) calls attention to important evidence.

> There is no inscriptional evidence for *kanēphoria* in the rituals of Artemis's festivals, but there is compelling evidence in the form of votive stelai that it was, in fact, a constant feature of Artemis at Brauron. These stelai ... [are] dedications by women during the fourth century BC ... In each of these, Artemis is depicted greeting a group of devotees ... At the rear of the group in each case stands a young woman or girl who bears on her head a cylindrical object, about twenty inches in diameter, and of the same height. This I believe to be a *kaneon* [basket of reed].

In addition, Kahil (1983: 237) describes a scene on a fragmentary vase from Brauron:

> Women and girls alternate in position, the girls in short chitons either preparing to "take-off" or already running; the women surveying their dresses, hold ritual objects, among them baskets.

Those holding the baskets are "older women" (Hamilton 1989: 465). Several scholia testify to the participation of older women/women of marriageable age as *kanephoroi* at Brauron or in the Artemis cult (Philochorus *FGrH* 328 F 100 and 101; scholion on Theocritus 2.66–68b; discussed by Parker 2005: 248–49). As at Thera, the wicker baskets were suitable to harvest crocus flowers for Artemis at Brauron.

Of course, this is at best circumstantial evidence for cult-sponsored saffron production and, as far as I am aware, no saffron dyeing works have been found in the (incompletely excavated) remains at Brauron[19] (or, for that matter, at Thera but see Smith and Tzachhili 2012: 142). However, the long narrow stoa behind the main stoa (mentioned earlier) would have been suitable for drip drying saffron dyed textiles and the numerous loom-weights found at Brauron might have been used to prevent the dyed material from shrinking (see the discussion by Monaghan 2001: 70–71).

That international traders visited the port at Brauron is confirmed by Herodotus's (4.145, 6.138) report that Athenian women celebrating an unnamed festival were "seized" and carried off and taken to Lemnos to be *pallakas*.[20] A trading role for the

19. See Ekroth (2003: 102–18) for a survey of the archaeological remains at Brauron.

20. There is reason to believe that the "seized" women became *pallakas* voluntarily. This, I believe, is the implication of another version in which the women were "rescued" by the god of marriage, Hymenaios (Scholiast Homer *Iliad* 18.493; Sourvinou-Inwood 2004: 142–43 with n. 5). That the descendants of the Lemnian "rapists" had inherited a *xoanon* of Artemis from Brauron (Plutarch *On the Bravery of Women* 247D–E) suggests that the Athenian women and Lemnian men had been married under the goddess's auspices. The *xoanon* served as a kind of passport to Greece and hence could hardly have been stolen property. In *Odyssey* 22.421–23 we find slaves being taught cloth-making skills: "Fifty women servants (*duōai*) hast thou in the halls, women that we have taught (*didaxamen*) to do their work, to card the wool and bear the lot of slaves

Lemnians is confirmed in the *Iliad* (7.467–75), wherein Euneos "Ship-man," the ruler of Lemnos and "son" of the adventurer Jason, gives wine to the Achaean kings before selling the main part of his cargo.

An indirect indicator of international commercial connections is the report in a scholium on Aristophanes *Peace* 874 that in Brauron there were

> many prostitutes [*pornai*]. And there the Dionysia used to be staged too, and in each deme, in which they were drunk ... and, while drunk, they used to grab many prostitutes (tr. N.F. Jones 2004: 136).

Although this is possible, it is not obvious that the "prostitutes" only occupied Brauron at festival-time. *Peace* 874 is rather obscure but there is a sense that diverse individuals were drawn from everywhere[21] to participate in the revelry at Brauron. As Dillon (1997: 214) notes,

> Any festival in the Greek world might also be accompanied by a market. This is true of pilgrimage festivals as well where markets sold not only simple foodstuffs for the pilgrims but other items as well, and so worship and trade were combined.

It is also possible that the *pornai* were actually *hetairai* (single women) who earned their living by producing textiles for the market but were sexually active. For Corinth, an even greater commercial center, Strabo claims that the numerous women who sell (sex? cloth? both commodities?) are called *hetairai*.[22] The goddess Theōria—"Festival"—was visualized as an attractive sexually active woman (Aristophanes *Peace* 871–91).

Significantly, with respect to the potential for textile production, the sanctuary of Artemis in Brauron possessed facilities capable of accommodating live-in workers.

> Ten so-called dining rooms, dating to the Classical period, were found among the remains of a sanctuary dedicated to Artemis Brauronia ... These rooms are notable because they are

(*doulosunē*)." Linear B texts from Pylos and Knossos dealing with cloth and wool sometimes refer to working women by "ethnics," some of which refer to foreign lands including places in the eastern Aegean: Knidos (*ki-ni-di-ja*), Miletus (*mi-ra-ti-ja*), and Lemnos (*ra-mi-ni-ja*; probably La-mniai) (see e.g. Billigmeier and Turner 1981: 4–5; Smith and Tzachili 2012: 147).

21. Note the mention in line 874 of *hupopepōkotes* "half-seas over" (Platnauer 1964: 142). In commercially oriented Delos the "hand-maidens of the Far-shooter; for when they have praised Apollo first, and also Leto and Artemis who delights in arrows, they sing a strain telling of men and women of past days, and charm the tribes of men. Also they can imitate the tongues of all men and their clattering speech: each would say that he himself were singing, so close to truth is their sweet song" (*Homeric Hymn to Apollo* 3.156–64; tr Evelyn White *LCL*) The vistiors to Delos were multilingual and, apparently, so were the Delian maidens.

22. Strabo 8.6.20: "And the temple of Aphrodite was so rich that it owned more than a thousand temple slaves, courtesans, whom both men and women had dedicated to the goddess. And therefore it was also on account of these women that the city was crowded with people and grew rich; for instance, the ship captains freely squandered their money, and hence the proverb, 'Not for every man is the voyage to Corinth'" (tr. Jones *LCL*).

> very well-preserved; thresholds are still visible, tables remain *in situ*, and the indications of couch legs are still present ... The dining rooms ... had ninety-nine couches. If there was a second story, the couches could have numbered nearly two hundred (Kilker 2008: 87, 91, 272).[23]

An inscription (*IG* 1^{3} 403) refers to a *Parthenon*, "Room for Unmarried Women/Girls," possibly a reference to (undiscovered) living quarters for women fed in the dining rooms.

Obviously, there is no direct evidence that Attica's Artemis cult at Brauron marketed textiles produced by single women. While far from constituting the proverbial "smoking gun," it is clear, however, that Brauron had the geographic advantages, financial resources, commercial connections and physical facilities plus a source of young woman labor-power capable of implementing this kind of commercial specialization. Further support is provided by finds of implements used in spinning and weaving and of pottery bearing depictions of women engaged in spinning and weaving.

23. In the *Iliad* (16.179–84), we learn that the unmarried women associated with Artemis had bedrooms on an upper story: "And of the next company warlike Eudorus was captain, the son of a girl unwed [a *parthenios*], and him did Polymele, fair in the dance, daughter of Phylas, bear. Of her the strong Argeiphontes [Hermes] became enamoured, when his eyes had sight of her amid the singing maidens, in the dancing-floor of Artemis, huntress of the golden arrows and the echoing chase. Forthwith then he went up into her upper chamber [*huperōon*], and lay with her secretly [*lathra*]" (tr. Murray *LCL*). I see no indication that the seduction took place in the house of Polymele's father Phylas as does Lefkowitz (2007: 57–58). The upper floor, like the dance, belonged to Artemis.

XV. Legal Status of *Nothoi* "Bastards"

Hesychius (s.v. *nothogennēta*) lists as *nothoi* the children of a *pallakē* together with those of a prostitute (*pornē*), a girlfriend (*philē*), and a slave (*doulē*). Pollux (*Onomasticon* 3.21) offers a more restricted definition: a *nothos* is a child born either to a foreign woman or to a *pallakē*.

Both definitions arguably reflect the post-PCL situation. I would hypothesize that prior to PCL, "*nothos*" was a legal designation reserved for the offspring of *pallakai*, whether citizen or foreign, who, it is argued below, routinely met Athenian citizenship requirements. After PCL, only *nothoi* born to citizen *pallakai* met the legal requirements for citizenship (Mossé 1991: 274; Wolff 1944: 88). A foreign woman could no longer be designated the *pallakē*-wife of a citizen. However, her children by citizens continued to be referred to as *nothoi*.[1] Hall (2016: 75 citing a fragment of Polemon) suggests that after PCL,

> [T]he disenfranchised aristocratic *nothoi* had formed a kind of alternative community, which had, by the time of this decree [of Alcibiades], reached a stage where its replication was seen as a possibility.

In the remainder of this chapter, the *nothos* is understood to be the child of a *pallakē* legally kept for the procreation of free children (Demosthenes 23.53). That is, the status of the offspring of any "unkept" *pallakai* and of *parthenioi*—"children of unmarried women"—who might be called *nothoi* is not considered.

Might nothoi be citizens? One view is that in the polity, *nothoi* had *astos* status—that is, they were Athenian citizens with fewer rights than a *politēs* who could elect and be elected to political office but, on the other hand, possessed more rights than *xenoi* "free foreigners" (see E. Cohen 2000: esp. 49–54, 71–72 who cites Aristotle *Politics* 127b 18–20; cf. Wolff 1944: 83; Patterson 1990: 40–41). This is a most useful perspective. However, problems arise because the boundary between *astos* and *politēs* is difficult to demarcate (Blok 2005: 16 ff.; Kears 2013: 39–43 with references).

1. In Euripides *Ion* 1473, Ion says to his mother Creusa: "You gave birth to me as a virgin's bastard [*nothon me parthenium*]?" (tr. Potter *Perseus Project*). The translation is doubtful. Are we to understand that Ion is a *nothos* because his mother was not legitimately married? That is, Creusa had the legal status of *pallakē* (compare Ogden 1996: 16–17). Or, is the meaning that Ion is a *parthenios* because his mother was not married at all? Or, are the meanings of *nothos* and *parthenios* the same. For discussions of the still disputed definition of *nothos*/*nothē*, see Patterson (1990: 41) and, more recently, Blok (2017: 48–50).

Nevertheless, a number of considerations demonstrate that, before PCL, *nothoi* were citizens—that is, they qualified for citizenship as a matter of routine upon becoming eighteen years old (K.R. Walters 1983 with references; Carawan 2008: 399). In support of routine qualification for citizenship, note first that the reference to the offspring of *pallakai* as *eleutheroi* (Demosthenes 23.53) has implications for the grant of citizenship. *AthPol* 42.1 (cf. 26.3) explains:

> The present form of the constitution is as follows. Citizenship [*politeia*] belongs to persons of citizen [*astōn*] parentage on both sides, and they are registered on the rolls of their demes at the age of eighteen. At the time of their registration the members of the deme make decision about them by vote on oath, first whether they are shown to have reached the lawful age, and if they are held not to be of age they go back again to the boys, and secondly whether the candidate is free [*eleutheros*] and of legitimate birth [actually *gegone kata tous nomos*, meaning "born as prescribed by the laws"]; after this, if the vote as to free status goes against him, he appeals to the jury-court, and the demesmen elect five men from among themselves to plead against him, and if it is decided that he has no claim to be registered, the state sells him, but if he wins, it is compulsory for the demesmen to register him. (tr. Rackham *LCL* modified; cf. Rhodes 1981: esp. 499–502; Scafuro 1994: 160 with n. 44).

The eighteen-year-old son (*nothos*) of a designated Athenian *pallakē* is legally free (not a slave). Then, since the *pallakē* was married "according to the laws" (although not by *eggue*), her *nothos* (although not a *gnēsios*) must be granted citizenship by his deme both before and after PCL (opposed by Mossē 1991). Before 451/0 BCE, a *nothos* who was the free child of a legally designated foreign *pallakē* equally met the conditions for the routine grant of citizenship.[2]

A variation on this line of reasoning is that the intention of PCL was without doubt to disenfranchise *nothoi* procreated by foreign *pallakai*. Obviously, the "law on *nothoi*" (Plutarch *Pericles* 37.2) could have accomplished this result only if Athenian men had all along purchased foreign women to be their wives, not only Athenians, and legally designated them for the purpose of producing *eleutheros* children. This designation qualified the children for the grant of citizenship as a matter of routine.

That *nothoi* of mixed marriages became citizens finds support in Plutarch's *Pericles* 37.3–4 report:

> The circumstances of this law [concerning children born out of wedlock] were as follows. Many years before this, when Pericles was at the height of his political career and had sons born in wedlock, as I have said, he proposed a law that only those should he reckoned Athenians whose parents on both sides were Athenians (*politeia*). And so when the king of Egypt sent a present to the people of forty thousand measures of grain, and this had to be divided up among the citizens, there was a great crop of prosecutions against citizens of illegal birth (*nothoi*) by the law of Pericles, who had up to that time escaped notice and

2. There is no evidence to assume otherwise as the deme, not the phratry, decided citizenship. The citizenship law was an attack on foreigners not an attack on the *pallakē* institution, which continued to serve the interests of Athenian citizens and their gods.

> been overlooked, and many of them also suffered at the hands of informers. As a result, a little less than five thousand were convicted and sold into slavery, and those who retained their citizenship and were adjudged to be Athenians were found, because of this scrutiny, to be fourteen thousand and forty in number (tr. Perrin *LCL*).

A fragment of Philochorus (Fr. 119; scholion to Aristophanes *Wasps* 715–18) apparently refers to the (Egyptian) grain distribution as taking place in 445/4 (Harding 2008: no. 131, 114; Stadter 1989: 336). That such a massive scrutiny was launched and that it uncovered 4,760 persons of demonstrably illegal citizen status (perhaps 16% of all those enrolled) suggests that the granting of citizenship by the demes to children (*nothoi*) of mixed marriages had been standard practice, not mere fraud, or error.

K.R. Walters (1983: 334) maintains that Plutarch's mention of *nothoi* is a "typical error; he [Plutarch] has mistakenly assumed that the citizenship law declared *mētroxenoi* to be bastards" (cf. Rhodes 1981: 333–4).[3] I do not follow Walters's meaning. *Mētroxenoi*, those born to a citizen father and a non-citizen mother (*pallakē*), previously had a claim on citizenship.[4] What happened in the scrutiny is that these bastards (*nothoi*) were distinguished from bastards born to Athenian mothers; the latter, together with *gnēsioi*, remained legally entitled to their citizen status (doubted by Ogden 1995: 227 with n. 59, 1996: 44–45; Kamen 2013: 63–67 but compare 70). The specifics of the new social and legal status of *nothoi* disenfranchised by PCL is unclear (but see Kamen 2013: 68–70 and below on Kunosarges).

Second, the PCL was restated or reinstated in the decree (*psephisma*) of Nicomenes in 403/2. This decree specified an amnesty for those born before the archonship of Eucleides—that is, before 403/2 (Scholiast to Aeschines 1.39). Also in 403/2, the orator Aristophon authored/proposed a law (*nomos*) that children not born from a citizen (*aste*) would be *nothoi* (Athenaeus 13.38 p. 577bc). The purpose of this law/proposal is not clear. Possibly, it intended to restore fully the children of mixed marriages to citizen status in which case Nicomenes's decree represented a compromise in which citizen status was restored only to those *nothoi* born to mixed marriages before 403/2. In Demosthenes 57.30, Euxitheus in seeking to regain his citizenship (*politēn*) after a

3. *Nothoi* were always, that is even before PCL, legally the property of their *pallakē*-mothers. I suspect that this ownership lies behind the theme of the "old woman" who gives away her citizen daughter/granddaughter in *pallakia*. This interpretation seems especially likely in the case of Glycera in Menander's "The Girl with Her Hair Cut Short" (130–31). It is also possible in Plautus *The Ghost* 188–89 and in Terence *Phormio* 112 ff. wherein the "old woman" in charge of the girl is not her mother, who has died. The "old woman" might perhaps be identified with the Roman *materfamilias* in a marriage by purchase. On the other hand, especially in *Phormio*, the "old woman" may simply be a *promnestria*—"matchmaker". (A scholia on Aristophanes *Clouds* 41 adds the later synonym *proxenetria* [The *Suda* On Line (headword *promnestria*].)
4. Thus, Hegesistratus, the son of Pisistratus is (explicitly) a *nothos* born to a foreign woman (Herodotus 5.94.1; *AthPol* 17.3). Given that he participated in governmental affairs and held office (Plutarch *Solon* 32.3), I would assume that he was an Athenian citizen. A complicating factor is that Hegesistratus also had the "modified" (*parōnumios*) name Thettalus. Perhaps, he was adopted at some point.

scrutiny reminds the jury that if an individual were born before the archonship of Eucleides in 403 BCE then that individual was a citizen even if only one of his parents was an Athenian.

A third consideration pointing to the routine grant of citizenship is that *nothoi* might legally be adopted. This is indicated in Plutarch's *Moralia* (834ab):

> That Archeptolemus and Antiphon should neither of them be buried in Athens, nor anywhere else under that government. And besides all this, that their posterity should be accounted infamous, bastards (*nothoi*) as well as their lawful descendants (*gnēsioi*); *and he too should be held infamous who should adopt any one of their descendants for his son.*" (tr. Barcroft, available at http://www.attalus.org/old/orators1.html; emphasis added; compare Sealey 1984: 128).

The point is that under Athenian law only those eligible for citizenship might be adopted (Isaeus 7.16 and 8.19; see also Isaeus 6).

On the other hand, my argument is that after PCL *nothoi* born to mixed marriages were no longer citizens and, hence, no longer could be adopted. This argument provides a tool for the understanding of Diogenes Laertius (2.26):

> For they say the Athenians (*astēn*), because of the scarcity of men, wished to increase the population, and passed a vote that a man might marry (*gamein*) one Athenian woman but have children by (*paidopoiesthai*) another" (tr. Just 1989: 33–34).[5]

The decree is undated but several scholars link it to the defeat of the Sicilian expedition of 415/13. K.R. Walters (1983: 323) suggests that the decree was not intended to legalize "bigamy" but rather to make the offspring of the "extramarital relationship legitimate"—that is, "to grant such offspring rights of inheritance and succession." Kennedy (2014: 18) believes the decree is an exception to the citizenship law in 412 to 403 BCE to permit children borne by *pallakia* to be citizens or even to be legitimate (but compare Ogden 1996: 72–75).

Kennedy's intuition finds support in Carawan's (2008: 401 n. 69) hypothesis that *paidopoiesthai* might stand for *paida poissthai*—"adopt a child." Acceptance of this emendation opens a path to understanding the purpose of the decree.[6] As there was no legal barrier to the adoption of a citizen's children, the decree must have made it legal for citizens to adopt the children of non-citizens. Most obviously, if a citizen adopted a child borne by his foreign *pallakē* he would make that child (*nothos*) eligible for citizenship (under PCL) and succession. The decree cited by Diogenes Laertius

5. The earliest sources named in behalf of this decree are Hieronymos of Rhodes (third century BCE) and Satyros the Peripatetic (second century BCE).

6. Is *paidopoiesthai* a humorously intended play on words to suggest the legalization of bigamy? See the discussion in Chapter XIX.1 of the "bigamist" Socrates.

applied only to already born *nothoi*[7] and did not (even temporarily) restore the *pallakia*-institution to its pre-PCL status[8]—that is, the children of foreign mothers no longer qualified for citizenship.[9]

Fourth, in Plutarch's *Moralia* (834ab) *nothoi* and *gnēsioi* are separately included in the context of *atimia*. That both were subject to *atimia*—"deprivation of civic rights"—does not mean that these are two names for the same legal status but rather that *citizens* were subdivided into legally distinct status groups (MacDowell 1976: 89; but compare Rhodes 1978: 89–90).

Fifth, pointing to citizenship, Plutarch (*Themistocles* 1.1–2) tells:

> In the case of Themistocles, his family was too obscure to further his reputation. His father was Neocles,—no very conspicuous man at Athens,—a Phrearrhian by deme, of the tribe Leontis; and on his mother's side he was an alien [*nothos*], as her epitaph testifies:— "Habrotonon was I, and a woman of Thrace, yet I brought forth That great light of the Greeks,—know! 'twas Themistocles." Phanias, however, writes that the

7. Plutarch (*Pericles* 37.3) notes that after both of Pericles's legitimate sons (and many others) died of plague, an exception was passed whose terms permitted Pericles (and other Athenians without heirs) to adopt and legitimize their sons by foreign *pallakai*. The son of Pericles by Aspasia (Pericles II) is called *nothos* by Eupolis (Fragment 98 K).
8. The *pallakia*-institution is attested in Attica as early as the seventh century BCE under Draco.
9. An alternative interpretation is that the decree legalized surrogate motherhood (see Müller 1899: esp. 744 ff., 786 ff. on the "*Nebenfrau*"), perhaps along the lines of the ancient Near Eastern institution. Thus, in Genesis 30.3, Rachel says to Jacob: "Here is my maid Bilhah, consort with her that she may bear on my knees and through her I may have children" (Van Seters 1968: 403). For the functioning of the surrogate mother (Akkadian *shugītu*) in the second millennium, see Westbrook (1988: 63–66, 108–09). Note that the children of the surrogate mother were legitimate but became legally the children of the legitimate wife. Plutarch (*On the Bravery of Women* 21) suggests the existence of this institution in the Greek world: "Galatia produced also Stratonice the wife of Deiotarus and Chiomara the wife of Ortiagon, women that deserve to be remembered. Stratonice, well knowing that her husband desired children from her to succeed to the kingdom, but having no child herself, prevailed upon him to have a child by another woman, and to connive at its being passed off as her own. Deiotarus thought highly of the idea, and did everything in dependence upon her judgement, and she procured a comely maiden from among the prisoners, Electra by name, and sealed her to Deiotarus. The children that were born she brought up with loving care and in royal state as if they had been her own" (tr. Babbitt *LCL*). Note more openly *Odyssey* 4.10–15 wherein "Megapenthes, who was his (Menelaus's) son well-beloved, born of a slave woman; for to Helen the gods vouchsafed issue no more after that she had at the first borne her lovely child" (tr. Murray *LCL*). The surrogate mother institution underlies a provision in the Spartan Constitution whereby: "[I]n case a man did not want to cohabit with his wife and nevertheless desired children of whom he could be proud, he made it lawful for him to choose a woman who was the mother of a fine family and of high birth, and if he obtained her husband's consent, to make her the mother of his children" (Xenophon *Constitution of the Lacedaimonians* 1.8; tr. Bowersock and Marchant *LCL*). A citizen woman might designate her slave woman for the procreation of legitimate children. Of course, many years have passed since Silver (1992: 197) noted the reference to the surrogate mother institution in the myth of Oedipus's incestuous relationship with his "mother." Pausanias (9.26.3) mentions "the sons of Laios by *pallakōn*."

> mother of Themistocles was not a Thracian, but a Carian woman, and that her name was not Abrotonon, but Euterpe. And Neanthes actually adds the name of her city in Caria,—Halicarnassus. It was for the reason given, and because the aliens were enrolled [*synteleō*] at Cynosarges,—this is a place outside the gates, a gymnasium of Heracles; for he too was not a legitimate god, but had something alien about him, from the fact that his mother was a mortal,—that Themistocles sought to induce certain well-born youths to go out to Cunosarges and exercise with him; and by his success in this bit of cunning he is thought to have removed the distinction between aliens and legitimates [*nothoi* and *gnēsiōn*] (tr. Perrin *LCL* modified).

The question is why are (were) *nothoi* registered by the state as a distinct demographic in a special deme? Humphreys (1974: 89) notes (and dismisses) the possibility that Cunosarges played this role as indicated by the technical term *syntelein eis Kunosarges*. The hypothesis of special registration is supported in the The *Suda* On Line (translated headword phrase "into Cynosarges"):

> As if [into] Kunosarges, [sc. so named] from the incident when, after a lavish sacrifice, a dog went in and snatched the meat from the offering and took it away. A temple was established there too, and *nothoi* used to be judged there [to see in each case] whether he was truly the son of the man present (tr. David Whitehead modified).

The registration of *nothoi* in a special deme shows at the very least that valid *nothoi* were eligible for citizenship.[10]

Sixth, in Demosthenes 23.213 the speaker explains,

> whereas the people of Oreus, who inhabit only a fourth part of Euboea, dealing with this very Charidemus, whose mother belongs to their city,—I will not mention who his father is or where he comes from, for it is not worthwhile to make unnecessary inquiries about the man,—so that he himself contributed one-half of the birth-qualification, have never to this day thought fit to make up the other moiety, and to this very day he is on the bastards' list, just as here bastards were registered at Cunosarges [in the past] (tr. Murray *LCL* modified).

The mother is a citizen (*politis*) of Oreus and the father is as well. Charidemus is identified with his mother because she is a *pallakē*; her *nothos* son being the son of citizens is himself a citizen. I disagree with Humphreys (1974: 88) when she claims: "The context shows that *nothoi* did not have citizenship at Oreos." Clearly, they did. Also, Humphreys (1974: 89–90) maintains, "Demosthenes's passage should not ... be taken to indicate that for him the *nothoi* of Kynosarges were born out of wedlock but not necessarily to foreign mothers". That is precisely the analogy made by

10. *Apeleutheroi* were identified with *nothoi*—"bastards." The beginning of the 6th century CE Commentary of Pseudo-Nonno to the *Oratio IV*, Contra Iulianum 1.105 (=*PG* [Patrolgiae Cursus Completus] XXXV, col 641) of Gregory of Nazianzus suggests that outside the city walls at Cunosarges there was a registration of *nothoi* who seem to have been identified or assimilated to *apeleutheroi*.

Demosthenes. Demosthenes 23.213 shows that a *nothos* born to an Athenian *pallakē* or, in the past, to a foreign *pallakē*, was granted citizenship as a matter of routine.

The set of arguments confirming the citizenship status of the nothos serve at the same time to confirm the original contention that the pallakē is a legally married wife. The children of a pallakē could have become citizens only if she was considered to be legally married.

Moving from citizenship to the succession rights of *nothoi*, a number of important legalities need consideration. To begin, in Aristophanes's (legalistically phrased) *Birds* (1649–70) dating to 414 BCE:

> *Pisthetaerus*: Oh! by the gods! how he is cajoling you [Heracles]. Step aside, that I may have a word with you. Your uncle is getting the better of you, my poor friend. The law will not allow you an obolus of the paternal property, for you are a bastard (*nothos*) and not a legitimate child. *Heracles*: I a bastard! What's that you tell me? *Pisthetaerus*: Why, certainly; are you not born of a stranger woman? Besides, is not Athena recognized as Zeus's sole heiress? And no daughter would be that, if she had a legitimate brother. *Heracles*: But what if my father wished to give me his property on his death-bed, even though I be a bastard? [actually Heracles refers to the *notheia* "bastard's portion"]. *Pisthetaerus*: The law forbids it, and this same Poseidon would be the first to lay claim to his wealth, in virtue of being his legitimate brother. Listen; thus runs Solon's law: "A bastard shall not inherit, if there are legitimate children; and if there are no legitimate children, the property shall pass to the nearest kin." Heracles: And I get nothing whatever of the paternal property? *Pisthetaerus*: Absolutely nothing. But tell me, has your father had you entered on the registers of his phratry? *Heracles*: No, and I have long been surprised at the omission" (tr. O'Neill *LCL*; cf. Ogden 1996: 36).

Wolff (1944: 88, 89) agrees that the [Solonian] clause "'if there be lawful sons' logically demands a provision giving *nothoi* preference to collaterals if there are no *gnēsioi*" and he concludes: "If this interpretation is correct, the original Solonian law had given the *nothoi* a legal position in the family, although this position was not equal to that of the *gnēsioi*" (Demosthenes 46.14; Plutarch *Solon* 21.3–4; cf. Carawan 2008: 396–98).

In any event, whatever changes were made after Solon, Pisthetarius certainly exaggerates when he says that the *nothos* receives "Absolutely nothing."

> The Athenians had a law [or custom] that when there was a legitimate daughter and a *nothos* son, the *nothos* did not inherit the family property. Alternatively [the term *epiklēros* means] she who has no other brothers as fellow *kleros*-inheritors, but is the sole *kleros*-inheritor. Since it was not possible for *nothoi* to inherit the *kleros*, they gave [him] control of the money. It was Attic law [or custom] to bequeath [money] to *nothoi* up to the sum of 5 minas [500 drachmae] (*Suda* On Line headword *epiklēros*; tr. David Whitehead).

Other sources put the *notheia* "inheritance" at up to 1,000 drachmae (Harpocration s.v. *notheia*; Scholiast on Aristophanes *Birds* 1655–56). The *notheia* might be a substantial sum but even then, it would constitute only a small fraction of what was due from a large estate to the legitimate (male and female) heirs (Cox 1998: 172).

The sources on the *notheia* as an inferior inheritance are consistent with Odysseus fabricated story in the *Odyssey* 14.199–210. Although the term is not used, it is clear that "Odysseus" is a *nothos* and in this capacity, he received an inheritance inferior to that claimed by his father's "proud sons."[11] Solon (Plutarch *Solon* 22.4) made a law relieving *nothoi* of the responsibility to support their parents, which is only just if the parents (or at least the father) were relieved of the responsibility to provide *nothoi* with an inheritance.

Nothoi lacked the quality of *anchisteia* (roughly) "being next." Thus, Demosthenes 43.51:

> But no illegitimate child (*nothōs*) of either sex shall have the right of succession either to religious rites or civic privileges, from the time of the archonship of Eucleides [403 BCE]" (tr. Murray *LCL*; cf. Isaeus 6.47; Patterson 1990: 43 with n. 14, 55; Carawan 2008: 396–97).

Patterson (1990: 57) comments:

> Most likely this law is a reenactment or clarification of previously existing rules, just as, for example, the Periclean citizenship law was reenacted at the same time. So we have a *terminus ante quem* but no certain date of enactment.

11. The word *nothos* appears frequently in the *Iliad* but not all in the *Odyssey*.

XVI. Share the Wealth? Not with (Foreigner) *Nothoi*

Pericles's citizenship law was implemented "owing to the large number of citizens" (*AthPol* 26.3–4)—by this is meant that there had come to be too many claimants for state transfer payments.[1]

To begin with, Pericles had consciously employed the profits of empire for ambitious building programs to benefit the *demos:*

> And it is but meet that the city, when once she is sufficiently equipped with all that is necessary for prosecuting the war, should apply her abundance to such works as, by their completion, will bring her everlasting glory, and while in process of completion will bring that abundance into actual service, in that all sorts of activity and diversified demands arise, which rouse every art and stir every hand, and bring, as it were, the whole city under pay, so that she not only adorns, but supports herself as well from her own resources (Plutarch *Pericles* 12.4).

In addition, under the rule of Pericles pay was introduced for government service (*misthophoria*); first came pay for jury service that was then extended to the armed forces and elsewhere. These measures represented the unfolding of a strategy to consolidate his power (achieved in the late 440s) by increasing simultaneously the political power and disposable income of the *demos* (compare Blok 2009: 148–49 with n. 23; Humphreys 1974: 93–94).

After years of devastating wars, "conservatives" were not always willing or able to make available the required economic resources: many hid their wealth and others fled (Silver 2011a: 75–8). In the fourth century, Athenians were made to compete among themselves for assembly as well as jury pay (Pritchard 2015: 62).

Plutarch (*Pericles* 37.3) implicitly links the vigorous enforcement of PCL (451 BCE) to competition for increasingly scarce public resources by:

> And so when the king of Egypt sent a present to the people of forty thousand measures of grain, and this had to be divided up among the citizens [about 445 BCE], there was a great crop of prosecutions against citizens of illegal birth by the law of Pericles, who had up to that time escaped notice and been overlooked, and many of them also suffered at the hands of informers (tr. Perrin *LCL*).

1. It is not agreed whether this motive was operative in other Greek *poleis* that denied citizenship to children of mixed parentage (Vérilhac and Vial 1998: esp. 114–17), My belief is that the Spartan *partheniai*—that is, the offspring of unmarried Spartan mothers by foreign farmers—were stripped of their citizenship after the war with Messenia.

In Aristophanes's *Wasps* 718, first produced in 422 BCE, there is the joking complaint that (legitimate) Athenians claiming the grain dole were prosecuted as foreigners (MacDowell 1976: 88–89). The underlying reality is that public grain had become scarcer and applicants carefully vetted.

Again, a fragment of Lysias shows that at the end of Peloponnesian War a decree guaranteed state assistance (an obol per day) to orphans whose fathers were killed fighting in the civil war of 404/3 (*P.Hibeh* 1.14; Lysias fragment 10ab; tr. Todd; cf. Stroud 1971). Possibly Theozotzides wished to limit the assistance to those killed fighting on the democratic side against the oligarchy. However, as K.R. Walters (1983: 318) explains, the speaker in the Lysias fragment specifically

> inveighs against a motion to exclude bastards and adopted sons as war orphans. His outrage shows that *nothoi* had previously gotten the privilege (as does the motion; otherwise the exclusion would have been unnecessary).

Evidently the citizenship of *nothoi* borne by foreign *pallakai* did not stand on a very secure social foundation.[2] Why target them in particular? The main reason is that they could be identified easily as foreigners who were usurping economic resources rightfully belonging to native Athenians.[3] As Blok (2009: 150–51; cf. 165) explains in discussing previous research:

> The Athenian autochthony myth is taken to be a racial theory of sorts and of such ideological force as to induce the Athenians to protect themselves against non-Athenian blood (cf. Ogden 1996: 66).

Moreover, it did not help that *nothoi* were already second-class citizens in terms of succession and inheritance.

2. The cut directed against the allowance of *nothoi* is discriminatory even if part of a general effort to cut public expenditures (see Lysias Fragment 10.c with Todd 2000: 384 n. 10).
3. Demosthenes (59.89–90) reports a law that votes to grant citizenship to foreigners had to be confirmed at the next meeting of the assembly by secret ballot of 6,000 or more (cf. *IG* ii^2 102). Obviously, this law made it more difficult for foreigners to become citizens.

XVII. Case Studies in *Pallakia*: Homer's Penelope as *Pallakē*

In a controversial and, hence, often ignored passage in the *Odyssey* (Heitman 2005: 43–49) we learn that when Odysseus departed for Troy he grasped Penelope by her wrist and told, or rather, ordered her as follows:

> [S]o have thou charge of all things here. Be mindful of my father and my mother in the halls even as thou art now, or yet more, while I am far away. But when thou shalt see my son a bearded man,[1] wed whom thou wilt, and leave thy house" (*Odyssey* 18.255 ff.; tr. Murray *LCL*).[2]

So not only can Penelope remarry without being certain that Odysseus is dead, but she *must* do so (Lacey 1966: 63; compare Sealey 1990: 122).

It was argued earlier (in Chapter V) that the *cheir' epi karpoi* gesture signals that the bride whose wrist is grasped by the groom is a *pallakē*. I would now add that the performance of this gesture in a departure scenario is intended to recall the ritual/legal form of the marriage between Penelope and Odysseus. This connection remains unproven, however.

1. Homer makes clear in various ways that Telemachus has matured, most notably when he tells Penelope to go back into the house and not to interfere with matters under his authority and when he equips a ship and sails to Pylos and Sparta in search of news about Odysseus (*Odysseus* 1.346–50, 2.1 ff; cf. 4.744–57; cf. Sealey 1990: 123–25). See, most generally, Heath (2011).
2. In a remarkable painting on the interior of a kylix (London, British Museum 1843.1103.11; duplicated on the cover of this volume), a man wearing a *petasos*, a typical traveling hat, holds a spear in his left hand and his right grasps the wrist of an elegantly clad woman with an elaborate veil over her head and shoulders. The man has his mouth open as if speaking and the woman, clearly a willing bride, modestly looks down listening and perhaps replying. It is tempting to identify the couple as Penelope (with her image of *aidos*) and Odysseus (with his spear and *petasos*) and the scene with Odysseus giving instructions to Penelope before departing for Troy. More generally, however, the wrist-grasping gesture and the holding of the spear jointly testify that the husband is legitimately entitled to his wife. The exterior of the pylix depicts the vote over the arms of Achilles. Recall also two shield bands, in one of which a departing warrior grasps the wrist of a wreath-holding woman and, in the other, a woman holding a spindle and a wreath-grasps the wrist of a departing warrior. We may well think here of gestures that emphasize their marriage commitments while at the same time revealing the form of their marriage. However, in the case of Penelope and Odysseus the wrist-grasping is best understood as representing ownership and hence the right to command.

However, it must be noted that only if he (not her father) had been Penelope's *kurios* could Odysseus's (*inter vivos*) testament have freed Penelope to marry someone else. Additional evidence confirms that Odysseus owned Penelope. According to Pausanias (3.12.2), "because of their pollution" Icarius [Penelope's father] sent around a notice that he would not require payment (*hedna*) from Odysseus and the other suitors for Penelope:

> It is said that Icarius proposed a foot-race for the wooers of Penelope; that Odysseus won is plain, but they say that the competitors were let go (*aphethenai*) for the race along the Aphetaid Road (tr. Jones and Ormerod *LCL*).

Thus, the Spartan king Icarius transferred ownership of Penelope to Odysseus but waived the expected bride-price. In Apollodorus's version (*Library* 3.10.9), Tyndarus, in return for services rendered to him by Odysseus, solicited Icarius to give Penelope to Odysseus. Again, the meaning is that Icarius waived Odysseus's payment but granted him ownership of his daughter. Their marriage was not legitimate.

That Odysseus became Penelope's *kurios* finds further support in Pausanias (3.20.10–11) report that Penelope veiled herself when Icarius asked her to stay with him in Laconia and not to go to Ithaca with Odysseus (an aspect not mentioned in Apollodorus *Library* 3.10.9). At this spot on the road, Icarius dedicated a statue of Aidos. Lyons (2012: 97) notes "a kind of reverse *anakalypteria*" meaning,

> She covers her head to indicate her change in allegiance from father to husband. Here the usual ritual of incorporation into the husband's *oikos* is replaced with a gesture that emphasizes instead her separation from the *oikos* of her father.

The raising of the veil was arguably the usual *ritual* gesture of separation from the original *kurios*. It symbolized that the bride had chosen to inhabit a world of strangers in which her raised veil served to make her invisible. Thus, Helen went to the house of Paris "wrapping herself in her bright shining mantle, in silence; and she was unseen [*lanthanō*] of the Trojan women; and the goddess led the way" (*Iliad* 3.418–20: tr. Murray *LCL*). Constantinidou (1990) perceptively discusses *Iliad* 3, taking note of Pausanias 3.20.11, but she considers that the nuptial significance of Helen's veil lay in its luxury rather than in demonstrating the bride's *aidos*. The significance of Icarius's erection of a statue dedicated to Aidos is unclear except that he acquiesced in Penelope's permanent separation from his *oikos*—that is, he agreed to emancipate her.

Yet another important point is that the long and difficult journey (as is attested in *Odyssey* 2.15 ff.) between the *oikos* of Icarius in Sparta and the *oikos* of Odysseus in Ithaca significantly increased communication costs making it likely that a departing Penelope would have been sold by her father into *pallakia* rather than being given by him in legitimate marriage (see Chapter X).

The making of the *cheir' epi karpoi* gesture, the waived bride-price, the distance between Ithaca and Sparta, the "reverse *anakalypteria*" and that Penelope is in charge of Odysseus's *oikos* together provide grounds for concluding that Penelope was a *pallakē* whose *kurios* was Odysseus. A final clue to the status of Penelope is that the "nurse" Eurycleia addresses her as *numpha philē* "dear bride" (*Odyssey* 4.743). It was argued above that "nymphs" were understood to live outside male-headed households and to represent real world single women who were empowered to give themselves in marriage.

A most interesting aspect of Odysseus "testament" is that it has the form of the *paramonē* contracts familiar in historical Greece (Silver 2015: 153–55 with references). Under this type of contract, an owner promises to manumit his slave in the future on the condition that he/she *paramenein*—"remains with"—the owner to perform certain duties. Often the slave is to be manumitted upon the death of the owner. In our example, Penelope must perform duties for her owner Odysseus but becomes juridically free when Telemachus becomes an adult and able to fulfill his legal and familial duties.

Who has become Penelope's *kurios*? Not Telemachus, not Laertes, and not her father Icarius or her brothers. The latter figures are mostly confined to offering advice to Penelope about how, whether and whom she should marry (see e.g. *Odyssey* 15.16–26, 16.7307, 19.157–61; cf. Sealey 1990: 122–23). Because of having been freed/divorced by Odysseus, Penelope has become (again?) her own *kuria* and hence can choose to marry the highest-bidding suitor (*Odyssey* 16.76–77). She had been Odysseus's *pallakē* but now she has become a single woman. In classical Athenian terminology, Penelope is now a *hetaira*.

Indeed, Penelope, who is famed for her spinning prowess, presents herself to the suitors in a way that recalls the Spinning *Hetaira* (Chapter XI):[3]

> Now when the fair lady reached the wooers she stood by the doorpost of the well-built hall, holding before her face her shining veil [*krēdemnon*]; and a faithful handmaid stood on either side of her. Straightway then the knees of the wooers were loosened and their hearts enchanted with love, and they all prayed, each that he might lie by her side (*Odyssey* 18.209–14; tr. Murray *LCL*).

Following this display, the suitors showered Penelope with valuable gifts (*dōra*) (*Odyssey* 18.285–304). As her own *kuria*, Penelope is free to accept as husband the suitor who offers her the most valuable gift or, as advised by Athena and others, she may choose to reenter her father's household in the expectation of extracting an even larger payment (*hedna*) from the winning suitor.

True, Telemachus (*Odyssey* 2.223) says:

> But if I shall hear that he [Odysseus] is dead and gone, then I will return to my dear native land and heap up a mound for him, and over it pay funeral rites, full many, as is due, and give [*didōmi* possibly meaning "sell"] my mother to a husband (tr. Murray LCL).

3. I am not aware that any scholar has argued that Homer portrays Penelope as prostitute or courtesan.

However, there is no news of Odysseus's death and, more basically, to give away his mother Telemachus would need to "have a beard" at which time Penelope would already be free. Odysseus and Penelope both act to change her marital status without the permission of either her son or her father.

Telemachus is clearly portrayed as the biological son of Penelope by Odysseus (*Odyssey* 23.59–61) and, hence, in accordance with my interpretation, he is a *nothos*—"bastard". That Telemachus is a *nothos* finds support in a peculiarity in his Homeric identification. As noted by Higbie (1995: 148),

> The naming patterns for Telemakhos have a significant omission, nowhere in Homer is he identified by a patronymic adjective based on either Odysseus's or Laertes's name.

Various patronymic phrases are applied to him including the patronymic genitive ("Odysseus's son") but, unlike other heroes, his patronymic never takes the form of an adjective derived from his father's name (e.g. *Odysse-ides or Odysse-ion*; cf, Tsitsibakou-Vasalos 2007: 225–26).

Higbie (1995: 149) concludes,

> The cumulative evidence of these naming patterns for Telemakhos suggests that he has not been a major figure in the traditional epic stories about Troy and the return of the Greek heroes.

Another line of explanation is possible. Eudorus, one of Achilles's top officers, is introduced without being given a patronymic adjective. This, again, is significant because Eudorus was "the son of a girl unwed/son of a single woman (*parthenios*)" who, after Eudorus was born, was richly purchased from her father by a suitor (*Illiad* 16.179 ff.). The *nothos* (*Iliad* 8.284) son of the Greek Telamon and the Trojan mother Hesione (*Iliad* 13.173), the great fighter Teucer, is identified by the patronymic genitive ("Telamon's son," *Illad* 8.281) but not by the patronymic adjective. As noted by Wright (2016: 48 ff.), Teucer is the only specialized archer (*toxotēs*) to fight for the Greeks at Troy. Thus, the nomenclature of the *nothos* Teucer is linked with Telemachus whose name means something like "fighter from afar."

Arguably, Telemachos lacked a patronymic adjective not because he was unimportant but because he, like Eudorus and certainly Teucer was a *nothos.*[4] It is true that Telemachos, unlike Hesiod's Heracles, is not given the metronymic "son of Penelope." On the other hand, Penelope makes clear that Odysseus is not Telemachus's sole owner:

> Thou knowest how welcome the sight of him [Odysseus] in the halls would be to all, but above all to me and to his son, born of us two (*Odyssey* 23.60 f.; tr. Murray *LCL*).

4. There is one case in which an individual identified by Homer as a *nothos* (Doryclus) bears a patronymic adjective *Priamidēn*, "son of Priam" (*Iliad* 11.490; Ogden 1996: 26, cf. 93–94).

By stressing her motherhood, Homer is perhaps signaling Penelope's ownership of Telemachus.

Yet, despite his *nothos* status, Telemachus has the right to inherit Odysseus's *oikos*, as is recognized by the suitor Eurymachus (*Odyssey* 1.400–04) and by Eurycleia (*Odyssey* 4.744–57). It might be argued that this right contradicts my argument that Telemachus's mother Penelope is a *pallakē*. However, as noted above, a *nothos* could have a right of succession in the absence of legitimate brothers. Thus, in Sophocles's *Ajax* (1014–20), the *nothos* Teucer imagines that when he returns home without his deceased legitimate brother Ajax, his father king Telamon will verbally assault him as a cowardly betrayer who intended "with designs to govern your [Ajax's] domain and your house after your death" (tr. Jebb *LCL*). However, in *Odyssey* 16.117–20, Telemachus explains (to the disguised Odysseus) that neither Laertes nor Odysseus had brothers and that he is the only son born to Odysseus before he departed from Ithaca. So, most conveniently, Telemachus has no brothers and no paternal uncles; he has only his still-living grandfather Laertes. In this respect, Telemachos would be quite unlike the fabricated Odysseus (in *Odyssey* 14.199–210) who was the illegitimate son of a *pallakē* with numerous legitimate brothers. Outside Homer, we do find that Odysseus had additional sons (e.g. *FGrH* 1a49F fr. 10; Hesiod *Theogony* 1011–18).

The single son narrative seems contrived and the suspicion arises that Telemachus, like his celebrated father Odysseus, is fictionalizing. It is as if the poet had anticipated legal objections to his account and shaped it to make sure that Telemachus had no legitimate siblings who would take precedence over him in inheritance. This suspicion is only heightened by the fact that in the *Odyssey*, in striking contrast to the *Iliad*, the word *nothos* is never mentioned. In other words, the fact that Telemachus is denied siblings serves to confirm that he is understood to be a *nothos*.

However, since we can never be completely sure of the poet's intent, it is useful to consider an additional line of argument bearing on Telemachus's inheritance rights. When Telemachus meets opposition from the suitor Antinous, he does not press a claim to replace his father as *basileus* "king":

> Nay, it is no bad thing to be a king. Straightway one's house grows rich and oneself is held in greater honor. However, there are other kings of the Achaeans full many in seagirt Ithaca, both young and old. One of these haply may have this place, since goodly Odysseus is dead. But I will be lord of our own house and of the slaves that goodly Odysseus won for me (*Odyssey* 1.394 ff.; tr. Murray *LCL*).

For the present discussion, the important question is not what a "king" did or how Odysseus became "king" but that the holder of the kingship, a kind of property, might expect to experience an increase in wealth and prestige. If Penelope had been Odysseus's legitimate wife then, as Odysseus's legitimate son, Telemachus would not so easily dismiss his right to his father's kingship-property. He does so not because he is weak or stupid but because he is realistic (*pepnumenos*; cf. Heitman 2005: 54–55).

That is, as a *nothos* he is not legally eligible to inherit his father's kingship. Thus, Homer (*Iliad* 6.23–24) mentions that Boucolion the eldest son of Laomedon, king of Troy, was conceived *skotios* "in the dark" (see Chapter V.7; Ebbott 2003: 21) observes, "there is little doubt that Boukolion is illegitimate (and, perhaps, since he was the eldest son of Laomedon, this status is mentioned as a reason why he was not king of Troy)." More directly, Pausanias (2.18.6) explains,

> When Orestes became king of the Lacedaemonians, they themselves consented to accept him for they considered that the sons of the daughter of Tyndareus had a claim to the throne prior to that of Nicostratus and Megapenthes, who were sons of Menelaus by a slave woman [*Odyssey* 4.10–14] (tr. Jones *LCL*).

At the same time, it is possible that the *oikos* Telemachus hopes to inherit constitutes only a lesser portion of Odysseus's wealth—that is, it constitutes a *notheia*—"bastard's portion." In this respect, he would be like the fabricated Odysseus (*Odyssey* 14.199–210) who, in the end, did not, he says, receive a major inheritance share.[5]

To conclude, that Telemachus the *nothos* had an inheritance is consistent with his mother Penelope having been a *pallakē.*

5. One may well suspect that in *Odyssey* 14.199–210, Odysseus is the gracious father, Penelope is his *pallakē*-wife, and Telemachus is the fabricated Odysseus.

XVIII. Case Studies in *Pallakia*: Hera as Zeus's *Pallakē*

Hera refers to herself as Zeus's "wife" (*parakoitis*; *Iliad* 4.60) and Themis refers to Zeus as Hera's *akoitēs* "husband" (*Iliad* 15.91). It is clear, however, that Hera is not Zeus's legitimate wife—not only is there no reference to a betrothal, but also there is no sign of a male figure qualified to give Hera in marriage (*Iliad* 14.296, 15.12–23). Having given herself (auto-*ekdosis*) to Zeus (in a meadow or on a mountain) Hera could become only Zeus's *pallakē*.

Moreover, Hera was not Zeus's sole wife. In *Odyssey* 11.580, Leto is called Zeus's "wife" (*parakoitis*) and in *Iliad* 21.499 Leto is referred to as *alochos* "wife" of Zeus (cf. *Iliad* 21.499). Although *alochos* might mean legitimate wife, this is not to say that Leto or any of the other candidates (Alcmene, Metis, Themis, Eurynome, Demeter and Mnemosyne) had been viewed anciently in this light. In Euripides's *Heracles* 1–3, the raped Alcmene is *sullektros* "partner of the bed"/"wife" of Zeus, but at 1268 Hera is also described as Zeus's *sullektros*. There is no reason to assume that Hera in particular was Zeus's legitimate wife with the other women being *pallakai* or merely partners in extramarital affairs.

Hera plays a distinctly independent role and Zeus threatens her with violence for disobedience (*Iliad* 1.560–89). Indeed, Zeus had previously inflicted physical punishment on Hera with impunity (*Iliad* 15.12–23). Why did Homer have Hera play the role of the rebellious, abused and terrified wife?

> Even if we accept that the poet wanted indeed to parody the human dissension of the heroes, still his assumptions in opting to present and solve the heavenly strife in the way he does are indicative of some other realities which may have determined his choices (Synodinou 1987b: 19).

Unfortunately, with respect to the question of "other realities," the recent valuable study by Llewellyn-Jones (2011), Domestic Abuse and Violence against Women in Ancient Greece, does not focus on the form-of-marriage dimension of the problem of physical abuse. However, Llewellyn Jones makes an important connection:

> Zeus's punishment of Hera has striking similarities to the torture of Melanthius at Odyssey 22.170–90 and it may be that his intimidation draws inspiration from the threat of torture doled out to slaves. The vocabulary used at Iliad 15.17—*plēgēsin himassō* ("strike", "flog")—strongly suggests that in the past Hera's punishment was accompanied by prolonged

whipping, in the manner of slaves; see for instance Plautus, Asinaria 301–5 (Llewellyn-Jones 2011: 259 n. 53).

My hypothesis is that Homer's Hera is Zeus's *pallakē*-wife and hence a slave, albeit a privileged/autonomous slave.[1]

In an earlier fifth century BCE metope of Temple E in Selinus. Sicily (Plate 7) that is assumed to be a Heraion, a male figure seated on a large rock reaches up to grasp the wrist of a standing veiled woman. The figures are not labeled. However, the male figure is assumed to be Zeus and the simply garbed woman to be Hera (Avagianou 1991: N. 32, 93, 104–06). The outdoor location of the scene taken together with the wrist-grasping motif signal that a woman outside a male-headed household is giving herself into *pallakia*.[2]

The hypothesis that Hera is a *pallakē*-wife (slave-wife) finds support in one of the very few viable Indo-European etymologies of her name. Note first that "Hera" is known in Mycenaean texts as *e-ra*. Willi (2010: 243) explains that a successful etymology has to account "for the initial aspiration of Hera's name, so that only one possibility is left to postulate **sērā*, whose initial **s-* must have turned into */h-/* in Pre-Mycenaean times." This possibility has been taken up by Peters (2002) who begins with the verbal root **ser-* of Greek *aireō*—"to take with the hand, grasp, seize" [English "sell"]—and posits a related root noun **sēr* whose meanings include "(violent) taking, seizing, rape." The root noun would have served as the basis of a derivative whose feminine **sēr-ā* = Hera would mean "She of the seizure/rape/taking."[3]

Willi (2010: 244) finds Peters's theory "unobjectionable" but he finds it

1. Ypsilanti (2010: 223) has noted the similarity between Zeus's outbursts against Hera and Trimalchio's against his wife Fortunata: "Petronius's intentional sketching of Trimalchio as Zeus is strongly evident in the description of the host's outburst to his wife with the term *fulmen*, a 'thunderbolt' (*Sat.* 75.1)." However, Hera and Fortunata may have had more in common than subjection to abuse by pompous husbands. Trimalchio announces to his invited guests, "This chorus-girl (Fortunata) has no memory, yet I took her off the sale-platform and made her one of ourselves" (Satyricon 74; tr. Heseltine *LCL*). Thus, the abused Fortunata was arguably a wife *in manus*. On the other hand, Lysistrata tells the magistrate that she was threatened with violence by her husband for daring to interfere in matters of war-making (Aristophanes *Lysistrata* 520 ff). Even so, whether Lysistrata is a legitimate wife or a *pallakē* is indeterminate. The same indeterminacy applies to her married collaborators.

2. On an electrum ring from Mycenae (*CMS* 1 no. 101), a tall seated woman is grasped by the wrist by a youthful male. Scholars have interpreted the scene as a *hieros gamos* involving the youthful Zeus and, quite possibly, Hera (Koehl 2000: 139–40 with references).

3. It may be wondered whether by this logic Heracles should be understood as the "glorious/famous seizer." One may note that, according to Diodorus Siculus (4.10.1), Heracles's original name is Alcaeus, which is derived from the same stem as the name of his mother Alcmene (Kobakhidze 2010–11: 56). Heracles is a *nothos* fathered by Zeus (*Iliad* 19.95 ff.). As befits a *nothos*, Hesiod (*Theogony* 950) provides Heracles with the metronymic "son of Alcmene." Recall that the women who mothered the children of gods were not legitimate wives but rather *pallakai*.

Plate 7. Limestone metope from the Temple of Hera at Selinous of the mid-fifth century BCE featuring Zeus grasping the wrist of Hera. Palermo, National Archaeological Museum, Antonino Salinas 3921B (reproduced courtesy of the National Archaeological Museum, Antonino Salinas).

> most uncertain whether in the eyes of a (Proto-)Greek, a raped (booty) woman could have become one of the legitimate wives who are protected by Hera. Moreover, the derivation presupposes that Hera must have been imagined as a 'raped girl' at some point—for which there is no evidence at all in the iconographic, cultic, and literary sources—and it overlooks the fact that Hera is a goddess not *only* of brides, but of (married) women *throughout* their adult life.

However, Willi does not take into account that Hera *gave herself* in marriage to Zeus (= Zeus "raped" her) and that Zeus treats her like a (bought) slave.

Medea, a most famous *pallakē*, is closely linked with the cult of Hera Akraia in Corinth (or Perachora) where rites were held for her *mixobarbaroi* children whom Medea had taken to the temple in order to *katakruptein* "hide them away" (Euripides *Medea* 1378–83; Pausanias 2.3.11; scholiast on Pindar *Olympian Ode* 13.74g; Dunn 1994).

Again, Pausanias (5.16.2–4) closely links Hippodameia with the festival of Hera at Olympia:

> Every fourth year there is woven for Hera a robe by the sixteen women [*gunaikes* also meaning "wives"], and the same also hold games called Heraea. The games consist of foot-races for maidens ... To the winning maidens they give crowns of olive and a portion of the cow sacrificed to Hera. They may also dedicate statues with their names inscribed upon them. Those who administer to the Sixteen are, like the presidents of the games, married women (*gunaikes*). The games of the maidens (*parthenoi*) too are traced back to ancient times; they say that, out of gratitude to Hera for her marriage with Pelops, Hippodameia assembled the Sixteen Women, and with them inaugurated the Heraea. (tr. Jones and Omerod *LCL*).

Clark (1998: 22) explains:

> The theme of marriage operates on the levels of both myth and cult: the deity Hera is divine bride and wife and patron of mortal wives. The heroine Hippodameia plays an important role, since it is her marriage, which provides the *aition* for the whole festival. On the human level, it is married women who organise and participate in the festival, and who supervise rituals for the young girls who will eventually become brides in their turn.

I fully agree with this analysis. However, strong evidence shows that Hippodameia was not a legitimate wife who was given to Pelops as the winner of a chariot race but instead gave herself to Peleus. First, in a labeled Attic vase painting (Plate 8) Arezzo, Hippodameia calmly stands in Pelops's speeding chariot as he drives and looks back at her pursuing father Oinomaus, who, according to the myth (Hansen 2000), is determined to prevent the marriage. Second, Pausanias (5.17.7) says he saw an illustration in the temple of Hera in Olympia in which "Oinomaus is chasing Pelops, who is holding Hippodameia. Each of them has two horses, but those of Pelops have wings" (tr. Jones and Omerod *LCL*). Third, versions of the myth state that Hippodameia was in the chariot which was racing to the Isthmus of Corinth (Apollodorus *Epitome*

Plate 8. Athenian red-figure amphora of the late fifth century featuring "rape" of Hippodamia. Arezzo, Museo Nazionale Archeologico 1460 (Scala/Art Resource, New York).

2.3–2.9; scholiast on Euripides *Orestes* 990). Fourth, Hippodameia is depicted standing next to Pelops, not her father, before the "race" started (Glantz 1993: 541–42).

The myth of Proitos's daughters as told by Bacchylides provides additional evidence linking Hera specifically with marriage into *pallakia* of (untamed) single women. That the Protids become single women is made evident by their departure from the house of their kingly father and residence in the wilderness:

> All-powerful Hera drove these daughters in fear from the lovely halls of Proetus; she yoked their minds to a violent maddening compulsion. For, while still virgins (*parthenoi*), they entered the sanctuary of the purple-belted goddess, and said that their father far surpassed in wealth the golden-haired consort of holy, widely powerful Zeus. In anger at them, she put a twisted thought into their minds, and they fled to the wooded mountain with terrible screams, leaving behind the city of Tiryns and its god-built streets ... It was from Tiryns that the dark-haired unsubdued daughters of Proetus rushed in their flight ... For thirteen whole months his daughters roamed wildly through the shadowy forests and fled through sheep-nurturing Arcadia. But when their father came to the beautiful stream of Lusus, he washed his skin with its water and called on Leto's daughter with her crimson headdress, the ox-eyed goddess, stretching his hands to the rays of the steed-swift sun, and asked her to deliver his children from their deranged miserable madness. "I will sacrifice to you twenty unyoked red oxen." And the huntress, whose father is the highest god, heard him praying. She persuaded Hera, and stopped the godless mania of the bud-garlanded girls. They built her a sanctuary and an altar right away, and stained it with the blood of sheep, and set up choruses of women. From there you accompanied [*hepomai*—"followed"] battle-loving Achaean men to their horse-nurturing city; and with good fortune you dwell in Metapontion, golden mistress of the people. (Bacchylides *Ode* 11.44 ff., 80 ff; tr. Svarlien *Perseus Project* modified).

Bacchylides is not alluding to a standard "initiation ritual" in which all unmarried Argive women (all the "daughters of Proitos") were expected to participate (compare Seaford 1988: 119–20).

The participating women are described as *parthenoi* (47) and their transformation into maenadry begins with a visit to the temple of Hera who is referred to as Zeus's wife (*paredros*, literally "sitting beside" Zeus). The aim of their audience with Hera was that the Protids should emulate the goddess' marital status (Baumbach 2004: 57). We see Artemis playing an intermediary role in the process: at the appointed time, her specialized role is to convey the *parthenoi* (single women) to Hera to be married. "Artemis inspires a temporary virginity in the wild as a prelude to civilised sexual union" (Seaford 1988: 127).

Seaford (1988: 120), however, believes that in Bacchylides's narrative Hera fails to complete the marriage process (Seaford's "stage C"; Bremmer (1984: 283) disagrees). The omission is unexplained and, I think, inexplicable. Obviously, Bacchylides's Protids did not *legitimately* marry the "Achaean men." However, they did choose to "follow" them, which I take as a reference to marriage into *pallakia*. Note that in Hesiod (*Shield* 1–2), Alcmene left "behind her houses and her father's land, she came to Thebes following warlike Amphityron" (Hesiod *Shield* 1–2; tr. Most *LCL*). The point of the "following" is that Alcmene gave herself in marriage to Amphiyron. Again, Eurythemiste was "led-off" by "horse-taming" Thestius after he had presented "countless wedding gifts [*hedna*]" (Hesiodic *Catalogue of Women* Fragment 26 = Fragment 23 lines 34 ff.; tr. Most *LCL*). The point of the "leading-off" is that Eurythemiste married Thestius. Alcmene and Eurythemiste are slave-wives, not legitimate wives.

Hence, the Achaean men who led away the Protids/whom the Protids followed were bridegrooms not a special kind of military honor guard, as suggested by Seaford (1988: 123–24). Bacchylides did not forget the purpose of his narrative; he permitted Hera to carry out her specialized role of transforming untamed *parthenoi* into *pallakai*.

Hera was or became, among other roles, a goddess of legitimate wives However, evidence suggests that already in heroic times, her clients included *pallakē*-wives.[4] In order to better serve this constituency, Hera had to be a *pallakē* herself. In the same way, Heracles as the god of merchants had himself to be a merchant and, as gods of craftsmen, Athena and Hephaestus had to work with their hands (Silver 1992: 125–29; S. Lewis 2010: 16 ff.).[5]

Circumstantial evidence that Hera played a specialized role in the marriage market is provided by Kardara's (1960: 354) observation, "Nothing ... seems to suit the description of Andromache's headdress [in *Iliad* 22.469–72] better than does the headdress of the Samian Hera." Recall that Hector bought Andromache for "bride-gifts [*hedna*] past counting." That is, Andromache was not Hector's legitimate wife but his *pallakē*. The Samian Hera apparently dressed like a *pallakē*.

The unseemly and unfunny physical intimidation of the goddess by Zeus is not gratuitous but rather Homer intends it to emphasize Hera's special franchise. Homer's audience saw the point of this "other reality."

4. Clark (1998: 17–18) explains: "The *locus classicus* for the function of Hera Teleia as goddess of marriage is found in Aristophanes's *Thesmophoriazusai* [973–76]: 'Let us hymn Hera Teleia as is appropriate; she delights in the chorus and guards the keys of marriage.'" In fact, house keys are a characteristic find in Hera temples (Baumbach 2004: 81 f., 90). With respect to legitimate wives as clients of Hera, it seems significant that Demosthenes (59.122) refers to them as guardians (*phulaka*) of the household.

5. I would venture the thought that the goddess Eos who is frequently and uniquely depicted (winged or unwinged) in (gentle) sexual pursuit of a young male (Lefkowitz 2002) was, in "real life," a patron of single women (*hetairai*).

XIX: Case Studies in *Pallakia*: Classical Athens

Several much discussed and unresolved classical Athenian cases are analyzed below to determine whether the assumption of *pallakia* is consistent with the available evidence and facilitates a seamless understanding of the underlying issues.

1. Socrates the "Bigamist"

Several sources report that Socrates had two wives at the same time: *gunaikas ama* or *gametas gunaikas* or the plural *gametais* (Fitton 1970: esp. 60–61, 65; Woodbury 1973: 22).[1] Plutarch (*Aristides* 27.2) tells,

> Again, Demetrius the Phalerean, Hieronymus the Rhodian, Aristoxenus the Musician, and Aristotle (provided the book "On Nobility of Birth" is to be ranked among the genuine works of Aristotle) relate that Myrto, the granddaughter of Aristides, lived in wedlock with Socrates the Sage. He had another woman to wife (*sunoikēsai gunaika*), but took this one up because her poverty kept her a widow, and she lacked the necessaries of life" (tr. Perrin *LCL*).

Myrto was highborn but Xanthippe, the other named wife, was a citizen (*politin*) and "ordinary" (*koinoteran*) (*FGrH* 260 F11 = Theodoret 12.64–65). However, perhaps not so "ordinary" as the name Xanthippe brings to mind the aristocratic possession of horses (Fitton 1970: 64). Both wives bore children to Socrates.

Much else reported in the sources seems incomprehensible but Fitton (1970: 61) suggests that Aristoxenos wrote concerning the relationship between Socrates and Xanthippe not *prosplakeisan* but *pros pallakeisan* ["for *pallakia*"]—that is, "Xanthippe was said by Aristoxenos to be a *pallakē*." If Fitton's emendation is valid then Socrates had two wives and two households but only one could have produced legitimate children, as Xanthippe was a *pallakē*.

Woodbury (1973: 22) suggests that Fitton's conjecture is "unnecessary" as "Lampe's *Patr. Gk. Lex.* recognizes *prosplekō* and the sense '*be united with*; ref. sexual relations.'" More generally, as Fitton (1970: 61) notes, *prosplakeisan* (or *periplakeisan* in Cyril) has the sense of bodily intertwining but not only in the act of sexual intercourse. Thus, "Socrates took Xanthippe in an embrace and Myrto in marriage (*gamō*)".

1. Clearchus the Solensian credited the mythical Athenian king Cecrops with introducing male and female monogamy (Athenaeus 13.2 p. 555d). Herodotus (2.92.1) says, "Those who inhabit the marshes have the same customs as the rest of Egyptians, even that each man has one wife just like Greeks" (tr. Godley *LCL*).

Fitton (1970: 61) thinks this rendering does not "make any reasonable sense". Let us recall, however, that in Pindar *Pythian* 9.13, marriage into *pallakia* relied on a distinctive terminology involving use of the verb *harmozein*—"to fit together"—in *gamos*—"marriage." *Prosplakeisan* seems to play the same role as *harmozein*—that is, "Socrates took Xanthippe as his *pallakē*-wife (embraced with her/joined with her) and Myrto as his legitimate wife".

That the intertwining of Socrates and Xanthippe refers to marriage into the status of *pallakē* finds support in Porphyry's report of their relationship as cited by Theodoret:

> He says that he [Socrates] was rather keen on having sex, but did no wrong for he only made use of women to whom he was married [*gametais*] and common prostitutes [*aphrodisiōn* "belonging to Aphrodite"]. He says that he had two wives [*gunaikas*] at the same time, Xanthippe, a citizen woman, *who had a number of lovers*, and Myrto, daughter of Aristides and granddaughter of Lysimachus. He took Xanthippe in marriage, *after she had attached herself to him* [*prosplakeisan labein*], and from her Lamprocles was born. And he married [*gamētheisan*] Myrto, from whom Sophroniscus and Menexenus were born. (Thedoret *Graecarum affecionum curatio* 12.64–65; tr. Ogden 1996: 189–90; italics added).

From Aristoxenus, our earliest source, and those following him we learn that the two women were simultaneously Socrates's wives (*gametai*). From the account of Porphyry, we understand that Xanthippe had been a sexually active single woman who chose to join herself to Socrates—that is, to become his *pallakē*.

The chatter about "bigamy" is probably a devious play on the fact that both Socrates's wives were daughters of citizen parents.[2] As Harrison (1968: 17) points out, if the objective was to permit bigamy the decree cited in Diogenes Laertius (2.6) could easily have said, "an Athenian may marry a second legitimate wife."

2. Archippe as *Pallakē*

The banker Pasiōn's will explicitly gave his widow Archippe as a wife (*gunaika*) to Phormiōn, his banker-assistant (Demosthenes 36.8; cf. 45.28).[3] If Archippe had been

2. According to Gellius (*Attic Nights* 15.20), Euripides also had two legitimately born wives simultaneously, as did Callias, son of Hipponicus (Andocides 1.124).

3. "If an alien shall live as husband with an Athenian woman in any way or manner whatsoever, he may be indicted before the Thesmothetae by anyone who chooses to do so from among the Athenians having the right to bring charges. And if he be convicted, he shall be sold, himself and his property, and the third part shall belong to the one securing his conviction. The same principle shall hold also if an alien woman shall live as wife with an Athenian, and the Athenian who lives as husband with the alien woman so convicted shall be fined one thousand drachmae" (Demosthenes 59.16; tr. De Witt and De Witt *LCL*). To understand this law, it helps to assume that the Athenian state sought to limit a benefit, probably economic, that had been made available to Athenians who were married (*sunoikein*), not merely cohabiting (but compare Bakewell (2008/09 107). Whitehead (1986: 113) suggests that the law stated in Demosthenes 59.16 [in no later than 343–340 BCE] may not yet have been in effect at the time of the marriage of Archippe with Phormiōn in c. 368 BCE and that PCL contained no analogous

a legitimate wife, she could have been legally transferred to a new husband only by her *kurios*—that is, by her father or brother. If Archippe had been a metic, as assumed by Ogden (1996: 132), then, as a free person, her husband Pasiōn could not legally transfer her to anyone.

E. Cohen (1992: 103, 104 with n. 216, 106) observes, "Pasion's arrangements are *prima facie* patently unlawful" and he refers to the status of Archippe as a "conundrum resistant to solution" or as "ambiguous" (cf. Carey 1991: 89). I would suggest, however, that Pasiōn would have a *legal* right to transfer Archippe only if she was his *pallakē*-wife and, the other side of the nuptial coin, he was her *kurios*.[4] Direct testimony indicates that Archippe was a *pallakē*. Libanius (*Hypotheses to the Orations of Demosthenes* §36.1), a Greek scholar of the fourth century CE, reports that Pasiōn "gave Phormio the boy's mother (a *pallakē* who had been his) as a wife along with a dowry" (tr. Gibson, http://www.stoa.org/projects/demos/article_libanius?page=37&greekEncoding=UnicodeC).

Archippe's children by the metic Pasiōn were legally either slaves or (when emancipated) metics. As such, they were not eligible for Athenian citizenship under the terms of PCL. However, her two sons, Apollodorus and Pasicles, received citizenship together with their father under a decree of enfranchisement for "Pasiōn and his descendants." Apollodorus is a self-described "citizen by decree" (Demosthenes 53.18, 59.2). The decree did not apply to Archippe who was currently Pasion's slave and, as is argued next, was already a citizen.

The question is whether the slave-wife Archippe was of alien or citizen origin. Carey (1991: 84, 85) is "sure that she was not of Athenian birth" but his reasoning cannot sustain the weight of certainty:

> At some date in the fourth century it became punishable by death for an alien of either sex to contract a formal marriage with an Athenian [Demosthenes 59]. It is unlikely that the law in question was in existence at the time of Pasion's marriage to Archippe. But even so it is quite inconceivable that Archippe's parents would marry her to the metic Pasion if she were of citizen birth, for they would be aware that under existing legislation the marriage would be invalid for the production of legitimate or citizen issue; any children would be bastards and aliens (similarly Kapparis 1999: 10).

provision against mixed marriages. Whitehead (1986: 111) points out that Apollodorus, a rabid opponent of his mother's marriage to Phormiōn, never challenged its legality. Carey (1991: 85 with n. 10) takes a similar position and notes that the law was not in effect in about 395 when Archippe married Pasiōn. I will also assume that the marriages of Archippe were legal.

4. Similarly, in Demosthenes 28.15–16, Demosthenes claims that his father Demosthenes the elder gave (actually "pledged"—*egguōn*) his wife Kleoboulē in marriage to Aphobus. Demosthenes the elder could not have transferred Kleoboulē unless she was his *pallakē*. Demosthenes is not being open about the status of his mother. That Demosthenes was a *nothos* is supported by comments made about him by other orators, especially Aeschines (2.79): "But you [Demosthenes] find fault with my service as ambassador to Arcadia and my speech before the Ten Thousand, there, and you say that I have changed sides—yourself more slave (*andrapodōdēs*) than freeman, all but branded as a runaway!" (tr. Adams *LCL*). Aeschines (3.171–72) asserts that Demosthenes's mother was Scythian—the daughter of a Scythian mother by an Athenian father.

This is a suspect and most unrealistic objection. As proven by the generous dowry (*proix*) he bequeathed to Archippe, Pasiōn was a very rich man and this probably mattered quite a bit to Archippe and/or to her parents. It is not anachronistic to suggest that life in ancient Athens was full of trade-offs, just as it is today. For this point we have the observation of the poet Theognis of Megara (1.183–90) in the sixth century BCE:

> A good man does not hesitate to marry a base woman from a base father, provided he gives much money, nor is a woman ashamed to be the wife of a base man if he is rich, preferring wealth to birth (tr. Blundell 1995: 68).

In addition, among the motives inherited or devised by Euripides, Clytemnestra married herself (arguably by self-sale) to the wealthy Aegisthus for money (*Electra* 929, 1086 ff.; *Chapter VII*).

Even affluent, free (Athenian and foreign) persons might volunteer for slavery to obtain lucrative but otherwise unattainable sensitive positions such as banker. Owners of banks preferred to employ slaves because, unlike free employees, they could not legally quit and take clients and confidential information with them to other banks (E. Cohen 1992: 72).

> So a servant (*diakonon*) must be faithful and be such and keep his master's [or owner's—*despotēs*] business secret (Euripides *Eurystheus* Fragment 375; tr. Collard and Cropp *LCL*).

Moreover, slaves were subject to torture if suspected of peculation (Silver 2011b: 89–90). Similar considerations applied to the wives of bankers. There is ample reason for believing that slave status was a credential for entry into a banking household. E. Cohen (1992: 104), citing Demosthenes 36.29–30, explains:

> Archippe's situation was not unique or insignificant: Demosthenes (36.28–29) makes clear that for bankers such arrangements were actually the norm, at Athens and elsewhere, as evidenced by such archetypical exemplars as the Athenian bankers Sōkrates, Satyros, Sōklēs, and Timodēmos.[5]

Socrates and Socles arguably willed their wives to their slaves (or former slaves) Satyrus and Timodemus. A final point is that commercially oriented marriage partners would be attracted by the legal advantages of *pallakia* (including the rights to comingle assets and serve as agents).

---

5. Public banks as well as private banks relied on slaves: The Delphians made the temple-slave Ion the "steward" (*tamias*) and "gold-keeper" (*chrusophilaka*) of Delphi's rich treasury (Euripides *Ion* 54–55). Homer tells that the double doors of the *thalamus*—"treasury"—in Odysseus's *oikos* were under the charge of a *tamiē*—"treasurer/steward"—named Eurycleia, the daughter of Ops the son of Peisenor (*Odyssey* 1.345ff. cf. 19.30; 21.387). Eurycleia, a slave, had been purchased (*priamai*) as a young woman by Laertes for twenty oxen (*Odyssey* 1.430–35; cf. 19.483).

That Archippe could inherit a tenement-house (Demosthenes 45.28) goes far to dispel the remaining uncertainties by demonstrating that she possessed citizen status as only a citizen had the right to own Athenian real estate (*enktēsis*). Real property could not be owned by a metic and surely not by an enslaved person of metic origin (E. Cohen 1992: 104 with n. 215).

The best explanation is that an Athenian citizen who consented to become a slave or slave-wife (*pallakē*) retained certain residual rights of citizenship. This was the case in Rome. At the time of the jurist Gaius, a woman who entered *manus* via *coemptio* underwent *capitus deminutio minima* which did not completely remove her citizenship rights (Treggari 1991: 28).[6] Much closer in time and place to classical Athens, it appears that the Gortynian laws made it possible for an enslaved person to retain a claim on his citizenship (Kristensen 2015).[7] For Athens itself, Meyer (1993: 113–14 with n. 41) cites (with sources) a general agreement among scholars that *atimia* involved/came to involve not only full outlawry (total *atimia*) but also, more mildly, the loss of specified citizenship rights either temporarily or permanently (partial *atimia*). For examples, the loss of the right to give evidence or the right to enter the Agora. The point being that Athenians, like Romans, were capable of recognizing legal gradations in citizenship rights. Consequently, one may hypothesize that an Athenian who contracted into *pallakia* retained certain citizenship rights including the right to retain ownership of real property.

Concretely, when the citizen Archippe sold herself to the metic Pasiōn she either owned the tenement house or else it was part of the price she received. As a citizen, she was legally entitled to own real property and it could not be confiscated by the state when she became a slave-wife. The house together with other valuables she received formed her *peculium* and, legally speaking, it was classified as dowry, which she could recover at Pasiōn's death. By including the tenement house in his will, Pasiōn, an experienced businessman, took it for granted that Archippe could legally own the house just as much as his other property (see E. Cohen 1992: 108–09).

Having come this far let us take an extra step and consider the status of Phormiōn. Pasiōn had purchased (*onios*) Phormiōn to be his slave and trained him in letters, taught him the banking business, and placed him in control of large sums of money (Demosthenes 45.71–72). The transfer into slavery took place in Athens at the temple of Castor and Pollux, the Anakeion (Demosthenes 45.80). The term *paradidōmi* used in connection with this transfer (Demosthenes 45.81) could have the meaning "he was handed over" or "he handed himself over." Phormiōn is referred to as *andrapōdon*

6. Gaius *Institutes* 2.162: "The least loss of civil rights results when both citizenship and freedom are retained, but a man's domestic condition is altered; which happens to those who are adopted, as well as to women subject to coemption, and also in the case of those who are given in mancipation and are afterwards manumitted; so that as often as anyone is mancipated, or remancipated, or manumitted, he suffers a loss of civil rights" (tr. de Zulueta).

7. Doubters such as D. Lewis (2013) have not considered whether the Gortynian slaves with property and marriage rights had such rights prior to becoming slaves (see also n. 10 below).

(Demosthenes 45.73), a term that might apply to enslaved prisoners of war or might apply to slaves with no reference to a forcible mode of acquisition (Pritchett 1991, 170–73). Given his subsequent advantages as a skilled banker, it is quite possible that Phormiōn chose to become an *andrapodon*—that is, to sell himself into slavery.

It is often assumed that at the time he married Archippe, Phormiōn had already been manumitted from slavery and had metic status. I think this is incorrect. All we know is that Apollodorus states: "Phormio became an Athenian citizen during the archonship of Nicophemus, in the tenth year after my father died [about 360]" (Demosthenes 46.13; tr. Murray LCL). How did Phormiōn bridge the sizeable gap between alleged metic status and proven citiizen status? There is no indication that he gained citizenship by means of any special naturalization decree as did his owner the banker Pasiōn and the latter's sons (Demosthenes 59.2, 53.18). No one, not even a rich banker, was automatically promoted from metic to citizen. J.K. Davies (1971: 437) adds:

> Phormion does not seem to have owed his citizenship to any exertions on his behalf by Pasion's sons (if he had, we should have heard about it from Apollodorus in the shape of a specific charge of base ingratitude).

Next, I consider two alternative frameworks for explaining how Phormiōn went from slavery to citizenship. Both frameworks take into account the high probability that Phormiōn had an Athenian patronymic: "son of Ktesiphon of Piraeus."[8] The first interpretation assumes that when Phormiōn became a slave he was already a citizen or, more likely, a youth eligible to become one. This position is my favored one notwithstanding Phormiōn's difficulty with speaking good grammatical Greek (Demosthenes 36.1; 45.30; but compare 34.1).[9] The second interpretation is in some ways more speculative. It assumes first, despite the absence of evidence, that

8. Trevett (1992, 14 with endnote 26), maintains that our Phormiōn "is almost certainly to be identified with Phormion son of Ktesiphon of Piraeus" (cf. J.K. Davies 1971: 436–37). This wealthy individual is attested in inscriptions as a trierarch (*IG* II2 1822, 472; 1623, 246–48; 1629, 645–56) and as a witness in a bottomry loan (Demosthenes 35.13–14). His identification with the banker Phormiōn finds rough support in Demosthenes 21.157 wherein the speaker implies the presence in Athens of only one extremely rich Phormiōn and it is secured by the fact that Phormiōn son of Ktesiphon had a son named Archippos who would reasonably be understood to be his son by Archippe, the widow of Pasiōn (Demosthenes 45.4).

9. With respect to Phormiōn's alleged inability to speak good Greek, note that Euxitheus who was accused of being an alien (in part) on the ground that his father had a foreign accent was nevertheless able to provide countervailing evidence that both his mother and father were citizens (Demosthenes 57). In addition, to be kept in mind is that many Athenians who were remote geographically from Athens retained their claim on citizenship. J.K. Davies (1971: 437) speculates that Phormiōn "was sponsored for membership of Peiraeus by a man who adopted him as his son." However, even if true, this does not solve the problem as under Greek law Ktesiphon could have adopted Phormiōn only if the latter was of native Athenian birth (Isaeus 7.16 and 8.19).

Phormiōn was naturalized by decree and that, again in the absence of evidence, that the naturalization-by-decree process ordinarily included the adoption of those naturalized by a prominent Athenian.[10]

"Pasiō's bank had been leased for eight years by the slave Phormiōn after he had become *ēdē chath heauton onti* ['of himself'/'on his own']" (Demosthenes 36.4). This means that he had become an autonomous slave with lifestyle freedom who was doing business on his own, not that he was *eleutheron* meaning he was manumitted/juridically free (Kazakévich 2008: 36 with n. 43 with references). Phormiōn was not at this time actually a citizen (Demosthenes 36.6). I suggest that Pasiōn's will promised the autonomous "of himself" slave Phormiōn full manumission provided he married Archippe and cared for her and 10-year-old Pasicles for a defined period of time. I assume that as an autonomous slave Pasiön had the right to marry.[11] At the end of this period, Pasiōn's will granted Pasiōn juridical freedom. That is, the will embodied a *paramonē* contract familiar in classical Greece (Silver 2015: 153–55 with references). Under this contract, a slave owner promised manumission to his slave in the future on the condition that he/she *paramenein*—"remains with"—a specified individual to perform certain duties. Given proper performance, the slave became juridically free. In the case of Phormiōn, this would have happened no more than ten years after Pasiōn's death. In Demosthenes 36.48 (also 36.28) wherein the legal status of Pasiōn and Phormōn is equated, *gignomai*—"to come into a new state of being"—must mean that they had both been manumitted from slavery (made juridically free).[12] At that

10. The first question is why the state would furnish new citizens with a patronymic. As noted by Lape (2002–03: 129), in classical Athens, the "citizen took his last name ['x' of the deme 'y'] from the state rather than from the father." Looking at evidence, it seems possible that naturalization-by-decree included adoption by a citizen sponsor (*prostatēs*) in the case of the banker Pasiōn. The latter individual, a Greek-named slave of obscure origin who was manumitted and became a metic, was naturalized by decree and possibly had a patronymic. A short letter written by Pasiōn is translated by Jordan (2003) as follows: "I, Pasion (son) of <->ikaiarchos, am sending you a letter for Satyrion to punish and to prosecute both Nikostratos, Deinon's brother, and Arethousios, because they are wronging me and plotting (against me) and Glauketes and Aiontodoros and they are plotting and (or also?) for the X not to be paid before." However, Sosin (2008) has advanced technical arguments raising doubts about the text of the letter, and specifically about whether Pasiōn really had the patronymic "son of Dikaiarchos." Such arguments are by their very nature inconclusive. On the other hand, Pasiōn's letter is the only evidence suggesting that new citizens received a patronymic in addition to a demotic. Pasiōn himself was enrolled in the deme of Acharnai (Demosthenes 59.2; *IG* ii^2 1609.87). Interestingly, Pasiōn had a citizen associate named Pythodorus whose deme was Acharnai (discussed by J.K. Davies 1971: 430; Trevett 1982: 21–22).
11. In Rome, a slave woman might have a marital relationship, termed *contubernium*, with a free husband (see Chapter X.1 at n. 2). As proven by the *anniculi probatio* procedure, Rome's Junian Latins (autonomous slaves) could marry (Gaius *Institutes* 1.79–81; Silver 2014: 241 n. 29); in the Prologue of Plautus *Casina* 68 we are told that "slaves" (*servi*) could marry in Greece, as well as in Carthage and Apulia.
12. Demosthenes 36.28–29: "Socrates, the well-known banker, having been set free by his masters just as the plaintiff's father [Apollodorus's father Pasiōn] gave [*didōmi*] his wife in marriage

time, now surely over eighteen years old, a free man (not a slave) and of Athenian ancestry Phormiōn applied for and was granted citizenship by Piraeus. The alternative view that Phormiōn had been naturalized by decree which process included adoption of beneficiaries by prominent Athenian patrons is possible but supported by little evidence and little logic.

Returning to the original problem, the hypothesis that best fits the facts as presented is that Archippe was a citizen who, motivated by love or financial security or both, consented to become Pasiōn's *pallakē*. As a citizen, she retained certain rights of citizenship including the right to own real property.

3. Plangon as *Pallakē*

Demosthenes 39 and 40 deal with two half-brothers born by different wives to the same father, named Mantias son of Mantitheus of the deme Thoricus. Both wives are highborn Athenian citizens. One is Plangon, the daughter of Pamphilus of the deme Keiriadai, and other is the unnamed daughter of Polyaratus of the deme Cholargus, who comes from a family both prestigious and wealthy. On the other hand, the estate of Plangon's father had been confiscated and sold. Mantias supported both households.

Plangon's son did not have inheritance rights because his father Mantias had not enrolled him in his phratry. The speaker explains that Plangon tricked Mantias and

> swore that not only the defendant (Boeotus), but his brother too, her other son, was my father's child. When she had done this, it was necessary to enter them among the clansmen (the phratry), and there was no excuse left. My father did enter them; he adopted them as his children and (to cut short the intervening matters) he enrolled the defendant at the Apaturia as Boeotus on the list of the clansmen, and the other as Pamphilus (Demosthenes 39.4; tr. Murray *LCL*).

In Demosthenes 40.10, Plangon is said to have promised (in return for thirty *minae*) that she would get her brothers to adopt her sons by Mantias. The point of this promise is left unclear. Is it that the brothers were offering Boeotus an inheritance?

---

to Satyrus whom he had freed from slavery [*gignomai*]. Another, Socles, who had been in the banking business, gave [*didōmi*] his wife in marriage to Timodemus, who is still in being and alive, whom he had freed from slavery [*gignomai*]" (tr. Murray *LCL* modified). In the comparison of Pasiōn with Socrates and (probably) Socles, *gignomai*—"to come into a new state of being"—refers to manumission, the grant of juridical freedom. I suspect that in the instances of Satyrus and Timodemus, *gignomai* refers to the status of autonomous slavery. That the recipient of the banker's wife might be a current slave is confirmed in the last line of Demosthenes 36.29: "And it is not here only, men of Athens, that those engaged in this line of business so act; but in Aegina Strymodorus gave [*didōmi*] his wife in marriage to Hermaeus, his own slave (*oiketēs*), and again, after her death, gave [*didōmi*] him his own daughter" (tr. Murray *LCL*). Strymodorus's will assigns his wife (daughter) to this Hermaeus who is explicitly his current slave.

What is clear is that the argument made by the speaker makes no sense. Plangon's oath about the parentage of her sons *at the most* demonstrates that they qualified for citizenship. Plangon's oath could not have compelled Mantias to introduce her sons to his phratry (compare Patterson 1991a: 283 and Harrison 1968: 68–69). This would have been necessary only if Plangon had sworn they were Mantias's *legitimate* children, which the speaker does not claim either explicitly or implicitly. If, however, his two sons by Plangon were legitimate Mantias could have introduced them to his phratry with no need to adopt them.

Why did he adopt them? The explanation that seems most likely is that the speaker has left out an important detail: Plangon's oath asserted not only that Mantias was her children's father but also that Mantias had taken an oath that he would legitimize her sons so that they would have a legal share in his inheritance.[13] This would explain why he was so concerned about Plangon's oath that he bribed her. Adoption was necessary because Plangon was a *pallakē* (compare Mossē 1991: 283) and her son Boeotus was a *nothos*. Adoption was legally possible because Boeotus was a citizen. Contrary to Ogden (1996: 158), Plangon was a *pallakē* and a citizen.[14]

4. The Nuptial Relationship between Alcibiades and Hipparete

The Chapter ends on an interesting but uncertain note. According to Plutarch (*Alcibiades* 8.3–4):

> Hipparete was a decorous and affectionate wife, but being distressed because her husband would consort with courtesans (*hetairai*), native and foreign, she left his house and went to live with her brother (Callias). Alcibiades did not mind this, but continued his wanton ways, and so she had to put in her plea for divorce to the magistrate, and that not by proxy, but in her own person. On her appearing publicly to do this, as the law required, Alcibiades came up and seized her (*harpazō*) and carried her off home with him through the market place, no man daring to oppose him or take her from him. She lived with him, moreover, until her death, but she died shortly after this, when Alcibiades was on a voyage to Ephesus (tr. Perrin *LCL*).

Plutarch's account is similar to Andocides's (4.14):

> Then, after obtaining a dowry [*proix*] such as no Greek had ever obtained before, he behaved in so profligate a fashion, bringing mistresses, slave and free, into the bridal house, that he drove his wife, who was a decent woman, to present herself before the Archon, as she was legally entitled to do, and divorce him. At that he gave conspicuous proof of his

13. Such a promise would not be unprecedented. In Demosthenes 59.38, Stephanus convinces Neaira to leave Megara and come with him to Athens by promising to introduce her sons to his phratry.
14. Ogden (1996: 125), citing Isaeus 7.16, asserts that in Athens it was "not possible" to legitimize a *nothos* by means of adoption. This leaves unexplained the case of Philē and the fact that Plangon's children were adopted and then introduced into their father's phratry.

> power. He called in his friends, and carried off his wife from the Agora by force, showing the whole world his contempt for the magistrates, the laws, and his fellow Athenians in general. Nor was this one outrage enough for him. He went further (tr. Maidment *LCL*)

It appears from both accounts that Alcibiades treated his legitimate wife as if she were his purchased wife. Also, it appears that Hipparete's brother Callias who was Hipparete's *kurios* was afraid to assert his legal rights against Alcibiades. However, there may be more to the story of Hipparete's marital status than our sources reveal or admit.

Again, according to Plutarch (*Alcibiades* 8.2):

> But Hipponicus put away his wrath and forgave him, and afterwards gave him his daughter Hipparete to wife. Some say, however, that it was not Hipponicus, but Callias, his son, who gave Hipparete to Alcibiades, with a *dowry* of ten talents; and that afterwards, when she became a mother, Alcibiades exacted another ten talents besides, on the plea that this was the agreement, should children be born. And Callias was so afraid of the scheming of Alcibiades to get his wealth, that he made public proffer to the people of his property and house in case it should befall him to die without lineal heirs (tr. Perrin *LCL*).

Plutarch's account, unlike Andocides's, does not actually contain the word *proix*—"dowry". Callias gave (*dounai*) Hipparete to Alcibiades *epi deka talantois*—"on account of/because of ten talents"? Nevertheless, it is clear that Plutarch believes that wealth was transferred from Hipparete's *oikos* to Alcibiades's.

The split dowry mentioned by Plutarch, but not by Andocides, is unexpected and puzzling. Why did Callias (or his father) contract to pay an additional sum to Alcibiades in case children were born to the couple? Did not Alcibiades take Hipparete for bearing legitimate children? There must be answers but I cannot think of convincing ones. On the other hand, I find reasonable that the *purchaser* of a wife might contract to pay the full price only if she bore children to him. Indeed, Stol (1995: 120) believes such contracts were signed in the ancient Near East at mid-second millennium in eastern Assyria:

> It is my opinion that it [the brideprice] was a fixed price that could be paid in installments, the texts from Nuzi show that when the first child was born, another part of it was paid.

It is always risky and usually unwise to challenge the sources but I would propose that Alcibiades purchased Hipparete—that is, wealth moved from him to her *oikos*. This makes better sense of the nuptial installment contract and better explains why Alciabiades was not prosecuted for seizing Hipparate when she sought to divorce him. Callias took no action not because he was afraid to resort to law but because he knew that Alcibiades owned his sister and was within his legal rights to force her to return to his house.

Summary of Main Findings and Problems for Future Research

Under ancient Greek law, the legitimate wife is a "wife by loan" from the father (the *kurios*) to the husband. She remains under the control of her father and has suppliant status in her husband's household. The children of the legitimate wife inherit their father's name, household cult and property. The *pallakē* is a "wife by purchase," from the father or from herself by self-sale; she is legally owned by her husband and has slave status. More precisely, her position is that of a privileged or autonomous slave. Her children are *nothoi*—"bastards"—and have inheritance rights from their mother but not ordinarily from their father. As in the Roman *cum manus*-marriage, the children of a *pallakē* bear a metronymic, not a patronymic.

Even when the father chose the husband for his daughter, the marriage might not be legitimate. Also, ancient Greek society did not deny the validity of a marriage in which the husband and wife chose one another. Not only were their two distinct forms of marriage but there is no evidence that legitimate marriage was the "norm" in ancient Greek society.

The *pallakē* institution finds it primary socioeconomic rationale in the sexual and emotional needs of ancient Greek men who often spent large blocks of time away from their primary or legitimate households. Geographically displaced men enjoyed the benefits of marriage and family ties and local connections without diluting the inheritance rights of their children by legitimate wives.

Legitimate marriage is made recognizable by a distinctive betrothal terminology involving cognates of the verb *eggmalizein*—"to put into the hand". It is possible, even probable, that *pallakia* is made recognizable by use of the verb *harmozein*—"to fit together"—in *gamos*—"marriage" and by such cognates as *harmostēs*, meaning "husband". "To fit together" can express the outcome that the bride (a slave) merged into the household of the groom, unlike legitimate marriage, wherein she continued to belong to her father's *oikos*. Indeed, *harmozein* has the meanings "to rule" or "to govern."

Marriage by sale of the bride followed a distinctive ritual whose details are not yet proven. First, it is clear that the sale of the bride was solemnized by a handshake between the father and the groom or by the bride and the groom. Arguably, the handshake was followed by a procession in which the husband grasped the wrist/lower arm (*cheir' epi karpoi* gesture) of the *pallakē*, an act signaling that the groom has taken mastery/ownership of the bride-*pallakē*: Circumstantial evidence links wrist grasping with payment by the husband to the bride's father or to the bride herself. More research is needed into the role of wrist grasping and of the spear in the legalization of marriage into *pallakia*.

In legal form, the *pallakē*-wifeship transaction is a sale into slavery with a restrictive covenant mandating the employment of the sold woman as a wife. The general law of contract/contractual norm at Athens left ample room for writing and enforcing restrictive covenants. An important example is provided by a contract well attested in fourth-century Attica called *prasis epi lysei* "sale on condition of release" which is a sale of land (and/or structures) in which the seller reserves the option of repurchase. With respect to restrictive covenants in slave law, Athens knew the "sale [to a third party] for the purpose of [granting] freedom." In Euripides's *Electra*, Electra is the slave and wife of "Farmer," hence he is paid to divorce/emancipate her.

It is argued that wealth was typically transferred *to* the husband (groom-price/dowry) in the case of legitimate marriage and transferred *from* the husband (bride-price) in the case of *pallakia*. A key causal factor in determining marriage form is the distance of the groom's ancestral household from the *oikos* of the bride's father. Other things remaining equal, the greater this distance the greater the likelihood of bride purchase (*pallakia*) and, conversely, the smaller this distance the greater the likelihood of groom purchase (legitimate marriage).

A variety of evidence demonstrates that under Athenian law, the *pallakē*: (1) has a special status due to her being designated for the production of free children; (2) is a purchased slave who manages a secondary household for her owner/husband (*kurios*); (3) might be, before Pericles's Citizenship Law, either a foreigner or an Athenian woman; and (4) has the legal status of "wife." The children of a *pallakē* (*nothoi*) were routinely eligible for citizenship although they otherwise had lesser civil rights than the children of legitimate wives did. Euripides's *Electra* seems to refer to a historical trend in which marriage into *pallakia* grew in importance relative to legitimate marriage.

Demosthenes's formulation of point (2) does not make entirely clear whether there might exist Athenian "*pallakai*" *who* were *not* kept (legally designated/registered) for the procreation of free (*eleutheros*) children. There is evidence suggesting some were unregistered but it is either from very early or very late sources.

Were *nothoi* disenfranchised by PCL given the legal status of autonomous slaves because, while remaining free, they were the children of slave-wives? Alternatively, is it merely a coincidence that *nothoi* and autonomous slaves were registered in Cunosarges?

Some Athenian women who wished to marry had only *pallakē* status available to them because they *necessarily* lacked a male *kurios* who could give them in legitimate marriage. This latter group included women emancipated from the control of a male *kurios* and, hence, under their own ownership (*autē hautēs kuria*). Indeed, some women actively preferred placement outside a father's household—that is, to become single women—in order to act on their personal nuptial preferences. Other women were in households unable to offer a substantial dowry to ease their path into legitimate marriage. There are clear cases in which the motivating factor in sale (or self-sale) into *pallakia* is not the seller's poverty but access to the buyer's wealth.

The process by means of which the father emancipated his child remains unknown. The role and legal status of the "old women" mentioned in Menander and other sources remains an open question. Are they to be understood as *kuria* of women such as Glycera or Persephone? Were some "old women" specialized professional marriage brokers?

A large body of evidence demonstrates the presence in Greek antiquity of a class of respectable, socially and sexually active single women. These women were called *hetairai* whose literal meaning indicates that they were "companions" to one another. Their presence in classical Greece is signaled by the aetiological myths of the suppliant Danaids and the Amazonomachy. There is evidence, surprisingly, for Homeric times, of geographic mobility among single women. Nausicaa tells Odysseus about women who themselves go abroad to acquire "a husband from another people; for of a truth she scorns the Phaeacians here in the land, where she has wooers many and noble" (*Odyssey* 6.282 ff.).

It remains an open question whether Athenian *hetairai* (literally "companions") not only offered one another friendly but informal support but also were members of associations (*koina*) with corporate status like *orgeōnes, thiasōtai, eranistai* and others. Was there a name or term other than *hetaira* pertaining to the single woman? Might the more precise word be *anumpheutos* "unwedded" or better "removed from marriage"?

Also, was single woman status represented iconographically? The thought occurs that if the image of a male holding the breast of a woman (e.g. Zeus and Hera at Samos) signifies that her sexuality belonged to him then the image of an individual woman touching her own breast (the "Ishtar-Astarte type") might signify that her sexuality was in her own hands—that is, she is a single woman.

It also remains a question for further research to what extent cults participated in the courtship of mortal single women. Are *parthenoi* young women dedicated to a cult and is the erotic meadow with its flowers an idealization of a temple *alsos*? Does *parthenios* means the child of any mother not legally wed (as in the Spartan tale) or does it refer only to the child (e.g. Eudorus) of a woman dedicated to Artemis? My impression is that female deities such as Artemis controlled nymphs while maenads were controlled by Dionysius. However, real questions remain about how wild the maenads really were.

I am confident that this rich subject matter will provoke many additional issues in the minds of my readers.

Manhattan, New York September 21, 2017

Bibliography

List of abbreviations

A&A	Antike und Abendland
Acta Jurid.Hung.	Acta juridica Hungarica
AHB	Ancient History Bulletin
AJA	American Journal of Archaeology
AJP	*American Journal of Philology*
AntCl	L'Antiquité classique
CJ	Classical Journal
AntK	Antique Kunst
BICS	Bulletin of the Institute of Classical Studies, University of London
BMCR	Bryn Mawr Classical Review
BMFA	Bulletin of the Museum of Fine Arts, Boston
BSA	Annual of the British School at Athens
BSAS	British School at Athens Studies
ClAnt	*Classical Antiquity*
CP	*Classical* Philology
CQ	*Classical Quarterly*
CR	Classical Review
CW	Classical World
EchCl	Echos du monde classique. Classical Views
ELR	*Legal Roots, The International Journal of Roman Law, Legal History and Comparative Law*
EuGeStA	Eugesta: Journal of Gender Studies in Antiquity
ExClass	Exemplaria Classica
GaR	Greeece and Rome
GRBS	Greek, Roman and Byzantine Studies
Historia	Historia. Zeitschrift für alte Geschichte
HSCP	Harvard Studies in Classical Philology
ICS	Illinois Classical Studies
IGForsch	Indogermanische Forschungen
IncidAntico	Incidenza dellAntico
JAOS	Journal of the American Oriental Society
Jahrb.f.cl.Philol.	Jahrbuch für classische Philologie
JESHO	Journal of the Economic and Social History of the Orient

JHS	*Journal of Hellenic Studies*
JJurP	*Journal of Juristic Papyrology*
JNES	Journal of Ancient Near Eastern Studies
JRS	Journal of Roman Studies
Klio	Klio. Beiträge zur alten Geschichte
MAAR	Memoirs of the American Academy in Rome
MBAH	Marburger Beiträge zur Antiken Handels-, Wirtschafts- und Sozialgeschichte (Formerly Münstersche Beiträge zur Antiken Handelsgeschichte)
PP	La Parola del Passato. Rivista di Studi Antichi. Naples, Italy
QUCC	Quaderni Urbanati di Classica, Rome
RhM	Rheinisches Museum für Philologie. Frankfurt am Main: Sauerländer.
SO	Symbolae Osloenses
SyllClass	Syllecta Classica
TAPA	Transactions of the American Philological Association
TC	Trends in Classics
T.v.R.	Tijdschrift voor Rechtsgeschiedenis / Revue d'Histoire du Droit / The Legal History Review
WS	Wiener Studien
ZPE	*Zeitschrift für Papyrologie und Epigraphik*
ZRG	Zeitschrift der Savigny-Stiftung für Rechtsgeschichte: Romanistische Abteilung

Adams, J.N. (1983). "Words for 'Prostitute' in Latin." *RhM* 126, 321–58.

Aleshire, S.B. and S.D. Lambert (2003). "Making the *Peplos* for Athena: A New Edition of *IG* II^2 1060 + *IG* II^2 1036." *ZPE* 142, 65–86.

Alföldi, A. (1979). *Hasta—Summa Imperii*: The Spear as an Embodiment of Sovereignty in Rome." *AJA* 63, 1–27.

Arnaoutoglou, I. (1995). "Marital Disputes in Greco-Roman Egypt." *JJurP* 25, 11–28.

Arnott, W.G. (1997). "Final Notes on Menander's Sikyonioi (vv. 343–423) with Frs. 1, 2 and 7." *ZPE* 118, 95–103.

Aubert, J.-J. (1994). *Business Managers in Ancient Rome: A Social and Economic Study of Institores, 200 B.C.-A.D. 250*. Leiden: Brill.

Ault, B.A. (2016). "Building Z in the Athenian Kerameikos: House, Tavern, Inn, Brothel?" In Glazebrook and Tsakirgis (eds.), *Houses of Ill Repute*, 75–102.

Avagianou, A. (1991). *Sacred Marriage in the Rituals of Greek Relgion*. Bern: Lang.

Avilés, D. (2012). "The Athenian Las(s) on *Homologia*." *Mouseion* 12, 51–72.

Avramidou, A. and D. Demetriou (eds.) (2014). *Approaching the Ancient Artifact: Representation, Narrative, and Function. A Festschrift in Honor of H. Alan Shapiro*. Berlin: de Gruyter.

Bachvarova, M. (2009). "Suppliant Danaids and Argive Nymphs in Aeschylus." *CJ* 104, 289–310.

Badian, E. (2000). "The Rise to Prominence." In I. Worthington (ed.), *Demosthenes: Statesman and Orator*. London: Routledge, 9–44.

Bakewell, G.W. (2008/09). "Forbidding Marriage: 'Neaira' 16 and Metic Spouses at Athens." *CJ* 104, 97–109.

Bakewell, G.W. (2013). *Aeschylus'* Suppliant Women: *The Tragedy of Immigration*. Madison, WI: University of Wisconsin Press.
Barber, E.J.W. (1991). *Prehistoric Textiles: The Development of Cloth in the Neolithic and Bronze Ages with Special Reference to the Aegean*. Princeton, NJ: Princeton University Press.
Barber, E.J.W. (1992). "The Peplos of Athena." In J. Neils (ed.), *Goddess and Polis: The Panathenaic Festival in Ancient Athens*. Princeton, NJ: Princeton University Press, 103–17.
Barringer, J.M. (1995). *Divine Escorts: Nereids in Archaic and Classical Greek Art*. Ann Arbor, MI: University of Michigan Press.
Barringer, J.M. (1996). "Atalanta as Model: The Hunter and the Hunted." *ClAnt* 15, 48–76.
Baumbach, J.D. (2004). *The Significance of Votive Offerings in Selected Hera Sanctuaries in the Peloponnese, Ionia, and Western Greece*. Oxford: Archaeopress.
Beard, M. (1991). "Adopting an Approach II." In T. Rasmussen and N. Spivey (ed.), *Looking at Greek Vases*. Cambridge: Cambridge University Press, 12–35.
Bearzot, C. (2005). "Né cittadini né stanieri: apeleutheroi e nothoi in Atene." In M.G. Angeli Bertinelli and A. Donati (eds.) *Il cittadino, lo straniero, il barbaro, fra integrazione ed emarginazione nell'antichità*. Rome: Bretschneider, 77–92.
Beazley, J.D. (1931). "Corpus Vasorum Antiquorum: Athenes, Musée National, fasc. I." *JHS* 51, 121.
Beazley, J.D. (1947). "The Rosi Krater." *JHS* 67, 1–9.
Becker, G.S. (1991). *A Treatise on the Family*. Enl. ed. Cambridge, MA: Harvard University Press.
Belfiore, E.S. (2000). *Murder among Friends: Violation of* Philia *in Greek Tragedy*. New York, NY: Oxford University Press.
Ben, N. van der (1986). "Hymn to Aphrodite 36–291. Notes on the Pars Epica of the Homeric Hymn to Aphrodite." *Mnemosyne* 39, 1–41.
Benveniste, É. (1973). *Indo-European Language and Society*. Coral Gables, FL: University of Miami Press.
Bérard, C. (1989). "The Order of Women." In Bérard *A City of Images*, 89–108.
Bérard, C. (1989). *A City of Images: Iconography and Society in Ancient Greece*. Princeton, NJ: Princeton University Press.
Berg, R. (ed.) (2016). *The Material Sides of Marriage: Women and Domestic Economies in Antiquity*. Rome: Institutum Romanum Finlandiae.
Billigmeier, J.-C. and J.A. Turner (1981). "The Socio-Economic Roles of Women in Mycenaean Greece: A Brief Survey from Evidence of the Linear B Tablets." In H.P. Foley (ed.), *Reflections on Women in Antiquity*. New York: Gordon & Breach, 1–18.
Blasone, P. (2010). "On the Traces of Alcestis, between Eros and Thanatos." Unpublished paper available for download at: https://independent.academia.edu/PinoBlasone.
Blok, J.H. (2005). "Becoming Citizens. Some Notes on the Semantics of 'Citizen' in Archaic Greece and Classical Athens." *Klio* 87, 7–40.
Blok, J.H. (2009). "Perikles' Citizenship Law: A New Perspective." *Historia* 58, 141–70.
Blok, J.H. (2017). *Citizenship in Classical Athens*. Cambridge: Cambridge University Press.
Blundell, S. (1995). *Women in Ancient Greece*. Cambridge, MA: Harvard University Press.
Blundell, S. (2002). "Clutching at Clothes." In Llewellyn-Jones (ed.), *Women's Dress in the Ancient Greek World*, 143–69.
Bonfante, L. (2010). "Euripides in Etruria: Admetus and Alcestus." In G.M. Sifakis and S. Tsitsiridis (eds.), *Parachoregema: meletemata gia to archaio theatro pros timen tou kathegete Gregore M. Sephake*. Herakleion: Crete University Press, 463–78.
Botticini, M. and A. Snow. (2003). "Why Dowries?" *American Economic Review* 93, 1385–98.
Brauw, M. de and J. Miner. (2004). "Androtion's Alleged Contract: Aes, 1,165 and Dem. 22.23 in Light of P.Oxy. VII 1012." *ZRG* 121, 301–13.
Bremmer, J. (1983). "The Importance of the Maternal Uncle and Grandfather in Archaic and Classical Greeceand Early Byzantium." *ZPE* 50, 173–86.

Bremmer, J. (1984). "Greek Maenadism Reconsidered." *ZPE* 55, 267–86.

Brock, R. (1994). "The Labour of Women in Classical Athens." *CQ* 44, 336–46.

Brøns, C. (2015). "Textiles and Textile Inventories: Detecting an Invisible Votive Tradition in Greek Sanctuaries in the Second Half of the First Millennium BC." In J. Fejfer, M. Moltesen, and A. Rathje (eds.), *Tradition: Transmission of Culture in the Ancient World*. Copenhagen: Museum Tusculanum Press, 43–83.

Brøns, C. (2017). "Power through Textiles: Women as Ritual Performers in Ancient Greece." In Dillon, Eidinow and Maurizio (eds.), *Women's Ritual Competence in the Greco-Roman Mediteranean*, 46–64.

Brown, F.S. and W.B. Tyrrell. (1985). "*Ektilōsanto*: A Reading of Herodotus' Amazons". *CJ* 80, 297–302.

Buckland, W.W. (1908). *The Roman Law of Slavery*. Cambridge: Cambridge University Press.

Buckland, W.W. (1921). *A Text-Book of Roman Law from Augustus to Justinian*. 3rd ed. Cambridge: Cambridge University Press.

Buermann, H. (1877–78). "Drei Studien auf dem Gebiet des attischen Rechts." *Jahrbuch fur classischen Philologie*, Supplementband 9, 569–646.

Bundrick, S.D. (2008). "The Fabric of the City: Imaging Textile Production in Classical Athens." *Hesperia* 77, 283–334.

Bundrick, S.D. (2012). "Housewives, *Hetairai*, and the Ambiguity of Genre in Attic Vase Painting." *Phoenix* 66, 11–35.

Burnett, A.P. (1970). Ion *by Euripides*. Englewood Cliffs, NJ: Prentice-Hall.

Burnett, A.P. (1973). "Medea and the Tragedy of Revenge." *CP* 68, 1–24.

Burnett, A.P. (1994). "Hekabe the Dog." *Arethusa* 27, 151–64.

Burton, J. (1998). "Women's Commensality in the Ancient Greek World." *GaR* 45, 143–65.

Cairns, F. (1998). "Asclepiades and the *Hetairai*." *Eikasmos* 9, 166–93.

Calame, C. (1997). *Choruses of Young Women in Ancient Greece: Their Morphology, Religions Role, and Social Function*. Lanham, MD: Rowman & Littlefield.

Calame, C. (1999). *The Poetics of Eros in Ancient Greece*. Princeton, NJ: Princeton University Press.

Cameron, A. (1995). *Callimachus and His Critics*. Princeton, NJ: Princeton University Press.

Carawan, E. (2006). "The Athenian Law of Agreement." *GRBS* 46, 339–74.

Carawan, E. (2008). "Pericles the Younger and the Citizenship Law." *CJ* 103, 383–406.

Carey, C. (1988). "A Note on Torture in Athenian Homicide Cases." *Historia* 37, 241–45.

Carey, C. (1991). "Apollodoros' Mother: The Wives of Enfranchised Aliens in Athens." *CQ* 41, 84–89.

Carson, A. (1982). "Wedding at Noonin Pindar's *Ninth Pythian*". *GRBS*, 23, 121–28.

Clark, I. (1998). "The Gamos of Hera." In S. Blendell and M. Williamson (eds.), *The Sacred and the Feminine in Ancient Greece*. London: Routledge, 13–26.

Clément, P. (1934). "New Evidence for the Origin of the Iphigeneia Legend." *AntCl* 3, 393–409.

Cohen, A. (2007). "Gendering the Age Gap: Boys, Girls, and Abduction in Greek Art." In Rutter and Cohen (eds.), *Constructions of Childhood in the Ancient World*, 257–78.

Cohen, B. (2014). "Polyxena's Dropped Hydria: The Epic Cycle and the Inconography of Gravity in Athenian Vase Painting." In Avramidou and Demetriou (eds.), *Approaching the Ancient Artifact*, 15–29.

Cohen, D. (1998). "Women, Property and Statis om Demosthenes 41 and 57." *Dike* 1, 53–61.

Cohen, E.E. (1992). *Athenian Economy and Society. A Banking Perspective*. Princeton, NJ: Princeton University Press.

Cohen, E.E. (2000). *The Athenian Nation*. Princeton, NJ: Princeton University Press.

Cohen, E.E. (2015). *Athenian Prostitution: The Business of Sex*. Oxford: Oxford University Press.

Cole, S.G. (1984a). "Greek Sanctions against Sexual Assault." *CP* 79, 97–113.

Cole, S.G. (1984b). "The Social Function of Rituals of Maturation: The *Koureion* and the *Arkteia*." *ZPE* 55, 233–44.

Cole, S.G. (1998). "Domesticating Artemis." In S. Blundell and M. Williamson (eds.), *The Sacred and the Feminine in Ancient Greece*. London: Routledge, 17–33.

Cole, S.G. (2004). *Landscapes, Gender, and Ritual Space: The Ancient Greek Experience*. Berkeley: CA: University of California Press.

Connor, W.R. (1988). "Seized by the Nymphs. Nympholepsy and Symbolic Expression in Classical Greece". *ClAnt* 7, 155–89.

Constantinidou, S. (1990). "Evidence for Marriage Ritual in *Iliad* 3." *Topos* 19, 47–59.

Corbett, P.E. (1930). *The Roman Law of Marriage*. Oxford: Oxford University Press.

Cox, C.A. (1998). *Household Interests: Property, Marriage Strategies and Family Dynamics in Ancient Athens*. Princeton, NJ: Princeton University Press.

Cox, C.A. (2002). "Is Sostratus' Family Urban in Menander's 'Dyskolos'?" *CJ* 97, 351–58.

Croon, J.H. (1952). "The Palici: An Autochthonous Cult in Ancient Sicily." *Mnemosyne*, 5, 116–29.

Dalby, A. (1993). "Food and Sexuality in Classical Athens." In G. Mars and V. Mars (eds.), *Food, Culture and History*, Vol. I. London: Food Seminar, 165–90.

Dalby, A. (2002). "Levels of Concealment: The Dress of *Hetairai* and *Pornea* in Greek Texts." In Llewellyn-Jones (ed.) (2002), *Women's Dress in the Ancient Greek World*, 111–24.

Davidson, J.N. (1997). *Courtesans & Fishcakes: The Consuming Passions of Classical Athens*. New York, NY: St. Martin's.

Davidson, J.N. (2004). "*Liaisons dangereuses*: Aphrodite and the *Hetaira*." *JHS* 124, 169–73.

Davidson, J.N. (2006). "Making a Spectacle of Her(self): The Greek Courtesan and the Art of the Present." In M. Feldman and B. Gordon (eds.), *The Courtesan's Arts: Cross-Cultural Perspectives*. Oxford: Oxford University Press, 29–51.

Davidson, J. (2002). "Arrival at the Cave: Odyssey and Greek Drama." *WS* 115, 45–57.

Davies, G. (1985). "The Significance of the Handshake Motif in Classical Funerary Art." *AJA* 69, 627–40.

Davies, J.K. (1971). *Athenian Propertied Families, 600–300 B.C.* Oxford: Oxford University Press.

Dawkins, R. (1976). *The Selfish Gene*. Oxford: Oxford University Press.

Deacy, S. (2013). "From 'Flowery Tales' to 'Heroic Rapes'; Virginal Subjectivity in the Mythological Meadow." *Arethusa* 46, 395–413.

Delougaz, P. (1967). "Remarks Concerning Dating and Function of the Northern Palace." In P. Delougaz, H.P. Hill and S. Lloyd (eds.), *Private Houses in the Diyala Region*. Chicago IL: University of Chicago Press, 1966–98.

Diakonoff, I.M. (1986). "Women in Old Babylonia Not Under Patriarchal Authority." *JESHO* 29, 225–38.

Dietrrich, B.C. (1965). *Death, Fate, and the Gods*. London: Athlone Press of the University of London.

Diggle, J. (1970). *Euripides'* Phaethon. Cambridge: Cambridge University Press.

Dillon, M.P.J. (1997). *Pilgrims and Pilgrimage in Ancient Greece*. London: Routledge.

Dillon, M.P.J. (1999). "Post-Nuptial Sacrifices on Kos (Segre, *ED* 178) and Ancient Greek Marriage Rites." *ZPE* 124, 63–80.

Dillon, M.P.J. (2002), *Girls and Women in Classical Greek Religion*. London: Routledge.

Dillon, M., E. Eidinow, and L. Maurizio (eds.) (2017). *Women's Ritual Competence in the Greco-Roman Mediterranean*. London: Routledge.

Dover, K.J. (1971). *Theocritus, Select Poems*. London: Macmillan.

Dowden, K. (1997). "The Amazons: Development and Functions." *RhM* 140. 97–128.

Duffy, W.S. (2013). "The Necklace of Eriphyle and Pausanias' Aprroach to the Homeric Epics." *CW* 107, 35–47.

Dunn, F.M. (1994). "Euripides and the Rites of Hera Akraia." *GRBS* 35, 103–15.

Ebbott, M. (2003). *Imagining Illegitimacy in Classical Greek Literature*. Lanham, MD: Lexington.

Eckerman, C.C. (2011). "Treasure and Pleasure in Archilochus' 'First Cologne Epode'." *ZPE* 179, 11–19.

Edmonds, J.M. (1957). *The Fragments of Attic Comedy*. Leiden: Brill.

Edmunds, L. (2016). *Stealing Helen: The Myth of the Abducted Wife in Comparative Perspective*. Princeton, NJ: Princeton University Press.

Edwards, M. (2007), *Isaeus*. Austin, TX: University of Texas Press.

Ekroth, G. (2003). "Inventing Iphigeneia? On Euripides and the Cultic Construction of Brauron." *Kernos*, 16, 59–118.

Elderkin, G.W. (1935). "Oitosyros and Oiorpata." *AJP* 56, 342–46.

Erdmann, W. (1934). *Die Ehe im alten Griechenland*. Munich: Beck.

Evans-Grubbs, J. (2015). "Making the Private Public: Illegitimacy and Incest in Roman Law." In C. Ando and J. Rüpke (eds.), *Public and Private in Ancient Mediterranean Law and Religion*. Berlin: de Gruyter, 115–41.

Fantham, E. (1975). "Sex, Status, and Survivalin Hellenistic Athens: A Study of Women in New Comedy." *Phoenix* 29, 44–74.

Faraone, C.A. (1999). "Aphroditie's *Kestos* and Apples for Atalanta: Aphrodisiacs in Early Greek in Early Greek Myth and Ritual." *Phoenix* 44, 219–43.

Faraone, C.A. (2003). "Playing the Bear and Fawn for Artemis." In D.B. Dodd and C.A. Faraone (eds.), *Initation in Ancient Greek Rituals and Narratives: New Critical Narratives*. London: Routledge, 43–68.

Ferrari, G. (2002). *Figures of Speech: Men and Maidens in Ancient Greece*. Chicago, IL: University of Chicago Press.

Ferrari, G. (2003). "What Kind of Rite of Passage was the Ancient Greek Wedding?" In D.B. Dodd and C.A. Faraone (eds.), *Initiation in Ancient Greek Rituals and Narratives: New Critical* Perspectives. London: Routledge, 27–42.

Ferrari, G. (2008). *Alcman and the Cosmos of Sparta*. Chicago, IL: University of Chicago Press.

Fine, J.V.A. (1951). *Horoi: Studies in Mortgage, Real Security, and Land Tenure in Ancient Athens*. Baltimore MD: American School of Classical Studies at Athens.

Finley, M.I. (1954). "Marriage, Sale, and Gift in the Homeric World." *Seminar* 12, 7–33.

Fischer, M. (2013). "Ancient Greek Prositutes and the Textile Industry in Attic Vase-Painting, ca. 550–450 B.C.E." *CW* 106, 210–59.

Fitton, J.W. (1970). "That Was No Lady, That Was..." *CQ* 20, 56–66.

Fletcher, J. (2014). "Oaths, Gender and Status." In Sommerstein and Torrance (eds.), *Oaths and Swearing in Ancient Greece*, 156–79

Flory, S. (1978). "Medea's Right Hand: Promises and Revenge." *TAPA* 108, 69–74.

Folry, H.P. (1999). *The Homeric Hymn to Demeter: Translation, Commentary, and Interpretative Essays*. Princeton, NJ: Princeton University Press.

Foley, H.P. (2001). *Female Acts in Greek Tragedy*. Oxford: Oxford University Press.

Foster, B.O. (1899). "Notes on the Symbolism of the Apple in Classical Antiquity." *HSCP* 10, 39–55.

Franco, C. (2014). *Shameless: The Canine and the Feminine in Ancient Greece*. Oakland, CA: University of California Press.

Frier, B.W. and T.A.J. McGinn. (2004). *A Casebook on Roman Family Law*. Oxford: Oxford University Press.

Funke, M.K.A. (2013). "Euripides and Gender: The Difference the Fragments Make". Unpublished Ph.D. dissertation. Seattle, WA: University of Washington.

Furley, W. (2015). *Menander* Perikeiromene *or the Shorn Head*. London: Institute of Classical Studies.

Gagarin, M. (ed.) (1991). *Symposion 1990: Vorträge zur griechischen und hellenistischen Rechtsgeschichte (Pacific Grove, California, 24.-26. September 1990)*. Cologne: Böhlau

Gelb, I.J. (1965). "The Philadelphia Onion Archive." In H.G. Güterbock and T. Jacobsen (eds.), *Studies in Honor of Benno Landsberger*. Chicago, IL: University of Chicago Press, 57–62.

Glantz, T. (1993). *Early Greek Myth: A Guide to Literary and Artistic Sources*. Baltimore, MD: Johns Hopkins University Press.

Glazebrook, A. (2011). "*Porneion*: Prostitution in Athenian Civic Space." In Glazebrook and Henry (eds.), *Greek Prostitutes in the Ancient Mediterranean, 800 BCE-200 CE*, 34–69.

Glazebrook, A. (2014). "The Erotics of Manumission: Prostitutes and the *prasis epi eleutheria*." *EuGeStA* 4, 55–80.

Glazebrook, A. (2015). "A Hierarchy of Violence? Sex Slaves, *Parthenoi*, and Rape in Menander's *Epitrepontes*." *Helios* 42, 81–101.

Glazebrook, A. and M.M. Henry (eds.) (2011). *Greek Prostitutes in the Ancient Mediterranean, 800 BCE-200 CE*. Madison, WI: University of Wisconsin Press.

Glazebrook, A. and B. Tsakirgis (eds.) (2016). *Houses of Ill Repute: The Archaeology of Brothels, Houses, and Taverns in the Greek World*. Philadelphia, PA: University of Pennsylvania Press.

Goldfarb, B.A. (1992). "The Conflict of Obligations in Euripides' *Alcestis*." *GRBS* 33, 109–26.

Goldman, M.L. (2015). "Associating the *Aulêtris*: Flute Girls in the Classical Greek Symposium." *Helios* 42, 29–60.

Gödde, S. (2000). *Das Drama der Hikesie Ritual und Rhetorik in Aischylos' "Hiketiden"*. Münster: Aschendorff.

Granholm, P. (2012). "Alciphron. Letters of the Courtesans." Unpublished Ph.D. dissertation. Uppsala: Uppsala University.

Griffin, J. (1986). *Latin Poets and Roman Life*. Chapel Hill, NC: University of North Carolina Press.

Gomme, A.W. and F.H. Sandbach. (1973). *Menander, A Commentary*. London: Oxford University Press.

Goody, J. and S.J. Tambiah (1973). *Bridewealth and Dowry*. Cambridge: Cambridge University Press.

Gould, J. (1980). "Law, Custom and Myth: Aspects of the Social Position of Women in Classical Athens." *JHS* 100, 38–59.

Graninger, D. (2007). "Studies in the Cult of Artemis Throsia." *ZPE* 162, 151–64.

Green, J.R. (1995). "Oral Tragedies? A Question from St. Petersburg." *QUCC* 51, 78–86.

Greengus, S. (1969). "The Old Babylonian Marriage Contract." *JAOS* 89, 505–32.

Griffith, M. (2011). "Extended Families, Marriage, and Inter-City Relations in (Later) Athenian Tradgedy." In D.M. Carter (ed.), *Why Athens? A Reappraisal of Tragic Politics*. Oxford: Oxford University Press, 175–208.

Häge, G. (1968). *Eheguterrechtliche Verhaltnisse in des griechischen Papyri Agyptens bis Diokletian*. Cologne: Bohlau.

Håland, E.J. (2004). "Athena's Peplos: Weaving as a Core Female Activity in Ancient and Modern Greece." *Cosmos* 20, 155–82.

Halleran, M.R. (1988). "Text and Ceremony at the Close of Euripides' *Alkestis*." *Eranos* 86, 123–29.

Halleran, M.R. (1991). "*Gamos* and Destruction in Euripedes' *Hippolytus*." *TAPA* 121, 109–21.

Hamilton, R. (1989). "Alkman and the Athenian Arkteia." *Hesperia* 58, 449–72.

Hansen, W. (2000). "The Winning of Hippodameia." *TAPA* 130, 19–40.

Hansen, P.A. (1983). *Carmina epigraphica Graeca*. Berlin: de Gruyter.

Harding, P. (2008). *The Story of Athens: The Fragments of the Local Chronicles of Attika*. London: Routledge.

Hardwick, L. (1990). "Ancient Amazons – Heroes, Outsiders or Women?" *GaR* 37, 14–36.

Harris, E.M. (1988). "When Is a Sale Not a Sale? The Riddle of the Athenian Terminology for Real Security Revisited." *CQ* 38, 351–81.

Harris, E.M. (2013). "Were there Business Agents in Classical Greece? The Evidence of Some Lead Letters." In U. Yiftach-Firanko (ed.), *The Letter: Lam State, Society and the Epistolary Format in the Ancient World*. Wiesbaden: Harrassowitz, 105–34.

Harris, E.M. (2014). "Wife, Household, and Marketplace: The Role of Women in the Economy of Classical Athens." In U. Bultrighini and E. Dimauro (eds.), *Donne che contano nella storia greca*. Lanciano: Carabba, 183–207.

Harris, R. (1964). "The *Nadītu* Woman." In Robert M. Adams (ed.), *Studies Presented to A. Leo Oppenheim*. Chicago, IL: Oriental Institute of the University of Chicago, 106–35.

Harrison, A.R.W. (1968). *The Law of Athens: The Family and Property*. London: Oxford University Press.

Hatzilambrou, R. (2010). "Isaeus' Art of Persuasion: The Case of his Third Speech." *WS* 123, 19–35.

Heath, J. (2011). "Telelmachus *Pepnomenos*: Growing into an Epithet." *Mnemosyne* 54, 129–57.

Hedreen, G.M. (1992), *Silens in Attic Black-figure Vase-painting: Myth and Performance*. Ann Arbor, MI: University of Michigan Press.

Hedreen, G.M. (1994). "Silens, Nymphs, and Maenads." *JHS* 114, 47–69.

Heitman, R. (2005). *Taking Her Seriously: Penelope & the Plot of Homer's* Odyssey. Ann Arbor, MI: University of Michigan Press.
Heldmann, K. (2016). *Europa und der Stier oder der Brautraub des Zeus: Die Entführung Europas in den Darstellungen der griechischen und römischen Antike*. Göttingen: Vandehoeck and Ruprecht.
Henrichs, A. (1978). Greek Maenadism from Olympias to Messalina." *HSCP* 82, 121–60.
Hersch, K.K. (2010). *The Roman Wedding: Ritual and Meaning in Antiquity*. Cambridge: Cambridge University Press.
Hersch, K.K. (2013). "Introduction to the Roman Wedding: Two Case Studies." *CJ* 109, 223–32.
Higbie, C. (1995). *Heroes' Names.Homeric Identities*. New York: Garland.
Hoffner, H.A. Jr. (1968). "Birth and Name-Giving in Hittite Texts." *JNES* 27, 198–203.
Hollinshead, M.B. (1985). "Against Iphigeneia's Adyton in Three Mainland Temples." *AJA* 89, 419–40.
Hooker, J. (1990). "Cult-personnel in the Linear B texts from Pylos." In M. Beard and J. North (eds.), *Pagan Priests: Religion and Power in the Ancient World*. Bristol: Bristol Classical Press, 138–42.
Huebner, S.R. (nd). "Single Men and Eomen in Pagan Society: The Case of Roman Egypt." Available for download at: https://www.academia.edu/22765294/_Single_Men_and_Women_in_Pagan_Society_.
Humphreys, S.C. (1974). "The Nothoi of Kynosarges." *JHS* 94, 88–95.
Hunter, R. (2005). *The Hesiodic* Catalogue of Women: *Construction and Reconstruction*. Cambridge: Cambridge University Press.
Hunter, V. (1989). "Women's Authority in Classical Athens. The Example of Kleoboule and Her Son (Dem. 27–29)." *EchCl* 33, 39–48.
Ierulli, M. (1993). "A Community of Women? The Protagonist and the Chorus in Sophocles' *Electra*." *Mètis* 8, 217–29.
Ilievski, P.Hr. (1993). "The Origin and Semantic Development of the Term *Harmony*." *ICS* 18, 19–29.
Immerwahr, H.R. (1984). "An Inscribed Cup by the Ambrosios Painter." *AntK* 27, 10–13.
Isler-Kerényi, C. (2015). *Dionysos in Classical Athens*. Leiden: Brill.
Jackson, S. (1999). "Apollonius' *Argonautica*: The Theseus/Ariadne Desertion." *RhM* 142, 152–57.
James, S.L. (2012). "Sex and the Single Girl: The Cologne Fragment of Archilochus." In S.L. James and S. Dillon (eds.) (2012), *A Companion to Women in the Ancient World*. Malden, MA: Wiley-Blackwell, 81–83.
Jameson, M.H. (1977–78). "Agriculture and Slavery in Classical Athens." *CJ* 73, 122–45.
Jenkins, I. (1983). "Is There Life after Marriage? A Study of the Abduction Motif in Vase Paintings of the Athenian Wedding." *BICS* 30, 137–45.
Jenkins, I. and D. Williams. (1985). "Sprang Hair Nets: Their Manufacture and Use in Ancient Greece." *AJA* 89, 411–18.
Jentoft-Nilson, M. (1983). "A Krater bu Asteas." *Occasional Papers on Antiquities*, 1. Greek Vases in the J. Paul Getty Museum, 139–48.
Jeppesen-Wigelsworth, A.D. (2010). "The Portrayal of Roman Wives in Literature and Inscriptions". Unpublished Ph.D dissertation. Calgary, Alberta: University of Calgary.
Jim, T.S.F. (2012). "Seized by the Nymph? Onesagoras the '*dekatephoros*' in the Nymphaeum at Kafizin in Cyprus." *Kernos* 25, 9–26.
Johnstone, S. (2002). "Apology for the Manuscript of Demosthenes 59.67." *AJP* 123, 229–56.
Jones, J.E. (2007). "'Living Above the Shop': Domestic Aspects of the Ancient Industrial Workshops of the Laureion Area of South-East Attica." *BSA* 15, 267–80.
Jones, N.F. (2004). *Rural Athens under the Democracy*. Philadelphia, PA: University of Pennsylvania Press.
Jordan, D. (2003). "A Letter from the Banker Pasion." In D. Jordan, J. Traill and J. Kirchner (eds.), *Lettered Attica: a Day of Attic Epigraphy*. Toronto: Athenians, 23–29.
Joyce, C.P. (2011). "*Porne* or *Parthenos*: The Reputation of a Painted Lady." *Scholia*, 20, 25–51.
Just, R. (1989). *Women in Athenian Law and Life*. London: Routledge.

Kahil, L. (1983). "Mythological Repertoire of Brauron." In Moon (ed.), *Ancient Greek Art and Iconography*, 231–44.
Kakavoyannis, E. (2001). "The Silver Ore-Processing Workshops of the Lavrion Region." *BSA* 96, 365–80.
Kamen, D. (2013). *Status in Classical Athens*. Princeton, NJ: Princeton University Press.
Kamen, D. (2014). "Sale for the Purpose of Manumission: Slave-Prostitutes and Manumission in Ancient Greece." *CJ* 109, 281–307.
Kapparis, K.A. (1999). *Against Neaira: [D 59]*. Berlin: de Gruyter.
Kapparis, K.A. (2011). "The Terminology of Prostitution in the Ancient Greek World." In Glazebrook and Henry (eds.), *Greek Prostitutes in the Ancient Mediterranean, 800 BCE–200 CE*, 222–55.
Karamanou, I. (2006). *Euripides, Danae and Dictys*. Munich/Leipzig: Saur.
Kardara, C. (1960). "Problems of Hera's Cult-Images." *AJA* 64, 343–58.
Kazakévich, E.G. (2008/1960 in Russian). "Were the *khōris oikountes* Slaves." *GRBS* 48, 343–80.
Keaney, J.J. (1981). "Hymn Ven. 140 and the Use of *Apoina*." *AJP* 102, 261–64.
Kears, M.J. (2013). "Metics and Identity in Democratic Athens." Unpublished Ph.D. dissertation. Birmingham: University of Birmingham.
Kenens, U. (2012). "Greek Mythography at Work: The Study of Perseus from Pherecydes to Tzetzes." *GRBS* 52, 147–66.
Kennedy, R.F. (2014). *Immigrant Women in Athens: Gender, Ethnicity, and Citizenship in the Classical City*. New York, NY: Routledge.
Kennedy, R.F. (2015). "Elite Women and the Origins of the *Hetaira* in Classical Athens." *Helios* 42, 61–79.
Keuls. E.C. (1983). "Attic Vase-Painting and the Home Textile Industry." In Moon (ed.), *Ancient Greek Art and Iconography*, 209–30.
Keuls, E.C. (1984). "Male-Female Interaction in Fifth-Century Dionysiac Ritual as Shown in Attic Vase Painting." *ZPE* 55, 287–97.
Keuls, E.C. (1985). *The Reign of the Phallus: Sexual Politics in Ancient Athens*. Berkeley, CA: University of California Press.
Kilker, L.A. (2008). "Dining Like Divinities: Evidence for Ritual and Marital Dining by Women in Ancient Greece." Unpublished Ph.D. dissertation. Columbus, OH: Ohio State University.
Kirschenbaum, A. (1987). *Sons, Slaves and Freedmen in Roman Commerce*. Jerusalem/Washington, DC: The Magnes Press of the Hebrew University/The Catholic University of America Press.
Knigge, U. (1991). *The Athenian Kerameikos: History, Monuments, Excavations*. Athens: Krene.
Knigge, U. and K. Tancke (2005). *Der Bau Z*. 2 vols. Munich: Hirmer.
Knoblauch, A.-M. (2007). "Promiscuous or Proper? Nymphs as Female Role Models in Ancient Greece." In A. Cuffel and B. Britt (eds.), *Religion, Gender and Culture in the Pre-Modern World*. New York, NY: Palgrave Macmillan, 47–62.
Kobakhidze, E. (2010–11). "The Tradition of Foster Adoption in Ancient Mediterranean Area and Georgia." *Phasis* 13–14, 55–59.
Koehl, R. (2000). "Ritual Context." *BSAS* 6 (The Palaikastro Kouros: A Minoan Chryselephantine Statuette and its Aegean Bronze Age Context), 131–43.
Konstan, D. (1987). "Between Courtesan and Wife: Menander's Perikeiromene." *Phoenix* 41, 122–39.
Koschaker, P. (1937). *Die Eheformen bei den Indogermanen*. Tübingen: Mohr.
Kosmopoulou, A. (2001). "'Working Women': Female Professionals on Classical Attic Gravestones." *BSA* 96, 281–319.
Kovacs, D. (1985). "Castor in Euripides' *Electra* (*EL* 307–13 and 1292–1307)." *CQ* 35, 306–14.
Kozak, L.A. (2014). "Oaths and Characterizations: Two Homeric Cases." In A.H. Sommerstein and I.C. Torrance (eds.), *Oaths and Swearing in Ancient Greece*. Berlin: de Gruyter, 213–29.
Kristensen, K.R. (2015). "A Comment on Legal Identification in Ancient Crete." In M. DePauw and S.R. Coussement (eds.), *Identifiers and Identification Methods in the Ancient World: Legal Documents in Ancient Societies III*. Leuven: Peeters, 185–96.

Kron, U. (1996). "Priesthoods, Dedications, and Euergetism: What Part Did Religion Play in the Political and Social Status of Greek Women? In P. Hellström and B. Alroth (eds), *Religion and Power in the Ancient Greek World*. Uppsala: Axta Universitatis Upsaliensis, 139–82.
Kuenen-Janssens, L.J.Th. (1941). "Sone Notes upon the Competence of the Athenian Woman to Conduct a Transaction." *Mnemosyne* 9, 199–214.
Kulesza, R. (2008). "Spartan *Gamos* in the Classical Period." *Palamedes* 3, 135–66.
Kurke, L. (1997). "Inventing the '*Hetaira*': Sex, Politics, and Discursive Conflict in Archaic Greece." *ClAnt* 16, 106–50.
Kurke, L. (1999). *Coins, Bodies, Games, and Gold: The Politics of Meaning in Archaic Greece*. Princeton, NJ: Princeton University Press.
Lacey, W.K. (1966). "Homeric *hedna* and Penelope's *kyrios*." *JHS* 86, 55–68.
Lacey, W.K. (1968). *The Family in Classical Greece*. Ithaca, NY: Cornell University Press.
Lambert, W.G. and A.R. Millard (1969). *Atra-Ḫasīs: the Babylonian story of the Flood*. Oxford: Oxford University Press.
Lape, S. (2002/03). "Solon and the Institutions of the 'Democratic' Family Form." *CJ* 98, 117–39.
Lape, S. (2004). *Reproducing Athens: Menander's Comedy, Democratic Culture and the Hellenistic City*. Princeton, NJ: Princeton University Press.
Lardinois, A.P.M.H. (2011). "The *parrhesia* of Young Female Choruses in Ancient Greece." In L. Athanassaki and E. Bowe (eds.), *Archaic and Classical Choral Song: Performance, Politics and Dissemination*. Berlin: de Gruyter, 161–72.
Larson, J. (2001). *Greek Nymphs: Myth, Cult, Lore*. Oxford: Oxford University Press.
Larson, J. (2002). "Corinna and the Daughters of Asopus." *SyllClass* 12, 47–62.
Leão, D.F. (2012). "The Myth of Autochthony, Athenian Citizenship and the Right of *enktesis*L A Legal Approach to Euripides' *Ion*." In B. Legras and G. Thür (eds.), *Symposion 2011: Vorträge zur griechischen und hellenistischen Rechtsgeschichte (Paris, 7-10 September 2011)*. Vienna: Verlag der Österreichischen Akademie der Wissenschaften, 135–152.
Leão, D.F. and P.J. Rhodes (2015). *The Laws of Solon: A New Edition with Introduction, Translation and Commentary*. London: Tauris.
Levin, S. (1983). "Hebrew (*pi(y)léges*), Greek *pallakē*, Latin *paelex*: The Origin of Intermarriage Among the Early Indo-Europeans and Semites." *General Linguistics* 23, 191–98.
Mili, M. (2015). *Religion and Society in Ancient Thessaly*. Oxford: Oxford University Press.
Lee, M.M. (2015). *Body, Dress, and Identity in Ancient Greece*. New York, NY: Cambridge University Press.
Lefkowitz, M.R. (2002). "'Predatory Goddesses'." *Hesperia* 71, 325–44.
Lefkowitz, M.R. (2007). *Women in Greek Myth*. 2nd ed. Baltimore, MD: Johns Hopkins University Press.
Lewis, D. (2013). "Slave Marriages in the Laws of Gortyn: A Matter of Rights." *Historia* 62, 390–416.
Lewis, S. (2002). *The Athenian Woman: An Iconographic Handbook*. London: Routledge.
Lewis, S. (2010). "Images of Craft on Athenian Pottery: Context and Interpretation." *Bolletino di Archeologia On LineI Volume Speciale*, 26. Available for download at: www.archeologia.beneculturali.it.
Lindblom, A. (2007). "Public, Private, or Mythological Identities? On the Identity of Females Sexually 'Harassed' by Satyrs on Red-figure Attic Vases." In L. Larsson Lovén and A. Strömberg (eds.), *Public Roles and Personal Status: Men and Women in Antiquity*. Sävedalen: Åstroms, 231–54.
Llewellyn-Jones, L. (ed.) (2002) *Women's Dress in the Ancient Greek World*. London: Duckworth/Classical Press of Wales.
Llewellyn-Jones, L. (2007). "House and Veil in Ancient Greece." *BSAS* 15, 251–58.
Llewellyn-Jones, L. (2011). "Domestic Abuse & Violence Against Women in Ancient Greece." In S.D. Lambert; N.R.E. Fisher and D.L. Cairns (eds.), *Sociable Man: Essays on Ancient Greek Social Behaviour in Honour of Nick Fisher*. Swansea: Classical Press of Wales, 231–66.
Lloyd-Jones, H. (1971). "Review of James Diggle: Euripides *Phaethon*." *CR* 21, 341–45.

Lonsdale, S. (1993). *Dance and Ritual Play in Greek Religion*. Baltimore, MD: Johns Hopkins University Press.
Looper-Friedman, S.E. (1987). "The Decline of Manus-Marriage in Rome." *T.v.R.* 55, 281–96.
Loprieno, A. (1997). "Slaves." In S. Donadoni (ed.), *The Egyptians*. Chicago, IL: University of Chicago Press, 185–219.
Lyons, D.J. (2012). *Dangerous Gifts: Gender and Exchange in Ancient Greece*. Austin, TX: University of Texas Press.
Lyons, D.J. (2016). "Female Goods in the Ancient Domestic and Symbolic Economies." In Berg (ed.), *The Material Sides of Marriage*, 93–98.
McClure, L.K. (2003). *Courtesans at Table: Gender and Greek Literary Culture in Athenaeus*. New York, NY: Routledge.
McClure, L.K. (2015). "Courtesans Reconsidered: Women in Aristophanes' Lysistrata." *EuGeStA* 5, 54–84.
McClure, L. (2017). "Priestess and Polis in Euripides; *Iphigeneia in Tauris*." In Dillon, Eidinow and Maurizio (eds.), *Women's Ritual Competence in the Greco-Roman Medierranean*, 115–30.
MacDowell, D.M. (1976). "Bastards as Athenian Citizens." *CQ* 26, 88–91.
McGinn, T.A.J. (1990). "*Ne serva prostituatur*: Restrictive Covenants in the Sale of Slaves." *ZSav*, 107, 315–53. A revised version of this article focusing mainly on prostitution may be found in McGinn 1998: 288–319.
McGinn, T.A.J. (1991). "Concubinage and the *Lex Iulia* on Adultery." *TAPA* 121, 335–75.
McGinn, T.A.J. (1998). *Prostitution, Sexuality, and the Law in Ancient Rome*. New York, NY: Oxford University Press.
McKechnie, P. (2005). "Beau Monde and Demi-Monde in Alexandria, 323–116 BC." *AntCl* 74, 69–82.
MacKinnon, J.K. (1971). "Heracles' Intention inHis Second Request of Hyllus: *Trach.* 1216–51." *CQ* 21, 33–41.
MacLachlan, B. (2004). "Kore as Nymph not Daughter: Persephone in a Locrian Cave," (Proceedings from the Conference "Feminism and the Classics" 2004). *Diotima*. A Website for Women in Antiquity. Available for download at: http://www.stoa.org/diotima/essays/fc04/MacLachlan.html.
Malkin, I. (2001). "The *Odyssey* and the Nymphs." *Gaia* 5, 11–27.
Malul, M. (1988). *Studies in Mesopotamian Legal Symbolism*. Neukirchen-Vluyn: Butzon & Bercker.
McPhee, I. and A.D. Trendall. (1987). *Greek Red-figured Fish-plates*. Basel: Vereinigung d. Freunde Antiker Kunst.
Mansfield, J.M. (1985). "The Robe of Athena and the Panthenaic Peplos." Unpublished Ph.D. dissertation. Berkeley, CA: University of California, Berkeley.
Meo, F. (2016). "Alcune considerazioni sui ruoli del generi nella produczione tessile a *Herakliea* di Lucania." In Berg (ed.), *The Material Sides of Marriage*, 81–86.
Meyer, E.A. (1993). "Epitaphs and Citizenship in Classical Athens." *JHS* 113, 99–121.
Michel, C. (2001). *Correspondance des marchands de Kaniš au début du IIe millénaire av. J.-C.* Paris: Editions du Cerf.
Mili, M. (2015). *Religion and Society in Ancient Thessaly*. Oxford: Oxford University Press.
Miner, J. (2003). "Courtesan, Concubine, Whore: Apollodorus' Deliberate Use of Terms for Prostitutes." *AJP* 124, 19–37.
Mitford, T.B. (1980). *The Nymphaeum of Kafizin: The inscribed pottery*. Hawthorne, NY: de Gruyter.
Modrzejewki, J.M. (2010). "Greek Law in the Hellenistic Period: Family and Marriage." In M. Gagarin and D. Cohen (eds.), *The Cambridge Companion to Ancient Greek Law*. Cambridge: Cambridge University Press, 343–54
Monaghan, M.D. (2001). "Coats of Many Colours: Dyeing and Dyeworks in Classical and Hellenistic Greece." Unpublished Ph.D. dissertation. Leicester: University of Leicester.
Moon, W.G. (ed.), *Ancient Greek Art and Iconography*. Madison, WI: University of Wisconsin Press

Mossē, C. (1991). "Le place de la *pallake* dans la famille athenēnne." In Gagarin (ed.), *Symposion 1990*, 273–79.

Müller, O. (1899). *Untersuchen zur Geschichte des attischen Burger- und Eherects." Jahrb.f.cl.Philol.* Supplemantband 25, 662–811.

Murnaghan, S. (2005). "Women in Groups: Aeschylus's *Suppliants* and the Female Choruses of Greek Tragedy." In V. Pedrick and S.M. Oberhelman (eds.), *The Soul of Tragedy: Essays on Athenian Drama*. Chicago, IL: University of Chicago Press, 183–98.

Neils, J. (1996). "Pride, Pomp, and Circumstance: The Iconography of Procession." In Jenifer Neils (ed.), *Worshipping Athena: Panathenaia and Parthenon*. Madison, WI: University of Wisconsin Press, 177–97.

Neils, J. (2000). "Others within the Other: An Intimate Look at Hetairai and Maenads." In B. Cohen (ed.), *Not the Classical Ideal: Athens and the Construction of the Other in Greek Art*. Leiden: Brill, 203–26.

Nosch, M.-L. (2004). "Red Coloured Textiles in the Linear B Inscriptions." In L. Cleland and K. Stears (eds.), *Colour in the Ancient Mediterranean World*. Oxford: Archaeopress, 32–39.

Nosch, M.-L. (2009). "Approaches to Artemis in Bronze Age Greece." In *From Artemis to Diana: The Goddess of Man and Beast*. Copenhagen: Museum Tusculanum Press, 21–39.

Nosch, M.-L. (2014). "Linen Textiles and Flax in Classical Greece: Provenance and Trade." In K. Droß-Krüpe (ed.), *Textile Trade and Distribution in Antiquity*. Wiesbaden: Harrassowitz, 17–42.

Nótári, T. (2007). "The Spear as the Symbol of Property and Power in Ancient Rome." *Acta Jurid. Hung*. 48, 231–57.

Nótári, T. (2008). "Remarks on Roman Marriage and Divorce." *Annales Universitatis Scientiarum Budapestinensis de Rolando Eötvös nominatae, Sectio Iuridica*. 48, 319–40.

Oakley, J.H. (1995). "Nuptial Nuances: Wedding Images in Non-Wedding Scenes of Myth." In Reeder (ed.), *Pandora*, 63–73.

Oakley, J.H. and R.H. Sinos. (1993). *The Wedding in Ancient Athens*. Madison, WI: University of Wisconsin Press.

Ogden, D. (1995). "Women and Bastardy in Ancient Greece and the Hellenistic World." In A. Powell (ed.), *The Greek World*. London: Routledge, 219–44.

Ogden, D. (1996). *Greek Bastardy in the Greek and Hellenistic Periods*. Oxford: Oxford University Press.

Ogle, M.B. (1911). "The House-Door in Greek and Roman Religion and Folk-Lore." *AJP* 32, 251–71.

Ojennus, P. (2006). "Holding Hands in the 'Argonautica'." *CJ* 101, 253–70.

Olsen, B.A. (2014). *Women in Mycenaean Greece: The Linear B Tablets from Pylos and Knossos*. London: Routledge.

Olson, D.S. (2012). *The Homeric Hymn to Aphrodite and Related Texts: Text, Translation and Commentary*. Berlin: de Gruyter.

O'Neill, E. Jr. (1938). *Aristophanes*. New York, NY: Random House.

Ormand, K. (1996). "Silent by Convention? Sophocles' Tekmessa." *AJP* 117, 37–64.

Ormand, K. (1999). *Exchange and the Maiden: Marriage in Sophoclean Tragedy*. Austin, TX: University of Texas Press.

Ormand, K. (2004). "Marriage Identity and the Tale of Mestra in the Hesiodic *Catalogue of Women*." *AJP* 125, 303–38.

Ormand, K. (2009). "Electra in Exile." In D.E. McCoskey and E. Zakin (eds.), *Bound by the City: Greek Tragedy, Sexual Difference, and the Formation of the Polis*. Albany, NY: State University of New York Press, 247–73.

Ormand, K. (2014a). The Hesiodic *Catalogue of Women* and Archaic Greece. New York, NY: Cambridge University Press.

Ormand, K. (2014b). "Uncertain Geographies of Female Desire in the Hesiodic *Catalogue*: Atalanta." In M. Skempis and I. Ziogas (eds.), *Geography, Topography, Landscape: Configurations of Space in Greek and Roman Epic*. Berlin: de Gruyter, 137–63.

Osborne, R. (1985). Demos: *The Discovery of Classical Attika*. Cambridge: Cambridge University Press.

Osborne, R. (2005). "*Ordering Women* in Hesiod's Catalogue." In Hunter (ed.), *The Hesiodic* Catalogue of Women, 5–34.
Pache, C.O. (2011). *A Moment's Ornament: The Poetics of Nympholepsy in Ancient Greece*. Oxford: Oxford University Press.
Page, D.L. (1953). *Corinna*. London: Society for the Promotion of Hellenic Studies.
Parker, R. (2005). *Polytheism and Society at Athens*. Oxford: Oxford University Press.
Patterson, C.B. (1990). "Those Athenian Bastards." *ClAnt* 9, 40–73.
Patterson, C.B. (1991a). "Response to Claude Mossē." In Gagarin (ed.), *Symposion 1990*, 281–87.
Patterson, C.B. (1991b). "Marriage and the Married Woman in Athenian Law." In S.B. Pomeroy (ed.), *Women's History and Ancient History*. Chapel Hill, NC: University of North Carolina Press, 48–72.
Patterson, C.B. (2012). "Marriage in Sophocles: A Problem for Social History." In K. Ormand (ed.), *A Companion to Sophocles*. Oxford: Blackwell, 381–94.
Penrose, W.D. Jr. (2016). *Postcolonial Amazons: Female Masculinity and Courage in Ancient Greek and Sandkrit Literature*. Oxford: Oxford University Press.
Perlman, P. (1983). "Plato Laws 833C–834D and the Bears of Brauron." *GRBS* 20, 115–30.
Perlman, P. (1989). "Acting the She-Bear for Artemis." *Arethusa* 22, 111–33.
Perry, M.J. (2014). *Gender, Manumission, and the Roman Freedwoman*. Cambridge: Cambridge University Press.
Peters, M. (2002). "Aus der Vergangenheit von Heroen und Ehegöttinnen." In M. Fritz and S. Zeilfelder (eds.), *Novalis Indogermanica: Festschrift für Günter Neumann zum 80*. Geburtstag. Graz: Leykam, 357–80.
Petridou, G. (2004). "Adoption by Persephone. Adoption and Initiation Ritual in A1-A3 Zuntz and Pelinna 1–2." In D.-C. Naoum and G.M. Muskett (eds.), *Cult and Death: Proceedings of the Third Annual Conference of Postgraduate Researchers, the University of Liverpool, May 2002*. Oxford: Archaeopress, 69–78.
Phillips, D.D. (2009). "Hypereides 3 and the Athenian Law of Contracts." *TAPA* 139, 89–122.
Phillips, D.D. (2013). *The Law of Ancient Athens*. Ann Arbor, MI: University of Michigan Press.
Pieraccini, L.C. and M.A. Del Chiaro (2014). "Greek in Subject Matter, Etruscan by Design: Alcestis and Admetus on an Etruscan Red-figure Krater." In S. Schierup and V. Sabetei (eds.), *The Regional Production of Red-figure Pottery: Greece, Magna Graecia and Etruria*. Aarhus: Aarhus University Press, 304–10.
Pipili, M. (2000). "Wearing the Other Hat: Workmen in Town and Country." In B. Cohen (ed.), *Not the Classical Ideal: Athens and the Construction of the Other in Greek Art*. Leiden: Brill, 153–79.
Platnauer, M. (1964). *Aristophanes Peace*. Oxford: Oxford University Press.
Polignac, F. de (2008). "Polignac on Budin on Pironti". *BMCR* 2008.11.02.
Pritchard, D.M. (2015). *Public Spending and Democracy in Classical Athens*. Austin, TX: University of Texas Press.
Pritchett, J.K. (1991). *The Greek State at War*. Part V. Berkeley, CA: University of California Press.
Quiller, B. (1996). "Reconstructing the Spartan Partheniai: Many Guesses and a Few Facts." *SO* 71, 34–41.
Rabin, S. (1983). "Hebrew (*pi(y)legeš*), Greek *pallakē*, Latin *paelex*: The Origin of Intermarriage among the Early Indo-Europeans and Semites." *General Linguistics* 23, 191–97.
Radin, M. (1937). "Legal History of the Morganitic Marriage." *University of Chicago Law Review* 4, 597–617.
Rawson, B. (1989). "*Spurii* and the Roman View of Illegitimacy." *Antichiton* 23, 10–41.
Reckford, K.J. (1972). "Phaethon, Hippolytus, and Aphrodite." *TAPA* 103, 105–32.
Reeder, E.D. (ed.) (1995). *Pandora: Women in Classical Antiquity*. Baltimore, MD: Walters Art Gallery.
Reeder, E.D. (1995). "The Catalogue." In Reeder (ed.), *Pandora*, 121–419.
Rehak, P. (1999). "The Aegean Landscape and the Body: A New Interpretation of the Thera Frescoes." In N.L. Wicker and B. Arnold (eds.), *From the Ground Up: Beyond Gender Theory in Archaeology*. Oxford: Archaeopress, 11–22.

Rehak, P. (2007). "Children's Work: Girls as Acolytes in Aegean Ritual and Cult." In J. Rutter and A. Cohen (eds.), *Constructions of Childhood in the Ancient World*, Princeton, NJ: American School of Classical Studies at Athens, 205–25.
Relihan, J.L. (1990). "Menippus, the Cur from Crete." *Prometheus* 16, 219–24.
Reilly, J. (1989). "Many Brides: 'Mistress and Maid' on Athenian Lekythoi." *Hesperia* 58, 411–44.
Rhodes, P.J. (1978). "Bastards as Athenian Citizens." *CQ* 28, 89–92.
Rhodes, P.J. (1981). *A Commentary on the Aristotelian Athenaion politeia*. Oxford: Oxford University Press.
Ricks, S.D. (2006). "*Deciosis* and *Dextrarum Iunctio*: The Sacred Handclasp in the Classical and Early Christian World." *FARMS Review* 18, 431–36.
Rinon, Y. (2006). "Tragic Hephaestus: The Humanized God in the 'Iliad' and the 'Odyssey'." *Phoenix* 60, 1–20.
Roisman, H.A. and C.A.E. Luschnig. (2011). *Euripides* Electra*: A Commentary*. Norman, OK: University of Oklahoma Press.
Rosenmeyer, P.A. (2004). "Girls at Play in Early Greek Poetry". *AJP* 125, 163–78.
Rosivach, V.J. (1989). "*Talasiourgoi* and *Paidia* in *IG* 2^2 1533–78: A Note on Athenian Social History." *Historia* 38, 365–70.
Rosenzweig, R. (2004). *Worshipping Aphrodite: Art and Cult in Classical Athens*. Ann Arbor, MI: University of Michigan Press.
Rotroff, S. (2013). *Industrial Religion: The Saucer Pyres of the Athenian Agora*. Princeton, NJ: The American School of Classical Studies at Athens.
Rowlandson, J. (1998). *Women and Society in Greek and Roman Egypt: A Sourcebook*. Cambridge: Cambridge University Press.
Rubinstein, L. (1993). *Adoption in IV. Century Athens*. Copenhagen: Museum Tusculanum Press.
Rudhart, J. (1999/1978). "Concerning the Homeric Hymn to Demeter." In Foley, *The Homeric Hymn to Demeter*, 198–211. Original published in *MusHelv* 38/1, 1–17.
Rutherford, I. (2005). "Mestra at Athens: Hesiod fr. 43 and the Poetics of Panhellenism." In Hunter (ed.), *The Hesiodic* Catalogue of Women, 99–117.
Sage, E.T. (1916). "Advertising Among the Romans." *CW* 26, 202–08.
Scafuro, A.C. (1994). "Witnessing and False Witnessing: Proving Citizenship and Kin Identity in Fourth-Century Athens." In A. Boegehold and A.C. Scafuro (eds.), *Athenian Identity and Civil Ideology*. Baltimore, MD: Johns Hopkins University Press, 156–98.
Schaps, D.M. (1977). "The Woman Least Mentioned: Etiquette and Women's Names." *CQ* 27, 323–30.
Schaps, D.M. (1998). "What was Free about a Free Athenian Woman?" *TAPA* 128, 161–88.
Schlesier, R. (2013). "Atthis, Gyrinno, and Other *Hetairai*: Female Personal Names in Sappho's Poetry." *Philologus* 157, 199–222.
Schnapp, A. (1989). "Eros the Hunter." In Bérard *et al. A City of Images*, 71–87.
Scott, A.G. (2011). "Plural Marriages and the Spartan State." *Historia* 60, 413–24.
Seaford, R. (1988). "The Eleventh Ode of Bacchylides: Hera, Artemis, and the Absence of Dionysos." *JHS* 108, 118–36.
Seaford, R. (1990). "The Imprisonment of Women in Greek Tradgedy." *JHS* 110, 76–90.
Sealey, R. (1984). "On Lawful Concubinage in Athens." *ClAnt* 3, 111–33.
Sealey, R. (1990). *Women and Law in Classical Athens*. Chapel Hill, NC: University of North Carolina Press.
Sebesta, J.L. (2002). "Visions of Gleaming Textiles and a Clay Core." In Llewellyn-Jones, *Women's Dress in the Ancient Greek World*, 325–42.
Segal, C. (1994). "Bride or Concubine?" *ICS* 19, 59–64.
Sens, A. (2011). *Asclepiades of Samos: Epigrams and Fragments*. Oxford: Oxford University Press.
Silver, M. (1991). "The Commodity Composition of Trade in the Argonaut Myth." In M. Silver (ed.), *Ancient Economy in Mythology: East and West*. Savage, MD: Roman & Littlefield, 241–82.
Silver, M. (1992). *Taking Ancient Mythology Economically*. Leiden: Brill.

Silver, M. (2006). “Temple/Sacred Prostitution in Ancient Mesopotamia Revisited: Religion in the Economy.” *Ugarit Forschungen* 38, 631–63.

Silver, M. (2009). “Must Frequently Performed Economic Services Have Distinctive Names? A Probe of Finley’s Hypothesis.” *Historia* 52, 246–56.

Silver, M. (2011a). “Transaction/Administrative Costs in Greco-Roman Antiquity with Special Reference to the Implications of Atheism/Naturalism in Classical Athens,” *MBAH* 29, 49–93.

Silver, M. (2011b). “Contractual Slavery in the Roman Economy.” *AHB* 25, 73–132.

Silver, M. (2013). “Pittalacus the Slave and the Mother of the Gods: Between the Lines of Aeschines 1.54–66.” *MBAH* 31, 97–120.

Silver, M. (2014). “Autonomous Slaves in Greco-Roman Legal and Economic History.” *ELR*, 3, 233–68.

Silver, M. (2015). “‘Living Apart,’ *Apeleutheroi* and *Paramone*-Clause: A Response to Canevaro and Lewis.” *IncidAntico* 13, 139–61.

Silvestrelli, F. (2014). “Red-Figure Vases from Metaponto: The Evidence from the Necroplolis along the Coast Road.” In T.H. Carpenter, K.M. Lynch and E.G.D. Robinson (eds.), *The Italic People of Ancient Apulia: New Evidence from Pottery for Workshops, Markets, and Customs*. Cambridge: Cambridge University Press, 96–115.

Siron, N. (2014). “Girl with a Heron. Women and Animals on the Greek Seals and Attic Vases of the 6th–4th centuries BC.” Unpublished paper, available for download at: https://univ-paris1.academia.edu/NicolasSiron.

Sissa, G. (2013). “The Hymen is a Problem, Still. Virginity, Imperforation, and Contraception, from Greece to Rome.” *EuGeStA* 3, 67–121.

Skempis, M. (2011). “Ironic Genre Demarcation: Bacchylides 17 and the Epic Treadition.” *TC* 3, 254–300.

Smith, A.C. (2016). “Looking Inside on the Outside of a Pot.” In Glazebrook and Tsakirgis (eds.), *Houses of Ill Repute*, 143–68.

Smith, J.W. (2013). “Political *Parthenoi*: The Social and Political Significance of Female Performance in Archaic Greece.” Unpublished Ph.D. dissertation. Exeter: University of Exeter.

Smith, J.S. and I. Tzachili. (2012). “Cloth in Crete and Cyprus.” *BSAS* 20 (Parallel Lives: Ancient Island Societies in Crete and Cyprus), 141–55.

Smith, M.S. (1967). “Greek Adoptive Formulae.” *CQ* 17, 302–10.

Smith, T.J. (2014). “Myth into Art: A Black-figure Column Krater from Castle Ashby at the University of Virginia.” In Avramidou and Demetriou (eds.), *Approaching the Ancient Artifact*, 31–41.

Snodgrass, A.M. (1974). “An Historical Homeric Society?” *JHS* 94, 114–25.

Sommerstein, A.H. (2014). “Menander and the *Pallake*.” In A.H. Somerstein (ed.), *Menander in Contexts*. New York, NY: Routledge, 11–23.

Sommerstein, A.H. and I.C. Torrance (eds.) (2014). *Oaths and Swearing in Ancient Greece*. Berlin: de Gruyter.

Sosin, J.D. (2008). “The New Letter from Pasion.” *ZPE* 165, 105–08.

Sourvinou-Inwood, C. (1987). “A Series of Erotic Pursuits: Images and Meanings.” *JHS* 107, 131–53.

Sourvinou-Inwood, C. (2004). “Reading a Myth, Reconstructing its Constructions.” In S. Des Bouvrie (ed.), *Myth and Symbol II: Symbolic Phenomena in Ancient Greek Culture*. Bergen: The Norwegian Institute at Athens, 141–77.

Souza, R. (2016), “Hellenistic Sicilian Real Estate Contracts Inscribed in Lead Tablets: New Readings and Implications for the Economic Independence of Women.” *ZPE* 197, 140–66.

Stadter, P.A. (1989). *A Commentary on Plutarch’s Pericles*. Chapel Hill, NC: University of North Carolina Press.

Stafford, E.J. (1997). “A Wedding Scene? Notes on Akropolis 6471.” *JHS* 117, 200–02.

Stafford, E.J. (2012). “From the Gymnasium to the Wedding: Eros in Athenian Art and Cult.” In E. Sanders, C. Thumiger, C. Carey and N.J. Lowe (eds.), *Eros in Ancient Greece*. Oxford: Oxford University Press, 175–208.

Stanbury-O'Donnell, M.D. (2006). *Vase Painting, Gender and Social Identity in Archaic Athens*. New York, NY: Cambridge University Press.
Starr, C.G. (1978). "An Evening with the Flute-Girls." *PP* 33, 401–10.
Stears, K. (2001). "Spinning Women: Iconography and Status in Athenian Funerary Scupture." In G. Hoffman (ed.), *Les Pierres de l'Offrande*. Zurich: Akanthus, 107–14.
De Ste. Croix, G.E.M. (1970). "Some Observations on the Property Rights of Athenian Women." *CR* 20, 273–78.
Stewart, A. (1995). "Imag(in)ing the Other: Amazons and Ethnicity in Fifth-Century Athens." *Poetics Today* 16, 571–97.
Stol, M. (1995). "Women in Mesopotamia." *JESHO* 38, 123–44.
Stone, E.C. (1982). "The Social Role of the *Nadītu* Women in Old Babylonian Nippur." *JESHO* 25, 50–70.
Stroud, R.S. (1971). "Theozotides and the Athenian Orphans." *Hesperia* 40, 280–301.
Suter, A. (2002). *The Narcissus and the Pomegranate: An Archaeology of the Homeric hymn to Demeter*. Ann Arbor, MI: University of Michigan Press.
Sutton, R.F. Jr. (1981). "The Interaction between Men and Women Portrayed on Attic Red-Figure Pottery." Unpublished Ph.D. dissertation. Chapel Hill, NC: University of North Carolina.
Sutton, R.F. Jr. (1989). "On the Classical Athenian Wedding: Two Red-Figure Loutrophoroi in Boston." In R.F. Sutton (ed.), Daidalikon: *Studies in Memory of Raymond F. Schoder, S.J.* Wauconca, IL: Bolchazy-Carducci, 331–59.
Sutton, R.F. Jr. (1997/98). "Nuptial Eros: The Visual Disclosure of Marriage in Classical Athens." *Journal of the Walters Art Gallery* 55/56, 27–48.
Sutton, R.F. Jr. (2004). "Family Portraits: Recognizing the *Oikos* on Red-Figure Pottery." In A.P. Chapin (ed.), *Charis: Essays in Honor of Sara A. Immerwahr*. Princeton, NJ: American School of Classical Studies at Athens, 327–47.
Swift, L. (2015). "Negotiating Seduction: Archilocus' Cologne Epode and the Transformation of Epic." *Philologus* 159, 2–28.
Swift, L. (2016). "Poetics and Precedents in Archilochus' Erotic Imagery." In L. Swift and C. Carey (eds.), *Iambis and Elegy: New Approaches*. Oxford: Oxford University Press, 253–70.
Synodinou, K. (1986). "The Relationship between Zeus and Athena in the *Iliad*." *Dodona* 15, 155–64.
Synodinou, K. (1987a). "Tecmessa in the *Ajax* of Sophocles." *A&A* 33, 99–107.
Synodinou, K. (1987b). "The Threats of Physical Abuse of Hera by Zeus in the Iliad." *WS* 100, 13–22.
Thür, G. (2013). "The Statute on *Homologein* in Hypereides Speech Against Athenogenes." *Dike* 16, 1–10.
Tiersma. P.M. (1988). "Rites of Passage: Legal Ritual in Roman Law and Anthropological Analogues." *Journal of Legal History* 9, 3–23.
Todd, S.C. (2000). *Lysias*. Austin, TX: University of Texas Press.
Torrance, I.C. (2005). "Andromache *Aichmalōtos*: Concubine or Wife." *Hermathena* 179, 39–66.
Torrance, I.C. (2014). "Ways to Give Oaths Extra Sanctity." In Sommerstein and Torrance (eds.), *Oaths and Swearing in Ancient Greece*, 132–55.
Traill, A. (2008). *Women and the Comic Plot in Menander*. Cambridge: Cambridge University Press.
Trantalidou, K. (2006). "Companions from the Oldest Times: Dogs in Ancient Greek Literature, Iconography and Osteological Testimony." In L.M. Snyder and E.M. Moore (eds.), *Dogs and People in Social, Working, Economic or Symbolic Interaction*. Oxford: Oxbow Books, 96–119.
Treggiari, S. (1981). "*Contubernalis* in *CIL* 6". *Phoenix*, 35, 42–69.
Treggiari, S. (1991). *Roman Marriage*: Iusti Coniuges *from the Time of Cicero to the Time of Ulpian*. Oxford: Oxford University Press.
Trevett, J. (1992). *Apollodorus the Son of Pasion*. Oxford: Oxford University Press.
Truitt, P. (1960). "Attic White-Ground Pyxis and Phiale, ca. 450 B.C." *BMFA* 67, 72–92.
Trimble, J. (2017). "Communicating with Images in the Roman Empire." In F.S. Naiden and R.J.A. Talbot (eds.), *Mercury's Wings: Exploring Modes of Communication in the Ancient World*. Oxford: Oxford University Press, 311–30.

Trzaskoma, Stephen M. (2010). "Callirhoe, Concubinage, and a Corruption in Chariton 2.11.5." *ExClass* 14, 205–09.

Tsakirgis, Barbara. (2005). "Living and Working on the Margins of the Athenian Agora: A Case Study of Three Athenian Workshop Houses." In B.A. Ault and L.C. Nevett (eds.), *Ancient Greek Houses and Households: Chronological, Regional, and Social Diversity*. Philadelphia, PA: University of Pennsylvania Press, 67–82.

Tsitsibakou-Vasalos, E. (2007). *Ancient Poetic Etymology, The Pelpids: Fathers and Sons*. Stuttgart: Steiner.

Tucker, C.W. (1982). "Women in the Manumission Inscriptions at Delphi." *TAPA* 112, 225–361.

Tzachili, I. (2003). "Weaving at Akrotiri, Thera: Defining Cloth-Making Activities as Social Process in a Late Bronze Age Town." In C. Gillis and M.-L. Nosch, *Ancient Textiles: Production, Craft and Society*. Oxford: Oxbow Books, 190–96.

Urbanik, J. (2016). "Dissolubilty and Indissolubilty of Marriage in the Greek and Roman Tradition." In Z. Benincasa and J. Urbanik (eds.), *Mater Familias: Scritti Romanistici per Maria Zabłocka*. Varsavia Journal of Juristic Papyrology, 1039–68.

Van Seters, J. (1968). "The Problem of Childnessness in Near Eastern Law and the Patriarchs of Israel." *Journal of Biblical Literature* 87, 401–08.

Van Wees, H. (2005). "The Invention of the Female Mind: Women, Property and Gender Ideology in Archaic Greece." Paper presented at Center for Hellenic Studies, Conference on Women and Property Organized by Deborah Lyons and Raymond Westbrook. Available for download at: chs.harvard.edu/CHS/article/displayPdf/386.

Vaux, Roland de. (1978). *The Early History of Israel*. Philadelphia, PA: Westminster.

Veenhof, Klaas R. (1972). *Aspects of Old Assyrian Trade and Its Terminology*. Leiden: Brill.

Vérilhac, Anne-Marie and Claude Vial. (1998). *Le mariage grec du VIe siècle av. J.C. à l'époque d'Auguste*. Paris: Dépositaire, De Boccard Edition.

Vester, Christina. (2009). "Bigamy, Wives and Bastardy, Wives and Concubines: Civic Indentity in *Andromache*." In J.R.C. Cousland and J.R. Hume (eds.), *The Play of Texts and Fragments: Essays in Honour of Martin Cropp*. Leiden: Brill, 293–305.

Wallbank, M.B. (1981). "Artemis Bear-Leader." *CQ* 31, 276–81.

Walters, H.B. (1921). "Red-Figured Vases Recently Acquired by the British Museum." *JHS*, 41, 117–50

Walters, K.R. (1983). "Perikles' Citizenship Law." *ClAnt* 2, 314–36.

Watson, A. (1967). *The Law of Persons in the Later Roman Republic*. Oxford: Oxford University Press.

Watson, A. (1998). *The Digest of Justinian*. Philadelphia, PA: University of Pennsylvania Press.

Webster, T.B.L. (1966). "The Myth of Ariadne from Homer to Catullus." *GaR* 13, 22–31.

West, M.L. (1978), *Hesiod, Works and Days*. Oxford: Oxford University Press.

West, M.L. (1985). *The Hesiodic Catalogue of Women: Its Nature, Structure, and Origins*. Oxford: Oxford University Press.

Westbrook, R. (1988). *Old Babylonian Marriage Law*. Hom: Berger and Sōhne.

Westbrook, R. (2005). "Penelope's Dowry and Odysseus Kingship." In R.W. Wallace and M. Gagarin (eds.), *Symposion 2001: Papers on Greek and Hellenistic Legal History* (Evanston, IL, September 5–8, 2001). Vienna: Verlag der Österreichischen Akademie der Wissenschaften, 3–23.

Whitehead, D. (1986). "Women and Naturalization in Fourth-Century Athens: The Case of Archippe." *CQ* 38, 109–14.

Willetts, R.F. (1967). *The Law Code of Gortyn*. Berlin: de Gruyter.

Willi, A. (2010). "Hera, Eros, Inno Sororia." *IGForsch* 115, 234–67.

Williams, G. (1958). "Some Aspects of Roman Marriage Ceremonies and Ideals." *JRS* 48, 16–29.

Williamson, M. (1990). "A Woman's Place in Euripides' *Medea*." In A. Powell (ed.), *Euripides, Women, and Sexuality*. London: Routledge, 16–31.

Wilson, L.M. (1929). "An Unusual Marriage Scene." *MAAR* 7, 173–76.

Wistrand, E. (1976). *The So-Called* Laudatio Turiae: *Introduction, Text, Translation, Commentary*. Lund: Acta Universitatis Gothoburgensis.
Wohl, V. (1998). *Intimate Commerce: Exchange, Gender, and Subjectivity in Greek Tragedy*. Autsin, TX: University of Texas Press.
Wolff, H.J. (1944). "Marriage Law and Family Organization in Ancient Athens: A Study on the Interrelation of Public and Private Law in the Greek City." *Traditio* 2, 43–95.
Woodbury, L. (1973). "Socrates and the Daughter of Aristides." *Phoenix* 27, 7–25.
Woodbury, L. (1982). "Cyrene and the Teleuta of Marriage in Pindar's Ninth Pythian Ode." *TAPA* 112, 245–58.
Wrenhaven, K.L. (2009). "The Identity of the 'Wool-Workers' in the Attic Manumissions." *Hesperia* 78, 367–86.
Wright, T. (2016). "Homeric Kinship on the Margins of the *Oikos*." Unpublished Ph.D. dissertation. London, Ontario, Canada: University of Western Ontario. Available for download at http://ir.lib.uwo.ca/etd/4281.
Wyse, W. (1904). *The Speeches of Isaeus*. Cambridge: Cambridge University Press.
Yatromanolakis, D. (2008). *Sappho in the Making: The Early Reception*. Hellenic Studies Series 28. Washington, DC: Center for Hellenic Studies.
Yiftach-Firanko, U. (2003). *Marriage and Marital Arrangements: A History of the Greek Marriage Document in Egypt. 4th century BCE-4th Century CE*. Munich: Beck.
Yiftach-Firanko, U. (2005). "Judean Desert Marriage Documents and *ekdosis* in the Greek Law of the Roman Period." In R. Katzoff and D. Schaps (eds.), *Law in the Documents of the Judean Desert*. Leiden: Brill, 67–84.
Ypsilanti, Maria. (2010). "Trimalchio and Fortunata as Zeus and Hera: Quarrel in the *Cena* and *Iliad*." *HSCP* 105, 221–37.
Younger, J. (July 27, 2001). "Excavated Brothels." *AEGEANET* Available at: http://lsv.uky.edu/archives/aegeanet.html.
Zacharia, K. (2003). *Converging Truths: Euripides* Ion *and the Athenian Quest for Self-Definition*. Leiden: Brill.
Zeitlin, F.I. (1992). "The Politics of Eros in the Danaid Trilogy of Aeschylus." In R. Hexter and D. Selden (eds.), *Innovations in Antiquity*. New York, NY: Routledge, 203–80.
Zelnick-Abramovitz, R. (2015). "Public Registers of Land Sales in Ancient Greece." In E. Jakab (ed.), *Sales and Community: Documents from the Ancient World*. Trieste: EUT, 41–65.
Ziogas, I. (2013). *Ovid and Hesiod: The Metamorphosis of the* Catalogue of Women. Cambridge: Cambridge University Press.
Zulueta, F. de (1946). *The Institutes of Gaius*. 2 Vols. Oxford: Oxford University Press.

Index of legal and economic terms